# Paddling
## the Salish Sea

**80 Trips** in Puget Sound, the
San Juan Islands, Olympic Peninsula
& Southern British Columbia

**ROB CASEY**

**MOUNTAINEERS
BOOKS**

**MOUNTAINEERS BOOKS** is dedicated
to the exploration, preservation, and enjoyment
of outdoor and wilderness areas.

1001 SW Klickitat Way, Suite 201, Seattle, WA 98134
800-553-4453, www.mountaineersbooks.org

Printed in China

Fourth edition, 2024. Previous editions were published in different form as *Kayaking Puget Sound and the San Juan Islands* in 1991, 1999, and 2012.

Design and layout: Amelia von Wolffersdorff
Cartographer: Lohnes + Wright
All photographs by the author unless credited otherwise.
Cover photograph: *Paddlers explore the rugged shores and pocket beaches of the Strait of Juan de Fuca on Trip 46.*
Frontispiece: *Kayak landing on Alice Bight by the Cascadia Marine Trail site, Burrows Island*
Photos, page 8: *Raccoon Island in Indian Arm (Trip 79)*; page 352: *Solitude on the Salish Sea near Seattle with the Olympic Mountains in the distance.*
Illustrations on pages 28 and 34 are by Dennis Arneson. Illustration on page 37 is adapted from *Fundamentals of Kayak Navigation* by David Burch, with permission of the author.

Library of Congress Cataloging-in-Publication Data is available at https://lccn.loc.gov/2023042038.
The LC ebook record is available at https://lccn.loc.gov/2023042039.

Printed on FSC®-certified materials

MIX
Paper | Supporting
responsible forestry
FSC® C008047

ISBN (paperback): 978-1-68051-682-1
ISBN (ebook): 978-1-68051-683-8

*An independent nonprofit publisher since 1960*

# Contents

## South Puget Sound

## Middle Puget Sound

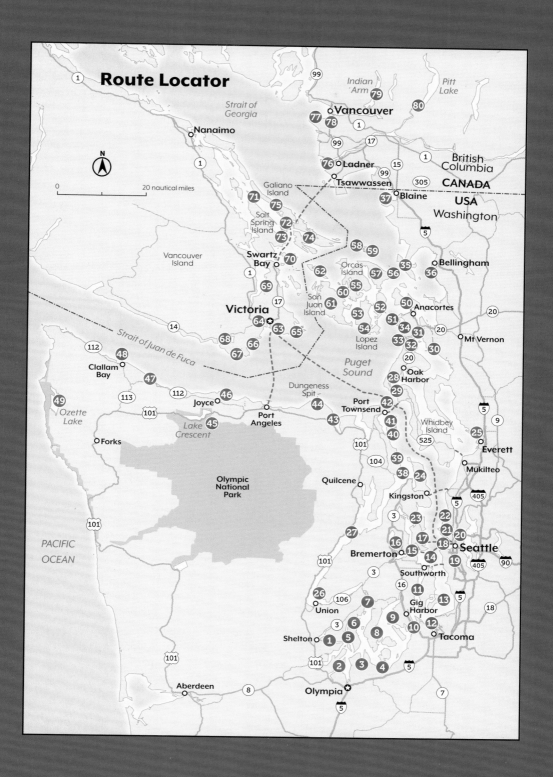

# Quick Trip Reference

Rating: P=Protected; M=Moderate; E=Exposed

| No. | Name | Rating | Duration | Camping |
|-----|------|--------|----------|---------|
| **SOUTH PUGET SOUND** | | | | |
| 1 | **Hammersley Inlet** | M | Full day to overnight | Walker County Park (CMT); Hope Island St Park (CMT) |
| 2 | **Eld Inlet** | P or M | Part day to full day | |
| 3 | **Henderson Inlet** | P or M | Part day to full day | |
| 4 | **Nisqually Delta** | P | Part day to overnight | Carlson Bay on Anderson Island (CMT) |
| 5 | **Hope Island (South)** | M | Part day to overnight | Hope Island St Park (CMT); Joemma Beach St Park (CMT); Jarrell Cove St Park (CMT) |
| 6 | **Jarrell Cove State Park** | M | Part day to overnight | Joemma Beach St Park (CMT); Jarrell Cove St Park (CMT) |
| 7 | **Case Inlet: Allyn to Vaughn Bay** | P | Part day to full day | |
| 8 | **Carr Inlet: Lakebay, Penrose Point State Park, Pitt Island, Longbranch** | P or M | Part day to overnight | Penrose Point St Park (CMT); Maple Hollow Park (CMT) |
| 9 | **Carr Inlet: Horsehead Bay, Cutts Island State Park, and Kopachuck State Park** | P or M | Part day | Kopachuck St Park (CMT) |
| 10 | **Tacoma Narrows** | M or E | Part day to overnight | Narrows Park (CMT) |
| 11 | **Gig Harbor** | P or E | Part day to full day | |
| 12 | **Commencement Bay** | P or M | Part day to full day | |
| **MIDDLE PUGET SOUND** | | | | |
| 13 | **Maury Island** | P, M, E | Part day to overnight | Saltwater St Park (CMT); Pt Robinson (CMT); Maury Island Marine Park |
| 14 | **Blake Island** | P, M, E | Full day to overnight | Blake Island St Park: 2 St Park sites and one CMT |
| 15 | **Eagle Harbor to Bremerton** | M | Full day to overnight | Manchester St Park (CMT); Fort Ward (CMT) |
| 16 | **Bremerton Port Washington Narrows and Ostrich Bay** | P or M | Part day | |
| 17 | **Eagle Harbor** | P | Part day | |
| 18 | **Elliott Bay** | M | Part day | |
| 19 | **Duwamish Waterway** | P | Part day to full day | |

| No. | Name | Rating | Duration | Camping |
|-----|------|--------|----------|---------|
| 20 | Lake Union | P | Part day | |
| 21 | Upper Salmon Bay: Ballard Bridge to Fremont Bridge | P | Part day | |
| 22 | West Point, Shilshole Bay, and Golden Gardens | P, M, E | Part day to full day | |
| 23 | Port Madison and Agate Passage | M | Part day to overnight | Fay Bainbridge Park (CMT) |
| 24 | Kingston to Point No Point Lighthouse | M or E | Part day to full day | |
| 25 | Everett Harbor: Jetty Island and Vicinity | P, M, E | Part day | |
| 26 | Southern Hood Canal: Annas Bay | P | Part day | Potlatch St Park (CMT) |
| 27 | Central Hood Canal: Quilcene Bay to Mike's Beach Resort | P or M | Full day to overnight | Mike's Beach Resort; Triton Cove (CMT); Seal Rock Campground; Herb Beck Marina: Dosewallips St Park |

## NORTH PUGET SOUND

| No. | Name | Rating | Duration | Camping |
|-----|------|--------|----------|---------|
| 28 | Whidbey Island: Coupeville and Penn Cove | P or M | Part day to full day | Windjammer City Park in Oak Harbor (CMT) |
| 29 | Whidbey Island: Keystone to Hastie Lake Boat Ramp | E | Part day to overnight | Fort Ebey St Park (CMT); Joseph Whidbey St Park (CMT); Fort Casey St Park |
| 30 | Skagit River Delta | P or M | Part day to full day | Pioneer Park (CMT) |
| 31 | Hope and Skagit Islands | M | Part day to overnight | Skagit Island (CMT); Ala Spit (CMT); Hope Island |
| 32 | Deception Pass | P, M, E | Part day to overnight | Bowman Bay (CMT); Deception Pass St Park |
| 33 | Deception Pass: Cranberry and Pass Lakes | P | Half day | |
| 34 | Burrows Island | M to E | Part day to overnight | Alice Bight (CMT); Washington Park |
| 35 | Lummi Island | M or E | Part day to overnight | Lummi Island DNR site (CMT) |
| 36 | Chuckanut Bay | P or M | Part day to full day | Larrabee St Park |
| 37 | Semiahmoo Spit, Drayton Harbor, Dakota Creek, and California Creek | P | Half day to full day | |

## OLYMPIC PENINSULA

| No. | Name | Rating | Duration | Camping |
|-----|------|--------|----------|---------|
| 38 | Hood Head | P or M | Part day to overnight | Hood Head (CMT) |
| 39 | Mats Mats Bay | P or M | Part day | |
| 40 | Indian Island | P, M, E | Full day to overnight | Kinney Pt (CMT); Oak Bay (CMT); Fort Flagler St Park |

| No. | Name | Rating | Duration | Camping |
|-----|------|--------|----------|---------|
| 41 | Marrowstone Island | P, M, E | Full day to overnight | Kinney Pt (CMT); Fort Flagler St Park (CMT); and Oak Bay (CMT) |
| 42 | Port Townsend to Point Wilson | P or M | Part day to full day | Fort Worden St Park (CMT) |
| 43 | Sequim Bay, Protection Island, and Diamond Point Loop | P, M, E | Part day to full day | Sequim Bay St Park |
| 44 | Dungeness Spit | P or M | Part day to full day | Dungeness Recreation Area |
| 45 | Lake Crescent | P to M | Half day to overnight | Fairholme Campground; Log Cabin Resort |
| 46 | Freshwater Bay to Salt Creek Recreation Area | P, M, E | Part day to overnight | Salt Creek Recreation Area; Crescent Beach and RV Park |
| 47 | Pillar Point and Pysht River | P, M, E | Half day to full day | |
| 48 | Clallam Bay Spit Community Beach County Park | P | Half day | |
| 49 | Ozette Lake | P or M | Half day to overnight | Ozette Campground; Ericson's Bay; Tivoli Island |

**SAN JUAN ISLANDS**

| No. | Name | Rating | Duration | Camping |
|-----|------|--------|----------|---------|
| 50 | Cypress Island | M | Full day to overnight | Cypress Head and Pelican Beach DNR sites (CMT), open year-round; Washington Park |
| 51 | James Island Park | M or E | Overnight | James Island St Park (CMT); Spencer Spit St Park (CMT) |
| 52 | Obstruction Pass | M | Part day to overnight | Obstruction Pass Recreation Site (CMT); Doe Island St Park |
| 53 | Lopez Island: Fisherman Bay | P | Part day | |
| 54 | Lopez Island: Mackaye Harbor | P | Part day | |
| 55 | Shaw Island: Circumnavigation | P or M | Full day to multiple nights | Shaw Island County Park (CMT); Blind Island St Park (CMT); Jones Island St Park (CMT); Turn Island St Park; Odlin County Park (CMT) |
| 56 | Clark Island | E | Full day to overnight | Clark Island St Park; Lummi Island Recreation Site (CMT); Doe Island St Park |
| 57 | Orcas Island: Cascade and Mountain Lakes | P | Half day | Cascade Lake; Mountain Lake |
| 58 | Point Doughty on Orcas Island | M | Part day to overnight | Pt Doughty DNR site (CMT) |
| 59 | Patos, Sucia, and Matia Islands | E | Overnight to multiple nights | Patos Island: Active Cove; Sucia Island: Fossil, Echo, and Shallow Bays and Fox Cove; Matia Island: Rolfe Cove |
| 60 | Jones Island | M | Full day or overnight | Jones Island St Park (CMT) |

| No. | Name | Rating | Duration | Camping |
|-----|------|--------|----------|---------|
| 61 | South and West San Juan Island | M or E | Part day to multiple nights | Griffin Bay (CMT); San Juan County Park (CMT); Posey Island St Park (CMT); Turn Island St Park |
| 62 | Stuart Island | P or E | Overnight or longer | Reid Harbor (CMT); Prevost Harbor; Posey Island St Park |

## VICTORIA AND THE GULF ISLANDS

| No. | Name | Rating | Duration | Camping |
|-----|------|--------|----------|---------|
| 63 | Victoria Harbor | P | Part day to full day | |
| 64 | Victoria: The Gorge Waterway | P or M | Part day | |
| 65 | Victoria: Outer Harbor to Cadboro Bay and Trial, Oak Bay, and Discovery Islands | P, M, E | Part day, full day, or overnight | Discovery Island |
| 66 | Victoria: Albert Head to Witty's Lagoon and Sitting Lady Falls | P or M | Half day to full day | |
| 67 | Victoria: Beecher Bay (aka Belcher Bay) | P, M, E | Part day to full day | |
| 68 | Sooke Harbor | P or E | Part day to full day | |
| 69 | Brentwood Bay to Tod Inlet | P | Half day to full day | |
| 70 | Portland Island | M | Full day to overnight | Arbutus Point; Princess Bay; Shell Beach (BC Marine Trail sites) |
| 71 | Salt Spring Island to Wallace Island | P or M | Part day to overnight | Cabin Bay; Chivers Point; east of Conover Cove (BC Marine Trail sites) |
| 72 | Salt Spring Island to Prevost Island | P or M | Full day to overnight | James Bay (BC Marine Trail) |
| 73 | Salt Spring Island to Chain Islands | P or M | Half day | |
| 74 | Pender, Saturna, and Mayne Islands | M | Part day to overnight | Beaumont Marine Park; Port Browning; Miners Bay (BC Marine Trail sites) |
| 75 | Galiano Island and Montague Harbor | P or M | Half day to overnight | Montague Harbor Marine Provincial Park |

## VANCOUVER, BRITISH COLUMBIA

| No. | Name | Rating | Duration | Camping |
|-----|------|--------|----------|---------|
| 76 | Fraser River, Ladner Marsh, and Deas Island | P or M | Half day to full day | |
| 77 | English Bay | P, M, E | Half day | |
| 78 | False Creek | P | Half day | |
| 79 | Deep Cove and Indian Arm | P or M | Half day to overnight | Bishop Creek; Granite Falls; Twin Islands |
| 80 | Pitt River to Widgeon Creek and Falls | P or M | Half day to overnight | Widgeon Creek |

# Introduction

For thousands of years, people have used human-powered watercraft to travel through Pacific Northwest waters, also known as the Salish Sea. The Salish Sea includes the Strait of Juan de Fuca, Puget Sound, and the Strait of Georgia. Native people sometimes refer to Puget Sound as Whulge (or Whulj), an anglicization of the Lushootseed name x̌ʷəlč (pronounced "whulcH"), which means "salt water." Whenever possible, to help honor the cultural history of this area's Native inhabitants, I list Coast Salish or other Native-language names for the regions, water-ways, and other natural features described in this book's trips. While not exhaustive, I hope you find these references interesting and informative and can use them as a launching point to conduct your own research into the fascinating history of the people who lived and still live along these shores.

The canoe was a vital part of Coast Salish life. Native peoples paddled dugout canoes for general transportation as well as to collect food. Families traveled seasonally to specific locations to fish and to pick berries, with some also paddling to places like the Puyallup Valley to harvest hops. The Makah from Neah Bay used canoes to hunt gray whales, sometimes several miles offshore. Tribes used canoes to make surprise raids on other tribes, to capture slaves or for retribution. In the mid-1800s, amateur anthropologist James Swan, who lived among several

Northwest tribes, reported one incident where the Makah used their canoes to raid the S'Klallam Tribe from the Port Angeles area.

Prior to the twentieth century, Coast Salish peoples constructed their canoes by setting fires in the trunks of old-growth cedar trees to burn out the interiors, afterward carving them to precision using hand tools. The canoes varied in length, depending on the region and the type of water in which they were paddled. Saltwater canoes were usually twenty to thirty feet long and designed for speed and stability in big seas.

The first contact the Coast Salish peoples had with Europeans was reported to be in the late 1700s, when many explorers, such as Captain George Vancouver and Spanish explorer Manuel Quimper, "discovered" the region. In July of 1790, Quimper anchored in a wide bay along the Strait of Juan de Fuca near the Elwha River. American Indians in canoes brought his crew salmonberries and fresh water from a nearby creek. The area was later called Freshwater Bay (see Trip 46).

By the mid-1800s, the European settlers who had begun to populate the shores of Puget Sound needed a way to get around. Before steam wheelers and ferry services existed, many settlers hired American Indians to take them in canoes to their preferred destinations. The two parties didn't necessarily agree on how or when to travel. In one incident, a European couple was told by their Native canoe guide that the day they intended to travel wasn't a favorable time. The couple insisted on going anyway, and while they were underway, a strong gale began, eventually capsizing the canoe and drowning all aboard. Another time, a settler was in a hurry to get to a destination, but tribal customs required the paddlers to take a longer, slower route around superstitious landmarks. In 1847, Canadian artist Paul Kane hitched a ride in a canoe across the Strait of Juan de Fuca and experienced a harrowing, eleven-hour crossing in huge seas and gale-force winds.

In time, the new residents of the Salish Sea area learned how to get around on their own, using a variety of watercraft. In 1867, Samuel Jerisch rowed a flat-bottomed skiff from British Columbia to stake the first claim in the protected inlet of what is now Gig Harbor. In 1895, Ethan Allen and his wife, Sadie, moved to Waldron Island. As the county superintendent of San Juan Island Schools, Allen rowed more than 10,000 miles over the years in his homemade rowboat to check on each school.

Northwest paddler Bill Walker once showed me a photograph of his grandfather, Forrest Goodfellow, who in 1907 rode a canoe down the log flume separating Lake Washington from Portage Bay in Seattle. The Montlake Cut was built in the same location in 1909. Bill commented, "My brother Dee and I followed in his paddle strokes in the 1960s and 1970s while rowing for the University of Washington Husky Crew."

Sea kayaks didn't become commonplace in the region until the latter half of the twentieth century. Prior to this time, kayaks weren't readily available for purchase, so many people built their own. In the early 1970s, George Dyson immigrated to British Columbia to avoid the draft. Living in a tree house east of Vancouver, British Columbia, Dyson studied the history of the baidarka kayak, an Aleutian kayak originally used for hunting in the Arctic. Working with materials such as metal tubing, fabric, locally cut lumber, old metal stop signs, and nylon twine, he made several baidarkas and eventually, in 1975, he completed the forty-eight-foot Mount Fairweather. Kenneth Brower's books about Dyson's exploits, including *The Starship and the Canoe*, illustrate his superb craftsmanship and innovative kayak designs.

In the early 1970s, Tom Derrer relocated from Colorado to Seattle to work for Werner Furrer Sr., where he was tasked with building sea kayaks. Originally a whitewater paddler, Derrer was soon hooked on sea kayaking the coastal waterways of the Pacific Northwest. By the late 1980s, as sea kayaking finally hit the mainstream, Werner Paddles and Derrer's company, Eddyline Kayaks, became household names in the outdoor recreation industry. Other local companies, such as Necky Kayaks, Northwest Kayaks, Easy Rider Canoe & Kayak Co., Pygmy Boats, Sterling Kayaks, and *Sea Kayaker* magazine, contributed to making the Northwest a center of the sea-kayaking industry. In the early 1990s, the Washington Water Trails Association (WWTA) founded the Cascadia Marine Trail (CMT) to provide campsites for people using human-powered watercraft to move between Olympia and the Canadian border. WWTA now has four other water trails throughout the region. The BC Marine Trails Network was opened in 2011 and offers access to many paddling destinations in Canada.

*Paddler's view of a row of tugs on Seattle's Duwamish Waterway (Trip 19)*

I grew up in Seattle with a view of Puget Sound. I finally got on the water and began sea kayaking in the late 1990s. Influenced by local writer and photographer Joel W. Rogers's books, *The Hidden Coast: Kayak Explorations from Alaska to Mexico* and *Watertrail: The Hidden Path through Puget Sound*, I wanted to explore the rocky, madrona-lined shorelines of the San Juan Islands and the lush green estuaries of south Puget Sound.

I purchased Randel Washburne's paddling guidebook for Puget Sound—the first and original edition of the guide you now hold—which opened the door for me to learn where to go, when to go, and how to get there. I carried one copy of the guidebook in my car and left another copy by my bedside at home. I spent countless hours studying each trip. Friends would call me after finding a trip of interest in their copy of the guidebook and we'd set a date and

*Lime Kiln Lighthouse, San Juan Island (Trip 61)*

go. Even though I am a Seattle native, Washburne's book, later updated by R. Carey Gersten, introduced me to places I had never heard of before. It's an honor to be taking the reins of this guide from my talented predecessors.

Some of my early trips included exploring Mats Mats Bay, Marrowstone Point, Point Whitney on Hood Canal, the Nisqually Delta, and running the currents of Hammersley Inlet. Intrigued by the idea of driving as little as possible to go kayaking, my neighbor Todd and I took overnight paddling trips to Blake Island from our neighborhood in Ballard, a one-way distance of 8 miles. After acquiring skills in surf and whitewater kayaking, I began paddling the advanced trips in the guidebook, such as maneuvering the swift tidal rapids of Deception Pass, rock gardening the rugged stretch west of Freshwater Bay, and surfing the waves at Crescent Beach.

While the focus of Washburne's guidebook was on kayaking, it was always a treat to see other types of watercrafts at the various campsites. On my first trip to Jarrell Cove, we camped next to a Boy Scout troop that had canoed there from Boston Harbor and a couple who had rowed a dinghy to the island from Olympia. Some friends paddle another type of canoe, the outrigger, in local races as well as on their own throughout the Salish Sea.

Nearly two decades after my first wanderings on Pacific Northwest waters, a new type of watercraft was introduced—the stand up paddle board (SUP). Since its introduction, stand up paddlers have been exploring the Salish Sea. I began paddling a SUP as another way to get on the water, and in 2011 I wrote the first how-to guide for the sport. Today, many paddlers continue to embrace SUPs for their simplicity and fitness benefits—and because you get to stand upright while paddling, SUPs offer better views than kayaks.

Some participate in long-distance races, such as Orcas Island–based Karl Kruger, who in 2017 paddled a seventeen-foot SUP for 766 miles in fifteen days, from Port Townsend to Ketchikan, for the Race to Alaska. He and other paddle boarders have completed the SEVENTY48 race several times. This all-paddle craft and rowing race runs from Tacoma to Port Townsend—70 miles in forty-eight hours—which requires a unique training regimen. In Port Townsend, a few friends started designing custom touring paddle boards of unlimited length (fourteen feet plus) for the race and to tour the Salish Sea throughout the year. This passion in fast touring boards led Chris Doree to take over Splinter SUP, which makes a sixteen-foot touring board with internal storage like a kayak.

As described earlier, Native peoples have used canoes in the Northwest for thousands of years. In an interesting blend of old and new technologies, US Geological Survey (USGS) scientist Eric Grossman from Bellingham attaches water-quality testing gear to the stern of Native canoes during the annual Tribal Journeys event and paddles alongside on his SUP. Tribal Journeys, held on the Salish Sea, marks a cultural resurgence of the canoe culture of tribes along the coasts of Washington, Oregon, and British Columbia. Canoe families travel the waterways, often in cedar replicas of their tribe's traditional canoes, to gather at a different tribal location each year.

However you get on the water, I hope you will use this book to learn about new places or to rediscover old favorites. This new, fully revised, and reimagined version of Washburne's original guide is intended for *all* types of paddlers, canoers, and rowers. All routes described in this edition are accessible by each of these types of crafts, except where noted.

Since the last edition, I have added twenty-two new trips and updated several existing ones. While prior versions of the book focused primarily on Puget Sound, this new edition covers a wider region encompassing most of the Salish Sea, pushing the previous boundaries farther to include journeys into the Strait of Juan de Fuca, more trips in the Gulf Islands and around Victoria, and a handful of routes on the British Columbia mainland near Vancouver. A new trip, Pillar Point and Pysht River (Trip 47), is dedicated to Randel Washburne, who originally recommended and promoted this trip. And there are so many other great trips out there, across the Salish Sea, that they could easily fill a few more books! Enjoy, and see you on the water!

OPPOSITE  *Clark Island views (Trip 56)*

# Our Pacific Northwest Marine Environment

The Pacific Northwest waters in and around the Salish Sea offer some of the most beautiful, rewarding paddling to be found. But this isn't tropical paddling—the waters here can be very cold and conditions changeable. And if you plan to venture out into Puget Sound or Canadian waters, you'll need to have not only more advanced paddling skills but also solid knowledge of wind, tides, currents, and more. If you're properly prepared, though, you'll experience some extraordinary places.

## Water Temperatures

Sea and lake temperatures in the Puget Sound region vary between 56 degrees (Fahrenheit) in August and 46 degrees in February and can go as low as 41 degrees. Late spring brings snow-melt, so May has the coldest water temperatures of the year. Summer temperatures usually don't warm the water up until mid-July.

*Paddlers enjoy the protected waters of Victoria's upper Gorge Waterway (Trip 64).*

## Wind and Weather

For paddlers, two of the most important variables are wind and the resulting sea state. Unfortunately, winds are difficult for meteorologists to forecast, especially in the Pacific Northwest. Visual cues that you can use to predict what is coming are even less reliable, though a few will be noted in this very brief treatment of our local marine weather. For a more thorough understanding of patterns, see Kenneth Lilly's book *Marine Weather of Western Washington*, local TV weatherman and sea kayaker Jeff Renner's book *Northwest Marine Weather: From the Columbia River to Cape Scott*, and Cliff Mass's book *The Weather of the Pacific Northwest* (see Resources).

The maritime Northwest's year is almost equally divided into two seasonal weather regimes, the summer regime and the winter regime, each with characteristic patterns. The two regimes are governed by two large atmospheric pressure cells: the Pacific High and the Aleutian Low. The Pacific High is always present off the California coast but expands north in the spring to dominate the entire northeast Pacific. In early fall it retreats south and is replaced by the growing Aleutian Low, which moves south from the Bering Sea to the Gulf of Alaska, extending over the Pacific Northwest through the winter.

The summer regime usually begins during April and gives way in September. Gales (winds stronger than 33 knots) decrease in frequency toward midsummer as the stable Pacific High pressure system blocks most disturbances from entering the area. Nonetheless, lows and fronts can still bring rain and strong winds, which almost always blow from a southerly direction.

Winds can still be quite fresh during fair weather, sometimes blowing 17 to 21 knots or more. As the interior landmass warms, air from high-pressure areas in the Pacific Ocean is drawn in through the Strait of Juan de Fuca. The resulting winds can blow 25 knots or more in the afternoon and spread to the north and south at the eastern end of the strait, sending southwesterlies up into the San Juan Islands and northwesterlies down across Port Townsend and into northern Puget Sound. Generally, except for areas influenced by the Strait of Juan de Fuca, winds tend to be northwesterly during fair weather in the summer regime.

Of course, topography also plays an important part in wind direction and force. As land heats up on sunny afternoons, it creates local onshore winds, called sea breezes; hence, morning is generally the least windy time for paddling. When the sea-breeze direction coincides with the prevailing northwesterly, local winds are intensified. Mountainous seasides, such as those of Orcas Island, channel winds and deflect them as much as 90 degrees. They may also cause intensified winds if air is forced through a narrow passage or over a saddle between higher hills. For instance, Orcas Island's East Sound often has stronger-than-average winds during prevailing northerlies.

Fog is most common in late July through September, particularly during clear weather when rapid land cooling occurs at night. This fog usually clears by early afternoon.

The summer regime eventually gives way to the winter regime. As the Pacific High yields to the Aleutian Low in early fall, prevailing winds shift to southeasterly, and disturbances with gale-force winds become increasingly frequent and intense. The first gales of the season usually occur in late September. By late fall, no weather pattern can be counted on for very long, as a procession of unstable fronts and depressions becomes the rule.

Strong winter winds are typically southerly throughout the area but can blow from almost any direction. One anomalous wintertime hazard to watch for is strong northerly winds on clear days, a result of outbreaks from Arctic high-pressure fronts located in the interiors of Washington or British Columbia. On the other hand, periods of very calm weather also occur during the winter regime, particularly since the low-angle sun has less power to generate local sea breezes. Fog is also possible, especially in January and February, and may persist for several days.

Remember that strong winds can develop from very localized circumstances. Weather problems are not necessarily the result of a bad weather system. Keep an eye out for impending bad weather—while not completely reliable, a few visual indicators suggest a change for the worse.

Oncoming winds can often be spotted on the sea in the distance. In general, be most leery of southerly winds, as these suggest the presence of unsettled weather with potential for strong winds. Rapid shifts in wind direction, particularly counterclockwise changes (*backing* winds in nautical parlance) to the southeast, suggest the arrival of a front. Whatever the wind direction, weather usually arrives from the west, so note the sky in that direction. The development of high clouds, or rings around either the sun or the moon, is a harbinger of a front.

## BEAUFORT WIND SCALE

The Beaufort Wind Scale is used to measure wind speeds. You will want to monitor the **Beaufort Wind Scale** to learn how different levels of wind can affect both land and sea and how this knowledge can help you make good trip decisions.

## WEATHER FORECASTS

One of the most effective weather predictors is the meteorologist's marine forecast via VHF radio. Continuous broadcasts and local weather reports for the Northwest inland waters of the

# Beaufort Wind Scale

Developed in 1805 by Sir Francis Beaufort of the United Kingdom

| Force | Wind (Knots) | WMO Classification | Appearance of Wind Effects | |
|---|---|---|---|---|
| | | | ON THE WATER | ON LAND |
| 0 | Less than 1 | Calm | Sea surface smooth and mirror-like | Calm, smoke rises vertically |
| 1 | 1–3 | Light air | Scaly ripples, no foam crests | Smoke drift indicates wind direction, still wind vanes |
| 2 | 4–6 | Light breeze | Small wavelets, crests glassy, no breaking | Wind felt on face, leaves rustle, vanes begin to move |
| 3 | 7–10 | Gentle breeze | Large wavelets, crests begin to break, scattered whitecaps (1–4 feet high) | Leaves and small twigs constantly moving, light flags extended |
| 4 | 11–16 | Moderate breeze | Small waves 1–4 feet becoming longer, numerous whitecaps (4–8 feet high) | Dust, leaves, and loose paper lifted, small tree branches move |
| 5 | 17–21 | Fresh breeze | Moderate waves 4–8 feet taking longer form, many whitecaps, some spray (8–13 feet high) | Small trees in leaf begin to sway |
| 6 | 22–27 | Strong breeze | Larger waves 8–13 feet, whitecaps common, more spray 13–20 feet high | Larger tree branches moving, whistling in wires |
| 7 | 28–33 | Near gale | Sea heaps up, waves 13–20 feet, white foam streaks off breakers | Whole trees in motion, resistance felt walking against wind |
| 8 | 34–40 | Gale | Moderately high (13–20 feet) waves of greater length, edges of crests begin to break into spindrift, foam blown in streaks | Whole trees in motion, resistance felt walking against wind |
| 9 | 41–47 | Strong gale | High waves (20 feet), sea begins to roll, dense streaks of foam, spray may reduce visibility | Slight structural damage occurs, slate blows off roofs |
| 10 | 48–55 | Storm | Very high waves (20–30 feet) with overhanging crests, sea white with densely blown foam, heavy rolling, lowered visibility | Seldom experienced on land, trees broken and uprooted, considerable structural damage |
| 11 | 56–63 | Violent storm | Exceptionally high (30–45 feet) waves, foam patches cover sea, visibility more reduced | |
| 12 | 64+ | Hurricane | Air filled with foam, waves over 45 feet, sea completely white with driving spray, visibility greatly reduced | |

trips described in this book are always available from at least one of three stations in the United States and two in Canada. Most weather radios or handheld VHF transceivers get at least three of these channels (WX1, WX2, and WX4). Forecasts are reissued every six hours, with local condition updates every three hours.

Additionally, you can check these websites for forecasts:

| Location | VHF Channel |
|----------|-------------|
| Neah Bay | WX1 |
| Astoria | WX2 |
| Olympia | WX3 |
| Seattle | WX1 |
| Port Townsend | WX4 |
| Victoria, BC | WX2 |
| Vancouver, BC | 21B (also WX4) |

- National Weather Service, Seattle: wrh.noaa.gov/sew
- Environment Canada, West Coast: weather.gc.ca/marine/region_e.html?mapID=02

While underway, you can use your phone to access marine weather apps for detailed hourly and almost-weekly forecasts, along with other data on tides, surf forecasts, and more. It's wise to monitor at least two of these apps or forecast models to get a range of potential weather predictions. Some can access regional NOAA buoy data. On most apps, you can choose from several forecast models that pull from different sets of data. High-Resolution Rapid Refresh (HRRR), a NOAA model, provides forecasts in real time and up to three days out. Some say the European Centre for Medium-Range Weather Forecasts (ECMWF) is more accurate. Choose whichever model works for you. Surf apps provide similar data, plus ocean-swell info like wave size, direction, and period (time between crests). See Resources for a list of recommended marine weather apps.

## Tides and Currents

In Pacific Northwest waters, staying in tune with tides and tidal currents is as important as keeping an eye on the weather and the marine traffic. Rough water, created by currents and made far worse by bad weather, can be an extreme hazard.

Tidal currents, the horizontal movement of water, result from the vertical movement of water. Pay attention to tide cycles to choose the safest traveling times. Tides in the inland waters of the Northwest are generally "mixed semidiurnal," which means there are two high tides and two low tides each day. Typically, one daily low is considerably lower than the other (see Figure 1 on next page), and the exact shape of the daily curve changes significantly throughout the month.

The strength of a current is roughly proportional to the difference between the most recent high and low tide. For example, in Figure 1, the flood current between lower low (l.l.) water and higher high (h.h.) water will be swifter than that during the exchange from higher low (h.l.) to lower high (l.h.) later in the day. Since the order of this mixed semidiurnal pattern varies, the tide graphs included in some tide tables, such as the *Tidelog* (see Resources), are helpful for getting an overview of the day's currents.

Another important factor is the duration of exchanges. The average time between high and low tide is about six hours, but in some places the interval can be as much as nine hours. In very small exchanges, during which there may be hardly any current, it can take little more than an hour.

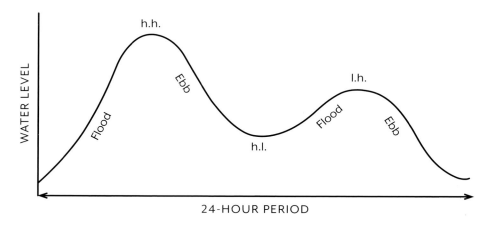

*Figure 1. Semidirunal tidal patterns*

Times of no current are called "slack water" or, in some documents, "minimum flood or ebb current," because the water may not completely stop flowing. The length of the slack is related to the strength of the currents before and after it. Slack water does not necessarily coincide with high or low tide. The unique characteristics of each waterway greatly affect the relationship between tides and currents. Hence, mariners use current tables to predict slacks and maximum currents. These are far more useful for travel planning than tide tables, though paddlers find the latter useful for timing launches and haul-outs.

You should also be aware of the bimonthly cycles in tide and current size caused by the alignment of the moon in relation to the Earth and the sun. Every fourteen days, when the moon is either full or new, a period of "spring" tides and bigger-than-usual currents occurs. In between are periods of "neap" tides and currents, which are smaller than average, occurring during quarter moons, when the moon is out of alignment with the sun and Earth. Spring and neap tide cycles exert their biggest influence on outer coastal waters; they have less of an effect on inland waters.

More important in the Northwest inland waters is the declination of the moon's orbit from the equator, which follows fourteen-day cycles independent of the spring-neap progressions. The difference between the two daily tides and their accompanying currents will be greatest when the moon is at its maximum north or south declination. Since the moon's orbit is elliptical, those periods of the month when it is closest to the Earth, "perigee," produce larger tides and stronger currents, particularly on inland waters.

All the factors discussed above can cause dramatic differences in tides and currents, particularly when they coincide. Currents can be more than twice as fast as they are on another day at the same stage of the tide. Take a close look at your monthly tide tables to keep track of trends and note that the two daily tide exchanges are somewhat independent of each other. Many tide and current tables also include calendars with astronomical conditions so you can predict their effects.

*A calm day in Sooke Basin, Vancouver Island (Trip 68)*

## RESOURCES FOR CURRENT PREDICTIONS

You can find predictions for tidal currents in two types of documents: current tables and current charts or atlases.

Current tables are composed of two parts. In the first part, a calendar indicates when slack water and maximum currents are expected, including predicted speeds at major reference points. In Washington's inland waters, for example, some common reference points are Admiralty Inlet, Tacoma Narrows, Deception Pass, Rosario Strait, and San Juan Channel. The second part of a current table offers correction factors for expected currents in many local places. Washington State tidal current tables are available to download from the National Oceanic and Atmospheric Administration (NOAA) as a PDF, XML, or TXT file. The Canadian Hydrographic Service (CHS) publishes its own tables, which are very similar in format to the NOAA tables; they are available online as a PDF or in print through a retailer. You can also refer to Saltwater Tides, *Waggoner Tables*, and various tide and current software programs and apps (see Resources). You can purchase current tables online at waggonerguidebooks.com/store/p400/CurrentAtlasTables.html.

Current charts or current atlases show schematic pictures of current flows at different stages of the tide. (See Figure 2 for an example of a current chart.) They are easier to use than current tables and are best for getting an overall picture of the flows during a particular time period. In some areas, such as the San Juan Islands' east and west channels, where flows are far from intuitive, current charts and atlases can be a great help. Another advantage is that these are perennial rather than annual. However, charts and atlases are less accurate for predicting slack-water times. For hazardous places, such as Deception Pass, use current tables.

For Puget Sound, Hood Canal, and Admiralty Inlet, NOAA has two sets of current charts that are used in conjunction with the annual current tables. For the San Juan Islands and the Gulf

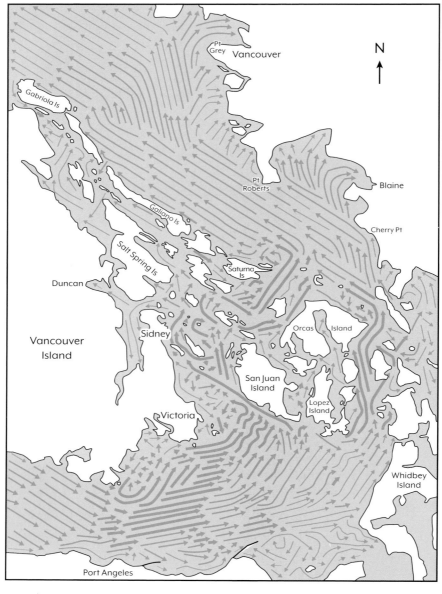

SPEED (KNOTS)

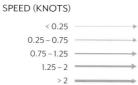

< 0.25
0.25 – 0.75
0.75 – 1.25
1.25 – 2
> 2

Figure 2. Example of a current chart

Islands, the CHS's *Current Atlas: Juan de Fuca Strait to Strait of Georgia* accurately locates both current streams and the large eddies that occur in this complex area. It also shows how current streams vary, both in strength and location, depending on the size of the tidal exchange. The major difficulty with this book is finding the right chart to use. To do so, you must have a Canadian tide table and make some calculations about the tide times and exchange size. As an alternative, consult the annual publication *Waggoner Tables* (see Resources), which takes you directly to the right chart for any hour of any day without the need for a tide table, calculations, or daylight-saving time corrections.

## HAZARDS FROM CURRENTS

Most paddling accidents in the Northwest are a result, at least in part, of currents aggravated by bad weather. The most common dangers are caused by the interaction of wind and currents.

When wind-generated waves encounter an opposing current—one moving against the wind—the waves are slowed down or, if the current is strong enough, prevented from advancing at all. The waves become steeper, larger, and may break heavily. The result is a much rougher and more difficult sea for small craft to handle. A channel may have moderate seas when the current is flowing in the wind's direction, but it could easily become untenable for paddlers after a significant current change.

Consequently, paddlers should plan to cross open water when the current and wind are moving in the same direction. Though the wind direction cannot be anticipated with certainty, currents typically can be predicted. It is important to note that in nautical publications, wind and current directions are customarily expressed in opposite fashion: winds in the direction from which they are coming; currents in the direction toward which they are going.

Many years ago, a kayaker died while crossing from Tumbo Island in British Columbia to Patos Island in the San Juan Islands, a stretch of water known for its strong currents. Though the 50-knot winds that caught the party in mid-channel alone could have caused the fatality, the heavy breaking seas were made worse by a large eddy that created opposing currents, during a time when the general flow was with the wind's direction. This eddy could only have been identified with the CHS's *Current Atlas*.

## USING RANGES

Learning to use ranges (see Figure 3) can help you know if and how your progress is being affected by the current during a crossing. First choose two fixed points; this is called a natural range. You can use them to determine your direction of drift: compare a fixed point in the middle ground, like a buoy or a rock, to another in the background, such as a hill or tree. Observe their movement in relation to each other. If the points become out of line, it means you're drifting due to current or wind. If the farthest point moves to the right, you're being pushed to the right. Some call this method "transits."

## TIDE RIPS

In certain situations, waves are forced to break in localized areas called "tide rips." Most tide rips occur where land obstructions or underwater shoals impede or change the current flow,

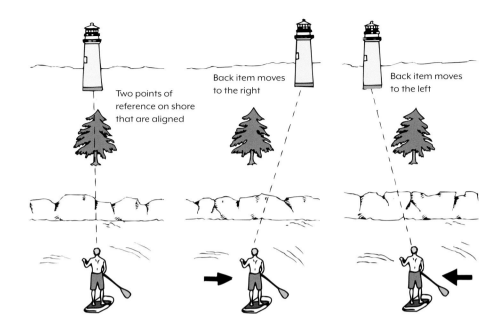

Two points of
reference on shore
that are aligned

Back item moves
to the right

Back item moves
to the left

*Figure 3. Using ranges to assess progress in currents*

causing the moving water to accelerate because it is being squeezed around a point, through a narrows, or over a shallows (see Figure 4). Waves may be able to advance against slower currents up to that point, but when they cannot get farther, they break, expending their energy and becoming trapped in rips that result in turbulence. (Note: A tide rip is different than a surf rip, which is a sand channel on a beach that draws water like a river out to sea, pulling unsuspecting paddlers with it.)

Where currents intersect, they form an eddy line at their edges. If the difference in current speeds is great enough, waves are unable to cross this barrier and a rip composed of stalled, multidirectional waves forms adjacent to it. The effect is reminiscent of vertical shorelines where intersecting waves are being reflected through the incoming ones. The waves become irregular and pyramid shaped. They leap up and disappear unpredictably. If you are paddling in these conditions, your kayak or SUP cannot find equilibrium on the rapidly moving surface, so the boat or board's movement will be jerky. At best, you'll get splashed a lot, at worst, you could lose your balance and capsize.

Sometimes you encounter rips on calm, windless days. Where do the waves come from? They may stem from very low, widely spaced waves that are barely perceptible until they become trapped and intensified in the tide-rip area. Or currents flowing over an irregular bottom may transmit the bottom features to the surface as standing waves—waves that stay in one place—which are simply another variety of tide rip. Occasionally rips are the result of a large eddy being swept downstream from the place where it was created, creating adjacent rips for quite some time and distance.

The rough water in rips may also be created or intensified by the wakes of ships or even pleasure craft. I've seen very minor rips turn into nasty ones after a powerboat passed by. Large ship wakes can make situations far worse.

It is difficult to predict tide rip locations with certainty, even if you know the direction and speed of currents; there is just too little information on charts about bottom features. However, some likely spots are shoaling areas, underwater reefs, the downstream sides of points or islands, and places where currents are fastest or intersect (such as where they rejoin after flowing around a large island). In the San Juan Islands, for instance, colliding currents from Spieden Channel and San Juan Channel regularly form dangerous rips. The particularly fast water at San Juan Channel's south entrance usually has rips that are at their worst on ebbs against southerly winds.

From a distance, tide rips can be heard as a low roar. Seeing them from the low viewing point of a kayak or SUP is difficult, particularly on windy days when distant rips are camouflaged by wind waves. If you find yourself heading for a rip, assess your drift in the current using ranges and then try to take evasive action while there is still time. If you cannot avoid the rip, head straight through it. Remember that you are moving with the current, whereas the rip is stationary. You will soon pass through it. With most rips there is more noise and splashing than real threat to your stability. A suggested defense is to paddle rapidly, each stroke serving as a mini brace to help maintain equilibrium and direction. This method also works for SUPs, where a shorter cadence provides stability.

## EDDY LINES

Usually, wherever currents are found, there are also eddies along the shore, made up of either still water or localized currents moving upstream for some distance. The more irregular the shore-

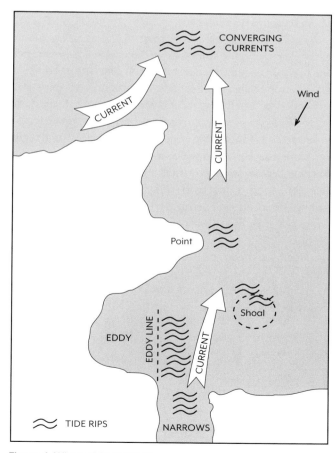

Figure 4. Where tide rips form

line, the more extensive the eddy system. Such eddies usually form on the downstream side of points, islets, or other obstructions. Sometimes the eddy system will extend out alongside the obstruction as well. Sharply defined boundary lines between the main current and the still or backward-flowing eddy are often accompanied by swirls, turbulence, or possibly whirlpools, although these may be difficult to see in slower currents. The southeast side of Pass Island in Deception Pass on a strong flood current is a good example of this situation.

Eddy lines can sometimes upset small craft such as paddle craft. The primary cause is inertia: crossing from current to eddy or vice versa involves a rapid transition in water direction. Consequently, the rule is to lean and brace downstream. The tremendous turbulence and up- and down-welling in some eddy lines can also focus strong torque on a kayak's hull, possibly causing it to capsize.

Crossing powerful eddy lines is best done quickly and at right angles. Keep paddling at a rapid pace so strokes can serve as braces. SUP paddlers should get as low as possible and use a short cadence while crossing an eddy line.

### Using Eddies to Go Upstream

Sometimes you can take advantage of eddies, using them to move quickly upstream. A good example is along the south side of Deception Pass where paddlers can use the irregular shoreline to move upstream on a strong ebb. Since most eddies are actually circling water, they can flow in many different directions. Eddies can also sometimes cover an extensive area, so you may need to hunt for the most favorable current. A good strategy when passing through large eddies is to move around to find the best currents. Kelp can be a good visual cue: the direction in which the kelp lies in the water indicates the flow or direction of the current.

More than likely, you will be forced to paddle hard to progress upstream from one eddy to the next, usually when you must round a point where, for a short distance, the current sweeps along the shore as fast as in midstream. Such "eddy hopping" requires some positioning, careful boat handling, and perhaps a burst of everything you have for a short, hard pull. Use the still water generally found just downstream from a point to build up some speed and inertia, then break out into the opposing current as far upstream and as close to the point as possible. Head as directly upstream as you can as you enter the main current; otherwise, the boat's bow, or nose, will be pushed out and you will find yourself heading perpendicular to where you intended to go, rapidly losing ground. If this occurs, rather than trying to recover, just continue to turn downstream, reenter the eddy you just left, and try again.

OPPOSITE  *A touring paddle boarder uses eddies to paddle up Snohomish River current (Trip 25).*

# Paddling Safety and Preparation

Learning to plan a safe day or overnight trip requires knowledge of marine weather, tides and currents, basic to advanced paddling skills, water safety, marine navigation, group dynamics, and on-water communication. Most incidents are preventable; being properly prepared for your trip allows you to have a memorable experience while staying out of the news.

## Paddling Skills

Every trip is unique, requiring different preparation, skills, and solutions to make it a safe and memorable experience. Taking the time to learn all the skills mentioned above will allow you to paddle farther and to more special places. Many trips have ended early, or even in disaster, due to paddlers' failure to learn about the location, watch the weather, bring adequate gear and clothing, or stay within their skill level.

For beginners, the best method for learning skills is to take a course from a reputable or certified paddling school or coach. This will save you tons of time in "figuring it out" and provide you with invaluable insights. After the class, go paddle! And consider a guided tour in areas

you're uncomfortable paddling in on your own. Kayak clubs offer affordable training and a skilled group to paddle with. Take time to practice your new skills and work out the kinks while becoming more comfortable with being on water. This will also give you a chance to improve your trip-preparation skills and learn from minor mistakes like forgetting your spray skirt or fin at home. Soon paddling will become less foreign and more natural to you.

Once you're comfortable with basic paddling skills, continue to improve your abilities with lessons or paddle clubs so you can paddle in more remote areas and in tougher conditions, such as in rough water, tidal rapids, surf, high wind, or by the coast. Learning to roll your kayak, paddle in rough water, remount your surf ski in any conditions, and maneuver your paddle board safely with control on rivers, tidal rapids, and surf will allow you to explore many magnificent destinations in the Pacific Northwest throughout the year.

*A strong flood current is visible against a channel marker on Sequim Bay (Trip 43).*

### KNOW YOUR LIMITS

Many unskilled paddlers see the blue sky and dart for the beach or lake. They don't know to check the wind speed or direction, water temperature, tide level, tidal currents direction, or river level. Many launch without life jackets, clothing for immersion, or SUP leashes, thinking nothing could happen to them. Recently, I heard "I'm a casual paddler and will be by shore, I don't need a life jacket." Skilled paddlers with experience in a variety of conditions always go through all the steps to prepare for specific situations and thus can have more fun and return home safely.

---

### GO OR NOT?

It's not uncommon for inexperienced paddlers to decide to go out in conditions well above their skill level after a long drive to the beach or after planning a trip for weeks. Upon arrival at the beach, if it looks sketchy, it probably is. Follow the adage, "When in doubt, don't go out." There will be another day, and with your increased knowledge of weather forecasting, you can better pinpoint the ideal conditions and location for your level. Don't let your buddies convince you otherwise!

---

## Safety

After a long winter, when the first warm, sunny days emerge, many seasonal Pacific Northwest paddlers dust off their gear and head for the water. And every spring there is a spike in cold-water fatalities because paddlers underestimate the effects of our chilly waters. Making sure

33

SAFETY

you are not only prepared for cold water (see the Gear section) but also that you know how to respond if you capsize are key to staying safe. Being visible to other craft, learning hand signals to communicate, and knowing how to respond in an emergency should also be part of your preparation.

## KNOW HOW TO REMOUNT QUICKLY

Well-practiced recovery techniques, whether you are properly dressed or not, are especially important in Pacific Northwest waters. If you fall in, getting out of the water quickly is critical, though the risk of hypothermia may continue due to wind chill. Kayakers should learn the Eskimo roll, but they shouldn't solely rely on it. Surf skiers and canoeists need a solid remount technique for all possible conditions. Paddle boarders should buy a flat-fronted, non-bulky life jacket to help them get back on the board. A leash can help keep the board close after a fall, especially in strong winds and currents.

## OUTFIT YOUR PADDLE CRAFT FOR SAFETY AND VISIBILITY

Add stick-on reflectors to the hulls of sea kayaks and SUPs. Fasten thick deck lines around the perimeter of sea kayaks so you have something to grab or hold onto during self- and assisted rescues. You can also affix a stick-on loop to the nose of SUPs to tie on a tow line; use it to attach to other boats or to the shore to prevent drifting.

## LEARN HAND SIGNALS

Hand signals (see Figure 5) can help you communicate when radios and phones don't work or when the wind and waves are too loud to talk over. They are also useful when paddlers in your group are spread far apart, and their voices can't be heard. Review the signals with your group before departure.

> **TIP**
>
> Paddle boarders should wear a quick-release leash attached to their personal flotation device (PFD) waist straps when paddling in tidal and river currents. Nearly all river and tidal current SUP fatalities happen when the paddler's ankle leash becomes entangled in logs, pilings, or other underwater obstructions. With the leash attached to your waist, you can release it much easier.

## BE PREPARED FOR EMERGENCIES

We all hope an emergency never happens, but we should be prepared just in case. It is wise to know at least the basics of first aid and cardiopulmonary resuscitation (CPR). Classes in these disciplines are taught on a regular basis by local chapters of the American Red Cross, through community service organizations like the local fire department, and by outdoor recreation groups and clubs.

In addition, the importance of taking classes to become proficient in fundamental sea-kayak rescues, such as the T-assisted rescue and paddle-float self-rescue, cannot be stressed

STOP

HELP/EMERGENCY

GO RIGHT

GO LEFT

ALL CLEAR

OK

*Figure 5. Hand signals help communicate over long distances.*

enough. Being prepared with a clear mind and a practiced response for that off-chance dunk into the water can literally be lifesaving.

Stand up paddlers should know how to tow another paddler. And you should always have the gear necessary to receive a tow yourself—waist-worn kayak tow ropes are ideal for this purpose. Be prepared to rescue people in other types of watercraft, such as kayaks, as well.

Beyond the unmistakable reality that the best help is the immediate aid of your paddling group, you can obtain assistance from a variety of sources when on or near the water. Who you call will depend on the nature of the emergency, your location, and the means of communication available to you.

In an emergency, you should be prepared to provide rescue workers with all relevant information. Some possible critical information includes the following:

- Nature of the emergency: injury (exact description), capsized boat, missing person, etc.
- When the problem occurred and how long people may have been in the water or suffering an injury
- Exact location or direction and distance from recognizable landmarks
- Description of persons and boats involved
- How many people and what kind of equipment, including survival gear and first-aid supplies, are at the scene
- Equipment needed
- Method of evacuation needed
- Local weather and sea conditions, including currents and wave action
- Names and addresses of members in the party and whom to notify

## Hypothermia

In the cold waters of the Pacific Northwest, hypothermia is a constant threat. It's important to know how to recognize and quickly treat it. Early stages of hypothermia include violent shivering, clumsy or slurred speech, and loss of dexterity. Warm up a hypothermic person with blankets and mild heat to avoid afterdrop, a condition where cold blood from the extremities rushes into the body core, causing a continued drop in body temperature and the potential for a heart attack. Consider carrying extra thermal garments designed for paddlers, such as a neoprene hood, a storm cag (a large-hooded, wind- and waterproof coat that fits over PFDs and extends down to the knees), and chemical hand warmers for yourself or others.

## Location

Knowing your precise location can be difficult at times, especially during the stress of an emergency. But it is essential information to have if help is to reach you in time. For an exact location, a global positioning system (GPS) receiver is ideal. Some cell phone systems can provide the location of the caller to 911. However, batteries and electronic equipment have a predisposition to fail in saltwater environments. There is no substitute for waterproof nautical charts and a compass to continually track your progress and position.

## Communication

In all emergencies, when feasible, call 911 for assistance. The dispatcher can contact the appropriate agency for aid. The county sheriff is the standard emergency responder in most areas of Puget Sound and the San Juan Islands. The US Coast Guard is tasked with providing emergency aid on the water.

*Kayaker off Washington Park with a view of Cypress Island in the distance (Trip 50).*

As common as cell phones are, do not rely on them totally, as you may be out of transmission range. If you do use a cell phone, tether it to your PFD in a waterproof case that allows for use on-water. A VHF-FM radio is invaluable for this reason. Handheld, waterproof, floating VHF radios are available, perfect for keeping strapped to your life jacket or within immediate reach.

But remember: don't just carry a radio; know how to use it and always keep it accessible. You should also carry flares and other emergency signaling devices. Know when and how to use them for maximum effectiveness.

## Navigating Marine Traffic

Other boats and ships can be as much of a danger to paddlers as anything nature can throw at us. Ships sometimes run down kayaks or paddle boards, or upset them in a near miss, because of their inability to see them or because they spot them too late for avoidance. Pleasure boats can do the same due to inattention at the helm or even in an innocent attempt to come in for a closer look.

### PREVENTING COLLISIONS

To determine what will happen as you approach a ship or other craft on a course perpendicular to your own, watch the ship's position off your bow as you converge; this is called the bow-angle method (see Figure 6). When a ship or boat is coming your way, point your paddle or arm toward it and note the angle between your paddle shaft and the front of your board. Continue checking this angle every few minutes as you paddle. If the angle appears smaller (the paddle shaft moves closer to the nose of your board), the vessel will pass behind you. If the angle gets larger, it'll pass in front of you. When the angle doesn't change, you're on a collision course. Alter your course immediately if a collision is imminent. Keep checking to see if the other vessel also changes its course.

Another method involves using your hand and fingers to determine how other vessels will cross your path. For a boat approaching on your right, face the nose or bow and place your right hand on your board or boat deck, with your fingers

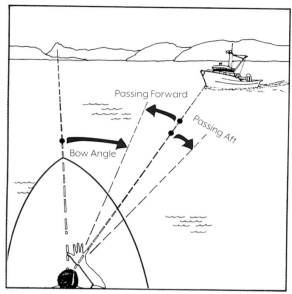

*Figure 6. The bow-angle method*

spread out and your thumb lined up with the center line of the board. Line up one finger with the incoming ship's bow. Use the center of the board or boat as a guide. If the angle between your thumb and finger increases, the boat will pass behind. If the angle decreases, the boat will pass in front of you. If there's no change, you're on a collision course.

At night, understanding the significance of port and starboard lights is essential. If you see a red (port) light on an incoming vessel, it'll pass to your left. If you see a green (starboard), it'll pass to your right. If you see both red and green lights, plus a white mast light in the middle, you're on a collision course.

## SHIPS

Large ships suffer from two major disadvantages in avoiding collisions: impaired visibility and slow reaction time. Visibility forward from the ship's bridge is partially obstructed by the hull—from some ships, a kayaker is not visible at all when less than a half mile ahead! And the chances that a ship will be able to pick you up on radar are slim. Even if you have a radar reflector, it will be too low to the water to produce a significant signal. Ships also cannot maneuver out of the way quickly; emergency actions, like throwing the engines into reverse, take some time and may put the ship out of control. Many ships require more than a mile to stop, even with full power astern. Tugs pulling barges are especially unable to change course or stop quickly.

The burden is on you to stay out of a ship's path. As with all other pleasure craft, you must stay at least a half mile from approaching ships and a quarter mile aside passing ones. Fortunately, large ship courses are usually predictable. The major shipping routes in Puget Sound, Rosario Strait, and the Strait of Juan de Fuca have defined traffic lanes, marked in red or purple on nautical charts. Some routes are divided into one-way lanes with a separation zone in between. Ships are supposed to stay within these lanes. If you can determine where you are in relation to a lane, you can predict where the ship will pass. Though pleasure craft are allowed to cross these lanes, they should do so as quickly as possible. Ships will sometimes deviate from their lane—to pass around a sailboat regatta, for example—so be sure to leave a margin of error for both you and any ships.

Suppose you see a distant ship coming down a traffic lane that you wish to cross. Should you try to cross ahead of it or wait for it to pass? Obviously, the latter is safest, but circumstances do arise when you find yourself needing to proceed ahead immediately. Can you make it?

To answer this important question, you need to know something about the ship's speed relative to yours, as well as its distance from your intended crossing point on the traffic lane. Most ships are much faster than they appear—16 knots is typical in our inland waters, though some freighters may move at their full 23-knot sea speed. Tugs with tows average 8 knots, with up to 10 knots possible. Assuming your speed to be 4 knots, ships may be traveling four to five times faster than you. Generously estimate the speed of the oncoming ship. Then estimate both your and the ship's distance from where you plan to cross the traffic lane. Use that information to calculate which of you will reach the crossing point first; be sure to add a quarter mile to your distance to guarantee you have enough clearance on the other side. Another option is to use the bow-angle method (see Preventing Collisions above).

If you find yourself in a situation where you believe you cannot get out of a ship's way, emergency signaling with flares—or orange smoke in sunny weather—may be your only remedy. However, it will probably bring the wrath of the Coast Guard down upon you, as well as attract the attention of the whole maritime community. The most effective solution is a marine VHF transceiver. Call the ship, let them know where you are, and then agree on a solution. Do this before it is too late for them to take evasive action. Though Channel 16 is the general calling and emergency frequency, ships in Washington's inland waters monitor Channel 14 (Seattle traffic) or Channel 13 (ships' bridge-to-bridge). If you cannot read the ship's name, call it by position (e.g., "the southbound black container ship off Foulweather Bluff").

Also consider using ship tracking apps that give visual updates on ships, pleasure craft, and some military craft—almost in real time. They also provide voyage routes and photos and details of the craft. (See Resources for a list of recommended ship tracking apps.)

Finally, you should be aware of the many restrictions, imposed by the Department of Homeland Security, on approaching military or commercial vessels. Most importantly, you must keep at least 100 yards away from all naval vessels and paddle at minimal speed within 500 yards. You may risk both fine and imprisonment if you approach closer. The 100-yard rule should also be applied to docked container ships, freighters and tankers underway, and ferries.

## FERRIES

Generally, ferries have much better visibility and maneuverability than ships of comparative size, but they can still be hazardous. When paddling in a group through narrow channels traversed by ferries, stay close together and avoid spacing out across their path. If you take evasive action, decide on a direction, and stay with it so the ferry can react accordingly. Be especially cautious

*Washington State Ferry storage in Eagle Harbor (Trip 17)*

around docked ferries; be sure they are not about to leave as you cross in front of them. As a safe practice, always give them a wide berth. Paddling underneath ferry docks is both illegal and dangerous, as the prop wash from a docking or departing ferry can easily wrap your boat around a piling. Check the BC Ferries and Washington State Ferries schedules to find a safe crossing time. Washington State Department of Transportation (WSDOT) has a great app that gives ferry departure and arrival times in close to real time (see Resources).

### PLEASURE CRAFT

Always yield to powerboats and sailboats, particularly in urban areas with heavy boat traffic and during the busy summer season. Kayaks and SUPs are both slower than most other boats. Many paddlers misjudge the speed of incoming powerboats and cross dangerously close in front of them. Pay attention to boating channels, where red and green buoys mark the path boaters must follow to avoid grounding on shallow shoals or sandbars. Below Seattle's Hiram M. Chittenden Locks, nicknamed the Ballard Locks (see Trip 20, Lake Union), kayakers and stand up paddlers regularly cross a busy channel in front of fast-moving boats. An outgoing current of 1 to 3 knots is continuously released from the locks; inexperienced paddlers find themselves being pushed more quickly toward oncoming boats than they expected. I've seen several near collisions as boaters swerve to avoid hitting the paddlers. Look both ways before crossing a boating channel—and when in doubt, let the boat traffic pass.

In open water, I've had larger boats turn directly toward me, giving me few options for how to react. Powerboats have cruised by me at full speed with no one at the helm, probably on autopilot. Remember that on sailboats, the captain is in the rear of the boat, with limited forward visibility. Make sure to wear bright colors, put reflective tape on your PFD and paddle, and pay attention to all the boat traffic around you.

## Types of Touring Paddle Craft

A variety of watercraft is available, depending on the type of paddling or experience you're interested in. Each type of craft has different requirements for gear. When planning what to pack, you'll also need to consider the length of your trip, the season, and current weather conditions. Knowing which gear to bring is essential to having a safe and enjoyable outing.

**Recreational Kayak.** The typical model is a plastic, open- or closed-deck kayak less than twelve feet long. While these can transport you a few miles, most don't have bulkheads to pre-

*Paddler enjoying a hot summer day on Jarrell Cove (Trip 6)*

vent water from traveling from the cockpit to the ends of the boat. If water gets in, the boat will sink. Float bags in the storage areas can help reduce this. (Oru Kayaks may look like traditional sea kayaks but lack bulkheads and can fill with water if capsized. Add float bags in the bow and stern to provide adequate flotation.) The relatively short length of recreational kayaks limits the distance you can travel and makes them unsuitable for rough seas.

**Rowing Craft.** Rowing shells and various row boats are commonly seen on the Salish Sea, as they are often fast and provide great fitness benefits. Row boats allow for ample storage. With a rowboat, you can stow a lot of gear and large amounts of water, get some great exercise, and enjoy an open-air feeling on the water. Many rowers make their own boats. Trailers and often a boat ramp are required.

**Outrigger Canoe (OC).** While less commonly seen on the Salish Sea, outrigger canoes provide another way to experience paddling. Many are fast but can only carry minimal gear. Adequate training is required for stability and remounts.

**Sit-on-Top Kayak or Pedal Kayak.** Plastic sit-on-top (SOT) kayaks and pedal kayaks can work for touring if their length allows for speed. Plastic SOTs are often very heavy, but some have hatches and efficient pedal drives. Some use a floor scupper to suck water out of the foot area while underway (see Resources for specific gear recommendations).

**Inflatable Kayak.** Inflatable kayaks tend to be very stable and comfortable—but not very fast. If speed isn't your goal, they're great for families and for taking it easy. And don't underestimate the advantage of being able to deflate and avoid needing a car rack.

**Sea Kayak.** A touring sea kayak can be plastic or composite, is usually fourteen to eighteen feet long, and has a closed deck. The paddler sits inside a cockpit, sometimes sealed by a spray skirt. Sea kayaks have stern and bow storage and often a day hatch—a small, easily accessed storage area behind the seat. Bulkheads prevent water from flowing through the length of the boat. Some have rudders, but others do not—it's a personal choice (see Resources for specific gear recommendations). Paddlers need solid training to learn how to "wet exit" and reenter sea kayaks safely.

**Touring Surf Ski.** Surf skis were originally designed as nimble, fast-racing, sit-on-top kayaks. Over the years, some paddlers found "skis" to be great for surfing. Now a few manufacturers make stable touring surf skis with storage hatches (see Resources for specific gear recommendations). Compared to closed-deck kayaks, surf skis are much easier to exit and reenter. They're also much lighter. Many skis weigh twenty-five to thirty-five pounds, making them easier to carry and lift onto car racks. These boats are in the twenty- to twenty-one-inch width range, so they are quite stable.

**Canoe.** Canoes are efficient for touring, offering ample storage and comfortable open seating. They are common on Salish Sea waters and very popular in Canada. Reentry after a capsize does require training. Weight can vary from surprisingly light to heavy, depending on the layup.

**Stand Up Paddle Board (SUP).** The advantage of paddle boards is that you can sit, kneel, and stand without being "in" a craft. Paddle boards under twelve and a half feet can move quickly, but only if the user has a good stroke. Boards fourteen feet or longer allow you to cover great distances more easily (see Resources for specific gear recommendations). Inflatable SUPs are handy for those who live in an apartment, don't have a car, or prefer to walk in their board. Two paddlers I know from Vancouver, BC, regularly walk their SUPs and camping gear onto BC Ferries with the help of a folding hand truck, saving them a hefty vehicle fee.

---

**TIP**

Get an inflatable paddle board with a standard fin box so you can choose which fin you want. Fins help with directional control, stability, and control while surfing and downwinding. Buy two fins in case you lose one. Store the backup in your car or backpack.

---

**Sails and Kites.** Why row or paddle when you can sail your paddle craft? Some kayakers use kites to help pull them along the waterways. Some companies have hybrid kayak/outrigger kits with sails that can carry more gear and travel very efficiently (see Resources for specific gear recommendations). Some paddle boards have a deck insert for a windsurfing mast.

## LONGER IS FASTER

You can enjoy paddling on craft of any length. But if you want to cover long distances easily and quickly, get an efficient kayak, canoe, or SUP. Aim for a craft with a longer waterline, fourteen feet or more, to maximize efficiency. Some surf skis and paddle boards are quite narrow, with a reduced "beam" (sides) to reduce drag, but this also makes them less stable. Find the right balance of length (speed) and width (stability) for you. Paddling a wide, short craft fast will require a lot of effort and you may injure your shoulders and back. Try out all gear prior to purchase; make sure it's comfortable and fits your paddling style.

# What to Pack

Kayaks and paddle boards have limited space for gear, so paddlers tend to focus on bringing only essential gear, clothing, and food. Know which marinas and campgrounds have water available and pack accordingly. Some paddlers prefer ultra-light tents, pads, and sleeping bags. Some go even lighter with floorless tents, or a just bivy sack or tarp, depending on the weather forecast. Think about your trip duration and length to determine which and how much gear to bring.

## LIFE JACKETS AND OTHER MUST-HAVES

The most fundamental item, of course, regardless of whether you're heading out for an hour or several days is a life jacket or personal flotation device (PFD). The US Coast Guard (USCG) requires all kayakers and paddlers of other small, human-powered watercraft to wear a PFD. They call it a life jacket for a reason. The thick foam in the more commonly used Type III PFDs adds insulation around your core and keeps you afloat when you're fatigued or injured. The bright color of these vests helps you be visible to boats and others when you're offshore, and pockets provide storage for essentials. You might also consider a PFD with reflective strips to provide more visibility in busy boating areas. Some PFDs have built-in short tow ropes and quick-release tow belt straps for rescues. But be sure your PFD isn't too bulky because that will make it difficult for you to climb on your craft. If you're paddling with kids, make sure they have a properly fitting PFD.

Inflatable Type V PFDs (also known as belt pack PFDs) are available for paddle boarders who prefer a minimalist feeling on the water. However, in the case of a sudden capsize or a head or shoulder injury, a paddler who is panicked or whose fingers are numb from cold may not be able to inflate the vest properly—and obviously this type of PFD won't do any good if a paddler is unconscious. If you use this type of PFD, practice using it by pulling the cord and putting it on while in the water. Clean the PFD with fresh water after each use and replace the PFD's $CO_2$ cartridges every few months; saltwater corrosion can cause the device to malfunction. There is one vest PFD that has both $CO_2$ and passive foam floatation (see Resources).

Many stand up paddlers choose to put their PFDs on their board. At the time of writing this edition, this practice is legal in some areas, but make sure you know the regulations in the area you're paddling in and that your PFD can be easily removed in case of an emergency. To help keep yourself hydrated while underway, add a hydration bladder to the rear of your PFD—some have built-in rear sleeves for hydration bladders (see Resources for specific gear recommendations). These PFDs still have adequate floatation for most body types.

You should always have a whistle tethered to your PFD, as required by the Coast Guard. Other items you can add to your PFD, depending on the type and duration of your trip: Tether a phone in a waterproof bag to the jacket and attach a floating, hand-held, 6-watt VHF radio on a tether or in a pocket. Add energy bars or gels, a small reflector, a strobe, smoke rocket flares or a laser signaling device, a light for night paddling attached to the exterior of the jacket, and a paddler's stainless-steel knife with a dull tip to avoid cutting yourself. For solo or remote trips, attach a rescue tracking device like a Spot Tracker.

## GEAR FOR YOUR CRAFT

Depending on what type of craft you have, you will need to add different types of gear.

**Kayak.** Paddle, extra paddle, spray skirt, sponge, pump, compact wheels, paddle float, pogies or gloves, storm cag, deck bag, dry bags, helmet, tow rope, rudder repair kit, kite.

**Paddle Board.** Paddle, leash, fin, small dry bag or deck bag, pump, patch kit, helmet, tow rope, compact wheels, or breakdown hand truck for ferry. Add a small repair kit with extra leash string, fin screws, ding repair kit.

*Chocolate Beach in the Chain Islands near Salt Spring Island (Trip 73)*

---

**TIP**

Get a nine-inch Surfco Superflex rubber fin for your paddle board for paddling through kelp beds and lake milfoil. These are also great for paddling near reefs or rocky areas.

---

**Touring Surf Ski.** Paddle, leash, helmet, tow rope, compact wheels, dry bags, ding repair materials, rudder repair kit, gloves, tow rope. Rudder repair kit should include an extra rudder, washers, locking nut, and bungie setup to attach to rudder yoke in case of a cable failure. A rubberized surf ski rudder works well in rough water, near reefs, and in rocky environments.

---

**TIP**

Make sure your name and phone number are on your paddling craft and paddle. The US Coast Guard has ID stickers to attach to kayaks, SUPs, and canoes. Almost every summer a random kayak or SUP floats off from a beach house or campsite, leading to a big Coast Guard rescue operation to find the owner.

---

## TEN ESSENTIALS AND MORE

Paddling guides often carry a "hypo-kit" (hypothermia kit) with extra synthetic clothes and accessories to make sure the paddlers stay warm and comfortable on a trip, and this is sort of the paddler's version of the Ten Essentials. Consider a similar kit for your trips. Items in these kits often include a VHF radio, energy bars, chemical heat packets, prescription medications, hydration tablets, a first-aid kit, extra warm synthetic clothing, neoprene hoods and gloves, and

*Low tide and an exposed erratic boulder on Freshwater Bay, Olympic Peninsula (Trip 46)*

a compact emergency blanket or bivy sack. Also include emergency signaling devices such as handheld rocket flares, a signaling mirror, and smoke canisters for daytime use. These items are in addition to the Ten Essentials, a list developed by The Mountaineers to prevent emergencies and respond positively should one occur (items 1–5) and to help you safely spend a night—or more—outside (items 6–10). Use this list as a guide and tailor it to the needs of your outing.

1. **Navigation:** The fundamentals for paddle touring are a marine chart, tide and current tables, compass, GPS device, and a personal locator beacon or other device to contact emergency first responders. Get to know your devices prior to departure. Carry extra batteries, a power bank, or a solar strip to keep your batteries charged.
2. **Headlamp or other light for night paddling and camp:** Include spare batteries or a solar charger, which can also work to recharge a phone.
3. **Sun protection:** Wear sunglasses with a head strap, a sun hat with a chin strap, sun-protective clothes, broad-spectrum sunscreen rated at least SPF 30, UV lip balm, and lip ointment.
4. **First aid:** Purchase a backpacker's or paddler's first-aid kit or assemble a custom kit. Basics include bandages; skin closures; gauze pads and dressings; roller bandage or wrap; tape; antiseptic; blister prevention and treatment supplies; nitrile gloves; tweezers; needle; nonprescription painkillers; anti-inflammatory, anti-diarrheal, seasickness, and antihistamine tablets; topical antibiotic; chemical heat packs; and any important personal prescriptions, including an EpiPen if you are allergic to bee or hornet venom.
5. **Knife:** Also consider a multi-tool, strong tape, some cordage, and gear repair supplies.

6. **Fire:** Carry at least one butane lighter (or waterproof matches or magnesium fire striker) and firestarter, such as chemical heat tabs, cotton balls soaked in petroleum jelly, or commercially prepared firestarter.

7. **Shelter:** In addition to a rain shell, carry a single-use bivy sack or mylar blanket.

8. **Extra food:** For shorter trips a one-day supply is reasonable—energy bars and gels are easy to carry in any paddling craft.

9. **Extra water:** Carry sufficient water and electrolytes and have the skills and tools required to obtain and purify additional water. Attach water bottles or a hydration bladder to your PFD.

10. **Extra clothes:** Pack additional layers needed to survive the night in the worst conditions that your party may realistically encounter.

Additionally, a tow rope is essential for you to tow a friend or another paddler who is in trouble, or for others to tow you in case of an injury, capsize, seasickness, fatigue, or other unexpected situation. Some kayaks have attachments for tow ropes, but most paddlers carry them in a fanny pack or waist pack or on quick-release straps on their PFDs. Tow ropes can also be used to dry gear in camp.

If you plan to stand up paddle offshore, outfit your board to carry extra warm clothing, camping and fishing gear, and water. Always wear your leash and PFD in case of a fall or in case a storm front catches you off guard. Consider carrying an extra break-down paddle in case of loss or breakage.

## GEAR FOR DAY TRIPS

In addition to items from the Ten Essentials, you may want to bring along some other things on short outings.

*Basics*
- ☐ Binoculars
- ☐ Fishing gear for adults and kids
- ☐ Insect repellent and/or bug net
- ☐ Keys/key fob in a waterproof dry bag (keep in a secure spot)
- ☐ Prescription eyeglasses with case and head strap
- ☐ Thermos of hot tea, cocoa, or soup
- ☐ Wallet
- ☐ Watch

*Shore gear*
- ☐ Bear spray
- ☐ Day pack
- ☐ Hand sanitizer
- ☐ Hiking boots
- ☐ Small shovel
- ☐ Walking sticks

*Camera gear (store in a dry bag with silicone packets)*
- ☐ Camera strap and bag strap
- ☐ Dry cloth to use on camera and lens exterior stored in a zip-top bag
- ☐ Extra batteries or solar battery charger
- ☐ Lens cloth

*Gear for kids*
- ☐ Bubbles
- ☐ Explorer's kit with binoculars, notepad, pencil, magnifying glass
- ☐ Games
- ☐ Kids' camera on a tether
- ☐ Snacks
- ☐ Water bottle
- ☐ Water shoes

Also, establish a hide-a-key location around your vehicle at the launch. Make sure you can find it in the dark if necessary. When you arrive back at your vehicle, it's also refreshing to have fresh clothes, hydration options, and snacks available. If you ran a shuttle, bring a duffel or backpack to store fresh clothes and snacks in the vehicle you'll use at the end of the trip.

## GEAR FOR MULTIDAY TOURS

For overnight outings, you'll need the Ten Essentials, some of the day trip items listed above, plus gear for camping:

*Gear for food prep and cleanup*
- ☐ Backpacking stove, fuel, and windshield
- ☐ Biodegradable liquid soap
- ☐ Can opener
- ☐ Coffee pot or French press
- ☐ Dish cloth
- ☐ Eating utensils
- ☐ Garbage bags
- ☐ Pot scrubber
- ☐ Sharp knife
- ☐ Titanium pots or a JetBoil (insulated cup or pot that is designed to cook food or liquid more quickly)
- ☐ Water filter
- ☐ Zip-top bags for food storage

*Gear for shelter and sleeping*
- ☐ Ground sheet
- ☐ Pillow

> **TIP**
>
> Plan your meals to limit how many pots and pans you need to bring. Get collapsible containers to save space. Choose pots that have multiple uses. While traveling, pack other items in empty pots and cups to save space.

> **TIP**
>
> Synthetic sleeping bags tend to stay warmer if damp but are heavier and take up more space. Double dry-bag your sleeping bag, as no kayak hatches are 100 percent dry.

- [ ] Reflective rope for tent and overhead tarp guy lines
- [ ] Sleeping bag with liner and cover
- [ ] Sleeping pad (air or foam, or both for better insulation)
- [ ] Tent, tarp, bivy sack, or hammock
- [ ] Toiletries

## What to Wear

The Salish Sea is cold most of the year, except for some areas like Hood Canal in late summer. Survival time in 50-degree water can be as short as a half hour without a full 5/4mm hooded wetsuit or dry suit. Wearing the appropriate clothing for the air and water temperature will allow you to extend your paddling season and enjoy each trip more.

A good practice is to dress for the water temperature, in case of unexpected immersion. This especially applies if you are paddling in rough water, through fast-moving currents, in surf, at night, or during open-water crossings. Clothing choices also depend on whether you're paddling fast or slow, and whether you're on flat water or in strong winds.

Several clothing options can provide adequate warmth without hindering movement. Dry suits keep you mostly dry and leave space for you to layer thermal garments underneath as needed. Always use insulating synthetic clothing underneath, such as polar fleece or polypropylene products. Full surfing wetsuits have come a long way in recent years with seam-sealed (not wet) suits, and there is a range of affordable styles made of warm, flexible neoprene in varying thicknesses; some are even fleece- or wool-lined. They come as hooded or hoodless, back zip, chest zip, or no zip for more warmth. Top and bottom neoprene paddling garments, insulating rash guards, or Farmer John/Jane armless neoprene wetsuits help but are not as warm as a full suit, though these may be fine options if you run hot or just plan on a quick dip in the water. If your duration in the water is longer or if your head is underwater, these will be effective for a shorter time than full-body options.

Neoprene booties, gloves, and hoods are recommended to provide insulation in cooler weather, on rough-water trips, during immersion, and in survival situations. Booties and gloves also protect your feet and hands from the Northwest's barnacled and gravelly shores.

Boost a wetsuit or dry suit's warmth with add-ons like a hooded vest, neoprene "skull cap" with a chin strap, or synthetic paddling jacket (with or without a hood to cut windchill and keep off the rain). Thin thermal tops can be worn under some wetsuits. If on a budget, many of these items can be borrowed from your hiking and bicycling gear, such as a pull-over raincoat and thermal beanies.

Remember to also carry some backup clothing in case someone in your group forgets or loses an item.

---

**TIP**

Make sure to follow your own experience and instincts when it comes to choosing paddling clothing. Asking a buddy what they're wearing won't help you if they run hot and you run cold.

## ADD EXTRA LAYERS ON SHORE

Bring along an extra thermal layer or shell to put on during breaks. Some kayak clothing companies have compact storm cags. An old foam camping pad works well to conserve warmth if you're sitting on the ground, rocks, or logs.

## WINTER CLOTHING

Clothing for the off-season—in fact for any season—should be able to shed water and wind. Winter's heavier precipitation and stronger winds mean you will want to wear a paddle jacket, dry top, full-hooded 5/4mm full surfing wetsuit, or dry suit most of the time. A good barrier against the substantially enhanced windchill factor, even in light breezes, is important for your safety as well as comfort. Gloves or pogies that guard against both wetness and cold air are also essential. If you don't like gloves, you can use sports tape to protect fingers during long paddles.

Head protection is extremely important; this is where most of the body's heat is lost. A wool or neoprene cap or hood serves most paddlers very well. You can adjust to a full range of temperatures and wetness conditions by wearing one of these items, both together, or neither. Neck gaiters help retain heat and block the sun as well. Neoprene booties are essential; to prevent foot injuries, choose booties with ankle support if you'll be doing a lot of walking on shore. Add a seam-sealed, insulated, neoprene sock under your booties to boost heat. Bring a warm jacket and hat, stored in a dry bag, to stay warm when you stop paddling at the end of the day or during shore lunch breaks.

## PADDLING IN HOT WEATHER BUT COLD WATER

Balancing clothing options for paddling in cold water but warm air can be a challenge. In hot weather, most choose not to dress for immersion but get a shock if they do fall off their SUP or capsize their kayak. Experienced paddlers who choose to wear a dry suit or full wetsuit on hot days know a quick roll or dip will cool them off. A good clothing compromise for summer days on flat water is to wear neoprene pants and a neoprene paddling or surf top, rash guard, or other quick-drying top. Consider dressing in layers so you can remove or add clothing easily if necessary.

## PADDLING IN WARM AIR AND WATER

For warm air and water days, wear light-colored, quick-drying, synthetic (no cotton) clothing and a wide-brimmed hat, which also helps minimize UV exposure. Some paddlers wear hats with neck coverings or a neck gaiter to keep the sun off. UV-block lip balm is also an option. Stash a small sunblock tube in your PFD to reapply after a few hours or a dip. Consider using sunblock products that are not harmful to the environment.

OPPOSITE *Low tide, Fry Cove (Trip 2)*

# Trip Planning and Using This Guide

Trip planning requires the consideration of many factors, including personal kayaking skills, navigation, group dynamics, and much more. It takes time to acquire these skills, but many are translatable from other activities like bicycling and hiking.

Develop a trip prep checklist to have a well-thought-out plan for your next trip. This list will help ensure you have the right gear, paddle with the right people, and take the time to review the trip details to determine if it's really the right one for you. A checklist will also remind you to get permits, make ferry reservations, do any necessary on-water training, and also to pack all of the gear, clothing, and food you'll need. See Resources for a sample checklist.

As you plan, start thinking about how you can better outfit your boat, board, or canoe. Paddle boarders need to consider how to attach all the gear to the deck and whether there will be enough standing room for controlling the board in waves and wind. Kayakers should look into adding deck bags to access gear more quickly and also into improving grab lines around the boat.

**A HARD-LEARNED LESSON**

One time, my partner and I camped for a night on Skagit Island. In the morning, I was in a rush to get home and we hastily left, not really looking at the currents. I knew we'd get to Canoe Pass in Deception Pass at the end of the ebb, and I told myself, "We should be able to make it!" Turns out the current had already started flooding and my partner lacked the more advanced skills needed to eddy hop to the other side. Once through Canoe Pass, we decided to portage from Lottie Bay to our parking lot at Bowman Bay. Lottie Bay was empty of water and a big mudflat. We trudged through sucking, knee-deep mud in 80-degree F heat, dragging our kayaks behind us. A lesson in the need for much better planning and training!

## Choosing a Trip

Carefully review the ratings and descriptions for each route in this guidebook when choosing a trip and be sure to select one that matches your abilities. Be especially conscious of this if you are new to paddling. Saltwater trips are more difficult to classify than those on rivers, where conditions can be somewhat accurately predicted. Saltwater can be mirror smooth on the best of days and a raging sea on the worst. There is no sure way to avoid the latter. Overconfidence comes easily on those glassy days, and many paddlers have gotten more than they bargained for by taking on challenging routes after enjoying better-than-average weather on earlier trips. It is wise to start out slowly and experience a range of weather conditions in protected situations before testing your skills in more-exposed places. If you're a beginner, or even an intermediate paddler, learn and improve your trip-planning skills by joining up with experienced paddlers or one of the many local clubs or commercial classes frequently offered.

Each route in this guide begins with an overview of what to expect, followed by more detailed information:

**Duration:** In calm weather with minimal wind and current, trip duration is based upon completing the trip at a rate of about 3.5 knots per hour, which is a common speed for touring paddlers.

**Rating:** With some trepidation, I have rated saltwater paddling routes in this book by the degree of hazard potential. Though much needed, this was as slippery a task as getting a footing on a kelp-covered rock.

All routes are rated with a *Protected*, *Moderate*, or *Exposed* rating, which reflects the numerous discrete and sometimes ethereal elements that are the sea environment. Unlike easily rated rivers with predictable conditions that are related to a particular rate of flow, sea conditions change by the minute as winds and currents shift in intensity independent of one another. Ratings are based on the potential for troubles that may express themselves only rarely, but with perhaps dire consequences: tide rips that spring up from nowhere or a sudden wind that delivers difficult sea conditions during a crossing.

There is a real danger that new paddlers, lulled by a placid first trip, might be drawn into traps laid by changing weather or tides. Weekend trips lacking a long but easy alternative route, coupled with the demand to be home by Sunday night, may lead to "going for it" on a nasty crossing. Sucia Island and its neighboring islands are frequented by weekend neophyte kayakers, yet the trip-rating criteria led me to rate this trip *Exposed*. (A kayaking fatality has occurred in this vicinity.) The ratings suggest the potential for trouble based on circumstances and paddlers' experiences. How you use them depends on your abilities and judgment.

Evaluate your own ability to counter the potential sea forces according to your awareness, strength, and survival skills on the water. Awareness is your ability to anticipate and avoid hazards—for example, to spot a dangerous tide rip far downstream and assess which way to paddle to avoid it. Strength is your ability to paddle hard against wind or current to escape a bad situation. Survival skills on the water are your boat-handling reflexes: balance, braces, and rolls. These abilities enable you to keep going despite the sea's energies around you, with the hope that conditions eventually moderate or you reach calmer water.

Trips are rated primarily on the potential for trouble from either weather or currents and also consider the availability of escape routes. Ratings also take into account the amount of protection provided by land in windy conditions, the route's distance from shore, and marine traffic hazards. Daily paddling distances, determined by either a minimum loop distance or the shortest distance between campsites, may be longer for trips with a more challenging rating.

Even the lowest rating presumes some kayak or SUP experience—solid instruction, the ability to perform assisted and solo rescues, and a saltwater trip with one of the many clubs or commercial outfitters for your first time or two in a kayak. A first-time kayaker should start by learning basic boat-handling skills, possibly in a pool, lake, or sheltered harbor that is likely to be warmer and smoother than the open Puget Sound.

These ratings are effective from late spring through early fall. Each trip moves up one difficulty rating during the off-season, October through April (see Paddling During the Off-Season below).

**Protected.** A trip designated as *Protected* is suitable for novice kayakers possessing basic rescue and boat-handling skills, as well as a rudimentary familiarity with nautical charts. Daily distances are 7 nautical miles or less and routes mostly follow the shore, with no crossings more than 1 nautical mile. Waters are largely protected by nearby landforms, and sea currents never exceed 1 knot. Tide rips are unlikely.

**Moderate.** A trip designated as *Moderate* is suitable for kayakers with well-established boat-handling skills, previous saltwater paddling experience, an awareness of current and weather patterns, and the ability to use current- and weather-prediction resources. This rating can include routes with wind and choppy seas, so you need to be able to stay on course and keep upright through balance and bracing. Daily distances may be up to 10 nautical miles. Routes sometimes require crossings longer than 1 nautical mile, and you may need to cross marine shipping lanes. Wind and current have the potential to create dangerous seas on these trips. For short distances, currents may attain 2 knots with tide rips possible, especially in opposing wind conditions. *Moderate* + indicates the presence of a localized hazard that can be avoided by wisely timing your travel or by choosing an alternate route.

**Exposed.** A trip designated as *Exposed* is suitable for experienced sea kayakers who have a thorough understanding of weather and currents and can interact with those elements. They need to be able to handle their boats in rough water. The potential for very rough seas is greater on these routes and long open-water crossings may require paddling for some time in these conditions. You may need to cross major marine shipping lanes. Daily distances may be 10 nautical miles or more, sometimes through exposed seas 1 nautical mile or more from the nearest shore. Currents may exceed 2 knots and tide rips are likely. Trips with this rating become very risky during the off-season and should only be undertaken if you have ample buffer time to wait for safe weather.

**Navigation Aids.** This includes information about which charts and current tables to use. The primary recommended resources are SeaTrails maps, NOAA and Canadian charts, and a few online apps.

**Planning Considerations.** These include how best to time your trip with tides, notes about shoreline access, and alternative launch points.

**Getting There and Launching.** Driving directions, parking permits, fees, restrooms, and other access information is detailed here. Note that all driving directions are in land miles.

**Route.** Learn my recommended route for each trip and what you'll see along the way, including historical references, natural history, and travel tips. Paddling distances are in nautical miles (nm), not the standard land miles you normally think in. A nautical mile equals 1.15 land miles. The route descriptions detail the various options you have, along with hazards, campsites, and so on.

## Navigation Plan

Find the best tools, resources, and methods for planning your trip and determining your route. Having a solid navigational plan will help make your trip safer and more memorable.

### NAUTICAL CHARTS

National Oceanic and Atmospheric Administration (NOAA) charts are issued for Washington waters, and the Canadian Hydrographic Service (CHS) issues charts for British Columbian waters, although there is some overlap. These charts are sold in many nautical supply stores around the region and are also available online. SeaTrails charts are designed for paddlers— they're waterproof, list distances for popular crossings, and mark Washington Water Trails Association (WWTA) sites, public and private shoreline areas, and hazards. SeaTrails stopped production some time ago, but it's worth finding them if you can. Maptech charts are essentially basic navigational charts; they are also waterproof and fold up small for easier use.

Two (and sometimes three) chart alternatives with different scales of coverage are available for any Pacific Northwest locality. For the least expensive coverage, use 1:80,000 charts, available in large, single sheets or in folios containing three sheets printed on lighter paper. The folios are called small craft (SC) charts and three of them combined—18423 SC and 18445 SC, and the CHS's 3310—cover all the waters discussed in this book. The detail at this scale is adequate for cruising (with the CHS chart a bit superior at 1:40,000) and their small pages and light paper make them easy to fold into a chart case. SC charts usually identify parks more thoroughly than the single-sheet equivalents.

# Map Legend

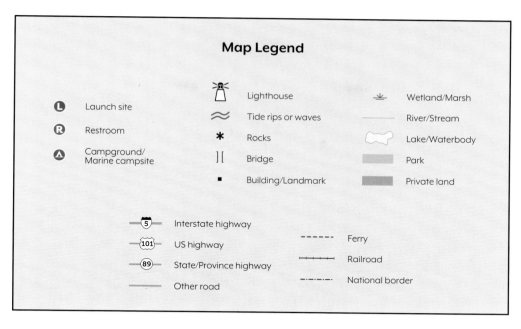

- **L** Launch site
- **R** Restroom
- **A** Campground/ Marine campsite

- Lighthouse
- Tide rips or waves
- \* Rocks
- ][ Bridge
- ▪ Building/Landmark

- Wetland/Marsh
- River/Stream
- Lake/Waterbody
- Park
- Private land

- (5) Interstate highway
- (101) US highway
- (89) State/Province highway
- Other road

- Ferry
- Railroad
- National border

Larger-scale charts—such as 1:25,000—give you a more intimate and detailed view of the shorelines but are more expensive and bulkier, which means frequent page-turning and refolding. To spot good landing sites on the wilder shores of British Columbia and Alaska, chart scales of 1:40,000 or larger are preferred, but the 1:80,000 chart is serviceable in Washington. Land-ownership is even more relevant to getting ashore in Washington and southern British Columbia than shoreline composition and foreshore extent (the area between high and low tide, which tells you how far you might have to carry your boat if the tide is out).

## DAILY DISTANCE

The distance you cover each day depends on how much time you are willing to spend in or on the boat or board. Time on the board is far more important than your paddling strength or the boat's speed. Most people cruise between 2.5 to 4 knots (nautical miles per hour). Accounting for stops to look around, rest, and stretch your legs, an average of 2 knots for the day is about right (the time between getting underway in the morning and hauling out for the evening, divided by miles traveled). About 12 nautical miles per day is a comfortable distance for most people in average paddling conditions, barring strong head winds or currents. Using the current can make a dramatic difference. Paddlers enjoying a favorable current (or those with a double kayak or surf ski) can reach up to 5 knots; at this speed, you can cover 10 miles in a relatively short time with somewhat leisurely paddling. Using the currents, paddlers have traveled the 21 miles from Anacortes to Friday Harbor in a few hours. Paddle boarders with a good stroke using a fourteen-foot-plus, displacement-hulled board can cover as much as 35 miles a day in favorable winds or currents.

*Vashon Island's Point Robinson Lighthouse (Trip 13)*

## WEATHER ALLOWANCES AND ALTERNATIVE ROUTES

The most dangerous situations paddlers get themselves into stem from the need to be some-place at a certain time. This self-induced pressure prompts them to paddle during unsettled weather in exposed places. For some trips, this book includes alternative routes that offer safer but longer ways back to your launch point, or to somewhere from which you can hitch a ride back to your car. Trip ratings in this book take into account the existence of such options.

Trips with more exposure and fewer route alternatives need an extra time allowance for bad-weather contingencies. How much time depends on the season and the current regional weather pattern. A large, stable, high-pressure area over the Northwest in July probably holds the least likelihood of causing trouble. During the summer months, you may want to consider the weather forecast and choose a trip rating accordingly. In January, however, weather patterns are too unpredictable to rely on forecasts even a day in advance. During the off-season, periods of bad weather should be assumed. Either build extra time into the itinerary or choose less exposed trips. Because of the increased hazard potential in the off-season, all trip ratings in this book move up one difficulty level between September and May.

# Picking Solid Paddling Partners

There's nothing worse than finding out in a high-wind scenario that your paddling partners can't self-rescue. Or that their paddling pace is twice as fast as yours. Do you like to paddle at an easy pace or get there as soon as possible? Choosing paddling partners who are on the same page makes all the difference in enjoying a trip. Shakedown trips, short test trips where you try out your gear before a longer expedition, are a great way to determine the strengths and weaknesses of your trip members and whether you click. All your paddle partners should know how to self-rescue and help others out of the water and have first-aid and CPR skills.

---

**UNSURE OF YOUR SKILLS?**

If you're unsure of your group's skills, hire a professional guide to come along or join a tour. This is a great way to get to know an area without having to purchase gear, figure out food, etc. Some tours also offer paddling instruction.

---

### PADDLING WITH KIDS

Paddle trips are a great way to introduce kids to the outdoors. Include your kids in your paddle training; learn the skills first and then teach them what you know. Be aware that learning styles and attention capabilities vary with age. The youngest kids, ages six through ten, often just want to come along for the ride and are less likely to respond to formal training. For this age group, little if any paddling gear is available. At ages eleven through fourteen, kids are sponges for learning and can fit in children's-size paddle gear. High schoolers are either very interested or not at all. Keep kids of all ages engaged with wildlife and sea life sightings, beach clean-ups (who can gather the most?), and counting games (how many harbor seals can you spot?).

### PADDLING SOLO

I started paddling solo because I have a work schedule that doesn't always allow me to meet others when they're free to paddle. Solo paddling also lets me paddle at my own pace and for longer distances than friends may be interested in. If I change my agenda while on-water, it doesn't affect anyone else. And sometimes I just desire solitude.

Some say you should only paddle in groups. But what if members of your group don't have the skills to rescue you? What if their pace is faster than yours and you're left behind? Groups are not free from safety issues if the members are not working as a solid team.

Solo means self-reliance: know your limits and don't push your luck. Only paddle solo if you have a 100 percent reliable self-rescue technique, strong communication skills, and can handle any conditions mother nature throws at you. As a solo paddler, you should leave a float plan with a friend before departure and check back in to cancel it after your return.

## Logistics

Planning ahead can make your trip safer and easier once on the water. Part of this preparation should include gathering information on the launch location, parking, and ferries.

### LAUNCHING AND PARKING

Finding a place to launch your kayak and leave your car while you are gone can be something of a problem. Some shorelines are well endowed with public facilities that provide both access to the water and convenient parking. Others, particularly in certain parts of the San Juan Islands, are limited in public shore access, parking areas, or both. Shaw and Orcas Islands have the least public access and parking, and private property is the probable option—at a cost. Bring your wallet with small bills and credit cards as one of your essentials on every trip, since almost every public or private launch and parking area requires a fee. Annual passes may be purchased from several agencies, including Washington State Parks and the Washington Department of Fish and Wildlife.

The Washington Water Trails Association has a guidebook for its trail system both in print and online (see Resources). The guidebook provides access points, locations, directions, a description of the specific type of launch (whether beach, road-end, ramp, or float), amenities at or near the site (such as water availability, restrooms, and grocery stores), any fees involved, and other useful facts. Whether planning a visit to a Cascadia Marine Trail site or just a quick day trip, it's a handy resource that can alleviate a lot of headaches.

## RESPECTING PRIVATE PROPERTY

Etiquette at access locations is very important. In the busy summer months, many launches become overwhelmed with human-powered and motorboat traffic. Parking can be tight and even unavailable, forcing paddlers to park in residential areas, sometimes inconsiderately blocking driveways. A few popular residential boat launches in this book include Boston Harbor, the Randall Drive Northwest ramp in Gig Harbor, and North Beach on Orcas Island. To avoid hassles, arrive early, carpool if traveling in a group, or use a less popular ramp if one is available nearby. Boston Harbor Marina requests paddlers to park end-to-end in the street lot west of the boat ramp.

Some maps, such as SeaTrails, mark which areas are public and private. The onX Hunt app (see Resources) displays US property lines. Respect private property, especially in boating-heavy regions like the San Juans, where there are few public access areas. As much as paddlers might feel they are less obtrusive than powerboaters, large paddling groups can be a nuisance and have been reported landing and even camping on private backyards in the San Juans. Many islands in the San Juans and Gulf Islands are private—some are well-signed; others are not. Check marine charts and with locals to confirm where public access is along your route.

## TRANSPORTING KAYAKS, CANOES, AND SUPS ON FERRIES

Both the Washington and British Columbia ferry systems allow foot passengers to carry kayaks, canoes, and SUPs aboard, preferably on a cart or dolly. Washington charges the stowage rate, equivalent to the motorcycle rate, for the boat. Get the WSDOT app for ferry schedules and see Resources for more contact information.

British Columbia ferries also charge a stowage rate, but it differs from their motorcycle rate, so you need to check the specific routes you will travel (see Resources for contact information).

In Washington, a couple with two kayaks or long SUPs, car-topped on one vehicle less than twenty feet long (including overhang) and less than seven and a half feet tall, will save money by driving on. In the San Juan Islands or Vashon and Bainbridge Islands, tolls for walk-on passengers are only collected on the mainland for westbound trips, so it's a free ride if you paddle out to any of these islands and take the eastbound ferry back.

The savings from leaving your vehicle behind are not as significant as the flexibility that carrying a kayak on board allows in choosing paddling routes. For example, you can have a

*San Juan Island's Roche Harbor kayak rental and the historic Hotel De Haro (Trip 61)*

fine excursion paddling from the town of Winslow on Bainbridge Island to Bremerton if you use the Seattle–Bainbridge and Bremerton–Seattle ferries to start and finish (see Trip 15). In the Gulf Islands, and to a limited degree in the San Juan Islands, you can leave your car on the mainland, ferry to one island, paddle to another, and ferry or paddle back to the car.

In the San Juans, opportunities to launch a kayak or SUP carried aboard the ferry are limited to Friday Harbor and possibly Orcas Island. Orcas Landing has intermittently allowed launching from a private dock near the ferry landing (for a fee), but it has been suspended due to congestion caused by paddlers loading inefficiently. Check with the ferry office at the Orcas Island terminal to see if the private dock is currently available. Access to the beach next to the ferry dock at Shaw and Lopez Islands is prohibited.

Carrying a kayak or SUP on board also provides a significant bad-weather fallback, particularly in the San Juan and Gulf Islands, where paddling to a closer or less exposed ferry terminal may be safer than paddling back to your car. Some paddlers always carry a stowable kayak or SUP cart in case bad weather prompts them to take a ferry back rather than paddle home. Paddle boarders with inflatables have the advantage of a carrying backpack. Some use folddown wheels if they're hauling overnight gear as well.

During the summer months, large numbers of foot passengers with kayaks and SUPs make the San Juan Islands ferry particularly hectic. The ferry staff recommend a few things to make it easier for everyone.

First, arrive at least one hour early. This will give you time to find parking and get your boat and gear ready to board. The biggest problem that carry-on kayaks and SUPs pose for the ferry staff is the multiple trips that paddlers make to get all their gear aboard, which delays loading cars. The staff asks that you consolidate as much as possible or use a boat cart to minimize trips. Consider using a mesh backpack or folding hand truck to carry your loose gear.

Due to the tremendous growth in San Juan Islands ferry use in recent years—and because walk-on kayak and SUP traffic has increased dramatically—paddlers now compete with cars for space. Westbound from Anacortes, crews are able to fit enough kayaks and SUPs into "void spaces," those not used by other vehicles, that paddlers stand a good chance of getting aboard. But eastbound from the islands, these void spaces cannot be filled readily. Since each island has a specific allotment of vehicle spaces for each ferry, paddlers must wait their turn to snag a space. You will not be required to line up with the cars; kayaks and SUPs can be staged near the ramp.

Paddlers who carry their boats onto the ferry need a put-in within walking distance of the terminal where they disembark. In many cases, but not all (including Shaw Island in the San

Juans), a nearby put-in exists—but there may be a fee for the privilege. If a trip in this book has a put-in fee, it's called out in the description.

## ENTERING CANADA OR THE UNITED STATES

Upon arrival in Canada, immediately use your cell phone (if you have coverage) or go to the nearest designated telephone reporting marine site to call the Canada Border Services Agency (CBSA) Reporting Centre (see Resources for contact information). Be prepared to provide details of your trip, the number of people in your group, and each paddler's declaration. You can get a list of telephone reporting sites by contacting CBSA prior to your departure.

To enter the United States from Canada, contact the customs office closest to your destination prior to landing. You can also contact the US Customs and Border Protection (CBP) (see Resources for contact information). Be prepared to report your date of birth, passport number, type of watercraft, home port, current location, the citizenship of all persons with you, and a return contact number. The NEXUS program expedites processing for pre-screened travelers; it may be a smart option if you cross the border frequently.

## PADDLING DURING THE OFF-SEASON

Paddling in Northwest inland waters during the off-season can be just as appealing as during the summer. In fact, there is much about it to be preferred.

During the winter, fewer boats crowd the waterways. A quiet wildness arises from the scarcity of people, and you may get whole marine park islands to yourself, something you would never expect in your wildest dreams in summer. If you meet other boaters, they are likely to be kindred spirits who appreciate the advantages of winter boating (or are just foolish enough to be out there too). Off-season boaters are more inclined to say a few words as they pass one another, acknowledging some sort of bond.

On some overcast November days, the air and the sea are languid, almost paralyzed, from dawn to dusk. Silence is broken only by the distant conversations of floating seabirds or the gentle breathing of a passing harbor porpoise. In the off-season, you can spot many seabird species rarely seen in the warmer months.

However, the question of imminent weather is seldom far from the winter paddler's mind. Winter in these waters is a stern, no-nonsense time of year. You do things on nature's terms or suffer the consequences.

Weather is simply more unpredictable during the off-season. Fronts and low-pressure systems follow each other in close succession. Conditions are more extreme and changeable. And you must paddle in rougher and more uncertain situations. There is also the pressure of time: twilight is never far away. Cloudy, low-pressure days can bring darkness sooner than clear days. With the stronger winds and the more fully developed seas, tide rips can occur where they rarely do in less windy times. And those admittedly reassuring passing pleasure craft that eagerly watch for the chance to rescue during the summer are now snug in their moorings.

Beaches, particularly gravel ones, become steeper in the off-season. The characteristically bigger waves tend to move the beach material more, piling it up at the current water level so there is a definite berm or steep drop-off. Driftwood is often found floating offshore, dislodged

*BC ferry approaching Salt Spring Island (Trips 72 and 73)*

by extreme high tides or wind-generated waves pounding the shore. Rivers may flow faster after heavy rains, creating a stronger outflow of current at river mouths, which can affect your route. Daily wind patterns from the summer no longer hold either, particularly the expectation of less wind in early morning. These summer cycles are largely generated by the heating of landmasses and subsequent convection currents. The low angle of the sun in the winter gives it far less heating power, so the land often remains as cold or colder than the sea and generates negligible convection.

Off-season camping likewise requires the acceptance of some austerities, but in return you're rewarded with your own private reserve of gorgeous winter wildlands. An evening spent sheltering from a continuous downpour seems like a fair barter for the privilege of a frosty morning walk along a marine park pathway without a single recent footprint. And the challenge of setting up a warm and comfortable evening nest despite rough weather is a large part of the season's appeal.

## PADDLING AT DUSK

Carry clip-on, waterproof, white LED (nonblinking) lights to attach to the rear shoulder of your PFD for night paddling. It's also wise to have one handheld waterproof flashlight to shine at a boater. Keep this light on a short string so you don't lose it. Keep an ear out for boats without running lights and learn boat and ship lighting setups.

Be particularly wary of being caught on the water at dusk in the winter since a quick weather change for the worse in the dark is especially unnerving and dangerous. Trying to paddle 10 miles a day requires every minute of daylight during the shortest days of the year. If you hate rising before dawn and it gets light at 8:00 AM, you'll likely get a 10:00 AM start on the water.

*Inner Victoria Harbor on Vancouver Island (Trip 63)*

Assuming a travel speed of 2 knots and a brief lunch stop, you should plan to reach your next camp at about 3:00 PM, with an hour of fading light left in which to get ashore and set up camp.

# Going Ashore

Paddlers are amphibious creatures, at home on both sea and land, with the ability to make the transition easily and frequently. In many other parts of the country, going ashore often puts you in somebody's front yard or private preserve. By contrast, the Pacific Northwest is well-endowed with public lands and camping sites hospitable to boaters, if you know where to look. The Cascadia Marine Trail, a "string of pearls," is a network of dedicated campsites for users of hand-carried, nonmotorized, beachable watercraft throughout Puget Sound and the San Juan Islands.

Many of the trips listed in this book take two days or more to complete, so you will need camping gear and outdoor skills for those. Though this book offers no primer on camping, a few peculiarities of kayak camping along these inland waters are worth noting, including things that paddlers can do to minimize their effects on these wildlands and their wildlife.

### WHERE TO CAMP

Most public lands are available for use by everyone, but some, particularly national wildlife refuges, are not. State parks provide the most extensive opportunities for both day-use and camping throughout Washington's inland waterways, and there are similar resources in the Gulf Islands. Although most of Washington's state park sites are developed, some of the marine (boat access only) state parks are totally undeveloped and overnight camping is not permitted. However, with a few exceptions, camping is allowed at the many small island parks, where sanitation such as a vault or solar composting toilet is provided. Most of these also have picnic tables and fire rings but no drinking water. Some are also included within the Cascadia Marine Trail System.

Fees for the use of campsites and trailheads vary depending on whose jurisdiction they fall within, whether it be the DNR (Department of Natural Resources), WDFW (Washington Department of Fish and Wildlife), or others. These fees, along with any additional site-specific fees, are usually noted on signage at the site or within the Cascadia Marine Trail guidebook (and online); you can also contact the supervising land manager to check.

**State Parks.** Almost all marine state parks charge a fee collected through self-registration stations. A few state parks with more highly developed campgrounds are popular with kayakers. These developed sites, usually with restrooms and running water, charge more. Most of these parks also have a Cascadia Marine Trail site near the water available for a per-night fee (see the Cascadia Marine Trail section). Campsite fees often change, so check the Washington State Parks website for current information: parks.wa.gov/166/Camping-fees.

Establishing your own campsite in the woods, also known as dispersed camping, is not permitted in any of Washington's state parks. This prohibition helps contain the impact of camping on wildlands and facilitates other management goals, such as eagle habitat management in the San Juan Islands.

**Gulf Islands National Park Reserve.** Policies and facilities are like those of Washington's state parks, with "full-service" campgrounds used by kayakers at Sidney Spit. Other island parks are less developed—a few have hand pumps for drinking water, and some have none. Camping is allowed at designated sites, though fires are prohibited unless an official fireplace is provided and no fire bans are in effect.

**Washington Department of Natural Resources (DNR) Recreation Areas.** The DNR manages some of the best-kept secrets along Washington shorelines; they aren't labeled on most nautical charts. Many DNR camping locations are also designated Cascadia Marine Trail sites. The DNR's recreation areas are picnic sites and campsites with most of the same basic amenities as those of state parks, and they are first-come, first-served. Facilities are simple (a pit or solar composting toilet and typically no water) and maintenance is infrequent, as the DNR covers a large area with a tiny staff.

Not all undeveloped DNR lands are open to camping. As an example, four-fifths of Cypress Island is undeveloped DNR land, but only two sites (Cypress Head and Pelican Beach) are open to camping. You can expect to be evicted by island staff if you camp elsewhere.

The DNR also manages the state's public tidelands, which are scattered throughout Puget Sound and the San Juan Islands. More than half of the tidelands in the San Juans are public, but few in Hood Canal are. Public tidelands are rarely signed, but booklets and maps showing their locations are available from the DNR (see Resources). Nearly all public tidelands extend only as far as the mean high-tide line unless the uplands are publicly owned too. In general, these are not very useful for kayakers except for a quick leg stretch or some clam digging. Remember, you will be trespassing if you wander above the high-tide line.

**The Cascadia Marine Trail.** The Cascadia Marine Trail system augments public waterfront campgrounds with a dedicated network of simple campsites, located an easy day's travel from the next, for sea kayakers and captains of other human- and wind-powered, hand-carried boats. It ranges from south Puget Sound to the British Columbia border.

Since the system's inception in January of 1993, the Washington Water Trails Association (WWTA), a volunteer organization, has facilitated the creation of more than fifty campsites stretching over 140 miles. About half of the campsites are located within Washington state parks, with the remainder in DNR, county, and city parks.

The Cascadia Marine Trail was honored in 1996 with an international Ecotourism for Tomorrow Award, and in 2000 it was named one of sixteen National Millennium Trails by the White House.

Benefits of membership in the WWTA include full access to their trails network online and in a downloadable PDF form. Visit wwta.org for additional information.

**BC Marine Trails Network.** Launched in the spring of 2011, the BC Marine Trails Network includes thirty access/launch and camping sites in the Gulf Islands, as well as more sites along the west coast of Vancouver Island. Visit bcmarinetrails.org for additional information.

## WHERE NOT TO CAMP (OR LAND)

As a paddler, it is your responsibility to research where you can legally camp, or even land at all. There are many areas where landing or camping is prohibited, and for good reason. Regardless of how careful and low impact you think you are, any human presence affects wildlife and the environment, so it's important to respect the rules that are in place to protect sensitive places like national parks and wildlife refuges. Some areas, such as land trusts, may or may not offer camping opportunities, so don't make any assumptions—reach out to them directly to ask. And it should go without saying that private property is off-limits unless you have explicit permission from an owner to camp.

**National Parks.** Washington State has one national park on its inland shoreline, the San Juan Island National Historic Park, commemorating the so-called Pig War of 1859 between Britain and the United States. There are two units, both on San Juan Island: American Camp at the southern end and English Camp on the northwest side. The park features historical reconstructions and interpretive programs, with facilities for picnicking but not for camping. Camping is also prohibited on the park's undeveloped lands.

**National Wildlife Refuges.** The Nisqually, Protection Island, San Juan Islands, and Dungeness National Wildlife Refuges all control shorelines along Washington's inside waters. The Nisqually refuge allows boating close to shore and walking onshore, if you don't disturb nesting sites. Areas may be closed during sensitive times of year. The Dungeness refuge restricts landings to one site, available through advance reservation only. No shore access is available at Protection Island. The San Juan Islands refuge includes eighty-three islets, rocks, and reefs, as well as some larger islands like Matia and Turn Islands. Landings are prohibited on most of these places without permission from the US Fish and Wildlife Service (USFWS); many of them are also part of the National Wilderness Preservation System. The USFWS requests that you stay at least 200 yards from these refuge islands. Portions of Matia Island and Turn Island are leased to the Washington State Parks Department. You may camp in these park areas, walk the trails on the rest of the island, and land on most of the beaches, as long as bird-nesting sites are not nearby.

These islands are particularly inviting to paddlers, but the USFWS will not compromise its goal of protecting birds' and seals' peaceful habitats for the sake of public recreation. You will be cautioned to keep away. Refuge areas in the San Juans are well marked with signs to that effect.

**Land Trusts.** Land trusts are becoming more common throughout the Salish Sea. These organizations purchase or are gifted property to manage and conserve. Some properties can be accessed and some, like those in the Capitol Land Trust, are off-limits. Check ahead to find out what's accessible and what's not. Some of the larger organizations in Washington State include the San Juan Preservation Trust, the Capitol Land Trust in the South Sound, the North Olympic Land Trust for the Olympic Peninsula, and the Whidbey Camano Land Trust. In British

*Whimsical piling views inside Tod Inlet (Trip 69)*

Columbia, they have many others, including the Islands Trust Conservancy (see Resources for land trust contact information).

**Private Property.** Public access is disappearing quickly in our region. The San Juan Islands have very few access points compared to other areas nearby and even fewer camping opportunities. For years, paddlers have camped illegally in the private backyards of waterfront residences, a situation that creates a negative image of paddlers and can affect future attempts to gain more public access. Some maps (such as SeaTrails) use shaded areas to delineate private and public waterfront property for the Puget Sound, the San Juans, and nearby waterways.

## Camping Etiquette

Maintaining and continuing to develop the Cascadia Marine Trail system depends on the goodwill and cooperative spirit of state, county, and city agencies, port districts, Native tribes, land trusts, and private citizens. To ensure their support, WWTA asks that its members, users of the trail system, or any other user of a human- or wind-powered, hand-carried boat to practice low-impact, "leave no trace" camping techniques and appropriate camping etiquette. Although as paddlers our mode of travel is low impact, we need to come ashore each evening to set up our temporary camping homes. Though the effect of a single sea kayaker is minimal, the sport's

*Driftwood dragon sculpture on Point Hannon, Hood Head (Trip 38)*

popularity continues to increase, and some problematic patterns are emerging. Each one of us must be aware of our personal impact on the environment.

**Water.** To be surrounded by water without a drop to drink is the ancient mariner's dilemma. It is shared by sea kayakers unfamiliar with camping along Northwest inland waters. Most campsites along these shores have no drinking water, and those that do, such as Jones Island State Park, often run out midway through summer or shut it off between fall and spring.

Unless you are going somewhere guaranteed to have drinking water, carry your own or bring filtration equipment if there is a running stream nearby. Take along enough to tide you over should you be unexpectedly delayed by bad weather. You don't want to have to beg people on yachts for water or be forced to head home in dangerous conditions.

Three quarts of water per person per day is usually enough if you are careful with it. Wash dishes in salt water, followed by a sparing rinse with fresh water to prevent corrosion. You can also add salt water to fresh water for cooking. A half-and-half combination is about right for cooking water that will be poured off, such as when boiling noodles. One part salt water to two or more parts fresh water is a good ratio if the water stays in the food, such as when cooking rice.

A collapsible, two- to three-gallon jug fits well in most kayaks. Soft hydration bladders are also handy for storing large amounts of water in your kayak. Some paddlers use flattened two-liter soda bottles, which fit easily in between gear or under deck bungees so they don't roll around inside or on top of your boat.

**Fires and Stoves.** Though most public campsites have fire rings or grates, firewood is not always available. It is also a better practice, environmentally, to use a backpacking stove. Downed wood provides homes for small creatures in the ecological web and returns needed materials to the soil as it decomposes. In most places driftwood is the only option, and during the busy months all pieces have usually been collected. If you do build an open fire, do so only where permitted and never leave it unattended.

Beach fires are generally prohibited, both because of the unsightly scars they leave and because they can get out of control and spread to the uplands. Wildfires are a particular fear in drier places, such as the San Juan and Gulf Islands during the summer.

**Dispersed Camping.** Another problem is independent or "guerilla" camping in undesignated sites. While common in areas without designated campsites, many paddlers also camp outside of established campsites in busy months when overcrowding occurs. This destroys plant life and scars the very landscape so many of us come out to enjoy.

Washington's coastline is simply too popular to provide the isolated camping that many kayakers seek. Opportunities for legal, independent camping exist on undeveloped DNR lands and in some British Columbia parks, but they are rare and often not very attractive. The rule is to stick to designated campsites and, when in doubt, ask.

**Garbage.** Boat it in, boat it out. Kayakers should cultivate their own best interests by being the most inoffensive campers possible. Be prepared to collect all the trash in your vicinity, whether left by your party or others, and avoid using the provided garbage cans if you can instead take your garbage with you. Many marine state parks now have a pack-it-out garbage program to combat the high cost of removing the mountains of trash left by boaters at the island parks. Another good practice is to repackage your food before you set out to lessen the burden on remote trash-removal systems.

**Human Waste.** As marine recreation has grown, so has stress on the land from improper disposal of human waste. Use only established tent sites and do not deposit feces anywhere but in a toilet facility or pack it out in a suitable container, as is now commonly practiced on some water trails in other parts of the nation. Serious health problems can arise from the contamination of groundwater and edible marine food sources.

**Campground Behavior.** Use camping areas in a compact way and extend a friendly welcome to others who arrive after you. Strive to preserve the serenity of the camping area and be considerate to others, particularly from dusk to morning. Encourage others through example and gentle correction, particularly members of your own party, to maintain appropriate, courteous behavior. Leave undisturbed any natural objects, flora, or fauna you find. Avoid trampling vegetation and respect any wildlife you may encounter, including intertidal life.

**LEAVE NO TRACE PRINCIPLES**

On land or on water, keep the principles of Leave No Trace in mind:
1. Plan ahead and prepare.
2. Travel and camp on durable surfaces.
3. Dispose of waste properly.
4. Leave what you find.
5. Minimize campfire impacts.
6. Respect wildlife.
7. Be considerate of others.

**Solitude.** One of the most sought-after elements of satisfactory camping, solitude is difficult to find during the summer months and particularly on major holidays. During peak times, aim for places less attractive to overnight boaters: sites without docks, moorings, or protected anchorages. Look to some of the lesser-known DNR sites, especially those with no overland access and poor landings for boats. Or head to the glorious south Puget Sound while everyone else crowds the San Juan Islands.

## Wildlife Etiquette

Birds and marine mammals (particularly seals) are most vulnerable when they are bearing and rearing their young. Mother seals may abandon their pups if they become separated from them or if the pups are handled by humans. Seal pups do not know enough to fear humans, and there have been reports of pups trying to climb aboard kayaks! Stay clear of mothers with young, and paddle away from pups if they approach you. Maintain a distance of 100 yards from seals, sea lions, and birds on land as prescribed by the Marine Mammal Protection Act. Report abandoned or dead seals to the Washington Department of Fish and Wildlife or the West Coast Marine Mammal Stranding Network. In Canada, contact the Cetus Society or the BC Marine Mammal Response Network.

**Whales.** Several organizations are working to educate the public about responsibly paddling near whales in Northwest waters (see Resources for contact information). The Whale Museum in Friday Harbor on San Juan Island has created a "Kayakers Code of Conduct." The code is designed to make paddlers aware of where they do and don't belong in saltwater environments and provides guidelines to avoid disturbing whales and other marine wildlife. Paddlers are required to stay 200 yards from whales and 400 yards from their direct path. San Juan County Park requires paddlers to watch a video about respecting and understanding these guidelines before launching at their site.

**Birds.** Birds are particularly sensitive to human encroachment when they are incubating their eggs. Bald eagles are of special concern to wildlife managers, as they may abandon their eggs if there is too much human activity in the vicinity of the nest. For this reason, camping is either prohibited or confined to one area in popular eagle-nesting areas like Patos Island. Eagles incubate between late March and late May, so be especially unobtrusive on shore or while paddling along shore in eagle country at that time.

Visitors to Cypress Island's Pelican Beach should note that the trail to Eagle Cliffs is closed from January to mid-July to protect peregrine falcon nests. This closure also affects going ashore on the beaches below Eagle Cliffs.

**Raccoons.** Cuteness is the sole virtue of the ubiquitous raccoon. You can expect a visit from these bold and persistent critters at any time, day or night. Their ability to cart off large food packages is notorious.

James and Jones Island State Parks are home to the commando elite of raccoons, well-known for their bravado and larceny—skills continuously honed on park visitors. The tenacity and deviousness of this cadre is unequaled in all the San Juan Islands. They never desist from their mission and apparently never sleep. Neither will you. Hanging your food only works if done cleverly enough to foil these excellent climbers. Another solution, if you have enough stowage space, is to store food in the animal-proof plastic containers commercially available or, as an inexpensive alternative, containers in which foods like Greek olives are shipped. These containers will hold several days' worth of food. Paddling guides have suggested tying zippers together and wrapping all loose gear in two layers of tarps with bungee cords or rope to prevent the animals from finding an access hole.

A final note to aid a half-decent night's sleep: bring anything that clanks or rattles (such as clean cookware) into the tent with you or be prepared to suffer through listening to the raccoons examining it all night.

As a well-prepared paddler, you will enjoy your trip more knowing all bases have been covered and nothing has been left behind.

*Great blue heron on Sucia Island (Trip 59)*

## A NOTE ABOUT SAFETY

Safety is an important concern in all outdoor activities. No guidebook can alert you to every hazard or anticipate the limitations of every reader. Therefore, the descriptions of waters, routes, and natural features in this book are not representations that a particular place or excursion will be safe for your party. When you follow any of the routes described in this book, you assume responsibility for your own safety. Under normal conditions, such excursions require the usual attention to currents, tides, shipping activity, weather, the capabilities of your party, and other factors. Because many of the lands in this book are subject to development and/or change of ownership, conditions may have changed since this book was written that make your use of some of these routes unwise. It is important to avoid putting in, taking out, or camping on private property. Always obey posted private property signs and avoid confrontations with property owners or managers. Keeping informed on current conditions and exercising common sense are the keys to a safe, enjoyable outing.

*—Mountaineers Books*

# South Puget Sound

The South Puget Sound region is the area south of the Tacoma Narrows, which separates Kitsap Peninsula from the city of Tacoma. It is known for its islands, protected backwaters, 450 miles of shoreline, and little to no crowds. Enjoy easy access from Seattle and Tacoma, avoiding long summer ferry lines.

# 1. Hammersley Inlet

The narrowest of the major Puget Sound inlets, Hammersley is a saltwater river ride that can transport you from one end of the inlet to the other—if you time the currents right. You can make it an easy round-trip by coordinating your return with the tidal exchanges; enjoy a snack and explore the shoreline at your turnaround point while you await the current's reversal. The Squaxin call the inlet Big Skookum. It was completely overlooked by Peter Puget's expedition and was not "discovered" for another fifty years, possibly due to the overlapping points of Cape Horn and Cape Cod near the inlet's entrance, which mask its true character. Once Hammersley Inlet was found, the fertile uplands quickly became and still are a primary source of timber.

**Duration:** Full day to overnight.

**Rating:** *Moderate* or *Moderate +*. During large tidal exchanges the current can flow at a swift 5 knots. Areas of tricky current and tide rips can be avoided.

**Navigation Aids:** SeaTrails WA 205; NOAA charts 18445 SC or 18448 (both 1:80,000), 18457 (1:10,000). The Narrows current table with adjustments for Hammersley Inlet.

**Planning Considerations:** Use the current tables to carefully plan the timing of your trip in either direction, traveling on the flood west to Shelton, and on the ebb east to the Arcadia launch. In this slender inlet, it is much more fun and exhilarating to paddle with the current than against it, which is impossible at high exchanges. Cape Horn, jutting out from the north shore about a half mile from the inlet's entrance, helps develop a strong tide rip that can be avoided by staying to the south shore. Also note that tricky eddies may form at other smaller protuberances along the inlet. If you paddle out to Hope Island, be aware of the strong current that builds on the west side of Squaxin Island and the long fetch of Totten Inlet, which can produce stiff southerly winds.

## GETTING THERE AND LAUNCHING

Four public launch sites provide access: three in and near Shelton at the inlet's west end, and one at the Arcadia boat ramp just south of the inlet's entrance on Puget Sound.

**Shelton:** The launch on Shelton's working waterfront is along Pine Street (State Route 3 to Bremerton) just north of the old downtown. Once you pass under a railroad bridge, take the first immediate right into the Oakland Bay Marina. At this public access gravel-and-dirt launch site you'll find plenty of parking. Visit the website for additional information about the marina: portofshelton.com/marina.html. Note that the mud below the boat ramp is deep. I recommend entering the water from the north side of the ramp.

**Jacoby Shorecrest County Park:** This launch is on the crook of the inlet's elbow across from Shelton. From SR 3 at the north end of Oakland Bay, head south on East Agate Road 3.4 miles,

OPPOSITE *Summer on Carlson Bay by the Cascadia Marine Trail campsite (Trip 4)*

*Low tide sea life and swift tidal rapids at Cape Horn, Hammersley Inlet*

then turn right onto East Crestview Drive and go 2.4 miles. Turn left on East Parkway Boulevard and then right onto East Shorecrest Park Way and you'll reach the county park, which has a paved boat launch.

**Walker County Park:** This small, wooded Mason County Park (closed in winter) is on the south shore of the inlet almost across from the Jacoby Shorecrest ramp. Drive SR 3 south out of Shelton and, as you reach the top of a long hill, turn left onto SE Arcadia Road. Travel for 1.5 miles and turn left onto Southeast Walker Park Road. In another 0.5 mile, enter the park. A brief walk from the parking lot gets you to the beach on the right side of the park. Cascadia Marine Trail campsites and overnight parking are available by prior reservation only. Call 360-427-9670 ext. 535. Year-round caretakers live across the driveway from the toilets. The park is small and may be crowded with day users.

**Arcadia Boat Ramp:** To reach this paved boat ramp, drive just over 7.5 miles from Shelton along Southeast Arcadia Road. At Lynch Road, turn left and proceed to the launch. The ramp is owned by the Squaxin Tribe and was improved in 2011. Park one block away from the ramp on the road's south side in the large gravel lot. There is one portable toilet.

## ROUTE

Your direction of travel is highly dependent on the current's flow and the time of day. The one-way route is just under 7 miles if you travel from Shelton to Arcadia (or vice versa). If you prefer to avoid Shelton, Jacoby Shorecrest and Walker County Parks are pleasant alternatives with picnic tables and sanitary facilities. Launching from either of these will shorten the route about 1 mile.

Starting in Shelton, you will immediately recognize this as a logger's town. The Simpson Mill dominates the waterfront and numerous logs floating on Oakland Bay are typically corralled into booms. The logs are often tended by one-man, lime-green work boats that are best described as pint-sized tugboats. It's fun to watch them push and prod the logs into obedience but remember to stay a safe distance away.

Looking to the north, you can see the wider expanse of Oakland Bay. Oysters are farmed in its uppermost beds. To the east lies narrow Hammersley Inlet.

As you paddle down the inlet for the next 4 miles, the shoreline is dominated on both sides by charming homes old and new, of various shapes and sizes, many hugging the beach. There is no public access, so be prepared to stay in your boat. The inlet maintains a somewhat even but cozy width of less than 500 yards along most of its length.

As you course the remaining 2.5 miles of the inlet after Libby Point, it gradually reverts to a more natural state, primarily due to the higher, steeper banks that discourage building. Nevertheless, houses appear sporadically at the tops, and a few have made inroads down the sides. Generally, the land feels a little wilder here and the paddling is pleasant, with plenty of shorebirds and waterfowl, often harbor seals, and sometimes eagles if you travel during a quieter time of the day or in the winter season.

Just before entering Pickering Passage from Hammersley Inlet, you will pass the jutting prominence of Cape Horn, which helps create a strong rip tide at high tidal exchanges. This is a place to practice paddling technique, or to be avoided, depending on your skills and intentions for the

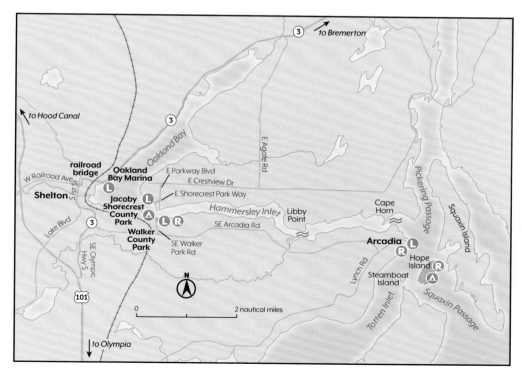

day. Just beyond Cape Horn is an area once called TEkEba'lo-stid or "aerial duck net mouth." Here the Squaxin once stretched a net across the inlet to catch flying flocks of ducks.

As you leave the inlet, Squaxin Island appears directly across Pickering Passage; to the southeast is Hope Island; and to the south lies Steamboat Island with its obvious long, low bridge connecting to the mainland. Bear south along the western shore of Pickering Passage to reach the Arcadia boat ramp in under 0.2 mile.

If your plan is a round-trip or overnight, the best spot to relax or camp before your return is the Cascadia Marine Trail site on Hope Island, which is 6 miles from Walker County Park (see Trip 5, Hope Island). However, this requires paddling across Pickering Passage and adds another 2.5 miles to your roundtrip journey. If you traveled from the other direction, either Jacoby Shorecrest County Park or Walker County Park will be a much more comfortable picnic spot compared to the barren launch at Shelton.

# 2. **Eld Inlet**

This is a pleasurable place to paddle with no real destination, or to explore the little mid-inlet coves and southern tidal estuaries. Only one boat ramp, a driveway through the yard of a private home and boat building shop, provides direct trailered boat access on Eld Inlet. This factor helps encourage greater tranquility than found elsewhere. The other access point, at Frye Cove County Park, is only suitable for hand-carried boats.

**Duration:** Part day to full day.

**Rating:** *Protected* or *Moderate*.

**Navigation Aids:** SeaTrails WA 205; NOAA charts 18445 SC or 18448 (both 1:80,000), 18456 (1:20,000). The Narrows current table with adjustments for Eld Inlet entrance.

**Planning Considerations:** Any trip into the southern tidal estuaries requires careful timing. Explore them only during a high tide. Extending your trip into these shallow channels too long into ebb risks dragging your craft through deep mud. The current can also be a concern, especially as the channels drain, which creates fast-flowing waters.

## GETTING THERE AND LAUNCHING

There are two launch sites for hand-carried boats: a very small commercial boat ramp open to the public and Frye Cove County Park.

**Commercial Boat Ramp at Young Cove:** From US Highway 101, take the Hunter Point/ Steamboat Island Exit and drive north 1.1 miles on Steamboat Island Road Northwest. Turn right onto Gravelly Beach Road Northwest, proceed another 1.6 miles to Gravelly Beach Loop Road Northwest, and turn right. A sign at the intersection directs you to the boat ramp. In another

*Low tide mudflat on Mud Bay in Olympia*

0.6 mile, arrive at the boat ramp where a marine repair shop and boat builder are clustered on the same property.

Park on the grass opposite the boat storage shed. There is limited overflow parking on the street and no portable toilet. Weekend parking is a little better, as the boat builders need the spaces during workdays. Overnight parking is allowed by permission of the friendly facility owners, who charge a small launch and loading fee to help maintain the facilities.

The ramp is concrete near the top and rugged rock below. Minus tides may be in the mud depending on the level. At higher tides, there's a float along the side to launch from. The floats are removed and stored in winter.

**Frye Cove County Park:** Once on Gravelly Beach Road Northwest, continue past the turn to the commercial boat ramp another 2.5 miles to the junction of Young Road Northwest and the other end of Gravelly Beach Loop Road Northwest. Turn right onto Young Road Northwest, proceed 0.7 mile, and turn right onto 61st Avenue Northwest (also known as Giddings Road). In 0.5 mile, at the end of 61st Avenue Northwest where it intersects with Boardman Road Northwest, find the park entrance to the right. Follow the park road to the main parking area. Wheels are recommended for carrying your boat down Cove Trail, a steep, rocky path. It's about a quarter mile to the small beach at the head of Frye Cove, plus another 200 yards during low tides. The well-maintained park is delightful, with a nice view out over Eld Inlet, restrooms, picnic tables, clamming on the beach (in season), and a great lawn for lazing on. For additional information about the park, call the Washington Department of Fish and Wildlife at 360-902-2200.

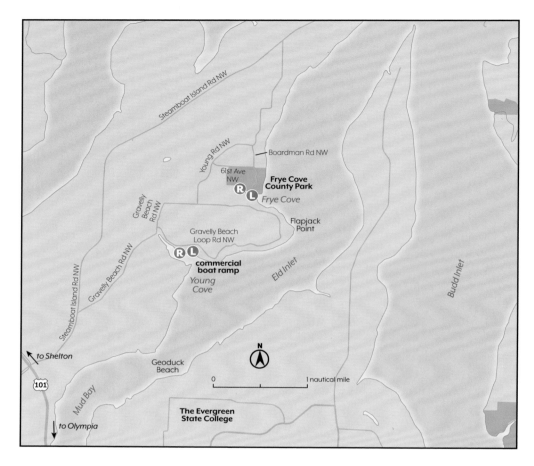

**Mud Bay:** Mud Bay is not a good option for launching. Buzz Inn discourages launching from their property and tow signs are posted in their lot. Capitol Land Trust does not allow launching from any of their properties, including Triple Creek. And Mud Bay dries to a mudflat in most lower tides.

## ROUTES

**Young and Frye Coves:** *Protected.* Great for novices, either of these snug little coves makes for a tranquil paddle of an hour or so. Time your trip for higher tides so the coves' inner reaches are accessible. Pass trees dripping with mosses and lichens, and small creatures foraging along the sheltered banks. The Young Cove ramp is also home to Devlin Designing Boat Builders, which designs classic wooden boats. The cove was called Q!a'bt!o by the Squaxin, meaning "abounding in food."

**Mud Bay:** *Moderate.* The distance to the head of the Mud Bay inlet and back is 8.5 miles. This route offers pleasant views of homes nestled in a wooded shore and backed to the south by gentle mountains. It is an easy paddle with no current to speak of until you approach the southern reaches and tidal channels passing beneath US 101. The ebb and flood of the tide creates a strong current that's difficult to paddle against, especially in the restricted passages near the highway during a large ebb. However, the southern reaches have ideal conditions for waterfowl and wading birds. Herons, kingfishers, and numerous other winged hunters reside in these shallows. Native people called Mud Bay Skwe-ail; McLane Creek, which feeds it, was called Sqwaya':iL.

Eld Inlet still produces a reasonable share of oysters, and you may see the markers that define growers' beds in the shallows and shoals here and there. However, the major harvests of old have long since dwindled. You will see evidence of this once-productive past intermittently along the shore as you pass the remnants of piers and pilings of oyster shacks, which you can identify by the mounds of sun-bleached oyster shells.

**Geoduck Beach:** *Moderate.* Directly across from Young Cove is Geoduck Beach, the western boundary of The Evergreen State College campus. This wonderful stretch of shoreline is fully wooded except for a couple of buildings. The buildings and the beach are part of the college's marine study/ecological reserve. To protect the marine and shore life, landing is prohibited, but simply paddling this edge of sandy shore and tall forest is pleasure enough. If you must walk the beach, save it for another day—the approach is by land, on maintained trails from the bluff above.

For a fulfilling roundtrip option, launch from Young Cove. Explore its waters and then paddle south across Eld Inlet to the southern end of Geoduck Beach. Follow the beach north, then recross Eld Inlet, rounding Flapjack Point (also known as Qwets-qs) to Frye Cove. Stop for a rest or picnic at Frye Cove County Park, then return south to your start by following the western shore and once again rounding Flapjack Point. The total roundtrip distance is about 7 miles.

# 3. Henderson Inlet: Woodard Bay Natural Resources Conservation Area

Henderson Inlet offers a serene place to paddle, especially as compared to other, more trafficked inlets of south Puget Sound. The serenity is partly due to the absence of public beaches or boat ramps, excepting a limited launch place for hand-carried boats. A fair amount of undeveloped and protected shoreline remains. Woodard Bay Natural Resources Conservation Area, a reclaimed gem along the western shore, was transformed from a Weyerhaeuser timber storage and transport facility into a lush oasis of wildlife, managed by the Department of Natural Resources (DNR). Waterfowl, seals, great blue heron, and numerous other shoreline and marine creatures call this area home, making it a prime wildlife-viewing destination. However, access is tightly restricted to protect sensitive wildlife habitat, so pay close attention to current regulations. Pets are prohibited.

In 2013, the DNR completed a restoration project to remove 2100 tons of creosoted material, including the Woodard Bay Trestle, 50 percent of the Chapman Pier, and 600 anchor pilings from Henderson Inlet. The project also involved the removal of 12,000 cubic yards of fill from Woodard Bay, the installation of fifty nesting boxes for purple martins, and the restoration of thirty acres of riparian and upland habitat. In addition, Woodard Point Park was created north of the original kayak launch. The park offers beach access, covered picnic tables, a native Salish canoe, and interpretive signs and trails.

**Duration:** Part day to full day.

**Rating:** *Protected* or *Moderate +*. Within Woodard and Chapman Bays and the south end of Henderson Inlet, the paddling is gentle and sheltered. Kayaking around Johnson Point exposes you to the possibility of tide rips and strong winds, depending on currents and weather.

**Navigation Aids:** SeaTrails WA 204, 205; NOAA charts 18445 SC and 18448 (both 1:80,000). The Narrows current table with adjustments for Dana Passage.

**Planning Considerations:** If the Woodard Bay Natural Resources Conservation Area is your planned launch, be aware that shoreline access is only permitted from April 15 through Labor Day to protect a varied and exceptional mix of wildlife. The alternative launch, from the marina on the east side of Johnson Point in the Nisqually Reach, requires paddling in possibly bumpy and exposed waters when the current is fast, the wind is blowing, or a combination of the two. It is easiest to paddle around Johnson Point into Henderson Inlet and back again by timing your trip with the respective flood and ebb. Be sure to watch the tide levels, as Woodard Bay can dry completely on lower tides.

## GETTING THERE AND LAUNCHING

Two launch sites provide access: a public site within Henderson Inlet at the conservation area and Zittel's Marina (on the east side of Johnson Point in the Nisqually Reach).

**Woodard Bay:** This launch provides access to Henderson Inlet below Woodard Creek, but as stated above, it closes right after Labor Day until April 15 to protect wildlife. From Interstate 5, exit at Olympia (Exit 105) and drive north on East Bay Drive Northeast for just over 2 miles. The road then becomes Boston Harbor Road Northeast; follow it an additional 2 miles. Turn right onto Woodard Bay Road Northeast and drive for just under 2 miles (watch for a right turn after 1 mile rather than going straight on Libby Road) to a bridge that spans Woodard Bay. Just before the west end of the bridge, turn left into the DNR lot, which provides parking next to the grassy launch slope. You'll need your Discover Pass. Signs in the lot warn of break-ins—make sure extra gear is secured to your car or out of sight. Note: Access to the water is on your left, over a five-foot-high metal gate that blocks vehicle access to the nature trail. Maneuvering over the gate can take some effort if you're solo. Be careful on the short, steep embankment leading to the beach. Low tides can make for a muddy entry. If you decide to walk over the bridge on the main road, watch for cars speeding down the hill on both sides.

*Woodard Bay at high tide*

**Woodard Point Park:** This launch provides direct access to Henderson Inlet at the entry to Chapman Bay. Woodard Point Park is accessible only by water or a quarter-mile walking trail from the Woodard Bay parking lot. Bring your Discover Pass and make sure to lock your car. The launch is closed right after Labor Day until April 15 to protect wildlife.

**Johnson Point:** The boat ramp at Zittel's Marina near the end of Johnson Point can be reached from I-5 by taking Exit 108. Drive north on Sleater-Kinney Road Northeast for 3.25 miles, turning right onto South Bay Road Northeast. In about a half mile, the road becomes Johnson Point Road Northeast and bends under the head of Henderson Inlet. In approximately 5 miles, turn right on 92nd Avenue Northeast. Follow it to its end at the marina. A fee is charged to use the boat ramp. Parking and toilets are available. Note: Parking can be tight during fishing season.

## ROUTES

**Woodard Bay Natural Resources Conservation Area** (or TsElE'gwIL). *Protected.* The paddling distance is a round-trip as short as 2.5 miles from Woodard Bay to Chapman Bay and back again, or longer as desired. Launching at Woodard Bay allows easy exploration of the two bays included within the conservation area, an ideal trip for novice kayakers. High tide is best for launching, as the bank is a potential slippery mudslide at lower waters. Paddling at high tide also allows you to explore the bays to their fullest extent. Summer water temperatures can get very comfortable in the bay.

After launching, begin by investigating Woodard Bay, with the option of paddling south-west under the car bridge back into its farthest reaches. On a flood tide, enjoy a mild tidal

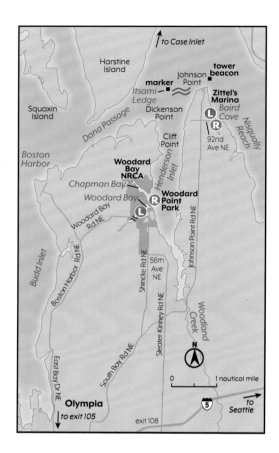

stream as the water squeezes through the narrow opening below the bridge into the back bay.

From Woodard Bay, paddle to the open water of Henderson Inlet, rounding the peninsula separating the bays to the north. The peninsula is named Su'pEks, meaning "blowing promontory," an homage to the sound of harbor seals expelling air as they come to the surface of the water. To protect sensitive habitat, paddlers are asked not to enter Chapman Bay. Return to your launch point by retracing your route.

The conservation area is the perfect place to immerse yourself in the intimate sanctuary these two bays provide for marine wildlife. The bays are well-sheltered, with a thick blanket of tall trees and natural vegetation guarding their perimeters. In places, the overhanging branches and fallen trees drip with lichens and mosses, dappled with sunlight highlighting their various greens, producing an almost southern feel of bayou. From either bay, when the skies permit, the white cone of Mount Rainier can be spied sitting atop the forest canopy on the opposing shore of Henderson Inlet.

You may spot smaller upland, perching, and clinging birds flitting within the branches and shrubs, while herons, eagles, and hawks deck the upper branches. Waterfowl grace the surface of the bays, including ducks, waders, and gulls. Seals and jellyfish are just two of the marine creatures likely to be encountered lurking within the water.

**Woodard Bay to the Head of Henderson Inlet:** *Protected* or *Moderate*. Paddle south to the head of the inlet for close shoreline viewing and wildlife observation. This is a round-trip from the Woodard Bay launch point of 5.75 miles or more, depending on how deeply you explore the bay and its shoreline convolutions. Visiting at higher tides is best to gain maximum entry into the tidal lands. If winds are strong from the north, seas can build over the long fetch and make the return trip a difficult one. Remember also that there is no public access along these shores, so you must be comfortable staying in your boat.

Here you can wander in the little channel formed by Woodland Creek emptying into Henderson Inlet and explore remnants of log booms left from the timbering days. Seals often inhabit these booms and breeding also takes place. Remember to maintain a distance of 100 yards from seals or other wildlife as prescribed by the Federal Marine Mammal Protection Act and DNR's posted instructions.

**Johnson Point to Henderson Inlet:** *Moderate* or *Moderate +* (depending on current and wind). The approach to Woodard Bay Natural Resources Conservation Area from the marina ramp adds 4.75 miles (one way) to the trip. The tidal flood and ebb passing between Johnson Point and the Key Peninsula, along with the long fetches of Case Inlet and Nisqually Reach, means you must plan your travel with the current's direction and an eye to the winds. Ideally, you would like a flood in the morning, high tide at midday, and an ebb in the afternoon for a full day's round-trip. Of course, a one-way trip in either direction is also easily accomplished with a shuttle.

Zittel's Marina is a pleasant place, as it is well kept and has a small store for last-minute provisions. You might even want to investigate among the docks or poke around a bit in Baird Cove.

As you leave the marina, you will see Mount Rainier looming up from the southeast across Nisqually Reach. Look to the right of the big volcano and you may also see a somewhat smaller one, Mount St. Helens. Proceeding north around Johnson Point, you will be facing the Olympic Mountains strung out across the far horizon.

Cormorants often perch on the tower beacon just off Johnson Point (Sqwa'tsqs) to dry their wings. As you head west around the point into Henderson Inlet, be aware that Itsami Ledge (marked by another light) is midwater between Johnson and Dickenson Points. If conditions are right, it can produce sharp waves. You can easily avoid it by staying along the gravel shore of Johnson Point.

Once you enter Henderson Inlet, you have two basic options: You may head diagonally across to Woodard Bay Natural Resources Conservation Area, passing by Cliff Point jutting from the opposing shore; or paddle south along the eastern shoreline to the bottom of the inlet, admiring modest and grand structures alike as you go. There are a couple of interesting little coves to explore as well.

*Exploring inner Woodard Bay via sea kayak*

*Abundant wildlife along the McCallister Creek shoreline with Mount Rainier in the distance*

# 4. Nisqually Delta

The Nisqually Delta (or Billy Frank Jr. Nisqually National Wildlife Refuge) is one of the finest estuaries in Puget Sound. Paddlers here can exploit their craft's shallow-water abilities to explore brackish back channels as few other boaters can. And this is a prime place for birders. In 2009, the Nisqually Tribe removed 8 miles of dike, including the Brown Farm Dike, opening the delta and freeing the river to flow naturally for the first time in a century. Visit fws.gov/refuge/billyfrank-jr-nisqually for additional information.

**Duration:** Part day to overnight.

**Rating:** *Protected*.

**Navigation Aids:** SeaTrails WA 204; NOAA chart 1844S SC (1:80,000); Seattle tide table (add 30 minutes).

**Planning Considerations:** Most channels are negotiable at ten to thirteen feet; high tide opens many others. Check the wildlife refuge website for landing restrictions. Nisqually Delta can be unpleasant in wind because of steep seas in the shallows and the chance of getting wet at the unprotected launch site. Waterfowl hunters are present in the Department of Fish and Wildlife portions of the delta from mid-October to mid-January.

## GETTING THERE AND LAUNCHING

From Interstate 5, take Exit 114 (Nisqually). Go south on Martin Way and follow it for just under 1 mile to Meridian Road Northeast—veer right through the roundabout. Turn right here and drive for almost 3 miles to 46th Avenue Northeast. Turn right again and go 0.25 mile to D'Milluhr Road Northeast, on the left with a sign pointing to public fishing. Follow it downhill for about a half mile to the parking area.

The Department of Fish and Wildlife's ramp at Luhr Beach has a moderate-size lot, restrooms, and a beach next to the ramp for launching. At high tide there is limited launching space on the rocky beach; at lower tides it becomes sandy and offers more space. To park here you will need a Department of Fish and Wildlife permit or a Discover Pass, which can be purchased online and at most sporting goods stores that sell hunting licenses. Next to the parking area, the Nisqually Reach Nature Center is open on selected days of the week, depending on the season.

## ROUTES

You can choose your own route and distance. This area is managed by the US Fish and Wildlife Service and the Washington Department of Fish and Wildlife. The federal Nisqually National Wildlife Refuge includes the mudflats in the lower delta and the meadows and woods of old farmland, found in the central portion above the dike that extends between McAllister Creek on the west and the Nisqually River on the east. State lands include most of the lower salt marshes and most of the land along McAllister Creek.

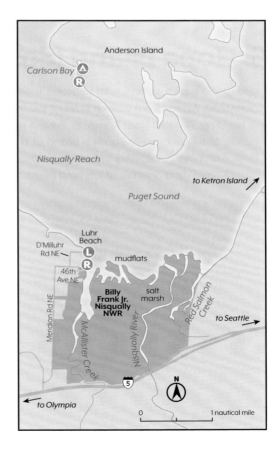

**Lower Delta:** *Protected.* If you arrive near high tide, you may wish to explore the myriad channels that wander across the salt marshes in the lower delta. At highest tides, you may be able to pick your way through shallow channels, though a spring tide is required to make it all the way across the delta by this inner route. Otherwise, head north to the lower flats to find your way to the eastern side of the delta, where you can head upstream on the Nisqually River or explore the connecting channel to Red Salmon Creek, farthest to the east. At the very northeast corner of the flats, still within federal refuge boundaries, find a sand jetty of old pilings and a beached concrete barge—a nice lunch and sunbathing stop. A few miles to the north is the tiny Ketron Island, which has no facilities and a few private homes.

**McAllister Creek:** *Protected.* If you care to venture inland, McAllister Creek at the western edge of the delta offers the possibility of many miles of small-stream paddling, using the last of the flood tide to assist you on the way in and then riding the ebb back out. The creek can be paddled easily to well inland of the freeway overpass. In autumn, salmon can be viewed under your boat in the creek. Settler James McAllister was the first white man to be killed in the Puget Sound Treaty War of 1855–56. Medicine Creek, a tributary of McAllister, was the location of the Treaty of Medicine Creek, which Governor Isaac Stevens used to trick the American Indian chiefs of the region into relocating their people onto reservations in the South Sound.

**Luhr Beach to Anderson Island:** *Protected.* An alternative route that can include an overnight stay is the paddle to Anderson Island, only 1.5 miles across from the boat ramp. Bear west along Anderson Island to Carlson Bay, which is 4 miles from Luhr Beach. The Cascadia Marine campsite, located on the end of the sand spit in Carlson Bay, is by reservation only. The site is limited to eight people and only one night. There is a portable toilet (in summer months only) located above the spit. Follow the old road at the southern end of the spit up a steep hill; the toilet is located on the right.

# 5. Hope Island (South)

Hope Island is a state park with beaches, meadows, forest trails, and the remnants of a farm homestead. Access from various sides of the South Sound is easy: you can launch from Latimer's Landing, Arcadia Boat Ramp, or Boston Harbor. Hope Island can be incorporated into a day trip around adjacent Squaxin Island or a multiday circumnavigation of nearby Harstine Island. Camping possibilities include two Cascadia Marine Trail sites: one at Jarrell Cove State Park (7.8 miles) and another at Joemma Beach State Park (7.6 miles) on the Key Peninsula.

**Duration:** Part day to overnight. There are two campsites that can host eight Cascadia Marine Trail users each. Fires prohibited.

**Rating:** *Moderate* or *Moderate +*. The Boston Harbor route requires an open-water crossing and exposure to possible tide rips in Dana Passage. Currents on the Peale Passage route may exceed 1.5 knots at times.

**Navigation Aids:** SeaTrails WA 205; NOAA charts 18445 SC or 18448 (both 1:80,000). Chart 18456 (1:20,000) covers the Boston Harbor route. Use current tables for the Narrows with adjustments for Dana Passage on the Boston Harbor route, or with adjustments for Pickering/Peale Passage.

**Planning Considerations:** Use the current tables to avoid maximum flows in Dana Passage on the Boston Harbor route. On the Pickering/Peale Passage route, travel to Squaxin Island on the ebb and return with the flood current.

*Paddler's view of Hope Island from Squaxin Island*

## GETTING THERE AND LAUNCHING

This area sits astride a portion of Puget Sound where island destinations are separated by only a few miles of water. Easily accessible by boat, they are hours apart by highway. Residents of the west side of Puget Sound can start from Latimer's Landing at the Harstine Island Bridge near Shelton and paddle the Pickering/Peale Passage route or launch at the Arcadia Boat Ramp just to the south of Hammersley Inlet. Those coming from the east will find Boston Harbor near Olympia most convenient.

**Latimer's Landing at the Harstine Island Bridge:** To reach the landing, turn onto East Pickering Road from State Route 3 about 8 miles north of Shelton (there is a sign for Harstine Island). Follow this road approximately 5 miles to the bridge. The county landing includes a public ramp, dock, seasonal portable toilets, and a parking lot located just north of the bridge's western end. The lot by the ramp is for day use only. For overnight parking, use the lot about a quarter mile up the road. Be cautious of swift currents here. The dock can be busy with fishermen, so leave your boat on the shore until you're ready to launch.

**Arcadia Boat Ramp:** To reach this paved boat ramp, drive just over 7.5 miles from Shelton along Southeast Arcadia Road. At Lynch Road, turn left and proceed to the launch. The ramp is owned by the Squaxin Tribe and was improved in 2011. Park one block away from the ramp on the road's south side in the large gravel lot. There is one portable toilet.

**Boston Harbor:** Take Exit 105B (Plum St.) from Interstate 5 in Olympia. Drive north after exiting the freeway; the rest of the route is essentially straight ahead. After passing through several intersections for approximately 1 mile, you will see water on the left. Plum Street becomes East Bay Drive, which eventually becomes Boston Harbor Road. Continue another 7 miles to 73rd Avenue NE and turn left. The boat ramp is on the west side of the Boston Harbor Marina building on your right. Arrive early on weekend mornings to get a parking spot and bring your Discover Pass. In 2024 the DNR added a new marina boat ramp, an expanded and paved parking area, two ADA parking spaces, restrooms near the boat ramp, and an ADA-accessible loading platform for boaters. If parking is tight, groups of paddlers should park end to end to save space. If you find street parking in the neighborhood, please be respectful of residents. The marina has a café, food and boating store, kayak rentals, and moorage.

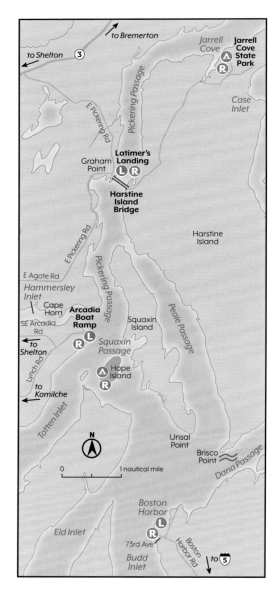

## ROUTES

**Pickering/Peale Passage (Latimer's Landing to Hope Island):** *Moderate.* The one-way distance is 4 miles. Currents can exceed 1.5 knots along this route. Using favorable currents can significantly lessen your required trip time, although eddies alongshore can be used to travel against the currents in most places. Tide rips are possible, especially when the current opposes the wind direction. The flood currents coming around both sides of Harstine Island meet in the vicinity of northern Squaxin Island.

To travel from Latimer's Landing to Hope Island via the west side of Squaxin Island, catch the flood current starting soon after Pickering Passage off Graham Point and return when the current begins to ebb at the same location. If you are circumnavigating Squaxin Island, note that Peale Passage has a quite different schedule, flowing north during most of the flood cycle and south during the ebb. Consequently, plan to head up the east side of Squaxin Island about two hours before the turn to the ebb at Graham Point, so you can ride the flood up Peale Passage and then the new ebb the remainder of the distance.

South of Latimer's Landing, the shores in Pickering Passage alternate between houses and steep, tree-lined banks—but the shore of Squaxin Island is a fine oasis of natural beauty. Paddling close to its shore, you can imagine yourself exploring Puget Sound two centuries ago with British explorer Captain George Vancouver.

Squaxin Island is an Indian reservation. Do not go ashore without permission. Squaxin's shoreline has escaped development except for an oyster-rearing operation in the bay midway down the island. The occasional dilapidated shack is the only sign of the island's sparse settlement, though you may see more-evident residents like river otters, blue herons, or even a coyote trotting along the beach.

Hope Island State Park is a 106-acre island that supported a working homestead until the 1940s. This addition to the park system includes meadows, orchards, and an old windmill on the west side, as well as extensive trails leading through the forests on the island. At lower tides, you can hike approximately 2 miles around the island on the beach. A caretaker's cabin is located above the beach on the flatter west side of the island. This area also has the Cascadia Marine Trail campsite, with several other sites for general use on the south side of the little cove here. There are vault toilets, but there is no water system. Make sure to bring your boat up to the site, as there is no beach at low tide.

An alternative camping option is to travel north from Latimer's Landing for 2.5 miles to Jarrell Cove on Harstine Island, which also has a Cascadia Marine Trail site (see Trip 6, Jarrell Cove State Park).

**Boston Harbor to Hope Island:** *Moderate +*. The one-way distance is 3.8 miles. Dana Passage currents can reach almost 3 knots at times, and rips can be lively here, especially with an opposing wind. Watch for heavy boat traffic in the summer.

The strongest currents can be avoided by crossing directly from Boston Harbor to Squaxin Island. This route, however, involves crossing 2 miles of open water. Also, an ebb current flows southeast from Unsal Point on Squaxin Island most of the time, averaging a little over 1 knot at its peak, making this route most practical for the return.

To avoid open water and the strongest currents, cross Budd Inlet from Boston Harbor and then cross the Eld Inlet entrance, where currents may reach 1 knot at times. Next follow the shoreline north and then west through Squaxin Passage, where the current may exceed 1.5 knots, flowing west during the flood. If you are circumnavigating Squaxin Island, expect a longer open-water crossing from Unsal Point back to Boston Harbor, or take a detour east to Dana Passage for a shorter crossing to Harstine Island at Brisco Point. Currents in Dana Passage may reach several knots, and tide rips can develop. Try to cross when the current is slack or at least flowing in the same direction as the wind. Note that Peale Passage flows north on the flood.

*Protected water awaits the paddler on inner Jarrell Cove*

# 6. Jarrell Cove State Park

Located along the western shore of Harstine Island, this 11.5-acre state park is a low-key destination that can be accessed easily from Tacoma or the Bremerton area via the Key Peninsula.

**Duration:** Part day to overnight.

**Rating:** *Moderate.* Requires a 1.5-mile open-water crossing. Currents along the route are weak.

**Navigation Aids:** SeaTrails WA 205; NOAA charts 18448 or 18445 SC (both 1:80,000).

**Planning Considerations:** McMicken Island is day use only; also be sure to keep an eye out for poison oak. Watch for heavy boating traffic in summer.

## GETTING THERE AND LAUNCHING

This trip originates at Joemma Beach State Park on the Key Peninsula, 8.5 miles from Jarrell Cove. From State Route 302, turn south in Key Center onto the Gig Harbor Longbranch Road (Key

Peninsula Highway Northwest) and follow it to Home. About 1 mile south of Home, turn right on Whiteman Road (there are signs for Joemma Beach here and at the next junction). After another mile, bear left at the fork, and then turn right a little less than a half mile later onto Bay Road Southwest. This road turns to gravel and then reaches a fork. Take the right-hand road and follow it downhill to the recreation area. Generally, there is ample parking in a lot just above the beach. Do not leave valuables in your parked car. A Cascadia Marine Trail campground in the park has four sites.

**ROUTE**

Follow the peninsula's shore north to a point opposite McMicken Island before crossing; on the return leg follow the Harstine Island shore south and cross opposite Joemma Beach, which involves a slightly longer crossing. The shoreline north of Joemma Beach is pleasantly natural, with a pebble beach below high bluffs; the remains of an old pier; and a shallow lagoon with water that warms to bathtub temperatures during the summer and, at upper tidal stages, a miniature tide race at its entrance. Harstine Island's shore offers a similar setting. Buffingtons Lagoon, less than 1 mile south of McMicken Island on Harstine, is another pleasant detour,

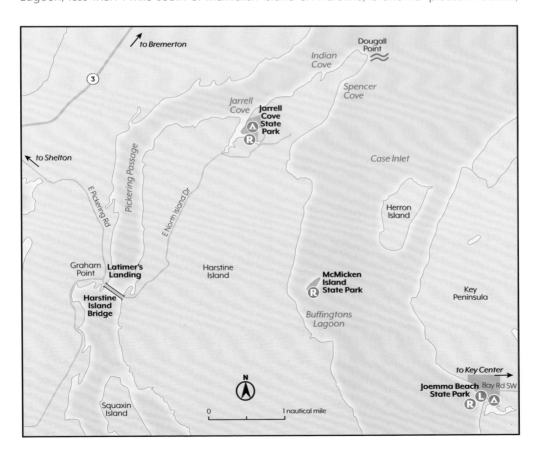

though accessible only at high tide. Keep in mind that tidelands on both shores are private, so stay in your boat.

McMicken Island is particularly attractive to boaters who like the isolation afforded by low levels of development. There is no dock or any drinking water, but there are two vault toilets. Be alert for poison oak. Fires are not allowed on the island. Landings and access to the island are practical only on the southwest side due to the steep bluffs above the narrow beaches elsewhere. Behind this pebble-and-shell beach find a meadow with the handiest picnic sites. The fenced-in area and buildings behind the meadow are private land. A trail network circles through the dense forest north of the meadow, with occasional views out over the bluffs. Xexpapa'i, meaning "many little cedars," was the Squaxin name for a place on the east side of the island.

Leaving McMicken and heading north, the Harstine Island shoreline for the next mile or so is maintained by the Department of Natural Resources (DNR). Enjoy Harstine's sandy shores and relative solitude. Turn into Spencer Cove and paddle toward Dougall Point, which becomes more residential. The point at low tide is sandy with some current swirls and eddies depending on the tide direction. The Squaxin called Dougall Point Sqwitqks, meaning "little promontory." Head south along the island to Indian Cove, a protected inlet with a marina. The remaining, medium-bank shore leading to Jarrell Cove has sand and gravel beaches with views across Pickering Passage. Pickering's flood current flows south and can reach 2.75 knots. Take advantage of the gentle push and enter Jarrell Cove.

The state park and Cascadia Marine Trail sites are on your left (north side) as you enter the cove. A kayak rack is provided above the water; look for one Cascadia tent site in the trees and another in an open area behind the rack. The park has nineteen reservable campsites. The restroom and other facilities are above in the main campground. The park provides two kitchen shelters and four sheltered picnic tables. Groceries and supplies are available at a marina on the opposite shore from Labor Day to Memorial Day.

The cove cuts nearly a half mile into the island, providing boaters and paddlers with a very protected gunkhole. A side inlet on the north side curves around Jarrell Cove State Park. Explore the cove and its peaceful waters. DE'xudExwll is the Squaxin name for the bay, which was known for good cedar for making canoes. A few beach homes appear among pocket beaches and mini coves. Swamp-like overhanging trees angle over the water.

Jarrell Cove can also be accessed by Latimer's Landing and Boston Harbor to the south (see Trip 5, Hope Island South, for more information).

# 7. Case Inlet: Allyn to Vaughn Bay

If you like exploring tucked-away inlets, small coves, and mini islands, then Case Inlet is the place to go. An easy drive from Seattle and only a few miles south of Hood Canal, the inlet has multiple access points and a variety of both developed and quiet shorelines. If you can find it, check out the Case Inlet petroglyph, one of the few remaining petroglyphs in the region. The Native people in Case Inlet were called the Squawksin, part of the larger Squaxin people farther south.

**Duration:** Part day to full day.

**Rating:** *Protected* or *Moderate*.

**Navigation Aids:** NOAA chart 18448 (1:80,000).

**Planning Considerations:** Launch on medium to high tides, preferably on the flood to avoid low tides along Case Inlet's shores. The coves and bays on both sides dry out on lower tides.

## GETTING THERE AND LAUNCHING

You have many options for launching into Case Inlet. Port of Allyn is the best place to start if you want to view the petroglyph. Or you can combine several of these options to paddle a triangular route across Case Inlet.

**Allyn Waterfront Park:** From State Route 16 at Purdy, take SR 302 west to SR 3. Drive south a few short miles to Allyn and take a left on Drum Street. At the end of Drum Street, there is a boat ramp, restrooms, and picnic tables.

**Port of Allyn Kayak Park:** Just south of Allyn off SR 3, this launch has beach access, restrooms, and picnic tables.

**Port of Grapeview Boat Ramp/Fair Harbor Marina** (5054 E. Grapeview Loop Rd.): From Allyn, drive 3.5 miles south on SR 3. Turn left on Grapeview Loop Road and follow it to the boat ramp. Inside Reach Island, this launch also has a restroom and marina store.

**Vaughn Bay Ramp** (17999 Hall Rd. NW): This is a day-use Pierce County boat ramp on the north end of Vaughn Bay. There's limited parking along the road and no facilities. Dries out at low tides. From SR 16, take SR 302 west to Wright Bliss Road Northwest and turn left. Take a right on Hall Road Northwest and follow it to its end.

## ROUTES

**Allyn Waterfront Park to the Case Inlet Petroglyph:** *Moderate.* From Allyn, cross Case Inlet 0.5 mile to the east shore, aiming for the small point slightly southeast of Victor. The rock is visible at a 7-foot or lower tide. The faces can be hard to see as years of tides and weather have taken their toll on the petroglyph.

**Port of Grapeview Boat Ramp/Fair Harbor Marina to Vaughn Bay:** *Moderate.* Paddle around the south end of Reach Island and cross Case Inlet, heading 1.7 miles to Vaughn Bay. The opening to the bay is on the north end

*Ancient petroglyph on the beach at Victor*

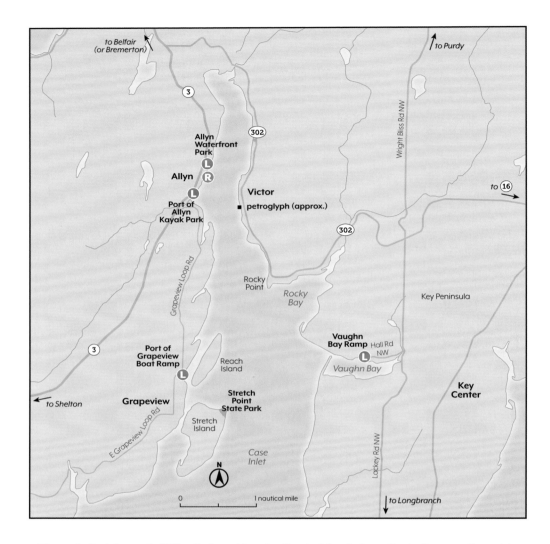

of the spit. Paddle north 0.75 mile from Vaughn Bay to 1.4-mile long Rocky Bay, another pictur-esque bay and estuary to visit. Both dry out on low tides. Return by paddling back across Case Inlet 1.49 miles to Fair Harbor Marina. Alternatively, paddle slightly south of Reach Island to visit Stretch Point State Park and Stretch Island.

**Four Coves—Fair Harbor Marina to Allyn:** *Moderate.* The western shoreline leading to Allyn has several interesting coves and estuaries worth exploring. Staying on the west side of the inlet, head north from the inside of Reach Island to the first cove, 0.44 mile from the launch. Continue heading north for another 0.75 mile to arrive at the second cove, which is protected by a sandy spit. The third cove is another 0.93 mile north, also somewhat protected by a sandy spit. Grape-view Loop Road crosses the south end of the cove. If you keep paddling 0.31 mile north, you'll find the fourth and final cove. SR 3 crosses its back end; Allyn is a half mile north.

*Vaughn Bay entry and spit*

**Case Inlet Triangle—Allyn to the Case Inlet Petroglyph to Vaughn Bay to Allyn:** *Moderate.* Launching from Allyn, cross Case Inlet 0.5 mile to the small point slightly southeast of Victor to view the Case Inlet petroglyph. This rock, visible at lower tides, is four feet tall and five feet long, with faces carved into its surface. From here, paddle 1.5 miles south to Rocky Bay, which is 1.4 miles long and lined with beach homes interspersed with green spaces. Another 0.75 mile south of Rocky Bay, keep an eye out for Vaughn Bay, which is protected by a long, sandy spit with an opening on its north side. Cross back across Case Inlet 1.49 miles to Reach Island. Alternatively, paddle slightly south of Reach Island to visit Stretch Point State Park and circumnavigate Stretch Island. Aside from the park, the island is private.

# 8. **Carr Inlet: Lakebay, Penrose Point State Park, Pitt Island, Longbranch**

This South Puget Sound gem on Carr Inlet is known for its protected, picturesque coves and sand spits. The inlet was originally Squaxin tribal land. With several launch options, camping, and shore access, this trip is ideal for all levels of paddlers. Southeast of Lakebay is McNeil Island Corrections Center, which (like Alcatraz) is surrounded by cold water and swift currents. In 1792 Peter Puget and his crew camped in Pitt Passage on the spit that overlooks McNeil Island. They called McNeil Island "Pidgeon Island," for the pigeons that live in the holes of the island's steep banks. In the morning, Puget's crew launched their boats but were quickly stopped by the tidal currents that flow between the islands, not realizing they often run opposite to common thinking.

Lakebay, which is on Mayo Cove, was named in 1871 by its first homesteader, William Creviston; the name refers to Bay Lake, which drains into Lakebay. After the construction of a sawmill in 1875, Lakebay flourished. Steam-powered mosquito fleet ferries, among other boats, were built in the bay by the Lorenz-Berntson Navigation Company. An active marina for decades, Lakebay Marina fell into disrepair for years and was purchased in 2022 by the Recreational Boating Association of Washington (RBAW) and the Washington State Department of Natural Resources (DNR), which plan on improving the marina to open again for public use. The nearby town of Home was founded in the 1890s as a utopian community for anarchists and free thinkers seeking an alternative lifestyle.

**Duration:** Part day to overnight.

**Rating:** *Protected* to *Moderate*.

**Navigation Aids:** NOAA chart 18448 (1:80,000). The Tacoma Narrows current table.

**Planning Considerations:** Launch on medium to high tides, preferably on the flood to avoid low tides. All the coves and bays in this area dry out on low tides. Currents in Pitt Passage are light, but nearby Balch Passage can flow much faster—with maximum ebb at forty minutes before maximum ebb in the Narrows— and can run as high as 3.6 knots. Maximum flood is sixty-seven minutes after maximum flood in the Narrows.

## GETTING THERE AND LAUNCHING

All launches are on the Key Peninsula and are accessed via Key Peninsula Highway Southwest. Avoid rush-hour traffic, which jams up on Purdy Spit entering or leaving Key Peninsula.

**72nd Street Southwest Boat Ramp:** A mile south of Longbranch, take a left on 72nd Street Southwest. Explore the quiet, forest-lined coves and backwaters, including one particularly picturesque cove that can be seen from the boat ramp. The ramp is 1 mile south of the bay's

*Pitt Island in Pitt Passage*

entrance. The Filucy Bay Reserve lines the shores of the most northern cove. Also from the boat ramp, you can see Eagle Island 2 miles to the east between McNeil and Anderson Islands. Pitt Island (restricted) is visible 2.2 miles to the north. No facilities available.

**Home Boat Ramp:** The town of Home is just north of Penrose Point State Park; it has a simple boat ramp with a small dirt parking lot for four to five cars (no facilities). From Key Peninsula Highway Southwest, take a left on 9th Avenue Northwest and then a right at A Street Northwest. Bring your Discover Pass; it is a Washington Department of Fish and Wildlife site. Beaches on both sides of the ramp are signed as private.

**Penrose Point State Park:** From Key Peninsula Highway Southwest, take a left on Cornwall Road Southwest and then a right on Delano Road Southwest, which will take you to the park entry. For beach access, take a left on 158th Ave Southwest, following it to the right where it ends in a parking area. There's no boat ramp, but there are restrooms, picnic tables, and one Cascadia Marine Trail site. Bring your Discover Pass. Access the water from the parking and lawn area.

**Lakebay and Longbranch** do not have launches at the time of writing this edition. However, the RBAW recently purchased the Lakebay Marina, so access could become available once they've made improvements to the marina.

Starting from **Kopachuck State Park,** it's a 3.8-mile crossing to Penrose Point State Park. From **Horsehead Bay,** it's a 3.3-mile crossing. (See Trip 9, Carr Inlet: Horsehead Bay, Cutts Island State Park, and Kopachuck State Park.)

## ROUTE

Case Inlet's shorelines are lined with little coves and bays, sometimes surrounded by long sand spits and sandy beaches littered with erratic boulders and drift logs. Homes dot the shoreline

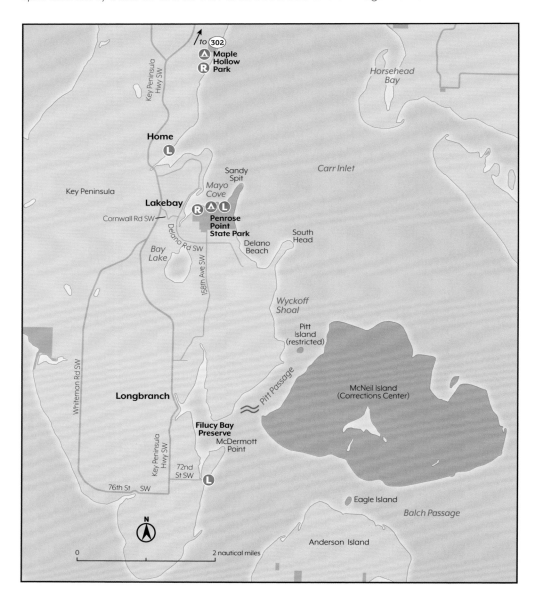

on medium- and high-bank bluffs. There are plenty of opportunities to explore, with two camping options and numerous access points, including crossing Case Inlet from **Kopachuck State Park or Horsehead Bay** (see Trip 9, Carr Inlet: Horsehead Bay, Cutts Island State Park, and Kopachuck State Park). Check out **Maple Hollow Park** 1 mile north of Penrose Point State Park, which has two Cascadia Marine Trail sites on eight-by-eight-foot tent pads and picnic tables. There's one vault toilet, no water, and fire pits. Black bears have been seen in the area, so bear containers are recommended. Look for the carsonite sign near the beach.

From the **Home Boat Ramp,** head south and cross Van Geldern Cove around the point with homes above into Mayo Cove. Paddle around the historic Lakebay Marina and the cove's quiet shores, enjoying the protected bay and its scattered old and new beach homes. The cove was called Suba'qob by the Squaxin people, meaning "prairie."

During higher tides, explore the madrone- and conifer-lined shorelines and inner cove of **Penrose Point State Park.** At low tides, skim along the sandy spits, where you'll see sanddabs, flounders, and other small fish shooting out from under your craft. Oysters can be spotted as well. The book *Gunkholing in South Puget Sound* mentions a difficult-to-spot petroglyph on Sandy Spit, which dries at a minus-five tide. Penrose Point State Park is a beautiful park with madrone, cedar, and fir trees along the shore and extensive beaches and sand spits to explore at low tides. Camping is available, including one Cascadia Marine Trail site with restrooms, showers, and no fires (four people maximum). The site is between Penrose Point and the smaller sand spit.

Exploring south of Penrose, you'll find Delano Beach, a sweeping, sandy crescent beach with erratic boulders leading up to narrow **South Head.** The bay here is home to two summer camps and a few waterfront homes, with plenty to see and enjoy. The distance between Penrose Point and South Head is one nautical mile. Southwest of the head is **Wyckoff Shoal,** a popular fishing spot marked by two shoal markers: "1" and "3." The shoal dries at minus-five feet. From South Head to **Pitt Island,** homes line the shoreline on medium to high banks. The tiny, scenic, and tree-lined Pitt Island, in the middle of Pitt Passage off a long sand spit, is 1.5 miles south of South Head. A large sign on the island's west side warns you to stay 100 yards away because of the corrections center a quarter mile east on **McNeil Island.**

Enjoy viewing (but not landing on!) McNeil Island's undeveloped shorelines. Picking up swimmers here is not recommended. Driftwood Annie, known for helping escapees who swam across Pitt Passage from McNeil Island, had a home on the long sandbar across from Pitt Island for eighty years.

Continue south 1.3 miles beyond Pitt Island to reach protected Filucy Bay Reserve and the community of **Longbranch,** a popular summer boating destination. The bay has no paddling launches or facilities, but it does have a small marina. Explore the quiet, forest-lined coves and backwaters, including picturesque Filucy Bay Reserve, which can be seen from the **72nd Street Southwest Boat Ramp.** The ramp is 1 mile south of the bay's entry.

# 9. Carr Inlet: Horsehead Bay, Cutts Island State Park, and Kopachuck State Park

If you live south of Seattle, this is a short, easy trip, ideal for families or those with limited saltwater experience. Distances between stopovers are not long, and there are plenty of shore attractions and beaches with warm water for wading and swimming during the summer months. The route can be altered or shortened if the weather is inclement. Camping is available at Kopachuck State Park or the Cascadia Marine Trail site located there. The beach is expansive at low tide and is known for ample sand dollars. The Squaxin Tribe originally resided on the seven South Sound inlets.

**Duration:** Part day.

**Rating:** *Protected* or *Moderate*.

**Navigation Aids:** SeaTrails WA 204; NOAA charts 18445 SC or 18448 (both 1:80,000), 18474 (1:40,000); Seattle tide table (add about 30 minutes).

**Planning Considerations:** Consult the tide table before starting out, as low tides make for long hauls to the water. Poor planning may lead to getting stuck in the mud in nearby inlets.

## GETTING THERE AND LAUNCHING

Launching alternatives are boat ramps on Horsehead Bay and nearby Fox Island, or a short drive from the parking lot to the beach in Kopachuck State Park.

**Kopachuck State Park:** From State Route 16, follow Rosedale Street Northwest 2.3 miles and take a left on Ray Nash Drive Northwest. Go 2.3 miles to 56th Street Northwest and turn right into the park. At the time of writing, signs for the park were hard to see when coming from the north. If you want to drop off boats at the beach, bring a cell phone to call the ranger at Kopachuck State Park for driving access. (The ranger phone number is 253-265-3606.)

**Horsehead Bay Boat Ramp:** From SR 16, take the Wollochet Drive Northwest exit. Follow past Artondale. Take a right on 40th Street Northwest, then a left on 92nd Avenue Northwest. Turn right on 36th Street Northwest and follow it past the intersection of Horsehead Drive to the boat ramp. A turnaround area is located just above the ramp. Limited parking is available along the west side of Horsehead Bay Drive. All property around the ramp is private.

**Fox Island/Towhead Island Boat Ramp:** From SR 16, take the Wollochet Drive Northwest exit. Follow past Artondale. Take a right on 40th Street Northwest, then a left on 70th Avenue Northwest, and then a right on Warren Drive Northwest. Veer left onto the Fox Island Bridge. Exit to the right at the boat ramp before you reach Fox Island; this is Towhead Island, which is

*Paddling Horsehead Bay on Carr Inlet with a view of the Cascade Mountains*

connected to Fox Island by a sand spit. The ramp is very rough and island residents are seeking funding to improve it. No facilities are available at the ramp. Parking is limited; arrive early on weekends and during fishing season.

If you want to avoid the 0.3-mile carry from the parking lot to the beach, you can drive down the gravel service road above the beach to unload and load your boat. There is a gate across the road. If it is locked, call the park ranger; the ranger's cell phone number is listed on the bulletin board by the gate. You can also call ahead to the park office: 253-265-3606. A Discover Pass is required for park use.

## ROUTES

**Horsehead Bay to Cutts Island and Kopachuck State Parks:** *Protected*. Launch alongside beach homes and docks in this narrow inlet and head north 1.2 miles to Kopachuck State Park. An impressive sand spit exposed at low tides juts out to the west entry of the bay. Don't land, as all property in this inlet is private. As you near Kopachuck State Park, Cutts Island will appear in the distance.

**Fox and Towhead Islands to Cutts Island and Kopachuck State Parks:** *Moderate*. Currents in Hale Passage can be as fast as 3 knots, stronger on the ebb. Base tidal predictions on the Tacoma Narrows. Watch for busy boating traffic on Hale Passage as you launch. The bridge may also create limited sight distance. Paddle along Fox Island to the sand spit at the island's end and cross north toward Green Point, where Hale Passage meets Carr Inlet. Resembling a horse head, Horsehead Bay is a result of a geological tombolo, a spit that has been built up by wave or tidal action over time and becomes attached to a neighboring island. At lower tides, wide sandy beaches lie around Green Point. Large mansions soon become obscured by a medi-

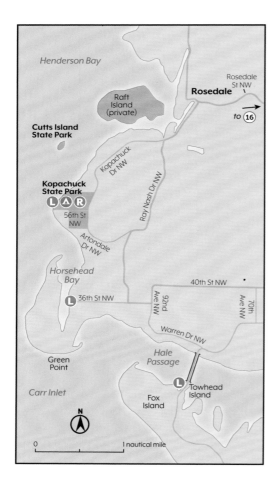

um-bank bluff, offering you some privacy from curious homeowners. The extensive sandy spit on the north tip of Horsehead Bay points to the southern edge of Kopachuck State Park. Cutts Island will appear in the distance offshore, just past Kopachuck.

Tiny Cutts Island seems larger than it really is. Steep bluffs, which increase in height toward the south end, limit the use of the island to either strolls in its madrona and fir woods above or beach hikes below. At the north end, a pebble-and-shell spit extends almost to Raft Island during the lowest tides; this is steeper but easier on boats than the rockier beaches to the south. Also known as "Deadman's Island," Cutts Island was a place where coastal Native peoples buried their dead in canoes placed in the forks of island trees. It was also called Qaqee'lts, or "Crow Island." Watch out for poison oak. This attractive little island cannot sustain camping or fires; both are prohibited.

Kopachuck State Park, barely a half mile from Cutts Island, brings you back to the bustle of road-accessible recreation. On a warm, sunny day, expect a lot of picnickers along the beach and kids splashing in the water. End the day here with a barbecue at one of the shoreside picnic sites. You may also camp at the Cascadia Marine Trail site if you have launched from another location.

The Cascadia Marine Trail site at Kopachuck is located above the beach on the north side of the park, just off the main access road leading to the beach. The seventeen-by-seventeen-foot site is large enough for a couple tents, but the carry from the beach to the site is a very steep, 75-yard haul. Keep your craft at the campsite to avoid vandalism on the beach: kayak storage racks are available. A fire ring and picnic shelter are also available at the site. Restrooms and water, available April through November, are located 500 feet south of the site. The day-use parking lot restroom is available in winter. Check ahead for current camping fees; the maximum group size is four people.

**Alternative Route:** Paddle across Carr Inlet to Penrose Point State Park, approximately 3.5 miles from the Fox Island and Horsehead Bay launches and 4 miles from Kopachuck State Park (see Trip 8, Carr Inlet: Lakebay, Penrose Point State Park, Pitt Island, Longbranch).

*View of the Tacoma Narrows Bridge from Narrows Park*

# 10. Tacoma Narrows

Famous for the 1940s film of the collapsing Tacoma Narrows Bridge, also called "Galloping Ger-tie," the Narrows is known for its tidal bottleneck effect. With Puget Sound squeezing through its mile-wide channel, currents can move swiftly. Four-hundred-foot-tall bluffs rise from both sides of the Narrows in some places, creating a wind tunnel. The modern Tacoma Narrows Bridge consists of a pair of suspension bridges that span 500 feet above the water. A Cascadia Marine Trail site is located on the west side below the bridge at Narrows Park.

**Duration:** Part day to overnight.

**Rating:** *Moderate* or *Exposed*.

**Navigation Aids:** SeaTrails WA 203, 204; NOAA charts 18440 (1:150,000), 18448 (1:80,000). Use the Tacoma tide table and the Tacoma Narrows current table.

**Planning Considerations:** Time the currents so they give you a push through the Narrows. Not doing so will be a slog. Avoid the Narrows when the currents oppose the wind, which can create dangerous conditions. Watch out for boating traffic. You should be comfortable with rough water, as boils, rips, and waves can develop.

## GETTING THERE AND LAUNCHING

**Owen Beach, Point Defiance Park, Tacoma:** From Interstate 5, exit at State Route 16 and drive 5.6 miles west to the Narrows Bridge exit. Exit right to North Pearl Street (SR 163) and follow it 4.9 miles north. Enter Point Defiance Park and follow signs to Owen Beach. Owen Beach has a ramp, plenty of parking, restrooms, picnic tables, and an easy-to-access gravel beach; it can be congested on sunny days.

**Narrows Park:** If going west across the bridge on SR 16, exit at 24th Street Northwest. Go over the freeway and then go left on Jahn Avenue Northwest (also called 95th Street Northwest). Turn left on Stone Drive Northwest and then turn right on Lucille Parkway Northwest. Follow this winding, forested road down to the park. Narrows Park has a Cascadia Marine Trail campsite. Please check with the WWTA site for campsite updates. If returning to Tacoma on the Narrows Bridge, note there is an eastbound bridge toll.

**Titlow Park, Tacoma:** From SR 16, exit at Jackson Avenue South, then take a right on 6th Avenue. Follow this to the park. A full-service park, Titlow has restrooms, a boat ramp, and picnic tables. Parking is limited. You will have to walk across the railroad tracks and down to the beach.

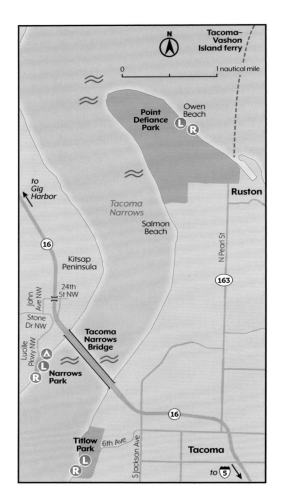

## ROUTE

Contrary to what you may think, currents don't necessarily run smoothly through the channel. On the east end of the bridge, an underwater shelf blocks currents flowing south, forcing the water to run in a counterclockwise direction near the north end of the Narrows. You can see the effect from above in Point Defiance Park. Note that ebb tides run stronger on the east side, while floods are stronger on the west side. The south end can have currents over 5 knots.

Launching from Owen Beach, take the flood southwest into the Narrows. Cross to the west side for a more efficient flow south, watching boat traffic as you go. Enjoy the canyon-like feeling of being in the Narrows below the forest-covered slopes. On the east side, you'll see the unique Salmon Beach community. The homes are on pilings above the water and a long wooden stairway up the hill provides access. Burlington Northern railroad tracks suddenly appear on the south side of Salmon Beach. The train tunnel runs from the Tacoma community of Ruston; it goes under Point Defiance Park and ends just south of the park.

As you near the bridge, stay clear of the concrete pillars. Eddies can form behind them, creating a section of bumpy water. As you pass the bridge, Narrows Park will come into view on the right (west). The Cascadia Marine Trail campsite is just past the house on the shore in the trees: it has two sites, a chemical toilet, no water, and fires are not allowed. Call 253-313-5090 to reserve. The site has a 1200-foot-long gravel beach and impressive views of the gigantic bridge to the north.

Titlow Park begins less than a mile south of the bridge on the east side. The park has a full-service marina and is a good take-out or launch point for the Narrows. Consider running a shuttle between Owen Beach and Titlow, or time your trip to take the ebb back north. The total one-way mileage from Owen Beach to Titlow using the west-side flood is 10.4 miles—but with the current assisting you on large tidal exchanges, it can feel like 5 miles.

# 11. Gig Harbor

In 1867, Yugoslavian immigrant Samuel Jerisch and two partners rowed a flat-bottomed skiff from British Columbia to what is now Gig Harbor. Samuel and his wife, Anna, began the fishing industry here, which later grew into a successful commercial fleet. The protected harbor has a narrow entry and is considered by boaters to be a perfect gunkhole. A quick jaunt from Tacoma's Point Defiance Park, the Narrows, Vashon Island, and Colvos Passage, Gig Harbor is a central location for many paddling routes. Gig Harbor also has a large surf ski community and annual races for all human-powered watercraft.

**Duration:** Part day to full day.

**Rating:** *Protected* or *Exposed*.

**Navigation Aids:** SeaTrails WA 203; NOAA charts 18440 (1:150,000), 18448 (1:80,000). Use Tacoma tide tables and the Tacoma Narrows current table.

**Planning Considerations:** The inner harbor is very protected but busy in summer with recreational boaters. Paddling outside of the harbor can be moderate during large tidal exchanges from the Narrows and Dalco Passage. Visit the tavern by the waterfront for a great view of the bay.

## GETTING THERE AND LAUNCHING
**Gig Harbor Jerisch Dock:** From State Route 16, take the Pioneer Way exit going north. Follow it 2.2 miles into Gig Harbor. Take a left on Harborview Drive and look for Skansie Brothers Park and the Jerisch Dock, on your right next to the Gig Harbor Marina. Use street parking, which can be

busy in summer. The park has restrooms, a public dock, a little beach, and PFDs for loan. Visit cityofgigharbor.net for additional information.

**Eddon Boat Park:** Continue west a few more blocks on Harborview Drive to this grassy little park with water access. Parking is on the street; no facilities available.

**Gig Harbor Public Boat Launch:** From the Gig Harbor waterfront, continue on Harborview Drive and follow it around the harbor. Take a right on Vernhardson Street, then an immediate right on Randall Drive Northwest. Follow Randall Drive to the boat ramp. Located in a residential area, the ramp has no facilities and limited parking; overflow parking is on the street. The day-use-only ramp and side streets get very busy in summer during fishing season.

**Alternative Launch:** Owen Beach in Tacoma's Point Defiance Park (see Trip 10, Tacoma Narrows).

### ROUTES

**Gig Harbor:** *Protected.* Centrally located, Gig Harbor has many paddling opportunities. The harbor itself is a pleasant place with beach homes and recreational boats lining the shores. Explore both ends and dip into the small inlet below Vernhardson Street. Paddle to the harbor entry and enjoy a dash of light current when pulling through on larger tidal exchanges. Use caution, as the entry may be a blind corner for boaters coming in and out of the harbor. In summer, rent kayaks and SUPs from Lee's SUP, located on the waterfront at 8829 N. Harborview Drive.

**Point Defiance Park:** *Exposed.* For longer routes, consider crossing from the outside of the harbor over to Point Defiance Park in Tacoma. A 3.1-mile paddle to Owen Beach on the north

*Skansie Brothers Park on Gig Harbor*

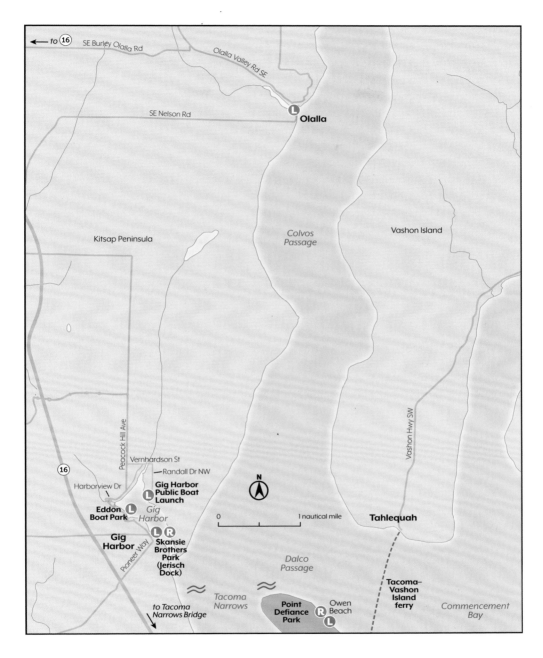

← to 16

SE Burley Olalla Rd

Olalla Valley Rd SE

SE Nelson Rd

L Olalla

Kitsap Peninsula

Colvos
Passage

Vashon Island

Vashon Hwy SW

Peacock Hill Ave

Vernhardson St
Randall Dr NW

16

Harborview Dr

L Gig Harbor
Public Boat
Launch

Eddon L
Boat Park

Gig
Harbor

N

Tahlequah

Gig
Harbor

L R
Skansie
Brothers
Park
(Jerisch
Dock)

Pioneer Way

0                    1 nautical mile

Dalco
Passage

Tacoma–
Vashon
Island
ferry

Commencement
Bay

to Tacoma
Narrows Bridge

Tacoma
Narrows

Point
Defiance R
Park

Owen
Beach

L

side, this trip crosses currents coming in or out of the Narrows to the south. You may encounter swirls and a push or pull, depending on the tidal direction. This trip is for intermediate to advanced paddlers.

**Olalla:** *Protected.* Run a shuttle to Olalla, a tiny waterfront community 11 miles north up Colvos Passage from Gig Harbor. The currents in Colvos Passage almost always run north. Use eddies along the shoreline to paddle back to Gig Harbor if paddling against the ebb.

In 1881, an American Indian approached settler L. P. Larson and offered him a *mamook olallie*, meaning a strawberry. In the early 1900s, strawberries ripened here three weeks earlier than those sold at Seattle's Pike Place Market and thus were in great demand. To reach the ramp at Olalla, take SR 16 north 12 miles and exit on Southeast Burley Olalla Road. Follow it 6 miles to Olalla. Park in the gravel lot on the south side of the road above the estuary. Launch or take-out at the boat ramp below. Aim for higher tides, as the bay empties out to a mudflat. There is a small store above the beach for basic supplies, but it burned in 2022. Call to confirm if it's open.

**Alternative Trips Nearby:** A short drive from Gig Harbor brings you to the head of Henderson Bay and Fox Island (see Trip 9, Carr Inlet: Horsehead Bay, Cutts Island State Park, and Kopachuck State Park).

# 12. **Commencement Bay**

Any expectations you may have of a polluted industrial wasteland will be pleasantly upended in Commencement Bay, which has a bit of everything. There are the wooded bluffs of Point Defiance, the "downtown" feel of the Thea Foss Waterway with its yachts and workboats, the melancholy quiet along the slag shores of the abandoned ASARCO smelter site, and the intense activity of one of the busiest ports in the Northwest. The bay and its adjacent waterways are enough to fill many days of exploration.

> **Duration:** Part day to full day.
>
> **Rating:** *Protected* or *Moderate.* The Moderate-rated Commencement Bay Loop requires crossing about 2 miles of open water.
>
> **Navigation Aids:** SeaTrails WA 203; NOAA charts 18445 SC (1:80,000), 18474 (1:40,000), 18453 (1:15,000).
>
> **Planning Considerations:** As Commencement Bay is a port of commerce, always stay alert to the locations and movement of other watercraft.

## GETTING THERE AND LAUNCHING

These are the most convenient launch sites around Commencement Bay. Most sites have limited parking, don't have restrooms, and are closed at dusk. Call Tacoma Parks for more info: 253-305-1054.

**Thea's Park:** This park at 405 Dock Street, just at the north end of the Thea Foss Waterway, has a ramp, sandy kayak launch, approximately twenty-five parking spaces, and no restrooms. Just a short walk down the street, at Foss Marina, you can rent kayaks and paddle boards.

*Thea's Park on the Tacoma waterfront*

**Waterway Park:** Located on the northeast side of the East 21st Street Bridge, this park has a public parking lot and a human-powered launch with a low dock into the waterway. The cross street is East D Street.

**Tacoma to Point Defiance Shoreline:** There are many alternatives to choose from on the shoreline between Tacoma and Point Defiance. The closest to the city is Jack Hyde Park (formerly Commencement Park), located at the point where Schuster Parkway becomes Ruston Way, a little less than 2 miles from downtown. There is a good sand and gravel beach here. Others include Dickman Mill Park—which has a ramp and parking that requires crossing Ruston Way— and Judge Jack Tanner Park, which has limited parking. For more info visit metroparkstacoma. org/place/ruston-way.

**Point Defiance Marina:** Located where the former ASARCO copper smelter operated and polluted the region for more than a hundred years, this facility includes a full boat ramp, ADA access, a marina store, ample day-use parking, overnight parking (for a fee), and restrooms in the marina store. The human-powered launch (adjacent to the boat ramp) requires a modest fee. The marina can get busy in summer. For more info, call the marina at 253-404-3960.

**Point Defiance Park:** You can set off from Owen Beach inside Point Defiance Park (closes at sunset). To reach it, continue into the park from its entrance on N. Pearl Street, pass the zoo and aquarium, and drive along the bluffs to a side road that drops down to the right to the beach. In summer months, it's usually busy and a concessionaire sells snacks and rents kayaks and paddle boards. The park has a ramp, a beach, and a lot of parking.

**North Side of Commencement Bay:** The Dick Gilmur Memorial Shoreline offers access to the north end of the bay. Rustic homes on stilts, small marinas, and views across the bay to downtown Tacoma make this a great place to paddle. The access point at 4700 Marine View Drive has parking (limited to four cars), no restrooms, and is closed at dusk. A smooth gravel ramp leads to the sandy beach. Navigate around the wooden boom to open water.

**Browns Point:** Along the northwest shore of Commencement Bay, picturesque Browns Point Lighthouse Park (part of the Tacoma Metro Parks System) is an appropriate launch for a loop tour of the entire bay. It's also the closest access point if you're coming from north of Tacoma. Watch for tide rips off the point on a strong flood.

From Tacoma, follow Marine View Drive (State Route 509) west 3 miles to Le-Lou-Wa Place Northeast. Turn left, then go about 0.75 mile, curving around to the right as the road becomes Tok-A-Lou Avenue Northeast. Parking is limited, but there are restrooms. Boats must be carried about 100 yards down a grassy hill to the steep gravel beach. Note that the park and lot close at dusk. Although there is no camping allowed, you can make reservations to stay in the park as a lighthouse keeper. Visit pointsnortheast.org/cottage-rental for additional information.

To reach Browns Point from the Seattle area, take Exit 143 (Federal Way) from Interstate 5. Go west on 320th Street for 4.5 miles until it intersects 47th Avenue. Go right for 0.5 mile and then

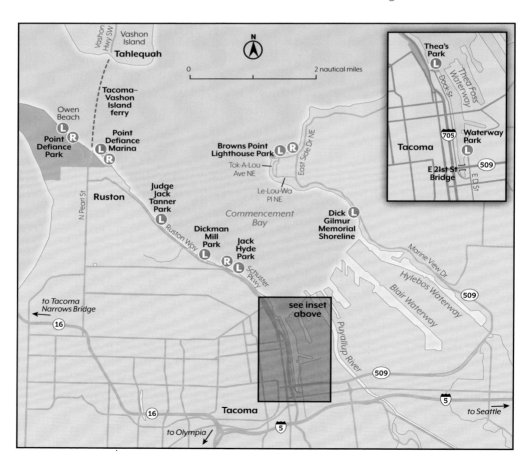

left on Dash Point Road. Follow this road for 3 miles, passing Dash Point State Park, after which it becomes East Side Drive. Proceed to Le-Lou-Wa Place Northeast. Turn right and drive 0.75 mile to the park.

## ROUTES

**South Shore Local Paddling:** *Protected*. Choose your own distance. Pick any of the launch sites described above along Ruston Way to Point Defiance Park.

One possibility is a short trip from Owen Beach west toward Point Defiance, following the gravel beach beneath steep, wooded bluffs that restrict access to the beach except for occasional trails. The current here, which is strongest during the flood, usually flows west and can be quite swift near the point.

Also consider paddling between Owen Beach and one of the parks along Ruston Way, perhaps in conjunction with a car shuttle. Many new restaurants have sprung up along the shoreline, offering dock space to lure in hungry boaters passing by. This route also skirts the former ASARCO smelter site, now a park and marina. The steep and jumbled shoreline is surprisingly pleasant and interesting: seaweed grows profusely, and waves have eroded sea caves large enough to paddle into cautiously.

A third and more urban alternative on Commencement Bay's south shore is the paddle from Jack Hyde Park southwest into Thea Foss Waterway, with a roundtrip distance of up to 4 miles. Or a much shorter exploration of the waterway can be made from the city dock at Thea's Park, perhaps on a Sunday morning when parking is easiest to find. You will pass bulk carrier freighters being loaded as you enter the waterway and the buildings of downtown Tacoma come into view. Thea Foss Waterway is the hub of recreational boating in the bay, so there are plenty of yachts to view in the many marinas along both shores. Commercial fishing boats have their own floats on the northeast side of the waterway.

**Commencement Bay Loop:** *Moderate* (due to 2-mile crossing). The loop distance is about 7 miles (not including any additional exploration into the waterways), but it can be shortened to about 5 miles by cutting across parts of the bay at any point. You can start from Jack Hyde Park on the south shore or from Browns Point Lighthouse Park on the north, depending on the direction from which you approach the area. This description begins at Browns Point.

Begin with the crossing from Browns Point toward downtown Tacoma via Jack Hyde Park, which offers only public facilities along the route. This course should take you past ships that usually are at anchor there. You'll also paddle past the Tacoma skyline and the Museum of Glass. Perhaps after a look into the picturesque Thea Foss Waterway, start northeast across the old Puyallup River estuary, now among the most active maritime industrial areas in the region. There may be a strong current outflow as you cross.

Beyond are the Blair and Hylebos Creek Waterways, where large container ships and car carriers unload. At the mouth of the Hylebos Creek Waterway is a small military station with US Army Corps of Engineers vessels. The north shore is mostly private marinas, one of which has interesting old ships positioned to form a breakwater.

# Middle Puget Sound

This section of Puget Sound is an easy getaway for city-dwellers, offering many paddles close to home. A few Cascadia Marine Trail sites are within paddling distance of Seattle. With epic views of the Olympic and Cascade Mountains, launches and campsites can get busy in summer.

# 13. **Maury Island**

A narrow isthmus connects Maury Island to Vashon Island, providing an age-old portage. The most challenging route here combines the quiet charm of Quartermaster Harbor with a more arduous paddle along the "island's" south coast for a circumnavigation that will leave you feeling like you have seen a great deal as well as had a good day's exercise. For a more relaxed alternative, dabble in the harbor. Launching from Saltwater State Park involves a more demanding crossing, traversing shipping lanes and possible tide rips.

**Duration:** Part day to overnight.

**Rating:** *Protected*, *Moderate*, or *Exposed*. The Moderate route may require committing to several miles of paddling in wind and choppy water. The Exposed area has potential tide rips and shipping traffic.

**Navigation Aids:** SeaTrails WA 203; NOAA charts 18445 SC or 18448 (both 1:80,000), 18474 (1:40,000); Seattle tide table (add 15 minutes).

**Planning Considerations:** Windy weather can make the east side of Maury Island unpleasant; the shallow beaches make offshore seas steep and landings wet and rough. If you are going to circumnavigate, plan for high tide to make the portage at Portage and to avoid the extensive tide flats on the Quartermaster Harbor side. Swift currents flow around Point Robinson. Check your current tables when paddling here or when crossing from Saltwater State Park. Use VHF channel 13 to monitor ship traffic.

## GETTING THERE AND LAUNCHING

Maury Island routes can be reached via Vashon Island by launching at either Portage, Jensen Point Boathouse, or Dockton County Park. They can also be reached from the east shore of Puget Sound from Saltwater State Park or Des Moines Marina, both of which require a 2-mile crossing.

To reach Vashon Island from Seattle, take Exit 163 from Interstate 5 and follow the West Seattle Bridge. In West Seattle, this becomes Fauntleroy Way Southwest and leads to the Fauntleroy ferry terminal. Take the ferry to Vashon Island and then drive south to the town of Vashon.

To reach Vashon Island from Tacoma, follow Ruston Way to Pearl Street, then turn right down the hill to the Point Defiance ferry landing. Take the ferry to Tahlequah and follow Vashon Highway Southwest north to the Quartermaster Harbor area.

**Dockton County Park:** To reach Maury Island from the town of Vashon, follow Vashon Highway Southwest south about 3 miles to Southwest Quartermaster Drive, where you turn left for Maury Island. For Dockton County Park, continue past Portage, where Southwest Quartermaster Drive becomes Dockton Road Southwest, for about 3.5 miles. Parking is ample; you'll

*A paddler crosses between Point Robinson and Des Moines on a calm morning.*

also find restrooms and a beach below a short sea wall. The park closes at dusk and no services are available in the town of Dockton.

**Point Robinson County Park:** Follow the directions above toward Dockton County Park to reach Portage and Dockton Road Southwest. Then take a left on Southwest Point Robinson Road, following this road to its end.

**Portage:** This launch is a popular beginning and end point for a Maury Island circumnavigation. There is limited parking along each of the two roads that cross the isthmus, which are connected by Portage Way Southwest. The carrying distance between high-tide lines is approximately 200 yards on pavement. Watch out for speedy traffic here. A high tide launch or take-out on the Quartermaster Harbor side is particularly desirable, since it becomes a large mudflat at low tide. The Shomamish people, who were native to Vashon Island, used the portage to save time when traveling through by canoe and raised 300-foot-wide nets made from bark and plant fibers to catch birds flying low over the portage.

**Jensen Point Park and Boathouse/Burton:** Take Vashon Highway Southwest to Southwest Burton Drive, turn left, and then turn right onto 97th Avenue Southwest, which becomes Southwest Bayview Drive. Turn right into Jensen Point at the sign for the park. There is usually plenty of parking. The park has a ramp, toilets, and a beach that gently slopes into Quartermaster Harbor. The Vashon Island Parks District has constructed a smart little boathouse—Jensen Point Boathouse—that provides human-powered boat rentals and storage for the local rowing club's fleet. Managed by Vashon Island Adventures, it has sea kayak and other small-craft rentals, and lessons are offered to the public on a regular basis. Call Vashon Island Adventures at 206-259-3978 for additional information.

**Saltwater State Park:** From I-5, take Exit 147 and go west 0.8 mile on South 272nd Street. Turn right at 16th Avenue South and proceed 0.7 mile. Turn left onto Woodmont Drive South. In 0.6 mile, bear sharply right onto Marine View Drive South (SR 509). At 1 mile, turn left onto South 252nd Street for one-half block, then turn left onto 8th Place South, which leads to the park's entrance. Saltwater State Park has vault toilets and easy access to a sand-and-gravel beach. Despite its nearly 300 parking spots, the lot may fill quickly on summer weekends. Unless you are camping, parking is for day use only. The Cascadia Marine Trail campsite is closed. Regular state park campsites along the forested hills at the east end of the park are only open in summer. Display your Discover Pass or purchase a day-use parking permit.

**Des Moines Marina Pier** (410 S. 222nd St.): From I-5, take South 216th Street west to Marine View Drive South (SR 509), where it becomes 7th Avenue South. Take a right on South 223rd Street and then another right on Cliff Avenue South to the Des Moines Marina Pier and Beach Park. This is the shortest paddle distance to Point Robinson from the east shore of Puget Sound. If you park on the pier, you must pay a fee by the restrooms. Enter down the gangplank to lower docks and put in on either side. It's a tight spot, especially if fishing boats are docked. Hose water

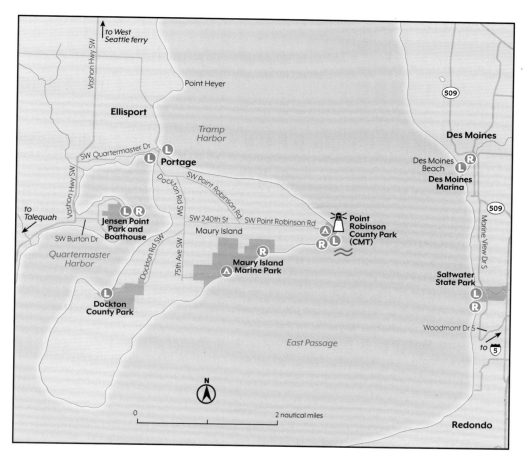

is available. Overnight parking is available with a parking pass; visit desmoinesmarina.com/paidparking.html for more parking info.

**Des Moines Beach Park:** Slightly north of the marina pier, enter the park through a pay gate. Park immediately on the left. Des Moines Beach Park has restrooms, a grassy area, picnic tables, and a gentle, sloping beach. Check the above link for parking fees.

## ROUTES

**Quartermaster Harbor:** *Protected.* Choose your own paddling distance. Quartermaster Harbor is a fine place for a leisurely paddle year-round. It features warm waters with the opportunity to swim during the summer and the quiet of still, overcast days in winter. The Burton Peninsula effectively breaks up the fetch, so seas are not likely to develop extensively. Both Jensen Point Park and Dockton County Park are good for a picnic, though Dockton offers more shoreside seclusion with its longer beach. Tables and restrooms are available at both.

**Maury Island Circumnavigation:** *Moderate.* The total paddling distance is 12 miles. The long, shallow bight of Maury Island's south side is an unusual mix of wildness amid the development of the central Puget Sound area. Though about half of the shoreline is occupied by residences, some are only accessible via long wooden stairways from the bluff above. The remainder are grassy or wooded bluffs that invite a climb for a magnificent view of East Passage, Commencement Bay, Tacoma, and Mount Rainier in the distance. Paddle 1.6 miles south of the Point Robinson Lighthouse to reach Maury Island Marine Park, which replaces a former gravel mine. There's one primitive campsite and restrooms, best accessible from the water. The park is run by King County Parks. On the southwest corner of Maury Island in Manzanita, there is a natural rock that Native peoples have said marks the spot where killer whales play.

A large part of this shoreline and the bluffs behind are occupied by huge, controversial gravel and sand pits below 300-foot cliffs. However, these do not detract in the least from the overall attractiveness and interest of the area. Grass, alder, and madrona are rapidly reclaiming most of the pits, while rusty, derelict conveyor systems descend through the brush to rotting terminals where barges once loaded. There are no public uplands or tidelands along this shore, so respect private property rights.

The south and north shores of Maury Island can turn into rough paddling in southerly or northerly winds, so you might want to time your circumnavigation to cover the portion most exposed to prevailing winds early in the day. Though currents for East Passage are described as weak and variable, tide rips are known to form off Point Robinson and are perhaps at their worst when ship wakes cross them. (See the Saltwater State Park to Point Robinson route below for information and cautions about Point Robinson.)

**Saltwater State Park to Point Robinson:** *Exposed.* The roundtrip paddling distance is 5 miles. The crossing from Saltwater State Park, about 2 miles at the narrowest point, is easy in moderate weather. Currents in the area are listed as weak and variable, though they do accelerate around Point Robinson as water is compressed around it. Rips and a light current wrapping around Point Robinson are possible. The primary hazard on this crossing is marine shipping moving to and from Tacoma. The traffic lanes are separated by the mid-channel buoy; northbound ships pass to the west. Wakes from ships and the many pleasure boats that ply this channel can create choppy seas. The surf from a passing ship's wake at Point Robinson can be quite large, a thrill to those who like to surf but a hazard to others. Be sure to look for boat traffic hazards before landing or launching. Pull your boat well up onto the beach when ashore.

The beach at Point Robinson and the grassy area behind the US Coast Guard's lighthouse are open to the public during the day. The lighthouse, which began operating in 1887, has keepers' quarters available for rent through the Vashon Parks District; visit vashonparks.org/pt-robinson-keepers-quarters for more info.

Up the hill, northeast of the lighthouse, is a Cascadia Marine Trail campsite. Access to the site is about 100 feet from the northwest side of the lighthouse in the trees below the hill. Signage is minimal. There is a boat storage rack by the beach, but the carry to the campsite is a long distance, upstairs, and across a grassy field to the sites overlooking the bluff. Consider carrying a backpack to transfer your gear to the site. There are two tent spaces; both require reservations from Vashon Adventures (206-259-3978). Camping is limited to one night and no fires are allowed.

# 14. **Blake Island**

Come to Blake Island for either a pleasant day trip or an overnight adventure. Some say Chief Sealth, whom Seattle was named after, was born on Blake Island in 1786. The island was logged in the 1850s and was later home to a wealthy Seattle lawyer, William Pitt Trimble. It became a park in 1974 and is visited by nearly 300,000 people a year. A quick escape from the city, the 475-acre island is a favorite among paddlers and boaters alike.

Blake Island, easily accessed from several locations, offers views of downtown Seattle and the Olympic Mountains. It also has one of the most unusual kayak-camping experiences on Washington shores. Pitch your tent at Tillicum Village, then take a hot shower in the heated restroom. Pre-COVID, Tillicum Village offered American Indian dancing and a salmon dinner. Too civilized for you? Choose the Cascadia Marine Trail site on the northwest corner of the island.

**Duration:** Full day to overnight.

**Rating:** *Protected*, *Moderate*, or *Exposed*. Tide rips may be encountered on the Moderate route; the Exposed route involves 4 miles of open water across shipping lanes, with the potential for rough seas in southerly or northerly winds.

**Navigation Aids:** SeaTrails WA 202, 203; NOAA charts 18445 SC or 18448 (both 1:80,000), 18449 (1:25,000); Seattle tide table.

**Planning Considerations:** Bring change for the coin-operated showers near Tillicum Village. Protect your food from the numerous raccoons. Argosy no longer offers boat trips to the island; call ahead to check if Tillicum Village's services have been restored. Contact the ranger in the main area for overflow camping.

*Paddle camping along the shores of Blake Island*

### GETTING THERE AND LAUNCHING

From West Seattle, launches can be made at either Alki Beach, along Beach Drive Southwest, or at Lincoln Park.

**Alki Beach or Alki Point Light Station:** Take Exit 163 from Interstate 5 and follow the West Seattle Bridge to the Harbor Avenue Southwest exit, then follow the road north (right). In 1.3 miles, the first launch is at the Seacrest Boathouse/Alki Kayak Tours on Harbor Avenue Southwest. Kayak and SUP rentals are available here as well. Or continue around Duwamish Head to where it becomes Alki Avenue Southwest and follow it west to the designated launch site between 54th Place Southwest and 55th Avenue Southwest. You can also access the water at the far west end of Alki Beach or just south of the Alki Point Light Station, along Beach Drive Southwest at Constellation Park. Public restrooms are available at 58th Avenue Southwest and 63rd Avenue Southwest, respectively. On-street parking is extremely difficult to find in the summer, so be prepared to launch early before the crowds arrive. Consider parking in residential areas if Alki Beach is too crowded.

**Lincoln Park:** This park has the unique advantage of being near the Fauntleroy ferry landing, so you can return on the ferry if necessary. Park in the south lot and follow the path at the park's southern boundary about 150 yards down to a defunct boat ramp and the sand-and-cobble beach. Restrooms are close by. Note that the park closes at night.

For ferry access to Vashon Island and Southworth, take the West Seattle Bridge and follow the signs to the Fauntleroy ferry.

**Vashon Island:** To launch your kayak here, use the small ramp just east of the north-end ferry dock. Parking next to the ramp is private, so unload and move your cars as soon as possible to the ferry parking area up the hill. There is no beach on either side of the ramp at higher tides; you must be prepared to launch quickly from the ramp at those times without delaying other users. Do not try to get to the beach from west of the ferry dock: this is private land.

**Southworth:** You can unload and load your boat at the dead end of Southeast Sebring Drive, parallel to the ferry entrance. Please be courteous, as private homes closely border this put-in and there is no parking. Park in the twenty-four-hour lot on the slight hill above the dock.

**Manchester:** Access to Manchester is from Port Orchard or Southworth. Park in the dirt overnight lot across from the restaurants. You can use the boat ramp (if it's not too busy) or the launch for small, hand-carried boats to the right of the boat ramp. Restrooms and a small park are nearby.

Alternative launches include Fort Ward Park on south Bainbridge and Manchester State Park, both of which have a Cascadia Marine Trail site.

## ROUTES

**West Seattle to Blake Island:** *Exposed.* The paddling distance is over 3 miles one way from any of the West Seattle launch points, across open water with heavy shipping traffic. Currents in this area usually are less than 1 knot; they are strongest on the ebb. Be prepared to use one of the alternative routes or to return to West Seattle by ferry if the weather takes a turn for the worse. You can monitor boat and shipping locations on channel 14 with your VHF radio to assure a traffic-free crossing.

**Vashon Island to Blake Island:** *Moderate.* The paddling distance is approximately 1.5 miles each way, with about 1.25 miles across open water. Currents in this area rarely exceed 1 knot, but rips can occur between the two islands, particularly near the Allen Bank off Vashon Island. Colvos Passage is unique in that the current flows only on the ebb (moves north) and becomes weak and variable at other stages of the tide. Hence, this area becomes roughest on northerly winds when the ebb current opposes it. Stay clear of Southworth and Vashon ferry traffic.

**Southworth to Blake Island:** *Protected.* The paddling distance is approximately 1.9 miles each way, with about 0.75 mile across open water. Currents here are weak and variable, as long as you stay west of Colvos Passage and head for the more westerly shore of Blake Island.

**Manchester to Blake Island:** *Protected.* Paddling distance is 2.2 miles to Blake Island. Watch for busy pleasure-boating traffic in summer.

Roughly triangular in shape, Blake Island has a paddling circumference of about 5 miles. Most of its shoreline consists of low bluffs above rocky beaches, but the west end has sandy beaches and a shallow high-tide lagoon. Once ashore, you can hike an extensive network of paths and trails.

There are two camping areas, both of which bear a camping fee year-round. Reservations are recommended. On the northwestern corner of the island is the Cascadia Marine Trail site (with three tent spaces), a state park public camping area with water (normally shut off during winter months), and restrooms located up the hill. The park sites here are titled "West Loop 37–51" and the landing is a nice sandy beach. Boaters tend to camp in the sites around the cor-

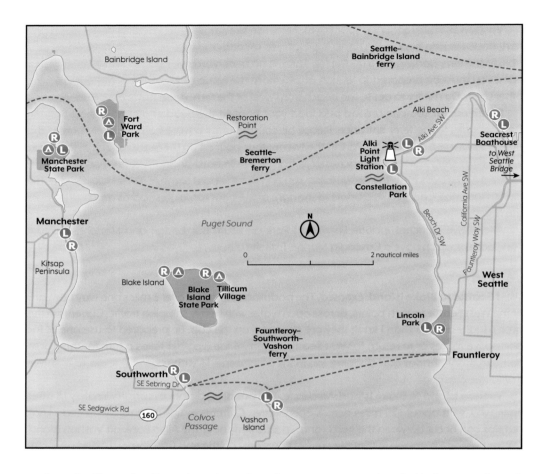

ner from the Cascadia site and can be quite noisy on summer weekends. No fires are allowed, and you're asked to respect the dune-grass restoration in progress.

The eastern point, by Tillicum Village, is the more developed state park site—expect it to be crowded with boaters and boat-in campers during the summer months. These sites are titled "Main Loop 1–32." A breakwater encloses a boat basin with floats for the boaters who come here year-round. The campground is between the boat basin and the stony beach to the south. If you are camping here, land on this beach unless there is a strong southerly wind and waves; in that case, use the beach in the boat basin. Most of the campsites here have little or no southerly wind protection, but they offer heated bathrooms with coin-operated showers and other amenities.

Nearby are semi-enclosed shelters for group picnics; they can be used for cooking during the day if not already reserved. Visit the state park website at parks.wa.gov/476/Blake-Island for camping reservations.

*Middle Point Torpedo building*

# 15. Eagle Harbor to Bremerton

This is one of the most interesting, long-range day trips in Puget Sound, and the ability to carry kayaks aboard ferries as a foot passenger opens up 10 miles of one-way paddling. Leave your car in Seattle, walk your boat aboard the Bainbridge Island ferry, paddle through Rich Passage and Port Orchard to Bremerton, then take the ferry back to the city. State parks along the way make nice picnic stops with old military installations to explore. To make this into an overnight, stop at one of three Cascadia Marine Trail sites: Fort Ward on the south end of Bainbridge Island, Manchester State Park on the south side of Rich Passage, or add a 2-mile side trip to Blake Island (see Trip 14, Blake Island).

**Duration:** Full day to overnight.

**Rating:** *Moderate*. Involves current with possible tide rips and heavy boat and shipping traffic in Rich Passage.

**Navigation Aids:** SeaTrails WA 202, 203; NOAA charts 18445 SC or 18441 (both 1:80,000), 18446 (1:25,000); Admiralty Inlet current tables corrected for Rich Passage.

**Planning Considerations:** Ferry schedules dictate your timing here, but runs are frequent, especially the fast ferry from Seattle to Bremerton. A favorable current in Rich Passage is desirable, as it can reach 3 or 4 knots. The flood flows toward Bremerton in Rich Passage.

## GETTING THERE AND LAUNCHING

This trip gives you two options for getting to Bainbridge Island from Seattle: wheel your kayak or SUP onto the ferry or car-top your kayak or SUP and drive on board.

If you are coming from downtown Seattle with your carted kayak or SUP on the ferry, weekends are preferred because parking close to the Seattle ferry terminal at Colman Dock is easier, especially early on Sunday morning. Check street parking and nearby garages for day or overnight parking. Be aware that there is a small kayak "storage fee" to wheel your boat aboard. Arrive one hour early and ask ferry personnel for loading directions.

**Eagle Harbor:** After leaving the ferry terminal with your carted kayak, turn left on the first street beyond the toll booths, signed "Eagle Harbor Condominiums." At the bottom of the hill, take a left at the Waterfront Trail before the condos. This leads to a small beach just south of the ferry terminal. Total carrying distance is about 300 yards. Respect private property at the put-in, as it shares a fence with the condos. There is no parking for this launch.

If coming by car off the ferry, follow traffic up the hill above the ferry dock and take a left at the light onto Winslow Way. Drive through the downtown corridor and take a left on Madison

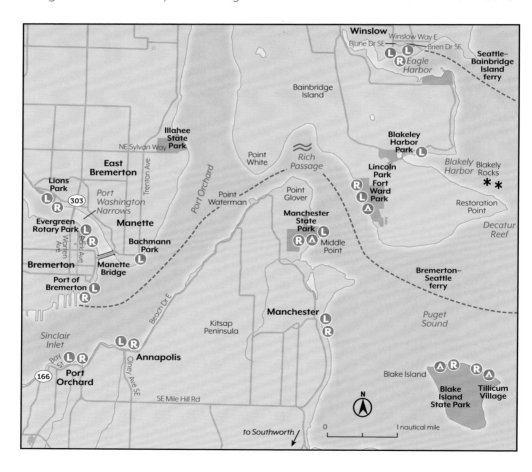

Avenue, then the next left onto Bjune Drive Southeast. In less than 0.1 mile, turn right onto Shannon Drive Southeast and follow it down to the ramp and circular parking area by the water at Waterfront Park. These are temporary parking areas to unload your boat and gear. Three-hour parking is located above the park on Bjune Drive Southeast and Brien Drive Southeast. Overnight parking is available in the ferry lot a few blocks away. There is no overnight parking in downtown Winslow. Contact the Harbormaster for more info: 206-780-3733.

**Blakely Harbor/Blakely Harbor Park** (10230 NE Country Club Rd.): Another option for day-use launching is on Blakely Harbor, just south of Eagle Harbor. Two public beach access spots here are a short distance from each other: one has a 50-yard carry and the other a 100-yard carry. There is a restroom, parking lot, and nice beaches. Low tides may make for a longer, muddy carry, as the bay empties out a bit.

**Bremerton:** In downtown Bremerton, gain water access via a natural-looking boat ramp in the Port of Bremerton Marina, just north of the ferry. There's a turnaround to drop your boat and gear adjacent to the ramp and restrooms on 2nd Street below Washington Avenue. Overnight parking is available above in two pay lots. Look for abundant starfish by the ramp below the docks.

Another option is to launch at the boat ramp north of the Manette Bridge in Evergreen Rotary Park on Park Avenue and 14th Street. Parking can be tight on sunny days. The park has restrooms and picnic tables. Port Washington Narrows flows by the park, usually with a few knots of current. Flood and ebb currents are stronger at the north end of the narrows, with speeds up to 4.5 knots on a flood and 3.1 knots on an ebb. Plan your launch to use the currents to get to your destination.

In East Bremerton, **Bachmann Park** provides a small put-in and a few parking spots but no restrooms. Access the park by taking Manette Bridge from downtown Bremerton. Take the first right at East 11th Street and follow it to Trenton Avenue. The park is two blocks farther near the end of the street. Look for the gazebo and picnic tables.

North of Manette, **Lions Park** at 251 Lebo Boulevard has a large lot, restrooms, picnic tables, a boat ramp, and shoreline access. Enter the park across from Oak Street. Watch tides here, as low tides make for a long carry to the waterline.

Across Sinclair Inlet, launch east of the **Port Orchard** Marina along Bay Street (State Route 160). There's also a boat ramp just east of Annapolis on Beach Drive East by the commuter ferry dock, which has plenty of parking but no restrooms.

## ROUTE

Paddling distance from Eagle Harbor to Bremerton is 10 miles. Add 4 to 6 miles for a side trip to Blake Island State Park, depending on which part you visit.

Eagle Harbor is a worthy destination in its own right; you may want to return on another day to explore it (see Trip 17, Eagle Harbor). But for this route, watch ferry traffic and cross to the south side and out of the harbor, passing the sandy, fenced-in site that was once the location of the world's largest plant for creating creosote-treated pilings. There's a restored sandy public beach just south of the point, one of several Eagle Harbor beaches once tainted by creosote chemicals. Head south from here, passing modern homes packed along the shore. Watch out for ferry wakes that can create sizeable surf waves along the shore. Stay close to shore, as ferries cruise parallel to this shore before turning into Eagle Harbor.

You'll soon pass Blakely Rocks at the opening of Blakely Harbor. In 1863, one of the largest logging mills in the region opened in the harbor, shipping lumber throughout the world. The Hall Brothers opened a shipyard in 1881, building seventy-seven vessels in twenty-two years. In 1889, the "Great Mill," the largest in the world, was built on the site and eventually employed more than one thousand workers. Remnants of both operations exist at the end of the bay. You can find a day-use park with two put-ins and restrooms on the north side of the bay adjacent to the old ruins. Stately homes now line the shorelines on both sides of the bay.

Continue to Restoration Point, being careful to stay out of the way of the ferries that run close to this shore for some way before turning east toward Seattle. Off Restoration Point is Decatur Reef, a long rocky spine that can produce breaking waves or tide rips. At high tide you can paddle close to shore over the reef. Or if conditions warrant, swing wide around the navigation marker. Note the white, sandy beaches on the north side of the homes by the point. Yield to the Bremerton ferry as you enter Rich Passage.

Both Fort Ward Park and Manchester State Park provide a Cascadia Marine Trail campsite, boat ramps, picnic tables, water, and restrooms, as well as interesting things to explore in the vicinity. The two parks are located across Rich Passage from each other. Look west of the pier to spot the picnic tables at Fort Ward. The Cascadia Marina Trail has five sites here near Battery Vinton, a coastal defense gun battery from before World War I. The boat ramp farther to the west is a good launch spot, also with restrooms.

Manchester State Park, on the south shore west of Middle Point, also has military origins: you'll find a gun emplacement and a large brick picnic shelter that originally housed torpedoes. Beach your boat at either side of this shallow bight (the center dries to a muddy foreshore). Be wary of boat and ferry wakes. Views along this route are mostly of beach homes, a few pocket beaches, and Mount Rainier to the southeast. Look for signs of the Cascadia Marine Trail site to the left of small buildings on the east end of the park; the two tent spaces are in the forest. No fires are allowed. Get tokens at the camp store to use the showers and toilets; both are only accessible in summer. Charge your devices outside the bathroom. And make sure to use the trail to the beach to prevent erosion on the banks.

Rich Passage makes a dogleg to the south and narrows just beyond the two parks, where currents become much swifter. Keep in mind that you could encounter an incredible array of large or small vessels coming through here—even huge aircraft carriers coming or going to the naval base at Bremerton. Currents themselves are not likely to be dangerous unless enhanced by adverse winds or ferry wakes; use them to your advantage while keeping an eye out for large vessels like the Bremerton ferry and the more frequent foot ferries, which must keep up some speed in order to stay in control in this flow. This is a good place to use a boat tracking app (see Resources for suggestions).

If you should encounter an opposing current, there are eddies north of Point White on the north shore and smaller ones along the south shore by Points Waterman and Glover. The latter may be preferable since you can continue along the shore, avoiding marine traffic into Port

Orchard, where the currents weaken. Watch your rudder or fins during low tide along the reef areas on the south shore. Make sure to look below the water's surface to view colorful sea life.

Public access (without facilities) is available at the pier nearly a mile northwest of Point White on Bainbridge. Cross to the East Bremerton shore 1 mile or so beyond the eastern end of Rich Passage. Straight across from the Point White dock, you'll find Illahee State Park, which has a boat ramp, dock, restrooms, and parking. If launching from here, display your Discover Pass.

The Bremerton Shipyard is an impressive sight with its rows of mothballed aircraft carriers and destroyers. The USS *Turner Joy*, a retired destroyer, is open for tours; find it in the marina just north of the ferry landing. But remember that this is a military installation, and you must keep a minimum of 500 feet from the perimeter of all naval vessels, piers, and other naval facilities. Consider a bite at the Boat Shed, a classic waterfront restaurant in East Bremerton under the Manette Bridge on Shore Drive. You can paddle to the restaurant and tie up to their dock; watch for currents.

# 16. **Bremerton: Port Washington Narrows and Ostrich Bay**

Bremerton's Port Washington Narrows is a tidal stream that can flow up to 5 knots on big tidal exchanges yet rarely gets rough. It's a great way to see Bremerton while getting a "free ride" on the current; it will feel as if you're on a horizonal escalator, moving from one end of the Narrows to the other as you pass under two bridges. You can use this watery escalator to travel to Dyes Inlet to the north or in reverse to access Sinclair Inlet and downtown Bremerton to the south. The Port Washington Narrows was the result of a large earthquake during the ice age that opened it up and drained the lake above, which became Dyes Inlet. Ostrich, Oyster, and Mud Bays northwest of the Narrows provide a laid-back alternative with narrow back bays to explore and easy shore access.

**Duration:** Part day.

**Rating:** *Protected* to *Moderate*.

**Navigation Aids:** SeaTrails WA 102; NOAA charts 18449 and 18452 (both 1:25,000), 18474 (1:40,000). Admiralty Inlet current tables corrected for Rich Passage.

**Planning Considerations:** Extreme low tides may make it difficult to access the water from Lions Park and other launches. Wind rarely builds waves, as the Narrows is mostly protected by high hills on both sides. Stick to the shore in summer when heavy boat traffic is common. Avoid the bridge supports because rips and eddy lines can occur behind them on stronger tides. Also avoid paddling around the Manette Bridge in late June or early July when the waterway is closed for setting up Bridge Blast fireworks and boat traffic is heavy. The tidal current in the north end of the Narrows is 30–45 minutes off from the south end. Ostrich, Oyster, and Mud Bays require medium to high tides. In summer watch for fast power boats.

## GETTING THERE AND LAUNCHING

**Tracyton Boat Launch** (701 NW Tracy Ave.): From the Warren Avenue Bridge (State Route 303), exit to Lebo Boulevard North and follow it 3 miles to pass Lions Park where it becomes Tracyton Beach Road Northwest. Turn left on Northwest Tracy Avenue and follow it to the launch. No facilities available.

 **Lions Park** (251 Lebo Blvd): From the Warren Street Bridge (SR 303), exit to Lebo Boulevard north and follow it 1.7 miles to Lions Park. Enter the park across from Oak Street; it has a boat ramp, parking lot, restrooms, and picnic tables.

 **Evergreen Rotary Park** (1500 Park Ave.): Exit the Seattle ferry onto Pacific Avenue. Go straight on Burwell Street and then right on Park Avenue before making a final right into the park on 14th Street. The park has restrooms, parking, picnic tables, and a gentle, sloping beach. The inner bay dries out at low tides.

*Paddlers exploring the south end of Port Washington Narrows*

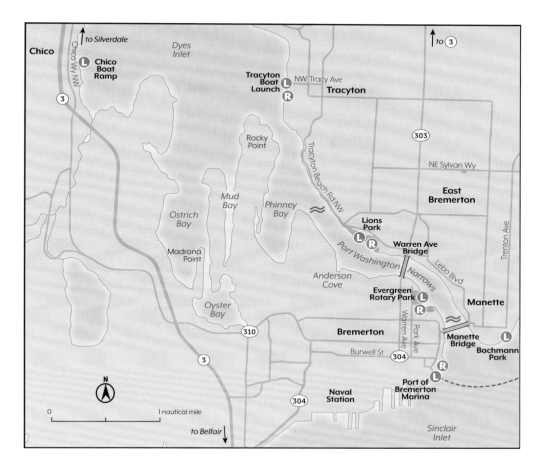

**Chico Boat Ramp** (5399-5201 Chico Beach Dr. NW): From SR 3, exit to Chico Way Northwest and turn east on Northwest Meridith Street, which takes you to ramp. Limited street parking and no facilities.

## ROUTE

**Tracyton Boat Launch and Lions Park to Sinclair Inlet:** Launch from either location on an ebb and return on the flood to enjoy an easy glide with minimal paddling. Float under Warren Street and Manette Bridges, heading south past the Boat Shed Restaurant to Sinclair Inlet. Stay to the side if heavy boat traffic is present and watch for kelp beds in summer. You can dock at the Boat Shed for a bite on their deck while enjoying views of downtown Bremerton, watching the current and boats float past. Bring a bow line to tie to the dock, as current flows underneath.

For an extra challenge, launch from Lions Park near the end of a flood and take the eddy along the east shore to the Boat Shed and return on the ebb. There are several options you can play with to take advantage of the current.

The west shore of Port Washington Narrows includes several picturesque features with minimal or no current, such as Phinney Bay and Anderson Cove with a few rustic older homes on stilts. Rudy Point on the east side of the bay was called PElkqs, meaning "boiling promontory," for the swift tidal currents in the Narrows. At low tides, a spring of water bubbles up from the rocks off the point and provides fresh drinking water.

**Ostrich, Oyster, and Mud Bays:** If you want to avoid the tidal current, launch from the **Chico Boat Ramp** to access Ostrich, Oyster, and Mud Bays. In summer watch out for northeasterly winds on Dyles Inlet. The Suquamish name for a long and narrow peninsula west of Oyster Bay is XoxayeqwEd, meaning "to cut the head off," a reference to the shape of the land. The long point separating Mud and Ostrich Bays was called BEqkwa, or "promontory with open spaces." The bays can get busy with boaters and various paddling craft on summer weekends, and they dry out at low tides, so aim for medium to high tides. After low tides on hot days, the incoming water will be warmed up to near bathtub temperatures, especially at the head of the bays. On maps and charts, it looks like you could portage from Mud Bay to Oyster Bay, but this narrow section of land is all private property.

# 17. **Eagle Harbor**

This excursion to a popular Bainbridge Island harbor is perfect for sea kayakers who love observing all sorts of boats, exploring pockets of wildlife, and viewing picturesque waterside structures old and new. All this can be found on Seattle's doorstep, yet it still feels far away from the urban bustle.

**Duration:** Part day.

**Rating:** *Protected*.

**Navigation Aids:** SeaTrails WA 202, 203; NOAA charts 18445 SC (1:80,000 with 1:25,000 Eagle Harbor inset), 18449 (1:25,000); Seattle tide table.

**Planning Considerations:** Higher tides allow exploration of the back bay and side coves in Eagle Harbor, which dry at lower tides.

### GETTING THERE AND LAUNCHING

If you are driving from the Bainbridge Island ferry dock, turn left at the first traffic light onto Winslow Way (turn right if you're coming south on State Route 305) and into downtown Winslow. After 0.3 mile of driving through the "downtown" shopping area, take the first left onto Madison Avenue at the four-way stop and then the next immediate left onto Bjune Drive Southeast. In less than 0.1 mile, turn right onto Shannon Drive Southeast and follow it down to the ramp at Waterfront Park.

*The Olympic Mountains form a backdrop to ferries docked in Eagle Harbor.*

Public parking for Eagle Harbor Waterfront Park is located along Bjune and Brien Drives Southeast. Within the park, most parking is limited to three hours (daylight hours only). Longer-term parking is difficult to find elsewhere in Winslow. Do not park in the trailered boat parking lot, or you risk suffering a stiff fine. The park is a lovely picnic stop with many options in Winslow for supplies and take-out food. Contact the Harbormaster for more info: 206-780-3733.

You may also leave your car on the mainland and wheel your kayak onto the ferry at Colman Dock in Seattle. When you exit the ferry, take the first left (before the light) onto a road signed for Eagle Harbor Condominiums. Follow it down a slight hill a very short distance. You may take either the left or right Waterfront Trail footpaths. The left footpath leads past the condo complex to public beach access right next to the ferry terminal. The right footpath leads to Eagle Harbor Waterfront Park and the public ramp and dock in about 0.1 mile. Either footpath, with a combination of hard pack and asphalt surfaces, is easily negotiated.

A final option is to rent a sea kayak from the barge moored at the public dock. With prior planning, you might even arrange for them to store your kayak if you paddle there for an overnight bed-and-breakfast stay.

## ROUTE

Choose your own route and distance. From Eagle Harbor Waterfront Park, you can paddle out in any direction and find interesting things to investigate. Just east are the state ferries' maintenance facilities, where out-of-service ferries dock. Here is your chance for a close-up look at the old veterans and the larger new ferries. Before approaching the ferries, look carefully for activity suggesting that one of them may be about to move. Never paddle in front of a ferry while it is underway.

Eagle Harbor is very popular with pleasure boaters due to its location and protection from wind. Several marinas, one directly across from the ferry docks and the others just west of the park, hold a wide assortment of fantastic yachts.

Along the shore are the remnants and reminders of past industry. At the harbor's south entrance, see if you can make out the location of a former plant site that once produced creosote-treated pilings used to build the Panama Canal. It's now an empty lot and Superfund site. Pritchard Park, which borders the western edge of the site, has restrooms just above the beach near Bainbridge Island Marina. Also visit the park's Japanese American Exclusion Memorial. Around the corner on the outside of the harbor is a pleasant public beach with restrooms, accessed from land via Northeast Eagle Harbor Drive.

A handful of other relics remain from the past—sheds and warehouses on pilings, some abandoned and some still in use. A tiny, shallow cove across from the ferry dock is particularly picturesque for its shoreline structures as well as its seclusion.

The very back of the harbor is quieter and less popular with boats because it dries on the lowest tides, but it is worth exploring when the tide is in. Midway back in the harbor, look for the eroding warehouse pilings that are all that remain of the vigorous berry-farming industry that once thrived in the vicinity. You can often spot eagles, ospreys, herons, and other birds dependent on a productive water environment.

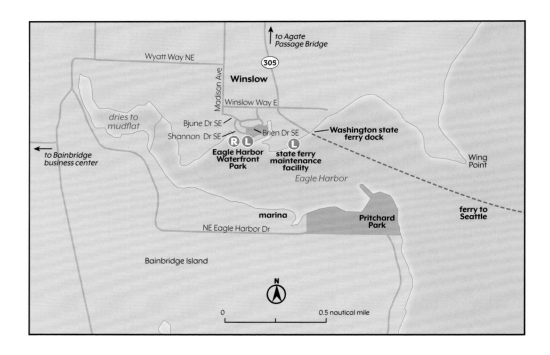

# 18. Elliott Bay

Shipyards with naval frigates and ferries in dry dock create an engaging scene in Elliott Bay, one that is in constant motion and change. Explore routes deep under the waterfront's piers, with the opportunity to make a stop along Alaskan Way South for fish and chips. You are sure to find plenty to enjoy if you like seaport cities. For a longer outing, you can paddle south around Harbor Island and the Duwamish Waterway (see Trip 19, Duwamish Waterway) or around Magnolia and West Point to Shilshole Bay (see Trip 22, West Point, Shilshole Bay, and Golden Gardens).

**Duration:** Part day.

**Rating:** *Moderate*. Ship and ferry traffic is heavy, landings are not allowed along much of the waterfront, and circumnavigating the harbor involves crossing 2 miles of open water and busy traffic.

**Navigation Aids:** SeaTrails WA 202, 203; NOAA chart 18450 (1:10,000), 18445 SC (1:80,000 with 1:40,000 inset); Seattle tide table.

**Planning Considerations:** High tide is more pleasant, but some riprap shores have small, low-tide beaches where landings are not possible at higher tides. There are no launches available in the immediate downtown corridor. Watch for ferry and other boating traffic. Expect a light to moderate current from the Duwamish River around Harbor Island.

## GETTING THERE AND LAUNCHING

There are two launch sites in downtown Seattle, two in Magnolia, five in West Seattle on the south side of the bay, and one at the downtown marina. As the city grows, new launches become available and others disappear. Check ahead to confirm launch locations are still available.

*Downtown Seattle and Magnolia*

**Myrtle Edwards Park:** The launch is by the northern entry to the park, close to the Magnolia Bridge. Myrtle Edwards Park skirts the waterfront and connects downtown Seattle to the Magnolia neighborhood. It offers access to the northern reaches of Elliott Bay, as well as Discovery Park, and has a popular biking and walking trail. From Elliott Avenue West, turn east one block south of the Magnolia Bridge, following signs to the cruise ship terminal and Port of Seattle. On the bridge, take the left fork. After the bridge crosses Elliott Avenue and curves around, take a right on Alaskan Way West. Then take another immediate right on West Galer Street, which takes you to the park and the Elliott Bay Trail. You can park in the garage at 1289 16th Avenue West and then walk to the adjacent beach to scramble down the steep bank to launch. The garage has an entry clearance of eight feet and three inches; if the garage overhead bar is too low, unload your gear by the shore and have a friend watch it while you park your car in the garage. Two steep and rocky entries to the beach are located north of the garage entrance.

*Bainbridge Island ferry on Elliott Bay with the Seattle skyline*

Watch for high-speed bicyclists along the bike path. Restrooms should be available in the garage; if not, there are vault toilets along the bike trail a few hundred yards south and around the bend at the Elliott Bay Fishing Pier. Make sure to lock your car.

**30th Avenue West Street End in Magnolia:** Located in the very west end of the Palisade restaurant parking lot, this launch has plenty of free day-use parking. The beach entry is from the sidewalk, which takes you down a slight slope to the rocky beach with concrete blocks and sand. You'll receive protection from the northerly winds here.

**32nd Avenue West in Magnolia:** This launch provides access near Smith Cove at the north end of Elliott Bay. From downtown Seattle, drive north on Elliott Avenue West and bear right onto the overpass for the Magnolia area (15th Avenue West). From the overpass, follow West Garfield Street and then West Galer Street for a total of 0.9 mile to Magnolia Boulevard West. Bear right on Magnolia Boulevard West and follow it 0.4 mile before turning left on West Howe Street. Take the next immediate left onto 32nd Avenue West, following it downhill to the water. There is usually parking available in the dirt pullout alongside the road. The small lot by the beach is for residents of the walk-in waterfront homes to the west. The beach is rocky with concrete slabs. Note that the lot fills quickly on summer weekends.

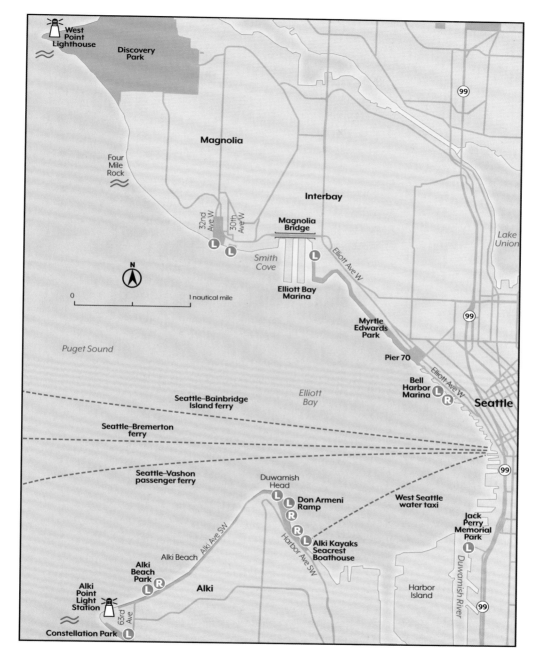

**Jack Perry Memorial Park Public Access/Alaskan Way:** Just south of the downtown ferries and across from Harbor Island, find the launch at the Jack Perry Memorial Park. It is located at the point where Alaskan Way South becomes East Marginal Way South, adjacent to the south side of the US Coast Guard station. There's ample parking but no restrooms. The park provides easy access to the Duwamish River mouth and the rest of Elliott Bay. A steep, rocky slope leads down to the water and the launch. Make sure to lock your car. The park closes at 11 PM.

See Trip 19, Duwamish Waterway, for more launches south of Elliott Bay.

### West Seattle

**Seacrest Boathouse,** northwest of Salty's Restaurant, is also home to Alki Kayak Tours, a full-service kayak and paddle board facility with lessons, tours, and rentals. Visit kayakalki.com for more information. Park in the lot south of the building or along the street. You can put-in at the finger dock below the fishing pier or via the pocket beach west of the shop. This location has restrooms and a restaurant and is popular with divers. Parking is tight on summer days.

Immediately west of Alki Kayak Tours along Harbor Avenue Southwest are two more put-ins. The **Don Armeni Ramp** has parking and restrooms. **Duwamish Head,** where Harbor Avenue Southwest curves left and becomes Alki Avenue Southwest, has on-street parking and a nice viewpoint deck overlooking Elliott Bay, but no restrooms are available. Enter the beach down a short set of stairs on the left side of the viewpoint.

There are several opportunities to launch off Alki Avenue Southwest if you can find parking. **Alki Beach Park** may be the most popular. Be watchful of the busy bike path as you carry your boat to the beach. South of the Alki Point Light Station, **Constellation Park** is another popular put-in. Street parking can be tight. Enter on the north side where the walkway slants to the beach. The beach is rocky and has a reef, which is part of a fault line. There are no facilities.

### Bell Harbor Marina (Downtown)

You can launch from the marina, use it as a rest stop, or leave your gear here overnight. The Port of Seattle has made provision for paddlers to moor at the marina for a few hours or overnight. The fee is insignificant, generally less than parking a car, and is a special bargain when you consider the included twenty-four-hour security for your craft. A hotel across from the marina on Alaskan Way South and several restaurants nearby offer places to sleep and eat. Pike Place Market and the aquarium are also an easy walk from here. The gate to the marina is locked, so plan to launch during normal business hours (7 AM to 5 PM, seven days a week) so that one of the staff members can give you access to the docks. Watch for boat traffic when leaving the marina. If you are arriving from the water, you can call the marina at 206-787-3952 or hail them on radio channel 66A so they can direct you to a safe place to land.

### ROUTE

Paddle locally from any of the launch points or circumnavigate as much of the bay as desired. A good option is to launch at Seacrest Park, then paddle straight across Elliott Bay toward Pier 70 or a point farther south. There's a nice, improved rest beach along Myrtle Edwards Park with restrooms just above the waterline.

Follow the waterfront south, with the option of taking a break at Bell Harbor Marina or perhaps strolling along Alaskan Way for a snack of fish and chips.

Though fun to observe, be careful of the varied private and commercial boats coming and going from the numerous piers, especially in the summer months. Plan your trip when a large naval or ocean liner is docked at the marina to get a waterside view few have seen. Make sure to keep a proper distance between yourself and the vessel for safety and security reasons, keeping in mind river currents.

At the container terminal, Pier 17, and Vigor shipyards on the north end of Harbor Island, you must stay at least 100 yards to seaward. You will still be close enough to ogle the dry-docked ships with propellers, bow thrusters, and sonar domes exposed for all to see.

If circumnavigating Harbor Island, watch for two low bridges in the southeast corner under the West Seattle Bridge. Paddle under the bridges past the support pilings. Yield to boats and ships in the main channels.

From West Seattle, consider paddling west to the Alki Point Light Station or for a longer trip, south to Lincoln Park. Constellation Park is known for its tidal pools and marine life at low tides. The point off the lighthouse can be rough in strong winds. Ferry wakes create three- to four-foot-high surfing waves at Duwamish Head on lower tides—enjoyable to some, a hazard to others. Avoid the surf by paddling around the outside of the navigational marker 200 yards off Duwamish Head. The beach here is also a popular tide pool and wading area in summer during low tides.

From Myrtle Edwards Park, either paddle south to the city or west past a few shipping termi-nals. Here military troops from past wars departed for the Pacific. You'll soon paddle past the Elliott Bay Marina—watch for departing boating traffic. After the marina, you'll see a boat ramp on your right; this is the 32nd Avenue West launch (see details above). From 32nd Avenue, pad-dle west past the walk-in waterfront homes below Magnolia Bluff. Mudslides in the early 1990s destroyed many homes along Perkins Lane, littering the beach with patios, lawn mowers, and other oddities.

A large erratic rock nearly twenty feet across named Four Mile Rock marks where the land turns north to West Point and Discovery Park. Shallow water around the rock has grounded a few boats. Watch for a light current flowing around the bend, as well as rough water and surf from strong southerlies or shipping traffic. The local Duwamish people called Four Mile Rock LE'plEPL or Tele'tla (meaning "rock"). Legend states that a hero named Sta'kub could throw a giant cedar and hazel branch over it while standing on the beach. In 1923, the steamship *Astoria* sunk a half mile off the rock.

# 19. Duwamish Waterway

The Duwamish River was once a curvy, slow-moving, flood-prone river that provided water access and subsistence for the Duwamish people. In Lushootseed, a Puget Sound Salish lan-guage, the name Duwamish (or Dkhw'Doow'Absh) means "People of the Inside." Pioneers set-tled in the area in the 1850s and soon changed this once-pristine landscape forever. The dredging of the waterway, completed in 1920, straightened all but one of the original curves in the lower river. In the years following, the river became an industrial center for the city of Seattle and a home for companies such as Boeing. In 2001, a 5-mile stretch was listed as a federal Superfund site. Since then, the Duwamish River Community Coalition has made considerable improvements to the river, reverting sections to their natural state. The coalition has also created public access and a few human-powered boat launches.

**Duration:** Part day to full day.

**Rating:** *Protected.* Although the paddling is easy, ship and barge traffic is heavy in this confined waterway. Novice kayakers should ensure they have sufficient boat control to stay out of the way before venturing into the waterway, especially during times of ebb current.

**Navigation Aids:** SeaTrails WA 202, 203; NOAA chart 18450 (1:10,000), 18445 SC (1:80,000 with 1:40,000 inset); Seattle tide table.

**Planning Considerations:** A strong ebb current (the flood current is negligible) can make upstream travel harder and may pose problems for novice kayakers, especially around pilings or ship or barge traffic. Consequently, you may wish to avoid these currents during periods of an ebbing tide. At low tide the shoreline is quite muddy. At the time of this writing, several of these parks were being developed, and it was unclear if restrooms would be added.

## GETTING THERE AND LAUNCHING

You have several launch points to choose from on both sides of the lower Duwamish Waterway. Using a shuttle makes a one-way paddle through the entire lower Duwamish possible. A trip could begin, for example, at the 1st Avenue South Bridge and end at Seacrest Park or Jack Perry Memorial Park.

**Jack Perry Memorial Park/Alaskan Way Public Access:** This access allows you to launch near the middle of the East Waterway and is also a good launch point for exploring Harbor Island and Elliott Bay. It is located about 0.7 mile south of the US Coast Guard facility, at the point where Alaskan Way South becomes East Marginal Way South. Look for the Jack Perry Memorial Park sign, only visible when traveling south. Access to the water is down a steep, rocky path. There is ample parking but no facilities. Make sure to lock your car.

**Tu?elaltx Village Park and Shoreline Habitat (Herring House Park)** (4570 W. Marginal Way SW): Formerly known as Terminal 105 Park, this access point is located off West Marginal Way Southwest less than a quarter mile south of the West Seattle Bridge interchange and just north of Southwest Dakota Street. The Duwamish Longhouse and Cultural Center is across from the park on Marginal Way. The park includes parking, a picnic shelter, and portable restrooms. Find the hand-carry launch through the trees just left of the parking lot south of the Longhouse. At low tide, this launch becomes muddy: plan accordingly. Be especially careful of a barge operation just to the north and shipping traffic, which cuts very close to the north end of the park.

*North Winds Weir and rapids on the upper Duwamish Waterway*

**sbəq̓ʷaʔ (sbaqwah) Park and Shoreline Habitat** (4663 Diagonal Ave. S.): Formerly known as Diagonal Park, this is the closest access for visiting Kellogg Island, which is directly across the waterway. To get there, follow State Route 99 for about a quarter mile south of the Southwest Spokane Street overpass and turn west on Diagonal Avenue South. Follow Diagonal Avenue South about three blocks to its end at the waterway. Public access and parking are to the left and center of a tiny bay. The carry is down a rocky embankment and low tide can be muddy.

**Duwamish River Boat Ramp (also called the 1st Ave. S Bridge Boat Launch)** (125 S. River St.): Look for South River Street off East Marginal Way on the east side of the river. A wide, paved boat ramp is located under the 1st Avenue South Bridge. Make sure to lock your car.

**Duwamish Waterway Park (in South Park)** (7900 10th Ave. S.): This renovated park has a great sandy beach and a simple carry from easy-to-find street parking. Park features include public art with a Duwamish tribal theme, picnic tables, and access to the South Park neighborhood. Find the park at the intersection of South Kenyon Street and South Elmgrove Street. The park site suggests cleaning all gear and clothing after use.

**Duwamish River Peoples Park and Shoreline** (8700 Dallas Ave. S.): As the largest habitat restoration site on the river, this park opened in 2022 with a hand-carried watercraft launch on the north end. Two paddle craft drop-off parking spots are just above the launch, and there is plenty of street parking. The launch may be muddy at lower tides.

A good alternative access point in Elliott Bay is Alki Kayak Tours at Seacrest Boathouse on Harbor Avenue Southwest.

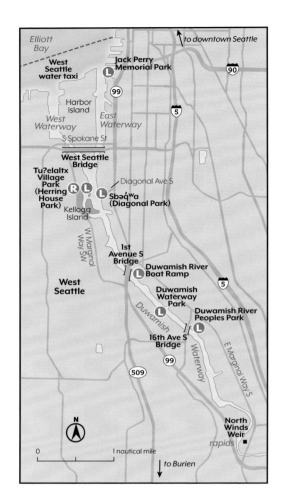

## ROUTES

Choose your own route in the waterway; there are shipyards, barge-loading docks, moored container ships, cement plants, green areas, derelict ships, and much more.

**Circumnavigation of Kellogg Island:** The island is close to the west side of the waterway, across from and slightly south of the sbəq̓wa? (sbaqwah) Park and Shoreline Habitat (formerly Diagonal Park). Kellogg Island was originally much larger than Anderson Island and was the approximate northern edge of the Duwamish estuary before the filling of Harbor Island and the development of the South Seattle industrial area. The waterway was dredged to the east of the original channel bend, creating Kellogg Island. The island's original height, formerly just above high tide, was raised by dredging spoils dumped on the south end. This wilderness of brambles, brush, and hidden grassy glens is worth a peek.

The shore on the west side of the old channel bend behind Kellogg Island is also a park, called **Tu?elaltx Village Park and Shoreline Habitat (aka Herring House Park),** formerly known as Terminal 105 Park. The park has restrooms and a dock for easy access to the water. The Duwamish Tribal Office and Longhouse are across from the park on West Marginal Way Southwest. The longhouse and store are worth a visit. Visit duwamishtribe.org/longhouse or call 206-431-1582 for more information.

The old channel course behind Kellogg Island may dry on low tides. Though the ebb current in the Duwamish can run up to 1 knot, the flow in the old channel is slight and a good way to get upstream. Ride back down in the main channel.

**Circumnavigation of Harbor Island:** Starting from Jack Perry Memorial Park, head north up the Duwamish East Waterway. The piers on both sides of the waterway are usually busy with incoming and outgoing container ships. At the West Seattle Bridge, paddle under the Southwest Spokane Street Bridge, which is held up by two sets of wooden pilings. If the current is running swiftly, paddle along the edges to avoid stronger current. Past the bridge, look to your right to find Western Towboat's Harbor Island dock. At the south end of Harbor Island, head north down the Duwamish West Waterway, enjoying the light push of the Duwamish River. Paddle past

Harbor Island Marina, under the West Seattle Bridge, by more container ships, and out into Elliott Bay adjacent to Vigor Shipyards. Vigor often builds and repairs navy ships and local ferries. Yielding to boat traffic, return to Jack Perry Memorial Park.

**Alternative Route:** Two miles upriver from Duwamish River Peoples Park and Shoreline you can find North Winds Weir, an ancient Duwamish fishing spot and the only whitewater rapid on the lower river. The shoreline has been restored recently. There is no easy water access here or accessible restrooms. At high tides you can paddle past the rapids.

# 20. Lake Union

The origins of Lake Union go back twelve thousand years. The lake was carved by the Vashon glacier, which also created Lake Washington. The Duwamish people called it "small lake," and the portage from Portage Bay to Lake Washington was called Skhwacugwit (portage). Chesheeahud was a renowned Duwamish chief who, along with his wife, Madeline, lived in a village called hehs-KWEE-kweel (meaning "skate") on the east side of what is now Montlake Cut. Their group was called hlooweelh-AHBSH, and they called the area of the Montlake Cut sxWatSadweehL, which translates to "carry a canoe." In the 1850s, pioneers began to populate the region. In 1854, pioneer Thomas Mercer predicted there would be a "union of waters," with canals connecting Lake Union to Puget Sound. Bill Boeing founded his airplane company on the

*Surf skier paddling through Montlake Cut below the Montlake Bridge*

lake in 1915. Leading up to the opening of the Ballard Locks 1916, the waterways from Lake Washington to the Puget Sound were completely transformed. Lake Washington was lowered by nine feet, the portage was made into the Montlake Cut, and Salmon Bay in Ballard was raised nine feet. Ross Creek, which drained the lakes into Salmon Bay, was dredged and made into the concrete-lined Fremont Ship Canal we see today.

The modern Lake Union is home to marinas, floating homes, dry docks, Gas Works Park, and a seaplane terminal. Many paddlers in Seattle have taken their first strokes here, where summer water temperatures can rise into the 70s. A tour of Lake Union can be combined with excursions either east to Portage Bay, the Washington Park Arboretum, and Lake Washington; or west along the ship canal toward the Hiram M. Chittenden Locks.

**Duration:** Part day.

**Rating:** *Protected.*

**Navigation Aids:** SeaTrails WA 202; NOAA chart 18447 SC (1:10,000). A Seattle street map is also useful.

**Planning Considerations:** Lake Union has little protection from the wind. A strong southerly or northerly can build enough chop to make paddling unpleasant if you're uncomfortable with rough water. Watch out for seaplanes, which land in the middle of the lake and take off from the Kenmore Air terminal on its southwest corner. Stay clear of the seaplane runway: lighted buoys run the length of the lake from south to north. The lake is very crowded with sailboats on Tuesday evenings from May to September for the Duck Dodge race. When paddling under drawbridges, stay to the sides to avoid the busy main boating channel.

## GETTING THERE AND LAUNCHING

There are several public shoreline areas suited for launching and two sea-kayak rental companies on the lake and another on nearby Portage Bay. Parking can be difficult to find on busy summer weekends. Centrally located in Seattle, the lake can be easily reached by Interstate 5, State Route 99, Fremont, the University District, and downtown.

**South End of Lake Union/Lake Union Park/Goose Beach** (900 Westlake Ave. N.): For the south shore of Lake Union, take Exit 167 (Mercer St.) from I-5. Take the first right (north) onto Fairview Avenue North and go one block, then take a left (west) on Valley Street. Get in the far-right lane and take the next right (north) to Westlake Avenue North. There is a fee for parking Monday through Friday between 9 AM and 4 PM. Look for the sandy beach, good for small-craft launching, and a ramp to a small dock. If the wind is up, tuck into the small cove to your right under the footbridge. Watch for seaplanes taking off just north of this launch. Visit atlakeunionpark.org for additional information.

**West Side of Lake Union/Northwest Outdoor Center:** Halfway down Westlake Avenue North, between the Fremont Bridge and Lake Union Park, is the Northwest Outdoor Center. A

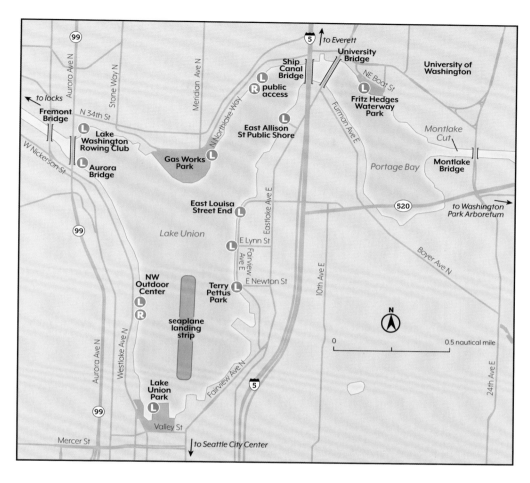

paddling shop, they offer SUP and kayak rentals, storage, and a public launch. Visit nwoc.com for additional information.

**North End of Lake Union/Waterway 19/Gas Works Park:** For the north shore of Lake Union, take Exit 169 (45th St.) from I-5. Go west on North 45th Street for 1 mile to Stone Way North. Turn left and follow Stone Way almost another mile to the lakeshore. Pass through the light on North 34th Street and veer left onto North Northlake Way. Gas Works Park will appear on your right in about a half mile. Turn right into the main lot and park near the east end. If you're facing the park and its odd industrial features, walk your boat to the left through the trees parallel to North Northlake Way. Walk about 50 yards across a grassy lawn to a small, protected beach lined with houseboats, also called Waterway 19. For a shorter walk to the lake, you can drop your boat at the small, circular pullout across from the Urban Surf shop, then park in the main parking lot 25 yards to the west. Urban Surf offers SUP and wetsuit rentals and other gear such as sunblock. Visit urbansurf.com for additional information.

**Lake Washington Rowing Club** (910 N. Northlake Way): Located below the Aurora Bridge and tucked between a marine business and house boats, this low, easy launching dock in Fremont is in front of the Lake Washington Rowing Club, which allows SUPs and kayaks to access its dock. Paddlers must yield to rowers. Rowing program hours: 5 to 9 AM and 3 to 8 PM Monday through Friday, and 5 to 11 AM Saturday and Sunday. The gate closes at sunset or 8 PM, whichever comes first. Paid street parking is nearby.

**Public Access Beach Past Gas Works Park/Waterway 18:** Going east of Gas Works Park on North Northlake Way there is a public access launch site on the right, a few hundred yards past the park. Look for the dragon boats stored below the road. Park across the street in the dirt lot; there is no restroom. This is a very protected launch, great for practicing skills.

**Fritz Hedges Waterway Park:** New since the last edition, Fritz Hedges is an expansive waterfront park east of the University Bridge and close to the University of Washington on Northeast Boat Street by Agua Verde Café. No bathrooms are available; street parking is free on Sundays.

See Trip 21, Upper Salmon Bay: Ballard Bridge to Fremont Bridge, to find put-ins in Fremont and Ballard.

### East Side of Lake Union Options

Eastlake has several mini parks and launches, here's a few:

**East Allison Street Public Shore** (1-65 E. Allison St.): At the bottom of Allison Street, this launch has three to four day-use parking spots and a gentle concrete slope into the water between two docks.

**East Louisa Street End** (2373-R Fairview Ave. E.): This is the only launch with a bocce ball court! There is one parking spot and the path is a few easy steps to the water in between houseboats. The park has a picnic table and bench.

**Lynn Street Mini Park** (2291 Fairview Ave. E.): The launch is a small, narrow beach among the houseboats, three or four feet down from the sidewalk at the foot of East Lynn Street, accessed from Eastlake Avenue East. Parking on side streets may be difficult. The steps leading to the water are decorated with colorful tiles. The park has a picnic table. Boston Street offers a great spot for deli sandwiches and snacks.

**Terry Pettus Park** (2001 Fairview Ave. E.): Located on the south end of the houseboat strip of Eastlake, this is the largest of the Eastlake launches, with two small docks and three parking spaces.

### ROUTE

The lake is slightly less than 2 miles long and about 4.5 miles around if you follow the shores between the Ship Canal Bridge and Fremont Bridge. All shores have restaurants with dock access, ranging from burgers to seafood to gourmet dining. The north shore has Gas Works Park, shipyards, and plenty of yachts to view. The west side is primarily yacht moorage. The Lake Union houseboat community comprises much of the east shore. The south end has the Kenmore Air seaplane base, the Museum of History and Industry, and NW Seaport, which restores historic boats and provides maritime education. The last steam-powered Mosquito Fleet ferry, the *Virginia V*, is docked there, as well as the historic tug, *Arthur Foss*, more than a hundred years old. Notice also a halibut schooner and a retired fireboat, the *Duwamish*. South Lake Union is home to the Center for Wooden Boats, where all manner of small wooden craft can be rented. A new addition in 2023 is the Northwest Native Canoe Center.

Lake Union's mood changes with the pulse of the city. Try it on a fair summer's evening when the water is busy with all sorts of boats, especially when the myriad sails of the Duck Dodge race frame the sunset. Or visit on a calm winter morning, when both city and water are quiet, and you will meet few others besides hardy paddlers like yourself. On a stormy day, Lake Union is a good practice place for experienced paddlers who want to work on their rough-water paddling techniques in a reasonably safe setting.

For an extended trip, paddle under the University Bridge to Portage Bay, a waterway that is especially busy on sunny weekends. Note that Agua Verde Paddle Club doesn't allow the general public to land boats at their docks but does offer kayak and SUP rentals. There is a public access dock east of Agua Verde in the marina next to the houseboats. Adjacent paid parking makes this an easy put-in. Farther east through the Montlake Cut, the arboretum offers hours of fun paddling through heavily wooded, winding canals. Be cautious of paddling through the Montlake Cut; boat wakes bounce off the Cut's narrow concrete walls, a phenomenon known as clapotis, and the reverb can make for very rough conditions. You should only paddle here on busy summer weekends if you have advanced skills. West of Lake Union, you can paddle under the Fremont Bridge.

# 21. Upper Salmon Bay: Ballard Bridge to Fremont Bridge

Salmon Bay in Seattle was once a saltwater inlet that stretched from Shilshole Bay to Ross Creek, which is now the Lake Washington Ship Canal and Fremont neighborhood. In 1916, the completion of the Ballard Locks separated the inlet, creating an upper freshwater bay and a lower saltwater bay on either side of the locks. During the construction of the locks, the upper bay had to be raised nine feet to be the same level as Lake Union, Portage Bay, and Lake Washington.

The Sheel-shol-ashbsh or Shilshole people were a band of the Duwamish who lived here for centuries. A large village inside what is now the Ballard Locks was called sHulsHool, or "tucked away inside." This village was protected not only from marine weather but also from northern tribes that often raided the area. Longhouses constructed here ranged from 60 to 120 feet long.

As settlers began to populate the area in the late 1850s, logging and shingle mills and mostly Scandinavian boat-building companies sprang up on the north shore of Ballard. By 1870, Ballard was logged of all its old growth. In 1895, Ballard was called the "Shingle Capital of the World." Commercial fishing was also a large industry, with Fishermen's Terminal opening on the south side of the waterway in 1911. The bascule train bridge below the locks was completed in 1914 and the Ballard Bridge in 1917.

Today the shoreline is a mixture of fishing boats, marinas, houseboats, and tugboat companies like Foss and Western Towboat. The Fremont Ship Canal is bordered by tech companies like Google and Adobe, with the Seattle Elks Lodge #92 on the south shore. This trip will take you under two historic bridges, plus the Aurora Bridge, which can be a good turnaround point.

---

**Duration:** Part day.

**Rating:** *Protected*.

**Navigation Aids:** Sea Trails 104; NOAA charts 18447 SC (1:10,000), 18449 or 18446 (both 1:25,000).

**Planning Considerations:** This route is very protected; the only hazard is boat traffic, which is easy to avoid. Rarely does wind affect this waterway. Paddle boards are not allowed in the locks, but kayaks can pass through. Stay clear of the entry to the locks in summer and on busy weekends.

---

## GETTING THERE AND LAUNCHING

**28th Ave. NW Street End:** If coming from Ballard, this is a great access near the locks. Limited day-use parking (free if less than two hours) is available next to the put-in. More free spots can be found across the train tracks behind the building west of Market Street.

**24th Ave. NW Street End:** At the time of writing, an adjacent stormwater construction site is keeping this launch from being fully open, but water access may be possible in future.

**14th Ave. NW Street End:** A popular boat ramp east of the Ballard Bridge, this access has several free day-use parking spots on 14th Avenue Northwest and additional parking on the center strip across from Northwest 45th Street.

**Fishermen's Terminal:** On the south shore of Salmon Bay, launch from Dock 10 on the west end of the Fishermen's Terminal building, which has several four-hour day-use parking spots.

**6th Ave. W. Street End:** Closer to Fremont, this launch between docks provides easy access off West Nickerson Street, with three parking spots and free day-use street parking nearby. A few old tugboats are moored here.

**Westlake Ave. N. Street End:** Below the Aurora Bridge and Westlake Avenue North, this easy access launch has a lot of free day-use parking and no restrooms.

See Trip 20, Lake Union, for more put-ins on nearby Lake Union, including Lake Washington Rowing Club.

## ROUTE

Choose your own route. The waterway from the Ballard Locks to the Fremont Ship Canal is an interesting place to explore, with many ships, fishing vessels, high-end yachts, and houseboats tucked between maritime industry companies, marinas, and the historic Pacific Fisherman Shipyard. Visit Fishermen's Terminal on the south side of the waterway near the Ballard Bridge to view purse seiners, tenders, trollers, and (if in dock) the eighty-seven-foot *Vansee* and the seventy-three-foot halibut schooner *Polaris*, built by John Strand of the Jangaard brothers on Salmon Bay in 1913. Some of the famous crab boats in the *Deadliest Catch* TV show can be seen moored along the waterway. Fishermen's Terminal may be empty of purse seiners and trollers from June

*Bow of ship on Seattle's upper Salmon Bay*

to early October, when they fish in southeast Alaska. By the Ballard Bridge, you can see Seattle Fire Station 3 with its fireboats ready for action.

A light current flows west in the waterway, increasing after rains or snowmelt. If you are heading east, duck behind boats and docks to find an eddy to escape the current.

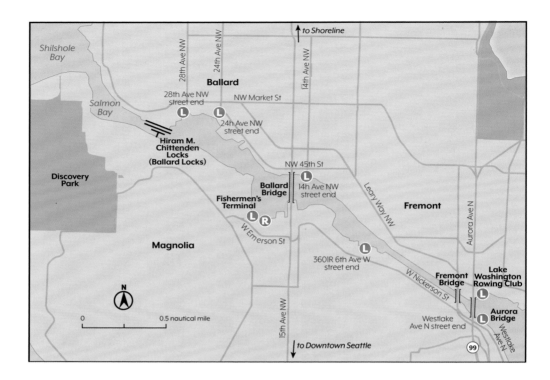

As you paddle under the Ballard Bridge, look up to see cars going over the metal grate. Stay clear if boats are passing through the middle or are waiting for the bridge to raise. Keep heading east to find the Seattle Maritime Academy and the 14th Avenue boat ramp. You can grab food and snacks a block north of the ramp. Farther east, you'll see the Foss tugboat dock on your right and the Western Towboat Company on your left. Western Towboat builds their iconic blue-and-yellow boats at this site.

Butud'aqt, or "spirit canoe power," was a creek than entered the north end of Salmon Bay near the old Ross Creek outlet (now the entry to the Fremont Ship Canal). This creek was said to have a power that enabled Indigenous doctors to connect with the world of the dead, allowing them to recover the souls of sick and struggling people. The outlet of what was later named Ross Creek was called gWaXWap. During the construction of the Ballard Locks in 1911, the creek was dredged to create the concrete-lined Fremont Ship Canal, which today leads to the Fremont Bridge.

Enter the concrete-lined ship canal, staying to the side if boats are present. Watch out for clapotis, a phenomenon caused by boat wakes reverbing off the concrete walls. And keep an eye out for rowers, who have a limited view and the right-of-way. At the Fremont Bridge, stay aside for boats. Colorful houseboats float on the east side of the bridge. The district of Fremont is on your left (north), but it has limited take-outs. Lake Washington Rowing Club has a low, private dock. Here you enter Lake Union. If you want to extend your trip east, see Trip 20, Lake Union.

*Sunset at West Point Lighthouse off Discovery Park*

# 22. West Point, Shilshole Bay, and Golden Gardens

This area, west of Seattle's Ballard neighborhood, is a good place for both cautious sea outings for new paddlers and lengthier and more challenging routes for experienced paddlers. Enjoy popular and secluded sunbathing beaches, pleasure boats galore at the extensive marina, and sunset views of the Olympic Mountains. The Lake Washington steelhead run at the locks in Salmon Bay attracts a notable "chorus" of California sea lions.

The Sheel-shol-ashbsh or Shilshole people were a band of the Duwamish who lived here for centuries. Sheel-shol-ashbsh means "threading the bead," a reference to the numerous sandbars that dominated the inlet, which were great for clamming but not for settlers trying to navigate their ships. Longhouses, some up to eighty feet long, were located above what is now the Ballard Locks, where they were protected from wind and raiding tribes. Before the locks were built, Salmon Bay reached nearly to Fremont.

The last of the Sheel-shol-ashbsh was Hwehlchtid, or Salmon Bay Charlie, and his wife, Madeline. After epidemics and devasting raids by northern tribes, few Native families were left by the time the settlers arrived in the 1850s. Charlie's Salish-inspired shack was located above a large sandbar near where Salmon Bay enters Shilshole Bay. The sandbars were dredged, and Salmon Bay Charlie's shack was burned down to prepare for the construction of the Ballard Locks, which opened in 1916.

The West Point beaches are lightly used and are backed by the woods and bluffs of Seattle's largest natural reserve, Discovery Park. Thanks to Fort Lawton, established in the 1890s, this land wasn't as heavily developed as other neighborhoods nearby. The park includes a gigantic shoreside sewer-treatment facility that has been landscaped to blend into the scene. From West Point, the route can also be extended into Elliott Bay (see Trip 18, Elliott Bay, for more information).

**Duration:** Part day to full day.

**Rating:** *Protected*, *Moderate*, or *Exposed*. The *Moderate* route may require rough paddling to return to the launch site.

**Navigation Aids:** SeaTrails WA 202; NOAA charts 18445 SC (1:80,000), 18446 (1:25,000), 18447 SC (1:10,000); Seattle tide table.

**Planning Considerations:** Winds and ships can create large breaking waves that produce rough paddling conditions, especially around West Point, Meadow Point, and near the entry to Salmon Bay below the Ballard Locks. Lower tides offer more beaches; many are backed by rock riprap that makes landing at high tide unsuitable. Allow plenty of leeway for both small and large boats and ships entering and leaving the Ballard Locks.

## GETTING THERE AND LAUNCHING

There are four easily accessible launch points for this trip:

**Golden Gardens Park:** Take Exit 172 for 85th Street from Interstate 5 and go west on Northwest 85th Street for about 3 miles. When it ends, turn right on Golden Gardens Drive Northwest and wind down the bluffs to the beach area.

At Golden Gardens, use the parking lots just behind the beach or, if they are full, park along Seaview Avenue Northwest. Launch at the beach or at the ramp just inside the marina breakwater to the south. The parking lots are closed at night. Bathrooms are located by the boat ramp and in the large beach building.

**Elks Beach:** The Elks Lodge farther south on Seaview Avenue Northwest has a small beach that can be entered from the left (south) side of their parking lot. The Elks own the beach but allow public access. Park on Seaview Avenue Northwest, as the lot is for Elks members only. The Elks will tow you if you load or unload in the disabled parking area or the fire lane by the beach entry. Don't park on the condo side of the beach; an increase of use in recent years has led to tension between the condo association and beach users. While this launch is protected, give caution to heavy boating traffic and a light outgoing current in the boating channel just outside the wooden breakwater. Lower daytime tides in summer will require a long walk to the waterline.

**Commodore Park/Hiram M. Chittenden Locks:** From 15th Avenue Northwest, take the West Emerson Place exit and go west toward Fishermen's Terminal. Take a right at 21st Avenue

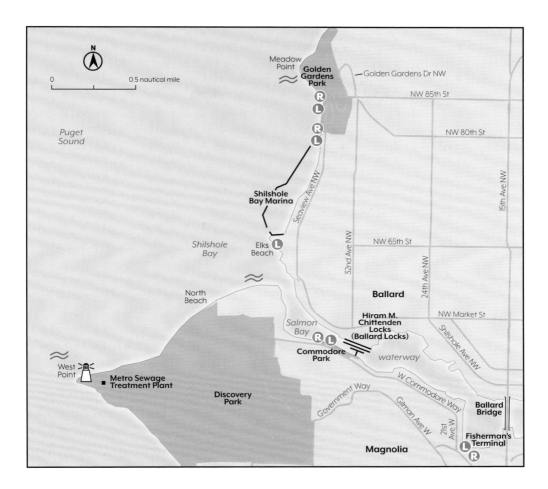

West, which soon curves to the left and becomes West Commodore Way. After about a mile, look for the park on your right side before the train bridge. Street and lot parking are available.

Put-in below the grassy slope on the left side of the lot. In lower tides, the beach can be muddy. Be cautious of heavy boating traffic on the other side of the wooden breakwater. A wire cable extends across the right (south) side of the locks in front of the spillways, marking a no-trespassing zone. If you get too close, the lockmaster will ask you to turn around. The spillways create a river hydraulic called a weir, or ledge, which draws water back to the wall, entrapping anything that gets too close. It's also a sensitive area due to fish runs: salmon go through the locks' fish ladder from June through November; steelhead and cutthroat trout from September through February. In autumn, make sure to paddle around the Muckleshoot Tribe fishing nets that extend from the shore into the middle of the channel. SUPs are not allowed in the locks. Kayaks and canoes are allowed only in the small lock but are not recommended by locks personnel.

## ROUTES

**Golden Gardens to Salmon Bay via Shilshole Bay Marina:** *Protected* to *Moderate*. Choose your own paddling distance; the full round-trip from Golden Gardens to Commodore Park at the Ballard Locks is about 4 miles. Novice paddlers may prefer to stay in the bay just off Golden Gardens beach, which gets some protection from both northerly and southerly seas. However, sustained northerly to northwesterly winds can produce large breaking waves and a lot of kite surfers. As an option, explore the Shilshole Bay Marina, being especially watchful for traffic entering and exiting at the breakwater entrance. A few hundred people live on boats in the marina; these people are sometimes called "live-a-boards." Show them respect by not looking in windows or holding onto boats. Only land on "guest docks." The back canal, which runs below the shoreside marina walkway, is ideal for avoiding wind when paddling to or from Ballard and Golden Gardens. Restrooms are available at Golden Gardens and Commodore Park.

An outflowing current is always present in Salmon Bay due to the drainage from the Lake Washington Ship Canal. Most of it can be avoided by using eddies close inshore, particularly in the shallows on the south side. Currents can get up to 3 or 4 knots after several days of heavy rain. Boat traffic may be very heavy in this area, so paddling along the shore is safest. Pleasure craft waiting for the locks may be numerous just below the railroad bridge. Make sure to give boaters the right-of-way when crossing the boating channel here.

Large surf from southbound ships is possible during low tides on the Magnolia (west) side of the channel below the large concrete retaining wall. Local surfers appear here in summer months to catch the waves. Strong northerlies can create large wind waves that refract off the cliff here at higher tides.

**Golden Gardens to West Point:** *Moderate* to *Exposed*. The roundtrip distance is 4 to 5 miles. Keep in mind launching is prohibited from the West Point beaches, but rest stops are allowed by Seattle's Department of Parks and Recreation. Tide rips are possible off West Point, and the sandbar directly west of the lighthouse can produce large surf from ships some distance from the point. Be especially watchful for ships' wakes when landing along this route.

Blue skies and high pressure in summer months create strong northerlies here in the afternoon. Make sure you can paddle back to Golden Gardens or Salmon Bay in these conditions before heading out.

Popular landing spots are the gravel-and-cobble North Beach, just past the rock riprap by the large erratic boulder, and at West Point itself by the lighthouse; choose whichever side is sheltered from the wind. During high tides with wind or a lot of boat wakes, stay offshore to avoid clapotis—reverb waves that bounce back from the shore. Restrooms are located 0.25 mile up the road from the point. For more seclusion, continue about 1 mile past the point and into the bight below the bluffs, beyond where most beach walkers usually venture. Lower tides leave an expansive sandy beach here, so you will likely have to carry your boat some distance if spending time ashore. Watch for the many boulders scattered throughout this intertidal area. This area is also great for surf: smaller waves will hold up over the shallow beach for some distance.

If you paddled through the marina on the way out, consider a straight course back across the bay from West Point toward Golden Gardens, but only if conditions are appropriate. Strong ebbs or southerlies can create a large bay-wide eddy or gyro with a current that circles to the north and then back to the point via the shoreline along Discovery Park. Sometimes paddling in a straight line isn't the most efficient way to get there. Use currents and wind protection along the shore to make your paddling experience easier.

Sea lions sometimes haul out on the buoys or riprap of the marina breakwater; it's best to stay clear of them. Harbor seals here are very domesticated due to all the human activity. If a seal tries to climb on your craft, paddle away. It is illegal to lure or have a seal on your craft and to feed them. At midtide, a sandy beach appears on the outside of the marina breakwater and provides the most secluded stop in this area, as it is not accessible by land.

# 23. **Port Madison and Agate Passage**

The northern shores of Bainbridge Island and the adjacent Kitsap Peninsula make an easy escape for locals and city dwellers alike. Though the area's shores are primarily residential with an emphasis on ritzy homes, two parks and an American Indian museum sit along the winding course of a narrow inlet and the fast waters of Agate Passage. Possibilities for short or longer paddles, perhaps with a car shuttle, are numerous.

**Duration:** Part day to overnight.

**Rating:** *Moderate* or *Moderate+*. The *Moderate+* route involves crossing Agate Passage in current up to 6 knots with possible heavy pleasure-boat traffic.

**Navigation Aids:** SeaTrails WA 203; NOAA chart 18446 (1:25,000), 18445 SC (1:80,000); Admiralty Inlet current tables with corrections for Agate Passage.

**Planning Considerations:** Strong wind, particularly from the south, can cause a wet launch or landing on the beach at Fay Bainbridge Park. Agate Passage has the only significant currents in this area, but they are strong enough to be worth planning around.

## GETTING THERE AND LAUNCHING

Launch choices are Fay Bainbridge Park on the northeast corner of the island, T'Chookwap Park in Port Madison or, for the Agate Passage area, Old Man House State Park or Suquamish Center. The car shuttle between Fay Bainbridge Park and the Agate Passage launch sites is about 8 miles.

**Fay Bainbridge Park:** Turn north from State Route 305 about midway between downtown Bainbridge Island and the Agate Passage bridge on East Day Road. Watch for signs to Fay Bainbridge Park. After 1.5 miles, go left onto Sunrise Drive Northeast. Go another 1.7 miles and turn right into the park. Restrooms, showers, drinking water (in summer), and picnic facilities are provided. The park has one Cascadia Marine Trail site and three hiker/biker campsites, plus a few rustic cabins for rent. Gathering driftwood for fires is prohibited. Camping is closed from October 15 to April 30. Reserve in person or online at biparks.org/fay-bainbridge-park-campground.

*2023 Tribal Journeys canoes at Suquamish*

Launch from Fay Bainbridge Park at a gravel beach facing east onto Puget Sound. A slight bulge in the shoreline offers some protection from northerly wind waves, but the launch is exposed to ship wakes and waves from the south.

**T'Chookwap Park (formerly Hidden Cove Park)/Port Madison:** Take SR 305 and turn east on Northeast Hidden Cove Road. After about a mile, look for the park sign on your left. The park has five parking spots, no restroom, and one picnic table. Launch from the old wooden float dock accessed from the east side of the park.

**Old Man House State Park or D'Suq'Wub (Suquamish Tribe):** Turn north from SR 305 about a quarter mile west of the Agate Passage bridge onto Suquamish Way. Follow the road 1.35 miles to Division Avenue. Turn right and drive another 0.35 mile to Old Man House State Park.

This small public park has room for just two cars, but fortunately it is little used. No alcohol is allowed and there are no facilities. Interpretive displays describe American Indian dwellings once located here, including Chief Sealth's. Launch from the sand beach about 100 yards from the parking area below a grassy hill on the north side.

**Suquamish Center/Charles Lawrence Memorial Boat Ramp:** Continue past Old Man House State Park for another 0.35 mile along Suquamish Way and turn right where the road makes a dogleg to the left as it enters this small town. Park in the public lot in front of businesses and the House of Awakened Culture (sgwədzadad qəł ʔaltxw). The walk to the beach is down a steep, paved boat ramp. No bathroom available.

Launch next to the boat ramp on a gravel-and-cobble beach. Cars can be driven to the water's edge briefly to unload. Cafés and grocery stores are nearby. Avoid launching on the long finger pier.

## ROUTES

You can choose between local paddling west of Fay Bainbridge Park or in Agate Passage. Connect the two areas for a 5- to 7-mile round-trip (half that distance if you use a car shuttle for the return).

**Fay Bainbridge Park:** *Moderate* or *Moderate +* (dependent on wind and ship waves). You might explore the high-tide lagoon at Point Monroe. On the ebb and lower tides, you can shoot the current out of the lagoon. The entrance is on the west side, close to the Bainbridge Island shore. Paddle into Port Madison to see the exclusive shoreside homes there. Once a company

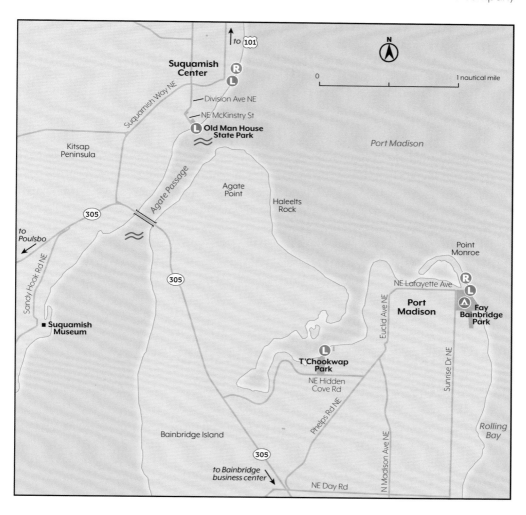

logging town, the bay was home to three hundred people who worked in the logging mill, or as shipbuilders and fishermen. The roundtrip distance is about 4 miles. Beyond Fay Bainbridge Park, there are no public shorelands or facilities on this route.

On Agate Point, you can find a petroglyph on a large erratic rock called Haleets Rock. One of thirty petroglyphs known in the region, the carving is thought to be 1500 to 3000 years old. Look for it at a bulge where the shore turns south, 100 yards northwest of the former Agate Pass steamer dock (shown on NOAA charts 18473 and 18446 as a "piling"). The bridge connecting Bainbridge Island to the Kitsap Peninsula south of the point was built in 1950.

**Agate Passage:** *Moderate* or *Moderate +* (dependent on current). You might launch at either Suquamish Center or Old Man House State Park and paddle locally or arrange a shuttle and paddle along the 3 miles of shoreline through Agate Passage. The sandy beach and picnic site at Old Man House State Park make a nice stop along the way. From the water, look for the park on the west shore between the inshore navigation marker and the "2" buoy at the north end of Agate Passage. Early explorers reported seeing a Suquamish longhouse here called "Old Man House" or D'Suq'Wub (dxʷsuqʼʷabš), which was six hundred to nine hundred feet long and sixty feet wide. The building had forty apartments, each with a fireplace. Every corner post of the chief's apartment was adorned with large carved Thunderbirds. The Suquamish thrived in this location for two thousand years, but Old Man House was burned down in the late 1800s by the US government as part of a campaign to remove American Indians from the area. South of the Agate Pass bridge, the Suquamish casino and hotel overlook Agate Pass.

Currents in Agate Passage can attain almost 6 knots under the highway bridge, but they rarely reach as much as 2 knots in the northern portion. You may cross between Agate Point and Old Man House State Park even if the currents are strong and unfavorable. A current flowing against either a north or south wind could make dangerous seas here, and the combination of strong currents, eddies around the highway bridge abutments, and heavy pleasure-boat traffic could present problems for less experienced paddlers. Most difficulties and hazards can be minimized by paddling as close to the beach as possible. However, currents under the highway bridge can sometimes be strong enough to slow your progress. I once surfed a sizeable tide rip in the main boating channel in front of Suquamish Center that was created by a flood opposing a strong southerly.

# 24. **Kingston to Point No Point Lighthouse**

An easily accessed paddle for those in the urban Puget Sound area, this route begins in a busy harbor and quickly sheds all signs of development. Enjoy views of Edmonds, Mukilteo, and southern Whidbey Island, as you pass by ships and the Point No Point Lighthouse, built in 1880. With three launches, you have plenty of options and routes to choose from. The route follows a Kitsap Peninsula National Water Trail (see Resources).

*Driftwood hut at Point No Point, looking south to Kingston*

**Duration:** Part day to full day.

**Rating:** *Moderate* or *Exposed*.

**Navigation Aids:** SeaTrails WA 104, 105; NOAA charts 18473 (1:25,000), 18440 (1:150,000); Puget Sound tide tables.

**Planning Considerations:** Watch for ferry traffic in Kingston harbor. The route can be exposed to wind and ship waves, especially off Apple Cove Point. Make sure to plan around the extensive tide flats that occur at low tides between Eglon Beach and Point No Point in the spring and summer months.

## GETTING THERE AND LAUNCHING

**Kingston:** From Seattle, take the Edmonds ferry to Kingston. Once off the ferry, take a left on Ohio Avenue Northeast and go two blocks to the Port of Kingston ferry parking lot. A self-pay parking kiosk includes two-hour and daily/weekly parking options. The marina also provides a boat facility with twenty-eight covered slips for small boats (eight to twenty-four feet long), for a modest monthly fee. A step launch and retrieval system gives easy access to the water. You can also pull out at the guest docks, where there is a hose for water and restrooms by the lawn area above. Visit portofkingston.org for more information.

**Eglon Beach Park:** From the Kingston ferry, continue off the ferry and follow State Route 104 for 3 miles to a stoplight and turn north (right) on Hansville Road Northeast. Drive for 4.3 miles and then take a right (east) on Northeast Eglon Road. Follow this winding yet scenic road to Eglon Beach Park (Port of Eglon), situated halfway between Point No Point and Kingston. The park has a boat ramp and beach, a restroom, picnic tables, and parking. Pilot Point, an undeveloped Kitsap County Park, is 1.5 miles north of Eglon Beach.

**Hansville and Point No Point:** From the Kingston ferry terminal, take SR 104 west for 3 miles to a stoplight. Turn right (north) on Hansville Road Northeast and drive 7.4 miles. Take a right on Point No Point Road Northeast and follow it for 1 mile to Point No Point County Park. The park has restrooms, picnic tables, walking trails, a beach, and parking. Parking will be tight during fishing season. Avoid landing in front of the homes just northwest of the lighthouse. These homes don't allow paddlers and beachgoers to loiter on their beaches. No camping is available, but you can rent the Point No Point Lighthouse for a minimum of two nights. Visit uslhs.org/about/point-no-point-vacation-rental/historic-keepers-quarters for more information.

## ROUTE

Put in from any of the three launches. If you start at Kingston, paddle to the end of the rock jetty and take a left to head north. Be very cautious when crossing in front of the ferry terminal. The best approach is to check the ferry schedule (visit wsdot.com/ferries/schedule) and pass by the terminal when no ferries are expected in the bay. If you do have to paddle by when a ferry is in dock, stay 200 yards away from the boat. Always give ferries the right-of-way. In a few hundred yards, you'll paddle past Apple Cove Point. Watch for waves from strong northerly or southerly winds. Shipping traffic can produce waves large enough to surf at lower tides. On the north side of the point, you'll pass a high-density housing development. From here on, there's only one other row of beach homes along a low bank. Continue north, paddling along

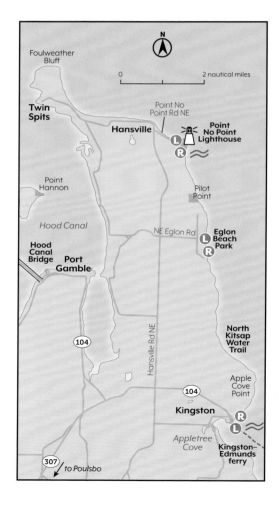

medium-to-high-bank bluffs and empty beaches for several miles to Eglon Beach Park and then Point No Point Lighthouse.

Just south of the lighthouse, you'll see a large erratic boulder on the beach left by a glacier. At extreme low tides, the beach north of Eglon extends 100 to 200 yards from the bluff. Pull out on the north side of the point just past the lighthouse. Picnic tables are above the beach. Go wide around Point No Point in fishing season. On a busy summer evening, you might see fishermen lined up shoulder to shoulder on both sides of the point. Light current and rips occur on large tidal exchanges. Keep an eye out for ship wakes, which can produce breaking waves on the beach. The point is not suitable for surfing freighter waves, as the beach descends too steeply into Puget Sound.

# 25. Everett Harbor: Jetty Island and Vicinity

Just beyond the industrial areas, US Navy base, and marinas of Everett's waterfront, Jetty Island is an interesting blend of wildness and history. Seabirds and sea lions float on barricades around navy ships and in the winter, the beach offers an excellent opportunity for a solitary hike. A manmade island, Jetty Island was built in the 1890s to create a freshwater harbor on the Everett waterfront. Old, rotting logs remain from when they were beached long ago to stabilize the shifting sandbars of the Snohomish River estuary. The Navy's homeport facility, on the west side of the Snohomish River channel and south of the marina, provides other big sea-going attractions but doesn't detract from the natural beauty of Jetty Island or interfere with access to the river's channels. The waters outside Jetty Island are popular with kite surfers seeking waves on high-wind days. Paddlers with the appropriate skill level can also enjoy paddling here while catching large wind waves.

Just south of Preston Point is the site of a former Snohomish village named Hibulb. Also called the "Heart of the Region," this was the main winter village for the Snohomish Tribe for thousands of years. The fortified village was abandoned in 1855 after the Treaty of Point Elliott.

*Touring paddle boarders traveling south along the inside of Jetty island*

At Legion Park, on the overlook above the north end of Jetty Island, the city has a kiosk describing what was called "The Eye of the Region." From this spot, Snohomish people had views of Priest Point to the north, Camano Island, Hat (Gedney) Island, and Whidbey Island. The sweeping glow of all the campfires of neighboring villages, stretching across what is now Port Gardner and beyond, inspired the name "Land of a Thousand Fires."

**Duration:** Part day.

**Rating:** *Protected*, *Moderate*, or *Exposed*.

**Navigation Aids:** SeaTrails WA 104; NOAA charts 18423 SC or 18441 (both 1:80,000), 18443 (1:40,000), 18444 (1:10,000); Seattle tide table.

**Planning Considerations:** Extensive tide flats make avoiding tides below three feet essential. Bring good footwear in case you have to walk out on mudflats. A five-foot or higher tide level allows circumnavigation of the island. To be safe, paddle in on a rising tide. Currents in the Snohomish River channels can be strong on both the ebb and flood tides. Strong winds, especially those opposing currents, can create very rough water and large, breaking waves on the outside of Jetty Island. A downriver current on an outgoing tide following a major rain event will increase the current significantly. Upriver currents are common on the rising tide. A free ride down the river current is the typical situation, but on many flood tides, the current will be traveling upriver. Be cautious of kite surfers, who are quite numerous on the western shores of the island on windy days.

If tides are below five feet, alternative options are to paddle upriver to Langus Riverfront Park or beyond the navy ships to Howarth Park or Mukilteo.

### GETTING THERE AND LAUNCHING

**10th Street Marine Park Pier:** From northbound Interstate 5, take Exit 193 for Pacific Avenue. Turn left (west) under the freeway and go about five blocks on Pacific Avenue to Broadway Avenue. Turn right and drive four blocks. Turn left and follow Everett Avenue (State Route 529) through downtown Everett and downhill toward the waterfront, where you bear right onto West Marine View Drive (SR 529). Follow this street for almost 1.5 miles, passing the marina on the left. Turn left onto 10th Street for the public launch ramp and marine park. Use the launch ramps and docks or, if they are very busy, the shoreline on either side. No fee is charged for hand-carried, human-powered boats if you walk your craft to the ramp. If you park on the ramp, you'll need to pay the fee; any other parking fees still apply. Also, parking rules at the Port of Everett have changed. Visitors can park two hours for free but must pay for additional time. Restrooms are available. Note the closing hours for the park and be sure to return before then.

The south marina docks are on the west side of Anthony's Homeport Restaurant. Launching from there is not recommended: water access is difficult, the current can be very strong, and the navy wharf is very close.

**Langus Riverfront Park on the Snohomish River:** Enjoy a free ride down the Snohomish River to Jetty Island from Langus Riverfront Park on the ebb but expect upriver current on

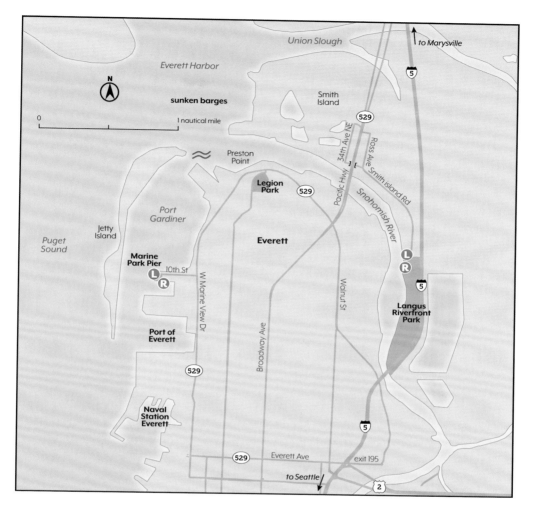

the flood. Located about 2.5 to 3 miles above the river mouth, the park provides restrooms, a boat ramp, and a picnic area. The Everett Rowing Association boathouse is at the south end of the park. Their low-profile dock for rowing shells makes launching human-powered craft much easier. Time your return to the park on the flood tide. To access the park from I-5 north, take Exit 195; from I-5 south, take Exit 198. Both lead to SR 529. Exit SR 529 at 34th Avenue Northeast, which takes you east. Take a right onto Ross Avenue, which parallels the freeway past Dagmars Marina, a dry boat storage. Ross Avenue soon merges into Smith Island Road, which takes you to the park.

## ROUTE

The Jetty Island circumnavigation at high tide is approximately 5 miles. Shorter excursions to northern Jetty Island and the vicinity are also a good choice. For the circumnavigation, plan your direction of travel in accordance with the Snohomish River channel flow direction, which is stronger than the flow on the west side of Jetty Island.

From the launching ramp at 10th Street Marine Park, to go counterclockwise around the island, paddle north toward the main Snohomish River channel, passing extensive log-storage facilities on the right. Jetty Island is across the channel. Its shore here is used for log storage, too, but less actively. Eventually, the water opens to the left as you round the north end of Jetty Island. A rip and back eddy occur on the inside of the northeast end on the ebb tide.

The seabed and land barely differ in elevation in this river outwash area. Jetty Island itself is hardly more than a long sandbar covered with salt grass, Scotch broom, and an occasional tree. Over the years, wooden barges were beached to control the movement of sand and silt. Walk inland toward the navigation marker tower at the north end of the island to find the old timbers, iron drift pins, and bolts of barges that were beached and burned here long ago, now completely surrounded by land.

Better-preserved barges are located about a half mile north of Jetty Island, beached in a line that extends north, along with countless pilings, most of the way to Tulalip's shore. In 1967, the eighty-seven-foot, two-masted ship the *Equator* was found in the line of barges. Robert Louis Stevenson sailed on the *Equator* during his South Pacific voyages. Learn more about this ship, which is in a covered building near the entry to the 10th Street boat ramp, by visiting historiceverettwaterfront.com/waterfront-special-features/the-equator.

The western edge of Jetty Island is an unbroken beach, with shallow waters warm enough in summer for a swim at high tide. At low tide, it becomes a sandy tide flat a mile or more wide. More hulks of old barges are found here and there along the beach.

The southern end of the island narrows to a stone jetty for the last 0.5 mile. If currents are strong against you for the paddle back upstream, you may want to shorten the loop by portaging across the island north of the stone jetty—a distance of 100 yards or less, depending on tides.

A large colony of sea lions may reside on the floating barricade that surrounds the navy ships in late winter and spring, usually from February to May. At lower tides they move offshore, floating in large clusters that should be avoided.

Once inside Jetty Island, you have the choice of following the wilder island shoreline to your left or crossing to inspect the fishing boats and extensive marina.

# 26. **Southern Hood Canal: Annas Bay**

Annas Bay, the elbow of the Great Bend of Hood Canal, has the largest river estuary in the area: the Skokomish River. Set against the spectacular backdrop of the immediately adjacent Olympic Mountains, this maze of winding channels and grassy banks abounds with birdlife and seals. At high tide, you can follow a meandering route all the way across the estuary through watery convolutions and miniature islets. Especially stunning are the fall colors of the wetland deciduous trees and shrubs in brilliant contrast to the mountains' greens.

*View of the Great Bend and the Olympic Mountains from Hood Canal Marina*

**Duration:** Part day.

**Rating:** *Protected.*

**Navigation Aids:** SeaTrails WA 201; NOAA charts 18476 (1:40,000), 18445 SC (1:80,000); Seattle tide table (add 10 minutes).

**Planning Considerations:** Best at high tide. Watch for windy conditions, which can create chop at the mouth of the river. Keep your distance from anglers.

## GETTING THERE AND LAUNCHING

Taking the Bremerton ferry from Seattle, you can reach the town of Union in about one and a half hours. Launch from sites in or near Union along State Route 106 or at Potlatch State Park on US Highway 101. The car-shuttle distance between these areas is about 5 miles.

Union: Launch from behind Hood Canal Marina at the Union Boat Launch, which offers parking. Find additional parking nearby on Highway 106. The full-service Hood Canal Marina has a café and store but no parking for paddlers. Alderbrook Resort operates the marina. Visit their website for additional information: alderbrookresort.com/union-city/union-city-market. The café, Hook and Fork, would be a nice spot for a beverage or bite after a paddle. It's closed on Tuesdays and Wednesdays (call 360-898-3500 to confirm their hours).

An informal roadside pullout along SR 106 about 1 mile south of Union gives the closest access to the eastern end of the estuary. In fishing season, outhouses are placed along this stretch for anglers. Access to the water is down a steep embankment. Make sure to display your Discover Pass.

**Potlatch State Park:** Use the beach in the day-use area (a Cascadia Marine Trail site is also located here).

**Note:** Avoid launching on the Skokomish River. Log jams and heavy river use by local anglers make it inadvisable. In the fall, the Skokomish Tribe lines the river shore with salmon-fishing nets. Flooding is common during heavy rains.

## ROUTE

The one-way paddling distance across the estuary is about 2.5 miles. Add another mile if you start from Union. The tidelands in the estuary are the property of the Skokomish Indian Reservation. Expect to see numerous gill nets set across the river channels during the fall salmon runs.

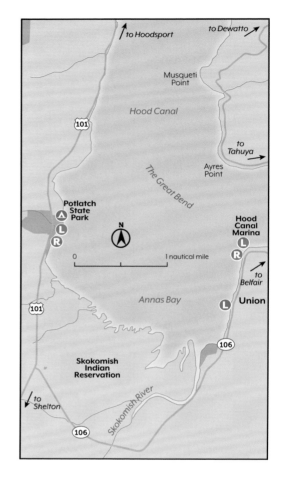

Depending on the tide height, pick your route along the fringe of channels and islands defining the northern edge of the estuary. If the water level is fairly high, you should be able to make it all the way across, except at the estuary's center, where a causeway requires you to skirt to the outside open water.

# 27. Central Hood Canal: Quilcene Bay to Mike's Beach Resort

With the Olympic Mountains towering overhead, this part of Hood Canal is the meeting place of land and sea. If you can take your eyes off this gorgeous backdrop, there is also plenty to see up-close: rich estuaries, lagoons, and a tideland renowned for its oysters. Be careful where you collect shellfish; most tidelands in Hood Canal are private. Check Washington Department of Fish and Wildlife regulations for the current season if you're interested in finding oysters. The routes described below focus on the west side of Hood Canal along US Highway 101.

**Duration:** Full day to overnight.

**Rating:** *Protected* or *Moderate*. *Moderate* may involve winds tunneling down the canal and producing sizeable wind waves.

**Navigation Aids:** SeaTrails WA 201; NOAA charts 18476 (1:40,000), 18445 SC (1:80,000); Seattle tide table (add 5 to 15 minutes).

**Planning Considerations:** Entering the mudflats, estuaries, and lagoons is best done at high tide. Check the forecast for wind, which can be either a benefit or a problem.

## GETTING THERE AND LAUNCHING

Coming from the Hood Canal Bridge, on State Route 104, take Center Road south to Quilcene. If coming from the north end of the Olympic Peninsula, stay on US Highway 101 south of Discovery Bay. From Olympia, take US 101 north and from Kitsap Peninsula, take SR 106 east and then US 101 north.

On the west side, at least five alternative launch spots are situated off US 101 between Quilcene and Pleasant Harbor.

**Quilcene/Herb Beck Marina:** This is the best launch for exploring upper Quilcene Bay. From Rodgers Road, take a left on Linger Longer Road. Follow it 1.5 miles to this small boat harbor. A full-facility marina, here you can find showers, restrooms, water, and overnight parking. Camping near Herb Beck Marina has been removed. Check in with the marina office before parking long-term. Launch at the sandy beach south of the marina. The facility is managed by the Port of Port Townsend: 360-756-3131.

Though roads lead directly to the shores of upper Dabob Bay, launching there is not advised since both the tidelands and shores are private. Local owners are concerned about trespassers wandering onto the rich oyster beds. You can, however, paddle to public access beaches managed by the Department of Natural Resources (DNR). On the Toandos Peninsula, across Dabob Bay from Quilcene, you can visit DNR beach 57 and, on the other side of the peninsula, DNR beach 57B.

**Point Whitney Shellfish Lab:** Start here for access to Dabob Bay or for paddling south toward Dosewallips and Pleasant Harbor. From Quilcene, follow US 101 south 8 miles to Bee Mill Road, which is marked for Point Whitney. Turn left and go 2.5 miles to the Washington Department of Fish and Wildlife Shellfish Lab at Point Whitney. The gravel beach next to the boat ramp is fine for launching in all but strong northerly winds when shore break may be quite large. Includes public restrooms nearby. Display your Discover Pass.

**Yelvik's Beach:** Located between Point Whitney and Seal Rock, Hood Canal Adventures operates their kayak tours and rentals from this beach. Find it on the shore of Right Smart Cove,

*Paddler's view of Pulali Point*

which is west of Jackson Cove. A private beach and campground, Yelvik's Beach charges a small fee to access the facilities and park. Yelvik General Store is a great place to resupply; their phone number is 360-796-4720. Launch from **Right Smart Cove County Park** adjacent to Yelvik's Beach off Hjelvicks Road.

**Seal Rock Campground:** One of the few Forest Service campgrounds on salt water, Seal Rock has a nice gravel beach with pleasant views of Hood Canal and points east. Camping, restrooms, and picnic tables are available. Launch on the north side of the beach by the small boat ramp. At high tide there is very little beach, so pull your boat up high and secure it to a tree or other anchor. Seal Rock is 2 miles north of Brinnon. Only open in summer. Display your Northwest Forest Pass.

**Pleasant Harbor:** About 2 miles south of Dosewallips State Park and 0.25 mile south of Pleasant Harbor Marina, turn off US 101 at Black Point Road. Immediately take the left fork, following the boat ramp sign to the lot below. Use the Fish and Wildlife boat ramp on the south side of the harbor. A Fish and Wildlife or Discover Pass is required here. There is a restroom but no other facilities.

**Triton Cove:** A few miles south of Pleasant Harbor, find Triton Cove State Park, a boat ramp, and a Cascadia Marine Trail (CMT) site. The CMT site is located on the south side of the park and has four tent sites; no fires allowed. A tall seawall directly above the beach is difficult to access during high tides or heavy seas. A picnic table is placed just above the wall, farther up the embankment on a nice grassy field. Vault restrooms are about 300 yards up the hill by the main parking lot. Display your Discover Pass.

**Mike's Beach Resort:** Located just north of the beautiful Hamma Hamma River mouth and near North Hamma Hamma Road, Mike's Beach Resort provides a public launch for a small fee. This access is crucial for exploring this side of the canal, where public access is limited. Cabins and tent camping are also available. Visit the website for additional information: mikesbeachresort.com.

**Scenic Beach State Park:** A scenic shoreline park by Misery Point and Seabeck, Scenic Beach has restrooms and a lot of camping. Display your Discover Pass. Find the boat ramp nearby at Seabeck Boat Launch (15376 Seabeck Hwy. NW).

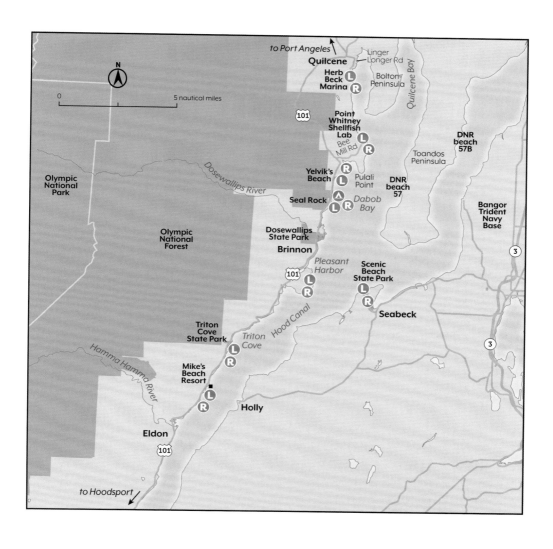

## ROUTES

Opportunities for both day and overnight trips abound along this stretch. Create your own trip, connecting day-use areas or overnight campsites such as the Cascadia Marine Trail site at Triton Cove.

**Quilcene Bay to Point Whitney to Jackson Cove:** *Protected* to *Moderate*. Quilcene Bay and its estuaries are perfect for beginning paddlers or for skilled paddlers seeking an idyllic, peaceful setting. North of Point Whitney, float past oyster-strewn beaches with nice views of Bolton and Toandos Peninsulas. Paddling south, follow a rugged, tree-lined shoreline with tiny pocket beaches. On a clear day, water visibility is quite good, allowing you to see far down below your boat. Beautiful Jackson Cove soon appears. Boy Scout Camp Parsons shares the north end of the cove. Yelvik General Store is a bit to the south if you need a snack, but a fee is required to access their beach and facilities.

**Scenic Beach–Dosewallips–Pleasant Harbor Triangle:** *Protected* to *Moderate*. (*Moderate* for possible winds on the crossing.) For this 8-mile triangular route, start at either Scenic Beach or Pleasant Harbor; both are fine at any stage of the tide. Launching from Dosewallips State Park is not recommended because the river channels leading to the beach here harbor sensitive salmon runs. Explore the delta offshore at higher tides for prime sea-life viewing. Scenic Beach and Pleasant Harbor both make pleasant lunch stops; Scenic Beach State Park has the most extensive and convenient facilities.

Amenities at Dosewallips are a short walk from the water, but to get there, you'll need to paddle up the Dosewallips River about a quarter mile (or up one of the dead-end side channels to the south of the river at high tide). Find the park's day-use facilities on the south side of the river. The river channel enters Hood Canal in the southern portion of the estuary; the portion of the estuary north of the river channel is primarily private land.

Take a little time to explore the back reaches of tiny Pleasant Harbor, gawking at the variety of yachts and working boats harbored in this all-weather shelter. Seal Rock is an alternative (but seasonal) launch and camping area for this trip; it's open from April to September. Another alternative launch is Point Whitney, only 3.6 miles north of Seal Rock.

**Pleasant Harbor:** *Protected*. Pleasant Harbor is a picturesque cove and full-service marina surrounded by thick forests. Very protected with a narrow opening, the harbor is ideal for beginning paddlers or those seeking glassy conditions when Hood Canal may be windy. The park is just inside and west of the narrow entrance. It consists primarily of the dock, a parking lot, and an outhouse.

# North Puget Sound

North Puget Sound is at the middle of the Salish Sea, and it's where four major straits—Strait of Juan de Fuca, the Strait of Georgia, Haro Strait, and Rosario Strait—converge into one waterway. Several large coastal defense forts from the pre–World War I to World War II look over this convergence zone. The region is known for strong tidal currents and wave action, miles of open water and protected areas, rich wildlife, and hundreds of small and large islands, bays, channels, inlets, and coves.

# 28. Whidbey Island: Coupeville and Penn Cove

Founded in 1852, Coupeville is the oldest town on Whidbey Island and it, along with the surrounding shoreline of Penn Cove, is within the Ebey's Landing National Historical Reserve that stretches to the west side of Whidbey Island. Coupeville's colorful, false-front buildings line the main street and extend to the gravel beach below. The Port of Coupeville Wharf reaches into Penn Cove with abundant sea life clinging to its pilings underneath. The museum inside the wharf has a full skeleton of a gray whale hanging from its ceiling. Penn Cove itself is mostly rural, with medium-bank bluffs punctuated by a few scattered homes. Enjoy distant views of Mount Baker to the north. A Cascadia Marine Trail site in downtown Oak Harbor is 4.2 miles to the north; otherwise, there is no water-accessible camping nearby.

**Duration:** Part day to full day.

**Rating:** *Protected* or *Moderate*.

**Navigation Aids:** SeaTrails WA 102; NOAA charts 18423 and 18471 (1:40,000 for Penn Cove).

**Planning Considerations:** A strong south wind can build rough swells as it sweeps up Saratoga Passage and into Penn Cove.

### GETTING THERE AND LAUNCHING

**Oak Harbor Windjammer City Park:** From southbound State Route 20, continue going straight onto Southwest Beeksma Drive when the highway turns right (west) in downtown Oak Harbor. If coming from Coupeville, once in Oak Harbor, take a right onto Southwest Beeksma Drive when the highway turns left (north). The launch is in Windjammer City Park, which has parking, restrooms, and a Cascadia Marine Trail campsite.

**Captain Coupe's Park and Boat Launch:** From SR 20, turn north onto North Main Street and go 0.5 mile, taking a right onto Northeast 9th Street. Drive 0.3 mile to the park and boat launch on the left. Named for Captain Thomas Coupeville, this day-use-only park offers restrooms, picnic tables, and parking. A ramp and float serve for launching boats.

**Mueller Park Beach Access (Coupeville):** This low-key launch spot is just off Madrona Way north of Captain Whidbey Inn. It opens at 6 AM, closes at dusk, and a Discover Pass is required. At lower tides a mudflat appears, making launching difficult.

### ROUTES

**Penn Cove:** *Protected.* Penn Cove, only open to the larger water of Saratoga Passage at its east end, is well sheltered from most major blows. Starting from Captain Coupe's Park and Boat Launch, you can explore the docks, wharfs, and overhanging buildings that compose Coupe-

*Erratic boulder and Coupeville Wharf*

ville's waterfront. You might want to secure your boat and visit the Island County Historical Society Museum at the foot of the wharf. Try the Penn Cove mussels at Toby's Tavern, a classic spot in town.

From Coupeville, you can paddle west past the many floating pens growing the famous and delicious Penn Cove Shellfish's mussels. Remember not to disturb or climb on the pens. Continue along the shoreline and stop for a bite at the dock of the historic Captain Whidbey Inn; for more information, visit captainwhidbey.com. Just before the inn and beyond the head of the cove, you can poke around Kennedy's and Grasser's Lagoons in search of waterfowl, raptors, deer, and other creatures inhabiting the shoreline. The lagoons harbor native littleneck clams, cockles, and horse clams. Check the Washington Department of Fish and Wildlife's harvesting regulations at wdfw.wa.gov/places-to-go/shellfish-beaches/240150. The one-way distance from Captain Coupe's Boat Launch to the lagoons is 2.6 miles.

**Penn Cove to Oak Harbor:** *Moderate.* You can follow this route as a one-way paddle from either end, with an easy car shuttle of only 11 miles between the two city launches, or as a round-trip. There are plenty of choices for food and drink at both locations. The relatively direct paddling distance from Penn Cove to Oak Harbor is 4.2 miles. Keep to the western shoreline and at 2 miles you will pass Klootchman Rock, a medium-sized erratic boulder left behind as the last glaciers melted, sitting beneath Blowers Bluff. On days when a south wind blows, the seas can build along this stretch, possibly breaking as they reach the shallow beaches.

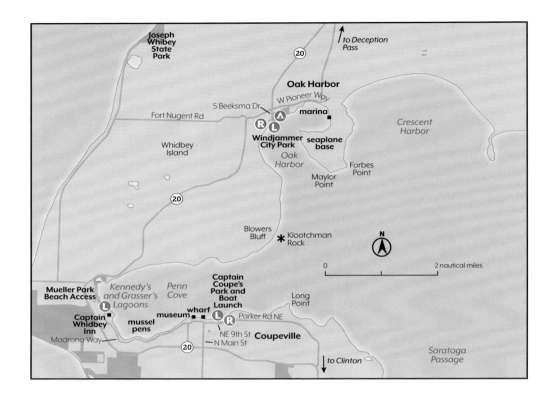

The Oak Harbor waterfront holds one Cascadia Marine Trail site, at the west end of the Windjammer Park west of the boat launch ramp. Bring ear plugs if you wish to stay overnight; the navy has a large air base nearby, and it is not uncommon to hear jets screaming overhead. Restrooms are available when the park is open, but you must bring your own water and no open fires are allowed. The campsite requires a reservation; sign up here: wta.org/sites/oak-harbor-city-park. If you're taking a longer trip, the city of Oak Harbor is a great spot for resupplying. No camping is available on Penn Cove in Coupeville.

# 29. Whidbey Island: Keystone to Hastie Lake Boat Ramp

This trip passes by Fort Casey Historical State Park, Ebey's Landing National Historical Reserve, and Fort Ebey State Park. Highlights include the historic lighthouse above Admiralty Head, the windswept grassy bluff and estuary of Ebey's Landing, and miles of vertical bluffs and empty beaches. With no areas of wind protection, this route is listed as *Exposed*. Swirling tidal currents and rips collide with wind swell from the Strait of Juan de Fuca and Puget Sound, and large surf is possible at Point Partridge.

**Duration:** Part day to overnight.

**Rating:** *Exposed*.

**Navigation Aids:** SeaTrails WA 102, 103, 104; NOAA charts 18441 (1:80,000), 18440 (1:150,000), 18471 (1:40,000); Port Townsend tide table.

**Planning Considerations:** This route can be glassy calm or have heavy seas with strong current, rips, and swell. Large surf may be present off Fort Ebey State Park and near Hastie Lake Boat Ramp. Know surfing etiquette (see Resources) before landing at Fort Ebey if surfers are in the water. Watch the currents and be comfortable with rough-water paddling.

## GETTING THERE AND LAUNCHING

**Keystone/Coupeville Ferry Terminal and Driftwood Park:** If coming from Port Townsend, take a right after leaving the ferry onto State Route 20, then another right into the day-use boat-ramp parking area adjacent to the ferry dock and Keystone Spit. From Coupeville, take South Main Street south past the high school and toward Fort Casey Historical State Park. Main Street becomes South Engle Road and after a few miles leads you to the Keystone/Coupeville ferry terminal. Just past the terminal, take a right into the boat-ramp parking area. Fort Casey State Park manages the ramp, so a Discover Pass is required to park; the lot has restrooms and picnic tables. Some also park on the street across from the ferry terminal. Camping is available in Fort Casey State Park adjacent to the ferry. Contact the park or reserve a campsite at parks.wa.gov/505/Fort-Casey.

Stay clear of the ferry when paddling in this area. Farther north of here is Driftwood Park and farther east is Ledgewood Park, both day-use areas with beach access. Both are Island County Parks with limited parking and no facilities; for additional information, visit islandcounty.net.

**Ebey's Landing National Historical Reserve:** From the Coupeville ferry terminal, take a left onto South Engle Road. In about a mile, take a left on scenic, winding Hill Road, which takes you above a bluff with epic bird's-eye views of the paddle route below. Keep following Hill Road as it drops to the beach and ends at the park. From Coupeville, take South Ebey Road off SR 20 and follow it to the park. The lot here is small, so park on the water side of the street if necessary. Restrooms, picnic tables, and hiking are available. Launching here can be easy (if the wind is light), or it can feel like going through a surf break (if wind is strong or swell is coming in from the Strait of Juan de Fuca). For additional information, visit the National Park Service website at nps.gov/ebla/index.htm.

**Fort Ebey State Park:** From SR 20 north of Coupeville, take West Libbey Road west. Follow signs to Fort Ebey State Park. If you don't have a Discover Pass, you must pay a fee at the booth or pay station. Follow signs to the beach. Parking is tight on busy days, but it is a short carry to the beach. A Cascadia Marine Trail site sits just below the beach parking lot; it has one tent site, but the lot and restrooms are day-use only. State park campsites are available on the south side of the park on the bluff, which has no water access. Wind waves and swell from the Strait of

*View from Point Partridge of the bluffs below Fort Ebey State Park*

Juan de Fuca can be quite large here. The beach is rocky with a few boulders and is a popular surfing spot for locals. Know surfing etiquette (see below) before launching here when surfers are present.

**Hastie Lake Road Boat Ramp:** From SR 20 just south of Oak Harbor, turn west on Hastie Lake Road. Drive 2.5 miles to the road end. To access the boat ramp from SR 20 near Fort Ebey State Park, continue west on West Libbey Road. Take a right on West Beach Road and follow it north for 2 to 3 miles to Hastie Lake Road. Turn left into the boat ramp area, which has a small lot and no facilities. Houses are on both sides; respect private property. If surfers are present, use good surfing etiquette: pass them on the outer water side.

## ROUTE

This trip can be completed in short segments or as one long paddle; choose your own route and launch location. If you want to make it an overnight, a Cascadia Marine Trail site is located above the beach launch at Fort Ebey State Park.

Check wind and currents prior to departing. Strong tidal currents and rips can swirl around Admiralty Head, stretching north past Fort Casey and creating challenging conditions. In summer, large kelp beds lie below the fort. If you're traveling near Fort Ebey and the Hastie Lake Road Boat Ramp, check swell conditions to avoid dealing with large breaking waves: a west or northwest swell above seven feet at Cape Flattery or strong southwest, west, or northwest winds can cause sizeable surf here.

When launching from the Coupeville ferry terminal, be cautious of a docked or moving ferry. Better yet, time your launch for when the ferry isn't there. The beach on Admiralty Head below

Fort Casey is strewn with driftwood. Look for interesting driftwood shelters here. Take a short hike up the bluff to explore the pre–World War I gun emplacements and pill boxes. The fort was part of the "Triangle of Fire," a three-fort system that included Fort Worden in Port Townsend and Fort Flagler on Marrowstone Head, both across Admiralty Inlet. The forts were designed to prevent invading fleets from entering Puget Sound.

The shoreline north of the ferry terminal rises to a bluff and stays steep until Ebey's Landing, where it drops to the beach. The beach is rocky with some sand and is minimal during higher tides. Across Admiralty Inlet, enjoy views of Marrowstone Island, Port Townsend, and the Olympic Mountains.

Take a restroom break at Ebey's Landing and hike up the short bluff trail for impressive views of Admiralty Inlet, the eastern entry to the Strait of Juan de Fuca, and the San Juan Islands to the far north. Along the bluff, you may see some small prickly pear cactus, indicative of the area's arid climate. The expansive Perego's Lagoon lies below, one of the few tidal lagoons not destroyed by development in the region.

Continuing north, the bluffs rise again to tall vertical cliffs. Savor the solitude of the seldom-visited sand-and-gravel beach. Bald eagles, hawks, and seagulls frequently fly over the bluffs, taking advantage of the pillow of air provided by the active beach below.

The bluff drops again at Fort Ebey State Park. Point Partridge is a rocky extension where waves often build, making this a popular surfing area. Go wide on the outside around the point if you're not skilled in dealing with breaking waves. Since good surf is hard to find inside of the coast, surfers may be unwelcoming to those who hog waves or can't surf safely; this spot is particularly known for its "localism." Sea kayaks are fast but can't turn well on waves, so they can be a hazard to others in the water.

Just around the point, look for a wooden-planked walkway leading up the hill. This is the path to the Cascadia Marine Trail (CMT) campsite. Restrooms are available in the parking lot during the day. The park's main hiking trail comes down just above the CMT site. If you're up for a hike, follow the trail up the hill. Poke around in the World War II observation bunker, a five-minute walk from the beach. A larger gun emplacement from the same era is on top of the bluff, about a quarter mile from Point Partridge.

Back in the water and moving north, the bluff remains lower, and homes appear above. A little over 2 miles north, reach the Hastie Lake Road boat ramp—a good rest stop or launch point. Another Cascadia Marine Trail site is 3.2 miles north in Joseph Whidbey State Park; it has one site, two vault toilets, and water. Bring ear plugs, as flights from the nearby naval base can be noisy.

# 30. **Skagit River Delta**

The Skagit River Delta is a birder's paradise. In this rich estuary country within the Skagit Wildlife Area, you can also find a maze of marshland channels, the shanties and floating houses of river dwellers, and even pre–World War II artillery emplacements.

*Old pilings at Goat Island mark the location of docks once used for the construction of 1890s-era Fort Whitman.*

**Duration:** Part day to full day.

**Rating:** *Protected* to *Moderate*.

**Navigation Aids:** SeaTrails WA 101; NOAA chart 18423 SC (1:80,000); USGS 7.5 Minute Series (1:24,000) topographic map for the Utsalady Quadrangle; Seattle tide table (add about 20 minutes).

**Planning Considerations:** Midtide or higher, at least four feet above mean low water, is required for paddling outside the main Skagit River channel and outside Swinomish Channel. Both Skagit River and Swinomish Channel reverse their currents with the tide. The channel current is not easily predicted, but typically reverses current at least one hour after the river. Currents affect paddling efforts to and from all launch locations. If you have to "buck" or go against current, paddle in the shore side eddies to move upstream.

You may wish to avoid the heavy bird-hunting period from mid-September through December; contact the Washington Department of Fish and Wildlife (WDFW) for specifics. Each member of your group must have a Discover Pass in his or her possession to go ashore in the Skagit Wildlife Area. Many paddlers don't time the tides correctly and end up struggling to paddle back to the launch. Keep in mind river flows are stronger after heavy rain and during spring runoff from snowmelt. Take the ebb downriver and the flood upriver.

## GETTING THERE AND LAUNCHING

Choose from launch sites along the Skagit River or in downtown La Conner. An approximately 10-mile car shuttle can be made between them.

**Skagit River:** From Interstate 5, take the La Conner–Conway exit and soon branch right to Conway. Continue about 5 miles on Fir Island Road. For the lower river launch at Blake's Skagit Resort and Marina, turn left on Rawlins Road. Located approximately 1 mile above the delta area, Blake's is the lowest launch point on the North Fork Skagit River. The resort charges a launch fee, which also covers parking for the first day. Call 360-445-6533 for additional information.

A WDFW launch site is located farther upriver. To reach it, turn right off Fir Island Road onto Moore Road about 0.35 mile beyond Rawlins Road, just before the North Fork bridge. Take the first unsigned dirt road to the left 0.25 mile beyond at the S curve. A Discover Pass is required to use this launch site. Follow the dike west and look for a sandy path through the trees to the river.

**La Conner:** To launch from La Conner, take Fir Island Road over the North Fork bridge. The road becomes Best Road. Take a left in 2.4 miles onto Chilberg Road and continue another 2.4 miles to La Conner. The La Conner public boat ramp is located below and just north of the Rainbow Bridge. After entering La Conner, turn left on Maple, then right on Caledonia Street, left on 3rd, and finally right on Sherman Street. The ramp is straight ahead at the waterfront. Parking in summer is difficult. If necessary, use the lot across the street or along the street beyond.

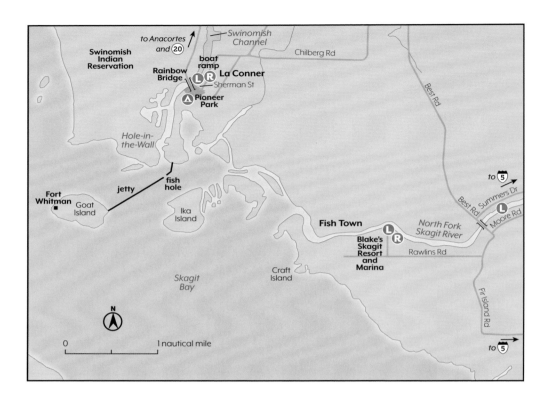

Pioneer Park in La Connor has a Cascadia Marine Trail site above the boat ramp with three to four tent spaces, water, restrooms, and a covered kitchen area. Bring a pack to carry your gear up to the campsite.

## ROUTES

**Skagit River to Craft Island:** *Protected.* The paddling distance is 3 to 5 miles one way. Time your start to ensure that you will have mid- to high tide in the delta once you get downriver. The distance to the shallow delta area is about 1.5 miles from Blake's and about 3 miles from the WDFW launch upriver. There is a downstream current from both river launch sites during the ebb and an upstream flow as far as the upper launch on larger flood tides (except during heavy river runoff), though this begins as much as an hour after low tide.

Head downriver and approximately 1 mile below Blake's, reach a sharp bend to the right; just beyond are pastoral farm buildings and river dwellers' houses and shacks on the right bank. This is the tiny community of Fish Town. Just downstream on the left is the first side channel into the delta. Take this channel for Craft Island and keep bearing left. Reach the island a little more than 1 mile after leaving the river.

Craft Island is really a hill jutting up from an otherwise flat marsh and tideland west of the river as it nears the mouth. From the top, you can enjoy a sweeping panorama of the marshlands to the north and south and, at low tide, the vast gray tide flats to the west. This and other upland islands are a particularly sensitive habitat for raptors, including bald eagles and red-tailed hawks. If you go ashore, avoid approaching or disturbing these birds, particularly when the nesting sites are in use.

The timing of your Craft Island excursion is important, as the side channel leading to it dries below midtide. If you have time, you may wish to head downriver at early ebb, paddle to the island, and spend the last of the ebb and early flood lunching, exploring, or just enjoying the view.

If your tide timing is off for paddling to Craft Island, you can walk there after returning to the launch point. Drive to the end of Rawlins Road beyond Blake's. A rough trail, accessible during lower tides, leads about 0.75 mile across the marsh meadows to the island.

A possible side trip along this route is to Ika Island, which is the large island to your west just beyond Craft Island. You can't land on Ika, but you can still enjoy the interesting rock formations and craggy shoreline around its base.

**La Conner to Goat Island to Skagit Delta:** *Protected.* The paddling distance for the loop is 7 miles; additional side trips are possible.

Most of this loop can be paddled at tide heights of three feet or more. Avoiding a lower tide is not as critical here as it is for the Craft Island route. However, you will be scooping sand much of the way in a foot or less of water; getting out to wade and tow your boat may prove easier in spots. Spending the low-tide interval exploring Goat Island is worthwhile if you can afford the time. If the tide is low, focus on following the main boating channel to avoid hitting a sandbar. As always, yield to boating traffic; this can be a busy waterway in summer months.

From the public launch at La Conner, follow the channel south through the twisting narrows of Hole-in-the-Wall. Beyond, the channel opens to flats with intertidal islets and shallow waterways that invite exploration if the tide is in. To the south, a log-storage area bounded by a stone jetty extends to Goat Island. The route later returns through a tiny gap in this jetty.

Goat Island has both the dense forest and the grassy meadows with madrona trees that are typical of the more arid San Juan Islands. On the northwest end sits Fort Whitman, part of the extensive Puget Sound coast artillery defenses built at the turn of the twentieth century. The emplacements have mounts for three guns, with associated rooms and tunnels similar to those found at Fort Worden and Fort Casey State Parks. Defenses like these were obsolete by World War II when aircraft became more effective than coast artillery against invading fleets.

To reach the emplacements, look for the old dock along the island's north shore. Behind it is a rocky, muddy beach and the start of a rough trail that climbs to the right. Follow this about 250 yards to the battery.

As with other islands in the Skagit Wildlife Area, this is a particularly sensitive habitat for resident raptors. The WDFW asks that you respect the privacy of these birds, particularly during spring nesting. As elsewhere within the Skagit Wildlife Area, no camping is allowed.

Paddling around the south side of Goat Island brings you into the shallowest part of this route, though enough water can be found in the shifting channels of the Skagit River on all but the lowest tides. On ebb tides and the first portion of floods, downstream currents will make moving up into the delta hard and slow work, with few eddies to assist your progress.

From here, you could take time to explore the many sloughs off the Skagit River's channel and perhaps cut through the delta to Craft Island, about 2 miles to the east, if the tide is high enough.

The return to Swinomish Channel from the Skagit River is via the "fish hole" in the jetty, a small opening allowing migrating salmon that made a wrong turn into Swinomish Channel to get back to the river. Located about 200 yards from the eastern end of the jetty, this gap is not visible as you approach from upriver but follow the jetty and you will find it. The fish hole is dry below midtide.

# 31. **Hope and Skagit Islands**

Though currents can be swift in this area, the protection of nearby Fidalgo and Whidbey Islands can bestow Hope and Skagit Islands with reasonable paddling conditions when other places are a bit on the rough side. These state park islands offer grassy hillsides with flowers in season, forest trails, and plenty of sand and gravel beaches for sunbathing. Skagit Island and nearby Ala Spit both offer a Cascadia Marine Trail campsite, which are easily accessible, wonderful overnight destinations.

**Duration:** Part day to overnight.

**Rating:** *Moderate+*. Currents can produce turbulence in certain areas and rough seas when opposing southerly winds. Avoid the strongest currents at the west end of Hope Island unless you have the skills to handle strong eddy lines and tide rips.

**Navigation Aids:** SeaTrails WA 101; NOAA charts 18423 SC or 18421 (both 1:80,000), 18427 (1:25,000); Deception Pass current table.

**Planning Considerations:** Currents here are thirty minutes different than at Deception Pass. The flood flows south. Stay off Dot Island, which is a wildlife refuge. If possible, plan to catch the flood current out to the islands and the ebb for the return. Strong wind that opposes current can create sizeable waves.

## GETTING THERE AND LAUNCHING

**Deception Pass:** Launch from the Cornet Bay area of Deception Pass State Park. From State Route 20 about 1 mile south of Deception Pass Bridge, follow signs to Cornet Bay and drive 1.25 miles to the launching ramp area. Use the gravel beach just below a timbered bulkhead in front of the parking area or, if the tide is high and covers the beach, use the launching ramp or floats. A Discover Pass is required to park in the state park. For overnight parking, there is a fee; use the lot across the road from the boat launch. Cornet Bay has a marine store, restrooms, and water.

**Snee-oosh Beach:** This gentle beach near La Conner is a pleasant alternative that avoids most of the current on the west side of the islands. Drive west from La Conner over the Swinom-

*The south side of Hope Island shows its beauty with madrone topped cliffs.*

ish Channel bridge on Pioneer Parkway for 0.6 mile to Snee-oosh Road; turn left and proceed another 1.9 miles. Bear left onto Chilberg Avenue for 0.3 mile and then make a U-turn onto the dirt access road to the beach. There are no amenities, but you can enjoy a beautiful view across the water to Hope and Skagit Islands.

## ROUTE

From Cornet Bay to Hoypus Point, the state of the current dictates how far offshore to paddle—head out 100 feet or so to catch a ride on the flood current. If it is ebbing, you can use eddies to ease your paddle along the tree-lined gravel beach to Hoypus Point, but you will have to fight the brunt of the current as you round the point. Watch for rocks and trees just under the surface to protect your rudder. In summer, busy boat traffic is also a concern. At Hoypus Point, pass by the remnants of an old ferry dock that took riders across to Fidalgo Island before the construction of the Deception Pass Bridge. South of the point toward Ala Spit, you can find eddies that will help against an ebb.

You may wish to cross directly from Hoypus Point to Skagit Island, adjusting to offset the effects of the current as you go. The current strength diminishes during the second half of this 1-mile crossing. On the ebb, Skagit Island will create an eddy or break in the current as you near it. The current runs strongest between the eastern point of the island by the Cascadia Marine Trail site and Flagstaff Point on Kiket Island.

Skagit Island is rocky and steep along its north and western shores, with gravel and shell beaches on its east and southeast ends. A trail circles the island, winding through fir and salal

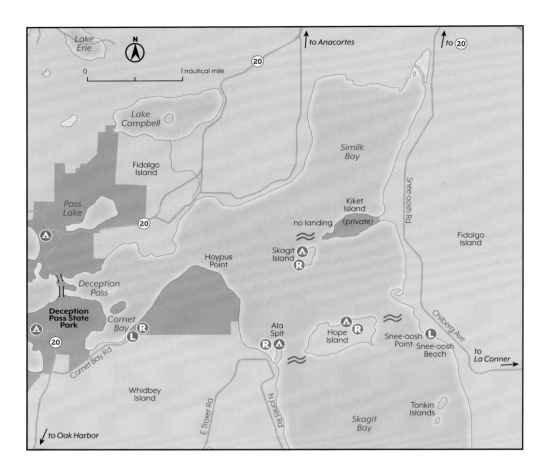

forest on the north side. On the south side of the island, a series of rocky meadows interspersed with madronas offer plenty of nice spots for lunch in the sun. Currents can run swift between Skagit Island and Kiket Island to the east. Landing on Kiket Preserve State Park Heritage Site is prohibited. Skagit Island has four Cascadia Marine Trail sites west of the vault toilet and one state park primitive site on the point facing Kiket Island. No water is available.

Hope Island is far larger than Skagit Island. Trails circle this island, but most visitors prefer hiking the beaches or paddling along the shore instead of walking in the thick forest. Gravel beaches, interesting rock formations, and caves on the south side of Hope Island are the biggest paddling attractions. The park has six primitive campsites on Lang Bay on its north side with a vault toilet nearby. Expect it to be busy on summer weekends.

During large tidal exchanges, currents at both the east and west ends of Hope Island can be swift and dangerous for anyone not skilled in dealing with moving water. Both ends can have sharp eddy lines and possible tide rips. Stay close inshore on the east end, where you will probably only need to cross one eddy line, and then paddle in eddies the rest of the way around. Watch your rudder near shore during low tides.

The west shore has a very strong eddy line that has capsized kayaks in the past. The current between Hope Island and Ala Spit, about 0.35 mile distant, may be as swift as you can paddle, requiring hard work to get across against an opposing flow. The flow along the spit is slower, but it still takes hard paddling upstream against a flood current to reach the eddies north of the spit.

# 32. Deception Pass

Deception Pass offers outstanding beauty that can be safely explored on the fringes of its high-current area. Beginners should avoid the pass; to paddle here, you must have strong tidal current skills and know how to correctly identify the slack current time. There are plenty of easy paddling options in areas of little current within view of Deception Pass's full magnificence, plus two beautiful lakes (see Trip 33, Deception Pass: Cranberry and Pass Lakes).

Experienced paddlers eager to expand their skills can expend some adrenaline practicing in Washington's strongest currents—crossing eddy lines, developing bracing reflexes in swirls and turbulence, and maybe descending into a whirlpool! Currents mostly average 5 or 6 knots at

*Group of kayakers paddling in Canoe Pass on a light flood tide*

their maximum, while the occasional strongest ones exceed 8 knots. Speeds rapidly decrease within 0.5 mile of both sides of the pass.

Routes in Deception Pass can be combined with those in the Hope and Skagit Islands area to the east (see Trip 31, Hope and Skagit Islands). The Cascadia Marine Trail campsite at Bowman Bay affords the opportunity to make extended trips.

**Duration:** Part day to overnight.

**Rating:** *Protected*, *Moderate+*, or *Exposed*. Heavy boat traffic, wind, or ocean swell in the pass may create rough conditions.

**Navigation Aids:** SeaTrails WA 101; NOAA charts 18427 (1:25,000), 18423 SC (see 1:25,000 inset for Deception Pass); Deception Pass current tables.

**Planning Considerations:** Seek or avoid strong current periods, depending on your skills and preferences, by using the Deception Pass current table. Launch and take-out locations depend on current flows, described below. The flood current flows east through the pass. Slack lasts ten to twenty minutes and is affected by Skagit River flows and wind direction. Note it could be slack in Canoe Pass while still flooding or ebbing in the main pass. Avoid times of strong wind from the west, particularly during ebb currents, which can produce particularly nasty seas and tide rips. Watch for boating and jetboat traffic in both Deception Pass and Canoe Pass. I recommend taking a class in the pass from a certified instructor to learn how it works and improve your safety protocols.

A Discover Pass is required to park at all launches. Mobile phone reception is poor; use a tethered VHF radio for on-water communication. For state park camping fees, visit parks.wa.gov/166/Camping-fees.

## GETTING THERE AND LAUNCHING

You have three launch sites to choose from within Deception Pass State Park. Which one you use depends on where you wish to paddle and the state of the current in the pass. Tactics for planning with the currents in mind are described in Routes below.

**Bowman Bay:** The launch is accessed from Rosario Road about a half mile north of the Deception Pass Bridge. This is a good place for protected paddling north of the pass or for launching a one-way paddle to Cornet Bay, which requires a car shuttle trip of about 3 land miles. Launch on the gravel beach in front of the parking lot. Plan for a morning arrival in summer, as the lot can be very congested. Groups of paddlers should park farther back, yielding to other visitors who may need ADA access. Restrooms, picnic tables, fire pits, and covered shelters are available, but the water has been shut off since the start of COVID.

**West Beach:** This is the easiest access to the pass from the west. Turn off SR 20 about a half mile south of the bridge and follow signs to the West Beach parking lot. In windy weather or when a large swell is penetrating the Strait of Juan de Fuca, the sand-and-gravel West Beach can have substantial surf. If it is not to your liking, a 200-yard-long path leads from the parking lot to a protected launch on North Beach just behind West Point. West Beach is day-use only and a Discover Pass is required for parking. Parking is tight on summer weekends.

**Cornet Bay:** This launch serves paddling to the east of the pass. From SR 20 about 1 mile south of the bridge, follow signs to Cornet Bay and drive about 1.25 miles to the boat ramp area. Use the gravel beach west of the boat ramp to launch. Cornet has restrooms, picnic tables, a shelter, and overnight parking (check for fees).

## ROUTES

**Bowman Bay:** *Protected.* Waters within this bay, located between Rosario Head and Reservation Head, should be relatively smooth. There is plenty of rocky shoreline to investigate, plus opportunities for lolling on the beaches: explore ashore at Sharpe Cove to the west, or at the isthmus adjacent to Lottie Bay to the east. Enjoy rock gardening opportunities south of Reservation Head, which has a coastal feel with small sea caves, rock slots, and surge channels. Swell from the Strait of Juan de Fuca can push against the rocks here, making for good coastal paddling practice.

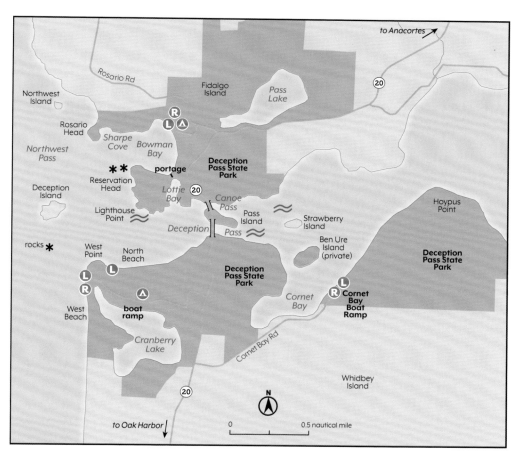

*Deception Island view of the Deception Pass Bridge in the distance.*

Portaging across to Lottie Bay is easy, and Lottie Bay is rated *Protected* to its mouth, where currents can be strong. Avoid portaging during extreme low tides, when the bay's thick mud can be a slog, especially if you're carrying a fully loaded boat. In addition, portaging the isthmus to the east of Lottie Bay is an easy way for experienced paddlers to enter or leave Deception Pass.

**West Area Exploration:** *Moderate +.* Currents west of Lottie Bay are generally less than half the strength of those predicted for the pass and probably are suitable for intermediate paddlers with some experience with currents. If there is any doubt about your party's paddling abilities, avoid times when currents in the pass exceed 3 knots or there are opposing winds. Crossing the mouth of the pass from Bowman Bay to North Beach should be done cautiously during flood currents, which can send you toward stronger currents in the pass. This area can be extremely rough when westerly wind or swells from the Strait of Juan de Fuca oppose an ebb current flowing out of the pass. Also watch for heavy summer boat traffic, which can create large wakes. At such times or in windy weather, the eastern portion of the pass area (Cornet Bay) is a more prudent choice.

Plan to spend some time exploring the rocky shores between Reservation Head and Lottie Bay, where you will find several pocket beaches for secluded lunch stops. Use the eddies when current is flowing in the opposite direction. Watch your rudders and fins on rocks and bull kelp. This area is accessed ashore by a trail from Bowman Bay. You can portage via a small, rocky cove behind Lighthouse Point if the rip or currents are too strong on the point. There's a fun, small, surfable standing wave on the flood on the west side of Lighthouse Point, directly below the navigational marker.

Deception Pass State Park extends north to include part of Rosario Head, as well as Northwest Island and Deception Island. Neither of the islands are developed and access is not easy. Gravel beaches on the north side of Deception Island offer fairly easy landings on lower tides, but it's a hard scramble to gain access to the island above. Currents in Northwest Pass, which separates Lighthouse Point and Deception Island, can be strong on the ebb. Watch for rips, kelp beds, boats, and reefs off the island.

**Cornet Bay:** *Protected.* Explore this bay as far north as Ben Ure Island (private) or east toward Hoypus Point, about 1 mile from the boat launch. Currents in Cornet Bay are weak and often flow in the opposite direction than in the pass to form a long, tapering back eddy on ebbs along the shore toward Hoypus Point. At Hoypus Point, currents may be strong and accompanying rips make it unsuitable for *Protected* -rated paddling. Likewise, the strong currents, eddies, kelp beds, and reefs around Strawberry Island are appropriate only for experienced paddlers. (See Trip 31, Hope and Skagit Islands, for info on currents east of Cornet Bay.)

**Bowman Bay to Cornet Bay (or reverse) through Deception Pass:** *Moderate +.* You can see it all in this 3-mile traverse through Deception Pass. Timing for at least near-slack in the pass is critical; you may want to catch the last of the current cycle going your way. Note that Canoe Pass and the main pass may run in opposite directions around slack. Allow plenty of time to explore the coves west of the pass. Stops ashore are easy on the beaches at surrounding Gun Point. Pass Island has fair access ashore on rocks on the east end; access at Strawberry Island is similar.

Boat traffic in the pass is a significant hazard, especially if the current forces boats to speed up or reduces their control. Canoe Pass, the smaller passage to the north of Pass Island, is the safer and more interesting way through, as little traffic goes this way. However, a bend in this channel reduces visibility for oncoming powerboats. If you paddle in Canoe Pass, move to the shore to let boating traffic go through. Boat wakes can get large here, so hold on to a rock or be prepared to brace.

**Deception Pass Current Play:** *Exposed.* Depending on the current strength and your skills, capsizing here is probable; a full wet suit or dry suit is essential. A helmet is a good idea as well because people drop things off the bridge, and it also protects you from accidental hits against your gear or rocks. Also recommended are neoprene gloves and booties, due to the water temperature and rocky, barnacle-covered shoreline. You should be prepared to rescue yourself and members of your party in case of capsize. Tether your VHF radio to your life jacket.

Several sea kayak outfitters and clubs (and the author's business, which offers paddle boarding instruction) hold classes for intermediate-level paddlers in Deception Pass, letting them practice negotiating currents and bracing. They usually seek current strengths up to 6 knots.

At 4 knots, eddy lines are strong enough to capsize an unprepared paddler, especially in narrower craft. When currents are 4 knots and above, strong leaning and bracing are required for all craft crossing eddy lines, and swirl zones and boils that may be intimidating to all but the most blasé whitewater boater can crop up. On ebbs, whirlpools form downstream from Pass Island but do not last. On strong floods, more persistent whirlpools form on the edge of the main channel east of Pass Island. These are a thrill for those who care to chase them down and put one end of their boat or SUP into the vortex.

Canoe Pass is preferred to the main channel for eddy play, primarily due to less boat traffic and cleaner eddy lines. Wakes can make big waves as they meet eddy lines on either side of the channel. On ebbs, Canoe Pass has eddies on both sides just west of the bridge, and ferrying back and forth from one to the other is easier. The flood is stronger than the ebb and creates a series of small eddies east of the bridge and close to the island's steep rock face, while a long back eddy forms along the opposite shore. Hopping from one to the other is possible but requires more maneuverability than during ebbs. Many who work the flood launch from Cornet Bay. For the ebb, Bowman Bay is preferred. You can also time it to get the end of the flood cycle and then play in the ebb when it begins.

Surfable standing waves can develop during lower tides in Canoe Pass when the ebb current collides with incoming swell or a strong wind. Experienced paddlers can enjoy a great surfing experience far from the ocean.

# 33. Deception Pass: Cranberry and Pass Lakes

Cranberry and Pass Lakes offer an alternative to the swift tidal paddling and other saltwater experiences of Deception Pass. Pass Lake is often calm with beautiful, forested shorelines, especially in the fall. The use of motors is prohibited on Pass Lake, so you can enjoy the quiet and solitude. Both popular fishing spots, these lakes are easily accessible and ideal for all types of paddlers and rowers.

*Cranberry Lake in Deception Pass State Park on a misty morning*

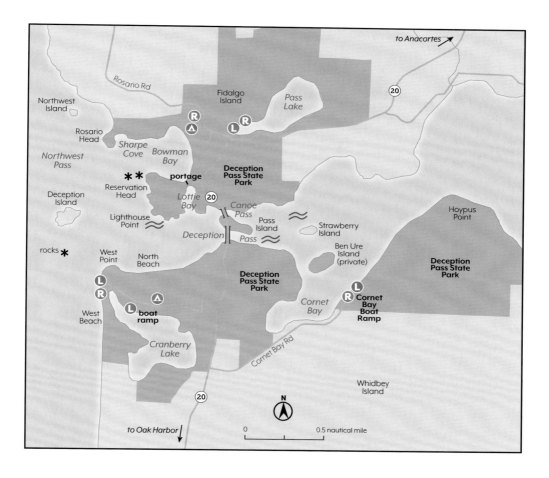

**Duration:** Half day.

**Rating:** *Protected.*

**Navigation Aids:** SeaTrails WA 101; NOAA charts 18427 (1:25,000), 18400 (1:200,000).

**Planning Considerations:** Check the Deception Pass State Park website at parks. wa.gov/497/Deception-Pass for lake closures, especially in late summer when algal biotoxins can create problems. The Washington Department of Fish and Wildlife lists fishing rules and regulations.

## GETTING THERE AND LAUNCHING

**Pass Lake:** The launch is accessed from State Route 20 about a half mile north of the Deception Pass Bridge. Turn right onto Rosario Road and immediately take a right into the parking lot. Restrooms and picnic tables are available. Display a Discover Pass or pay the day fee.

**Cranberry Lake/West Beach:** Turn off SR 20 about a half mile south of the Deception Pass Bridge; enter Deception Pass State Park on the right and follow signs to the West Beach parking lot. Launch by the public beach or the gravel boat ramp, located before the main park road merges into the parking lot. A few more pullouts can be found along the entry road as you drive in. There's camping nearby in Deception Pass State Park. Bring your Discover Pass or purchase a day pass. Parking is tight on busy summer weekends.

### ROUTES

**Pass Lake:** Pass Lake is across from the road entry to Bowman Bay on the north side of Deception Pass Bridge. A small parking lot and restrooms are available. This calm, wind-protected lake is a great alternative to Deception Pass. Paddle its tree-lined shores and enjoy views of Mount Erie. Often the lake is flat-calm with beautiful reflections, especially in autumn when the surrounding forest bursts into fall colors. This trophy fly-fishing and catch-and-release-only lake has stocked rainbow and brown trout averaging fifteen inches, with some up to twenty-eight inches. This was the first lake in Washington State dedicated to fly-fishing. No motors are allowed on the lake. A creek used to run down from here to Bowman Bay, but it was piped. The lake doesn't drain as low as before, instead holding its level for most of the year. In later summer months the lake may be closed due to algal toxins.

**Cranberry Lake:** Located on the south side of Deception Pass State Park behind West Beach, Cranberry Lake is a great alternative to paddling in Deception Pass. Once a saltwater inlet, this shallow lake is great for exploring. Paddle around and through its marshes, estuaries, and sandy west shores. In summer, enjoy its warm waters. There was once a village on the east side of the lake. Launch from the West Beach parking lot or a small pullout along the entry road. An alternative launch is from the East Cranberry Lake parking lot just inside the park entry. This is a popular fishing spot.

# 34. **Burrows Island**

The paddling at Burrows Island is interesting and exhilarating with both sheer rock and lively currents. Ashore you will find an abandoned US Coast Guard light station perched on a cliff on the west side. Hike beyond the station to steep, grassy shorelines or climb the hill above for a spectacular view of southern Rosario Strait. A secluded Cascadia Marine Trail campsite is on the east side of the island in a small cove with great tide-pooling opportunities nearby.

**Duration:** Part day to overnight.
**Rating:** *Moderate* to *Exposed*. Currents usually exceed 2 knots and tide rips are likely. Wind and a westerly swell can make this area quite dangerous during times of strong current.

**Navigation Aids:** SeaTrails WA 001; NOAA charts 18423 SC or 18421 (both 1:80,000), 18427 (1:25,000); Rosario Strait current tables with corrections for the Burrows Island–Fidalgo Head area.

**Planning Considerations:** Use the flood current to travel west in the channels on either the north or south side of Burrows Island and for rounding Fidalgo Head from the south. Flood currents here are generally stronger than the ebbs. The automated Burrows Island Light emits a white flash every six seconds at night. You can activate the fog signal by keying your VHF microphone five times on 83A. This emits a group of two flashes every thirty seconds for thirty minutes.

## GETTING THERE AND LAUNCHING

Choices for launching are either Skyline Marina, the closest to Burrows Island, or Washington Park, which adds another mile or so of paddling around Fidalgo Head. These two launch points are about a 0.5-mile walk apart, so consider starting at Washington Park and taking out at Skyline Marina.

**Skyline Marina:** From Anacortes, follow signs for the San Juan Island ferry, about 4 miles west of town. From Commercial Avenue, take a left on 12th Street (State Route 20), which becomes Oakes Avenue. Enjoy views on your right of Guemes Island, Cypress Island, and Bellingham Channel. At the Anacortes ferry terminal, continue going straight at the Y intersection. The road becomes Sunset Avenue. Take a left on Skyline Avenue and follow signs into the marina. At

*View of Burrows Island looking south toward Lopez Island and the Olympic Peninsula*

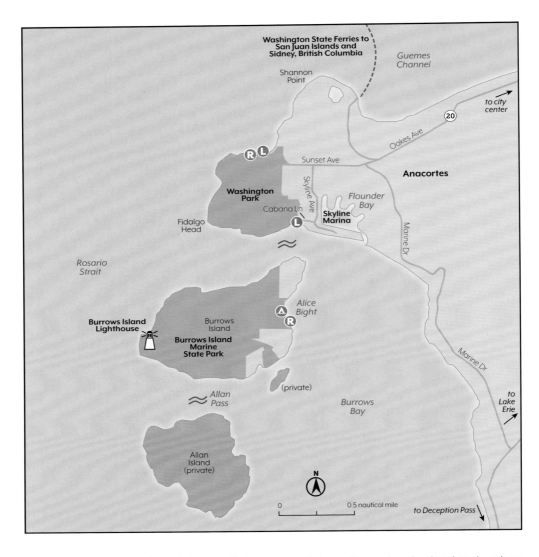

the bottom of the hill, take a right onto Cabana Lane. Drive to the end and unload and park on the street, or park in the pay lot by the water.

**Washington Park:** Follow the above directions to Skyline Avenue, but this time continue straight past Skyline Avenue and go right at the Y intersection. Park in the "A" lot to carry your boat across the lawn to the gravel beach. Then move your car to the "B" lot to park. There is a daily parking fee for the boat launch, and there is camping in the park.

## ROUTE

Most of the shoreline of Fidalgo Head, Burrows Island, and neighboring Allan Island is steep rock with grass and madronas growing above. Sharp drop-offs allow close-in paddling, but beaches are infrequent. All of Fidalgo Head west of Skyline Marina is in Washington Park; expect to see a lot of people along its shores. Public land on Burrows Island is restricted to the forty acres and 1000 feet of shoreline in Burrows Island Light Station State Park on the island's southwest corner. Visitors ashore Burrows Island are rare. There are no public lands or tidelands on Allan Island or the small island to the southeast of Burrows Island.

Expect to find strong eddy lines and nearby tide rips in the channels separating Burrows Island from Fidalgo Head and Allan Island. It is possible to ferry across these currents to reach the island, though you may have to work hard to maintain your position.

The only landing on the west side on Burrows Island is the gravel beach just north of the light station. The challenge here is scaling the steep rocks adjacent to the old supply-landing facility; these rocks can be precarious in wet weather. Above are the equipment shed and residence building, both boarded up since the station was automated. The lighthouse and a horn that operates in all weather are located at the point. The Cascadia Marine Trail campsite sits in Alice Bight on the east side of Burrows Island; please be respectful if staying here, as it is bordered by private land. A staircase leads up to three sites, served by a vault toilet farther above. The campsite is in a thick forest with a great view of the bay and the crescent-shaped sandy beach below. The three sites combined can hold up to eight people; they have fire rings but no water.

To the south are wild and rugged grassy slopes above cliffs that drop to the water: this is your chance to explore where few others go. If you want an excellent vantage point, follow this shore a few hundred yards around to the east and climb up the rocks and grassy slopes to the hilltop. To get there from the light station, walk on the path behind the lighthouse into the trees, as the shoreline here is not negotiable. Beyond, the trees and brush thin out as you continue. Be wary of steep drop-offs to the cliffs below—this is no place for small children.

# 35. Lummi Island

Originally called Skallaham by the Lummi people, Lummi Island may have had two longhouses on Village Point. Due to exposure, it was vulnerable to attack from the northern tribes. Lummi was first charted by Spanish explorers Galiano and Valdez as Isla de Pacheco in 1792. Although it has most of the amenities of the San Juan Islands, including a Cascadia Marine Trail campsite, Lummi Island is sufficiently off the beaten cruising path to be overlooked by many powerboaters; however, it is very popular with sea kayakers. The southern end has a rugged quality that makes alongshore paddling interesting. If desired, this trip can be extended to Clark Island (see Trip 56, Clark Island).

**Duration:** Overnight.

**Rating:** *Moderate* or *Exposed*. The *Moderate* route involves currents and some open-water paddling in a channel that can become very rough with southerly winds. The *Exposed* route involves more of the same, plus the potential need to paddle for miles in rough conditions.

**Navigation Aids:** SeaTrails WA 005; NOAA charts 18423 SC or 18421 (both 1:80,000), 18424 (1:40,000); Rosario Strait current tables or Canadian *Current Atlas*.

**Planning Considerations:** Moderate currents in Hale Passage affect paddling ease along these shores. Strong currents along Lummi Island's southwest shores can be hazardous against a contrary wind. Watch for the Lummi Island ferry from Gooseberry Point, which runs hourly. If you take the ferry to the island, be prepared to pay the roundtrip fee with cash.

## GETTING THERE AND LAUNCHING

**Gooseberry Point:** Launch from Gooseberry Point in the Lummi Indian Reservation. From Interstate 5, take Exit 260 (Lummi Island/Slater Road) and turn west onto Slater Road. After almost 4 miles, turn left onto Haxton Way and follow it 6.5 miles to the Lummi Island ferry landing at Gooseberry Point. For overnight parking, the launch is north of the Lummi Island ferry and is owned by the Lummi Nation. A parking attendant is in the small building by the boat launch. At the time of writing, there is a small parking fee, and the lot is monitored by a security guard. Park in the westernmost corner of the lot. Parking protocol in Gooseberry Point may change and is often not clear; check here for updates: lummi-island.com/ferry. You can also call 360-305-9703.

**Lummi Island:** You may also want to launch from Lummi Island. If you take the ferry across, note they don't take reservations. Read about ferry fees and parking at whatcomcounty.us/562/Ferry-Schedule. Once on Lummi, take a left onto South Nugent Road and then another left on Legoe Bay Road. After passing the beach community of Legoe, the road curves north to West Shore Drive. Follow it along the shoreline past Village Point. Look for an unmarked pullout along the west (left) side of the road. This is a public access area with a nice gravel beach. Make sure to fuel up and buy all your supplies before reaching the island, which has limited resources.

## ROUTES

**Hale Passage Loop:** *Moderate.* The total paddling distance is about 13 miles. This pleasant overnight trip follows Lummi Island's east shore south to a campsite at one of the more interesting Department of Natural Resources (DNR) recreation sites. You can return by the same route or, if weather permits, you can cross Hale Passage to Portage Island for the return to Gooseberry Point.

Although the crossing from Gooseberry Point to Lummi Point is only about 0.65 mile, swift currents of up to 2 knots can make paddling to the opposite shore tiring, and it can be dangerous in winds opposing the current. Some have experienced currents exceeding 4 knots and six- to eight-foot swells here. Flood currents run 350 degrees true and during extremes may reach 2.8 knots. Ebb currents run southeast 145 degrees and may reach or exceed 1.8 knots. A 100- to 300-yard-wide shoal extends from Lummi Point approximately 3.6 miles north across Hale Passage to Sandy Point. The shoal can create rough conditions when the wind opposes the current.

*Reef fishing off Lummi Island with Lummi Peak in the background.*

If possible, time this crossing for near the slack and then catch the ebb down Lummi Island's shore. Though the alongshore currents are not terribly swift, they are persistent with few eddies to assist and can be tiring against a contrary tide.

Northern Lummi Island is a mixture of farms and residences. A café, grocery store, and library are near the ferry landing. There is little wild shoreline on the northeastern side, as it's heavily developed with beach homes. Along Hale Passage, homes become sparser as you paddle south and come abreast of Portage Island on the opposite shore. The number of homes continues to diminish as the shoreline steepens; they disappear altogether just north of Inati Bay, where there is a large gravel pit. Round one more point of land and enter the wild southern portion of Lummi Island.

Inati Bay is a fine spot for a stretch onshore, though it is likely boats will be moored there during the cruising season. The Bellingham Yacht Club leases the head of the bay for a private boaters' shore stop. The woods behind are well worth a walk inland, and there is an old road that eventually leads to the main road from the north.

The Lummi Island DNR recreation site is less than 1 mile south of Inati Bay, nestled among rocky shores that gradually become steeper as you travel south. This DNR site, which also carries Cascadia Marine Trail status, is a particularly interesting one, as it is fitted into the rocky benches of a steep hillside. Steps and switchbacking trails connect two tiny coves to upland campsites that make use of every level spot. The result is a remote-feeling campsite especially attractive to paddlers. Other types of boaters tend to avoid the site because it provides poor moorage for them, offering no protection against southerly blows. The five campsites are more secluded

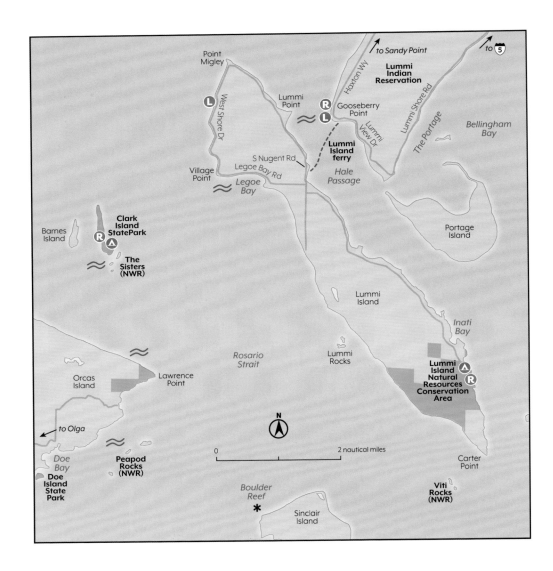

than those at similar recreation areas, making this a nice resting place even if others are present. Fire grates, picnic tables, and vault toilets are provided, but there is no water service. In the summer, this site becomes increasingly busy due to its easy access from the mainland. Practice minimum-impact camping. The Whatcom Association of Kayak Enthusiasts (WAKE) maintains the site.

At this point, the Hale Passage loop route turns back to the north. If currents are unfavorable, you can opt to cross to Portage Island for the return: currents will probably be slower along the shallow eastern shore of Hale Passage. Portage Island, part of the Lummi Indian Reservation, is quite wild with beaches fronting woods and meadows above. Landings are prohibited for nontribal members without permission. The island is connected to the mainland by a spit that dries at midtide.

**Lummi Island Circumnavigation:** *Exposed.* The total paddling distance is approximately 19 miles. The portion from Gooseberry Point south along Hale Passage is described above in the Hale Passage Loop route. The description continues south from the Lummi Island Natural Resources Conservation Area.

Venturing south toward Carter Point and around to the southwest side of Lummi Island, enter a world of unforgiving rocky shorelines and steep, narrow beaches backed by talus slopes. Should the weather turn against you, there are few opportunities for anything but an uncomfortable emergency bivouac. After rounding the point, the shore is a continuous scree slope punctuated by cliffs that rise abruptly to the ridgeline. It gradually ascends toward 1600-foot Lummi Peak as you move north. Viti Rocks, a San Juan Islands National Wildlife Refuge, can be seen offshore to the west.

Until you are opposite Lummi Rocks, where the country gradually flattens, few pullouts are available. Lummi Rocks is owned by the Bureau of Land Management and leased to Western Washington University for research and education. The rocks are closed to access for their protection.

Pastoral and residential developments appear gradually as you move north from Lummi Rocks, though most are blocked from the shore by bluffs until you start approaching Village Point.

Just south of Village Point, the eclectic beach community of Legoe is home to the Lummi reef-net fishing fleet. In salmon season, dozens of barges anchored to offshore reefs use ladder-like structures to catch schools of sockeye as they swim by. This has been a Lummi tradition for centuries—a few modern tools have been added, but the basic concept remains the same. Currents can run swiftly around Village Point.

As you round Point Migley, the shore is low—mostly sandy beach with residential housing. If a stiff north wind is blowing, crashing surf can easily build.

As you return to your start at Gooseberry Point, the same current advisories apply to Hale Passage as at the trip's beginning. Try to cross at near slack and time your return with an ebb to make for easy southward paddling.

# 36. Chuckanut Bay

The rocks around Chuckanut Bay make this Bellingham-area trip an interesting exploration. Investigate convoluted hollows, the fossilized remnants of ancient palm trunks, an old sculpture on a seaside rock, and the delicate, saltwater-eroded Chuckanut sandstone formations.

**Duration:** Part day to full day.

**Rating:** *Protected* or *Moderate*. The longer *Moderate* route is exposed to southerly seas. Rocky shores can make landings difficult if the weather takes a bad turn.

**Navigation Aids:** SeaTrails WA 005; NOAA charts 18424 (1:40,000), 18423 SC; Port Townsend tide table (add about 45 minutes) for the launch at Chuckanut Park.

**Planning Considerations:** Plan for higher tide levels or an incoming tide if paddling south of Wildcat Cove or in Chuckanut Bay. The southern portion of Chuckanut can dry out up to 1 mile from shore on lower tides.

### GETTING THERE AND LAUNCHING

All five launch points are accessible from State Route 11, also called Chuckanut Drive.

**Boulevard Park:** This waterfront park sometimes holds local paddling races. It has extensive parking, restrooms, picnic tables, and even a coffee shop. Enter the water on the north side. From Bellingham, take North State Street, which becomes Boulevard Street. Just past Adams Avenue, where Boulevard Street becomes 11th Street, take a right into the park.

**Community Boating Center (CBC)** (555 Harris Ave.): CBC is a nonprofit organization adjacent to the only boat ramp in Fairhaven. The center offers a no-dues and no-membership model for storing human- and sail-powered small boats, rentals, and instruction. Visit their website at boatingcenter.org for more details.

**Marine Park:** This tidy little park with picnic tables and restrooms is at the end of Harris Street, just past the Alaska Marine Highway ferry terminal and a boatyard. There is ample parking, yet it often fills on summer days. Launching is best done at mid- or low tides on the sand-

*Petrified palm tree trunks are embedded in the shoreline at Clarks Point.*

and-gravel beach. If you plan an overnight, pull your car back out onto the street or park in the paved lot across from the ferry terminal. On Wednesday evenings and high wind days from spring to fall, the park fills with surf ski and outrigger paddlers who meet to paddle together.

**Chuckanut Pocket Estuary:** This is not a recommended launch due to the extensive mudflat behind the railroad bridge. Locals call it "mud bay." Aim for high tides on a flood when departing and arriving.

**Wildcat Cove:** About 1 mile south of Chuckanut Bay, Wildcat Cove is part of Larrabee State Park. Follow SR 11 south from Fairhaven for 5 miles to Cove Road. Follow Cove Road downhill, turn left after crossing the railway, and go straight into the boat launch area. Launch on the gravel beach next to the boat ramp. Overnight parking is not allowed, but camping is an option at Larrabee State Park. For safety, there is a PFD (life jacket) loan kiosk for paddlers and boaters. Heavy seaweed builds on the shore in late summer, creating a mess for people trying to remove boats from the water. This is the locals' preferred launch for Chuckanut Bay.

## ROUTES

**Chuckanut Bay:** *Protected.* Stay within the shallow cove at Chuckanut Park or paddle

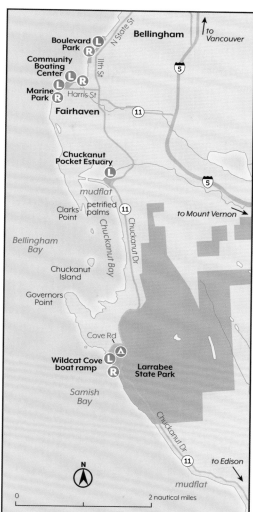

up to 4 miles around the entire bay. Except for the park and Chuckanut Island, all shorelines are private with some Burlington Northern right-of-way. Check out the rocks within the cove before paddling under the railroad bridge to the larger bay. Clarks Point has a very attractive inner bay with four fossilized palm-tree trunks in the rocks. They are easily examined from your boat. Across Chuckanut Bay, east of Clarks Point, find a rocky outcrop and some small beaches along the railroad. This area is known as Teddy Bear Cove.

Chuckanut Island is owned by The Nature Conservancy, which allows stops ashore but no camping or fires. No facilities are available here, and they ask that you stay on the trail that rings the island. At high tide, a small beach on the southwest side makes for the best landing spot, but there is a steep scramble to the island above. At lower tides, beaches on the north and southeast are uncovered. These beaches are surrounded by interesting rocks but lack access to the upper island.

**Fairhaven to Wildcat Cove:** *Moderate*: This 5-mile trip is best done with a 6-mile car shuttle between the CBC or Marine Park launch and Wildcat Cove. It can be shortened by 1 mile with a high-tide launch at Chuckanut Park. In Fairhaven, begin with a tour of the shipyards and the southern terminus of the Alaska Marine Highway.

As you paddle south, the railroad parallels the shore with two miniature coves behind it. They can be reached under low bridges; the second cove offers an exciting sluice under the bridge at midtide. Beyond, watch for a rock just above high tide that a sculptor rendered many years ago. Add as much of Chuckanut Bay as you like to your trip (see the Protected route above for highlights). Governors Point defines the south end of Chuckanut Bay. South of here the eroded rocks take on a delicate, lacy quality.

**Wildcat Cove South:** *Protected* to *Moderate*. Paddling south from Wildcat Cove, you'll see more interesting rock formations; craggy, forested cliffs rising far above the water; and a few tiny pocket beaches. In summer, college kids can be seen jumping off the large boulders that line the shore. Keep an eye out for otters and harbor seals, which are common in this area. There is no water access from the main section of Larrabee State Park or farther south until you reach Edison. Follow this route for as long as you like but beware of the extensive mudflats that develop in lower tides. Pass Taylor Shellfish Farms and notice the mini lighthouse in front of the facility. The steep, mountainous coastline below Chuckanut Drive continues to Colony Creek, where it begins to flatten into Samish Bay.

# 37. **Semiahmoo Spit, Drayton Harbor, Dakota Creek, and California Creek**

Located next to the Canadian border, 2.3-mile-long Drayton Harbor is a crescent-shaped bay protected by two sand spits and fed by two small streams—Dakota and California Creeks. The city of Blaine sits on the bay's northeast corner and Semiahmoo Resort is on the northern part of the western spit. The Peace Arch at the Canadian border can be seen in the distance beyond Blaine. Semiahmoo Spit and Drayton Harbor are prime bird-watching destinations; here you might spot bald eagles in winter or spring, brants, Barrow's goldeneyes, great blue herons, and more. North Cascades Audubon Society has dubbed the bay an "Important Bird Area."

Semiahmoo means "half-moon," a reference to the shape of Drayton Harbor, according to former Chief James "Jimmy" Charles. Others say the name means "water all around" or "hole in the sky." The principal village is at Semiahmoo Spit. A small ferry, the MV *Plover*, connects passengers between Blaine and Semiahmoo Spit. The Wilkes Expedition in 1841 stayed a week here, replenishing their supplies and enjoying the hospitality of the friendly Semiahmoo people.

**Duration:** Half day to full day.

**Rating:** *Protected.*

**Navigation Aids:** NOAA charts 18423 (1:80,000); NOAA tidal station 9449679.

**Planning Considerations:** Both spits can dry out at lower tides, including the two creeks. Launching on incoming medium tides is your best bet. The middle of the channel into the bay does not dry out. Wind outside the spit can whip up waves if the tide is low. Launch into Dakota or California Creeks on a flood no less than six feet.

## GETTING THERE AND LAUNCHING

**Semiahmoo County Park:** Take Exit 274 off Interstate 5 and drive south on State Route 548 (Blaine Road). Turn right onto Drayton Harbor Road, following signs to Semiahmoo County Park (or Semiahmoo Resort). Located at the beginning of Semiahmoo Spit, this day-use park has restrooms and a hand-carry launch area on its northwest corner. The beach is accessible from both sides.

**Semiahmoo Resort:** Take Exit 274 off I-5 and drive south on SR 548 (Blaine Road). Turn right onto Drayton Harbor Road, following signs to Semiahmoo County Park (or Semiahmoo Resort). This full-service resort is at the end of Semiahmoo Spit and offers a marina with a store, a café, and lodging. Non-guests can use the overflow lot near the water; it provides beach access and kayak and paddle board rentals at the adjacent Beach Activities Center. Visit semiahmoo.com for more information.

**Blaine Harbor Public Boat Ramp:** Take Exit 276 off I-5 and at the traffic circle, take the exit for Peace Portal Drive, following it under the freeway. At the next traffic circle, go right onto Marine Drive. Turn left on Milhollin Drive and follow it to the ramp. This two-lane boat ramp in the city of Blaine has a restroom, shower, boat and trailer rinse, and parking for up to two weeks. You can reach the harbor office at 360-647-6176. For launch fees, check portofbellingham.com/217/Rates.

**California Creek Estuary Park:** Take Exit 274 off I-5 and drive south on SR 548 (Blaine Road). Turn right onto Drayton Harbor Road and find the California Creek Estuary parking area.

## ROUTE

Drayton Harbor was named for Joseph Drayton, an artist who accompanied the Wilkes Expedition in 1841. Drayton Harbor and the mudflats out-

*Paddling below a train bridge in protected Dakota Creek*

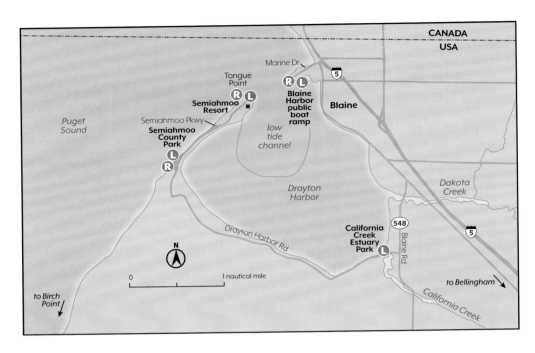

side the spit are known for holding warm water in summer, great for swimming and beach-combing. The bay is 2.3 miles long and more than 2 miles wide.

Choose your route, aiming for a medium to high flood tide to avoid getting stuck in the mud. Launching from Semiahmoo County Park into Drayton Harbor, paddle southeast 2.3 miles to California Creek to explore this lovely waterway for nearly 2 miles through rural and developed areas. Or launch from the California Creek Estuary for easier creek access. In 2022, Whatcom Parks purchased the land from Whatcom Land Trust to develop California Creek Estuary Park on the southwest side of the creek's mouth. "Soggy all around" was the Semiahmoo name for this creek. Continue paddling north into Dakota Creek, which runs about 1.3 miles through sim-ilar rural scenery. The Semiahmoo called this creek Tl'e'qx', or "place to get dog salmon." Enter both creeks on no less than a six-foot tide. There is no Dakota Creek direct access. Launch from the California Creek Estuary.

As you near Blaine, you'll begin to see more development. Eventually, Blaine's boat ramp and marina come into view, often busy with boat traffic in summer. Cross over to Tongue Point on the northeast corner of Semiahmoo Spit to return to the county park. Harbor seals line the floats near Semiahmoo Resort.

For a longer trip with a more coastal feel, paddle southwest from Semiahmoo County Park for 2.6 miles to Birch Point. The route is exposed to wind and waves, but the point is unlikely to become a mudflat at lower tides.

OPPOSITE *Exploring the majestic cliffs near Freshwater Bay in Port Angeles (Trip 46)*

# Olympic Peninsula

The Olympic Peninsula is a diverse region of small, picturesque port towns, remote waterways, and the towering, magnificent Olympic Mountains. With some of the peninsula located on Puget Sound and the rest on the more coastal Strait of Juan de Fuca, the region has dynamic waterways and beaches for all types of paddlers. The peninsula lies across the water from Vancouver Island, allowing easy access to trips in British Columbia.

*Bywater Bay in Shine Tidelands State Park*

# 38. **Hood Head**

Shine Tidelands State Park and Wolfe Property State Park, north of the Hood Canal Bridge, feature an interesting bay, a lagoon, and a gravel spit. Easy access makes this a nice afternoon destination or an easy overnight trip using the Cascadia Marine Trail (CMT) site adjacent to Hood Head. Ducks, herons, and other waterfowl are plentiful in the lagoon during the winter. Beaches are strewn with sand dollars and moon snails, and you might also spot harbor seals, river otters, or dolphins offshore. The easternmost point, Point Hannon, was once called Whiskey Spit and was a meeting and burial place for Native people. Documented as early as 1790 by European explorers, it later hosted a brothel and speakeasy and was a drop-off location for shanghaied crew. The alongshore paddling and largely protected waters make it a suitable trip for new paddlers. Hood Head can be combined with other paddling routes in the area, such as those around Port Gamble and Mats Mats Bay (see Trip 39, Mats Mats Bay).

**Duration:** Part day to overnight.

**Rating:** *Protected* or *Moderate*.

**Navigation Aids:** SeaTrails WA 105; NOAA charts 18477 (1:25,000), 18445 SC (1:80,000); Port Townsend tide table.

**Planning Considerations:** Midtide or higher is required to explore the inner lagoon. Respect private property signs and stay off the spit near homes. Watch for wind waves off Hood Head. Approach the CMT site from the north to avoid low-tide mudflats on the other side of the isthmus.

## GETTING THERE AND LAUNCHING

**Shine Tidelands State Park:** Access is simple: turn down Termination Point Road immediately north of the west end of the Hood Canal Bridge. Follow it north (left) to where it dead-ends at Shine Tidelands State Park. Launch on the gravel beach. This is a day-use-only park with a toilet and picnic table. A Discover Pass is required to park here.

Alternative launches include Port Gamble, Salsbury Point Park, Twin Spits on Foulweather Bluff, Port Ludlow, Shine, and Mats Mats Bay.

## ROUTES

**Bywater Bay Round-Trip:** *Protected*. Launching from Shine Tidelands State Park, the paddling distance is about 4 miles. Follow the beach north to the entrance just short of the spit connecting Hood Head to the mainland. You may encounter some current at the entrance to the bay but probably not enough to cause any problems. At higher tides, you can paddle southwest to grassy flats bordering alder forest—a good spot for a picnic, some birdwatching, and exploration. This inner lagoon area is called Wolfe Property State Park, which is undeveloped. The lagoon dries during lower tides. Stay off the spit where private property signs are posted.

**Hood Head Circumnavigation:** *Protected* to *Moderate+*. Add 2 miles to the Bywater Bay round-trip. As you round Hood Head, enjoy the large driftwood dragon sculpture on Point Han-

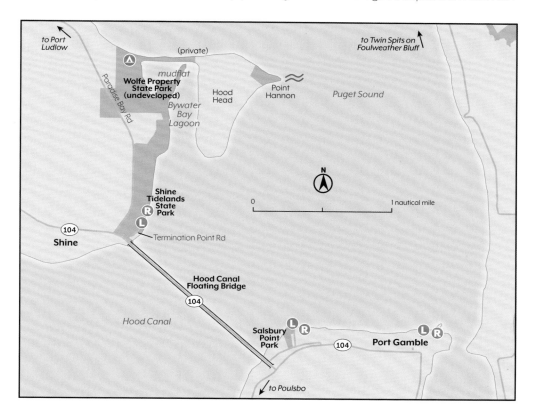

non, part of the Wolfe Property. Measuring nearly thirty feet long, the dragon is worth a peek. Wind waves can create surf south of the point. Make sure you secure your boat high on the beach if you plan on going ashore. Round the north side of the point (restrooms available) to find the Cascadia Marine Trail site on the northeast corner of the property where the lagoon spit begins. The campsite has a vault toilet, one site that fits four to five tents, and no water. Fires are in-pit only. From here, you can enjoy great views north toward Marrowstone and Whidbey Islands.

You might also get as close as you ever will to a passing Trident submarine, as the US Naval Bangor Base is nearby. Stay a considerable distance away from a sub if you do see one. You will be able to paddle across the spit only on the highest tides; otherwise, a short carry is needed. The mudflats are extensive south of the spit on the lowest tides. Some of the tidelands south of Point Hannon are privately owned and are marked accordingly.

# 39. **Mats Mats Bay**

This quiet little bay north of Port Ludlow is just right for paddling practice or touring anchored yachts. The bay has a pastoral feel to it, with residences generally low key and set back from the shore. A narrow, tree-lined entrance leads out to interesting offshore rocks, popular with divers, less than a half mile away. On the east side of the bay sits a closed basalt deep-bore mine, which started operations in 1934, and by 2005 had mostly ended. Reportedly, soil from the Seattle Alaskan Way tunnel project was transported here to cover the quarry. You can extend this trip by paddling to or from Port Ludlow, about 3 miles away.

**Duration:** Part day.

**Rating:** *Protected* to *Moderate.*

**Navigation Aids:** SeaTrails 105; NOAA chart 18445 SC (1:80,000; see 1:40,000 inset).

**Planning Considerations:** The steep, rocky shoreline outside the bay's entrance can create rough conditions during high tides due to refracted waves and offers few places to land. Aside from the boat ramp, there are no public shorelines along this route. Low tides can make launching from Mats Mats Bay a muddy endeavor.

## GETTING THERE AND LAUNCHING

From State Route 104, turn north on Paradise Bay Road just west of the Hood Canal Bridge. Drive 6 miles to the intersection with Oak Bay Road. Turn right and go another 2 miles, then turn right on Verner Avenue. Drive 0.5 mile to the launching ramp on Mats Mats Bay. The launch has a restroom, picnic table, a big parking lot, an antiquated boat ramp, and a floating dock. Put in on the beach to the right of the dock. No parking permits needed.

*Beautiful, protected Mats Mats Bay*

## ROUTE

Mats Mats Bay and its entrance offer plenty to see on their own. You can make a 2-mile loop following the shore, passing moored recreational boats, commercial fishing boats, and beach homes. The entrance to the bay narrows to less than 100 yards, with range markers to guide larger craft through.

A quarry and gravel operation occupies the real estate for almost a mile south of the bay entrance. Though there are a few beaches unaffected by the work, do not go ashore. Paddle out to Klas and Colvos Rocks if the weather isn't too windy, as these are great to explore on calm days. The rocks can be covered in harbor seals; keep a distance of at least 100 yards. As I paddled by on a trip there once, a dozen seals entered the water and followed me discreetly for a half mile. Enjoy views to the north of Marrowstone Island and to the south of Foulweather Bluff and Hood Canal. Colvos Rocks includes the largest of

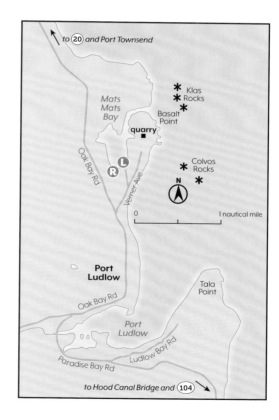

the offshore rocks in the area, making it a poor place to get out of your boat—the big rock is about fifty feet across, barren, and too steep for easy landings. The round-trip to Colvos Rocks from the Mats Mats Bay boat launch is 3 miles. You might also paddle south toward Port Ludlow.

# 40. **Indian Island**

Located less than two hours from Seattle, Indian and Marrowstone Islands are a quick getaway with scenery and paddling opportunities rivaling those of the San Juan Islands to the north. Somewhat off the beaten path, the islands provide solitude and miles of seemingly untouched beaches, tidal estuaries, protected coves, and a rural landscape. The southern section of Indian Island is known for its sandy beaches, interesting geological features, and madronas that overhang the shore. Swift currents run below the bridge connecting the island to the mainland, giving paddlers a free ride. The rest of the island is home to the US Naval Undersea Warfare Engineering Station, which is off-limits to the public. The naval base won a conservation award for management of its wildlands, and there's little visual evidence of any base at all. Two Cascadia Marine Trail sites are on Marrowstone Island and a third can be found on the mainland in Oak Bay Park.

Previously, Indian and Marrowstone Islands were known as Craven Peninsula and then later as the Scow Peninsula. In 1841, the Wilkes Expedition noted that Indian Island was connected to

*Looking across Port Townsend Canal from Indian Island County Park*

the mainland by a 450-foot-long gravel beach that stood three feet above the high-tide mark near the current location of Oak Bay Park. The Chimakum used to portage their canoes across this gravel bar; a Wilkes Expedition chart shows a village on it. The land was removed in 1915 to create the current channel and enhance commercial boating operations. Ferry service across the channel started in 1920 and ended when the bridge was built in 1952.

**Duration:** Full day to overnight.

**Rating:** *Protected*, *Moderate*, or *Exposed*. The *Moderate* route involves some fast-water paddling and possible tide rips for a short distance. *Exposed* paddling is on the east side of Marrowstone Island when the wind is strong.

**Navigation Aids:** SeaTrails WA 103, 105; NOAA charts 18423 SC (1:80,000), 18471 (1:40,000), 18464 (1:20,000); Port Townsend tide table and Deception Pass current table with corrections for Port Townsend Canal.

**Planning Considerations:** The current direction in Port Townsend Canal isn't always what you think. Consult local tide tables. At low tide, the portage is at least 300 yards of tide flats; high tide reduces it to as little as 75 feet. Make sure to stay 200 yards off the naval base on Indian Island.

## GETTING THERE AND LAUNCHING

From the Seattle ferries, follow signs to the Hood Canal Bridge. As soon as you cross the bridge, take the first right onto Paradise Bay Road. Follow it north and take a right onto Oak Bay Road (State Route 116). Keep following Oak Bay Road, eventually passing Mats Mats Bay (see Trip 39), and continue north. In a few miles, you'll see signs for Fort Flagler–Marrowstone and Indian Island. Take a right on Flagler Road.

From Port Hadlock, take Oak Bay Road (SR 116) south until you see the Fort Flagler–Marrowstone and Indian Island signs. Take a left on Flagler Road.

**Oak Bay County Park:** The first possible launch is from Portage Way, just before the turn to Indian and Marrowstone Islands if you're headed north. Oak Bay County Park provides access to the southern end of the islands and Port Townsend Canal. It also has one Cascadia Marine Trail camp area with a pit toilet and water. No fires are allowed. Choose your tent location wisely for high tides. Fort Flagler is 7.8 miles away and Port Hadlock is 1.6 miles away. Watch for boating traffic, fast current, and large rips in the canal. Use eddies to move up current.

**Port Hadlock Marina and Ramp:** This launch is on Oak Bay Road (SR 116) just before the turn to Indian and Marrowstone Islands if you're headed south. It's one block south of Port Hadlock's town center. Take a left on Lower Hadlock Road and follow it to the marina. Park on the dirt lot north of the Ajax Café by the estuary. There is one portable toilet by the lagoon. Launch at the beach between the dock and boat ramp. This puts you on the north side of the Port Townsend Canal.

**Portage Beach:** Take Flagler Road off Oak Bay (SR 116) and follow it over the canal bridge. After you cross the bridge, take an immediate right into the lot at Portage Beach. Watch for speedy traffic along Flagler Road. The boat carry is down a steep, grassy, 100-yard hill. A portable toilet is provided but no fires are allowed. The park, which is managed by the Washington Department of Fish and Wildlife, has extensive sandy beaches to the south, great views, and access to the canal. Public access ends and naval property begins 25 yards past the bridge to the north. Keep 200 yards off the shore beyond this point. Display your Discover Pass in the lot.

**Indian Island County Park:** Drive approximately 0.75 mile beyond the canal bridge. Ample parking and two toilets are available. Launch on sand or gravel beaches, which are dry for a considerable distance at low tide. Plan your launch or take-out for higher tides. This is also a popular clamming spot.

**Isthmus Park:** Follow Flagler Road to the south end of Indian Island and park off the right side of the road just before the isthmus that connects both islands. Enjoy views north to Port Townsend and south toward Mats Mats Bay. Watch for fast drivers here as they come off the hill on Marrowstone Island. Previous editions of this book recommended running the current through the causeway culvert below the road. Since the last edition, the old culvert under the roadway has been removed and a bridge now connects Indian and Marrowstone Islands. The new, more-open flow of water has reduced the number of lower-tide mudflats. The maximum water speed on bigger tidal exchanges is about 2 knots and is similarly timed with Port Townsend Canal. Local paddlers recommend using no longer than a 7-inch rudder or fin to avoid getting stuck. You can portage over the bridge if needed but watch for speedy traffic.

**Mystery Bay State Park on Marrowstone Island:** Use Mystery Bay State Park to access the water by Nordland. The park area has ample parking, vault toilets, picnic tables, easy access to a sand-and-gravel beach, and a boat ramp. Take Flagler Road north up Marrowstone Island and turn left just past Nordland and the oyster farm. A Discover Pass is required to park here. At the time of writing, the old Nordland General Store nearby was closed due to a recent fire.

**Fort Flagler State Park:** Take Flagler Road to the north end of Marrowstone Island and into Fort Flagler State Park. You have three options to launch here:

For Kilisut Harbor, take a left inside the park, following signs to the camping area. Launch from the boat ramp nearby. A Discover Pass is required for day and overnight parking. There is plenty of camping available here, including three Cascadia Marine Trail sites (water access only) on the east side of the campground. No fires are allowed. A small seasonal store, toilets, and other amenities make this a full-service launch.

The second launch from Fort Flagler is on the southeast side of the park. As you enter the park, take a right at the four-way stop on Wansboro Road and follow it to the beach. There is room for a few parking spots; the sandy beach is a short distance away. The wharf that used to be at this location was recently removed. There are no facilities.

The third launch is from Marrowstone Point south of the lighthouse. As you enter the park, continue on Flagler Road past the buildings and parade grounds, following signs to the lighthouse. After you go down the hill on the one-lane road to the beach, park on your right. Restrooms and picnic tables are provided. Display your Discover Pass. Watch for strong tidal currents off the point and ship waves on the east side of the point.

## ROUTES

**Indian Island Circumnavigation:** *Moderate*. The total paddling distance is 11 miles. Launch from any of the sites listed above: Oak Bay County Park, Port Hadlock, Portage Beach, or Indian Island County Park.

Indian Island is an interesting blend of attractive "forbidden fruit," a restricted government property surrounded by accessible public lands. Most of the island is occupied by the Naval Undersea Warfare Engineering Station, which stores ships' ammunition, reportedly nonnuclear. Piers and buildings line the northwestern shore, but the remainder of the shoreline is remarkably pristine. The navy employs a wildlife biologist to manage the island's habitat, and the station won a Department of Defense conservation award for its management.

Landings within the station boundaries are strictly prohibited and you must stay 200 yards offshore. Nonetheless, cruising along the station's shorelines makes for a pleasant interlude in a largely undisturbed environment. Plus, there are plenty of places not on navy property to stretch your legs. Look for river otters along the rocky shores.

The southern end of Indian Island, on both sides, has interesting sandstone formations with embedded nodules of harder rock that have eroded into studded surfaces, some forming tiny bridges like handles. Look for these south of Bishops Point on the Kilisut Harbor side and just north of the Port Townsend Canal on the west side.

If you are launching from the southern end of Indian Island, Mystery Bay State Park on Marrowstone Island is the first chance for a shore stop, about 2 miles north of the improved waterway and bridge now connecting both islands. Toilets and picnic facilities are available. Mystery Bay is lined with recreational boats, beach homes, and has a coastal New England feel.

*Indian Island shore and boulders along Port Townsend Canal*

Following the east shore of Indian Island south involves an hour or so of paddling along shores with no opportunities to get out. A good plan is to take a stretch break at Fort Flagler beforehand. It has a wonderful beach over a mile in length. In addition to a Cascadia Marine Trail camp area, Fort Flagler has picnic facilities, bathrooms with running water, and a concession stand that sells snacks during the summer. The Cascadia Marine Trail tent sites are secluded in the woods just east of the main campground.

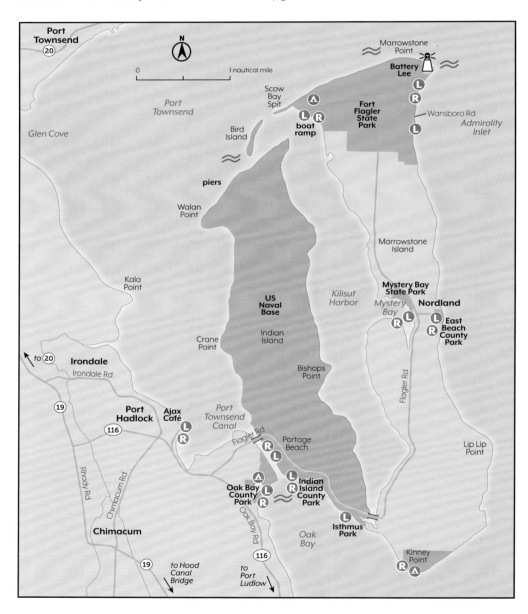

At the northwestern edge of Kilisut Harbor, arrive at a low sand spit covered with grass and connected to the Fort Flagler Park at low tide. Called Bird or Rat Island locally, its southern end is a popular place for large groups of seals to haul out. Paddling out through the channel, you may find yourself surrounded by fifty or more of them. On the flood, enjoy a light tide rip through a break in the spit. At the time of this writing, a bird flu was present, and it was suggested not to land on the island. Check for wildlife alerts prior to paddling here.

Be sure to honor the navy's requirement to stay 600 feet away from their docks at Walan Point and at Crane Point a mile to the south. Also remember that you must stay at least 200 yards away from any naval vessel. Just beyond Crane Point is an inviting park facility, but it's for naval personnel only.

From here, you could make a 1.5-mile paddle west to Port Hadlock before entering Port Townsend Canal. Port Hadlock has a private marina and the very popular shoreside Ajax Café; the town's center is a few blocks up from the water. The Northwest School of Wooden Boatbuilding has a campus across from the Ajax Café.

The navy's property line on Indian Island turns inland at the midpoint of a shell beach just north of the narrows of Port Townsend Canal. Immediately south are excellent stops ashore in the beginning of the county's parklands. Also south of this beach is the old Indian–Marrowstone ferry landing.

Port Townsend Canal (or PT Canal) has currents of up to 3 knots. Shore eddies form, except between the jetties at the southern end, where you have no choice but to fight the current if it is against you. If the water level is high enough, you can opt to paddle behind the jetty on the Indian Island side. Fairly large rips can form in the channel at the downstream end of the narrows, which may be dangerous for paddlers inexperienced with rough water. The canal's current is difficult to predict and often runs opposite to what you would expect, but good eddies can be found along both shores. Use them to your advantage when the current is running in the opposite direction. You can find a restroom up the hill at Portage Beach just south of the bridge.

Adjoining the southern end of the canal are Oak Bay County Park on the west side and Indian Island County Park on the east side. The sand and gravel tide flats are productive clamming areas. Both parks have outhouses, picnic tables, and fresh water. Oak Bay County Park is also the location of a Cascadia Marine Trail group area; it has two tent sites in summer and one from October 31 to May 1. Beware, during higher tides the sites may flood.

From the south entrance of Port Townsend Canal, it is a brief paddle back if your start was at Oak Bay County Park or Indian Island County Park.

A paddle-in-only Cascadia Marine Trail camp area is located at Kinney Point, on the south end of Marrowstone Island. Kinney Point has two tent sites and a vault toilet; no fires are allowed.

**Fort Flagler State Park and Kilisut Harbor:** *Protected*. Choose your own paddling distance. This area is popular for short trips in the warmer protected waters. It is also a good place for new paddlers to work on their skills. Be careful of the entrance channel to Kilisut Harbor, which can run at more than 1 knot.

# 41. **Marrowstone Island**

Previously named "Marrow-Stone Point" in 1792 by explorer George Vancouver, Marrowstone Island became known for the production of premium turkeys between 1920 and the 1940s. On the north end of Marrowstone is Fort Flagler, a coastal defense fort constructed in 1898 to keep invaders from attacking Puget Sound. Now a 784-acre state park, Fort Flagler provides hiking trails, beach access, building rentals for educational groups, and fortifications to explore. The rest of the island is composed of beautiful rural farms, vacation homes, and an oyster farm. Located less than two hours from Seattle, Marrowstone Island is easy to access for a quick escape.

**Duration:** Full day to overnight.

**Rating:** *Protected*, *Moderate*, or *Exposed*. The *Protected* route includes mellow Kilisut Harbor and Scow Bay; the *Moderate* route involves some fast-water paddling and pos-sible tide rips for a short distance. The *Exposed* route includes Marrowstone Point for its fast current, tide rips, and surf from shipping traffic, as well as the east side of Marrow-stone Island for wind and ship wakes.

**Navigation Aids:** SeaTrails WA 103, 105; NOAA charts 18423 SC (1:80,000), 18471 (1:40,000), 18464 (1:20,000); Port Townsend tide table and Deception Pass current table with corrections for Port Townsend Canal.

**Planning Considerations:** Plan your travel for the currents and for wind on the east side. Shipping traffic and high wind can produce large surf on Marrowstone Point and along the eastern side of the island.

## GETTING THERE AND LAUNCHING

From the Seattle ferries, follow signs to the Hood Canal Bridge. As soon as you cross the bridge, take the first right onto Paradise Bay Road. Follow it north and take a right onto Oak Bay Road (State Route 116). Keep following Oak Bay Road, eventually passing Mats Mats Bay (see Trip 39), and continue north. In a few miles, you'll see signs for Fort Flagler–Marrowstone and Indian Islands. Take a right on Flagler Road.

From Port Hadlock, take Oak Bay Road (SR 116) south until you see the Fort Flagler–Marrowstone and Indian Island signs. Take a left on Flagler Road.

After crossing the Port Townsend Canal bridge, follow Flagler Road down Indian Island and across the narrow isthmus connecting both islands. Curve north (left) on Flagler Road, driving past rural farms. In Nordland, you can rent kayaks for Mystery Bay, a quiet bay with an oyster-production business, fishing boats, and eclectic beach homes. About 300 yards north of Nordland, you will pass Mystery Bay State Park, which provides a protected launch for Kilisut Harbor.

**Fort Flagler State Park:** Continue north on Flagler Road to Fort Flagler State Park. Launch from the campground boat ramp (at Marrowstone Point south of the lighthouse), via the south-

*The Marrowstone Point Lighthouse lies at the end of the driftwood-lined beach.*

east side of the park from Wansboro Road, or on the west side of the park near Scow Bay Spit. Display your Discover Pass when parking.

**East Beach:** To launch from the east side of the island, go past Nordland about a quarter mile and take a right on East Beach Road. This will take you to the beach in about a mile. This is a day-use facility with picnic tables and a sandy beach.

If you prefer, launch at Oak Bay or Port Hadlock instead of driving to Marrowstone Island. Also consider Portage Beach or Indian Island County Park for launching from Indian Island.

## ROUTE

The circumnavigation of the island is 15 miles. Launch from any of the sites listed above and work with the currents and wind. There is a Cascadia Marine Trail (CMT) site on the northwest corner of Fort Flagler State Park and on the south side of the island on Kinney Point. (An alternative CMT site is at Oak Bay County Park on the mainland.)

Starting from the south end of Indian Island, head southeast past several estuaries with sloughs that empty to mudflats at low tides. As you near Marrowstone, the shore begins to rise to a medium bluff with a few homes above. On the southernmost part of Marrowstone Island, look for a seasonal stream, which is the location for Kinney Point, a CMT camp area. The trail leads you to a kayak storage rack. Kinney Point has a vault toilet, two CMT sites, and is best reached on higher tides to avoid a long carry. Campfires are not allowed, nor is sleeping on the beach. Round the point and head north along Puget Sound. Lip Lip Point is about three-quarters of a mile past Kinney Point. Known for its rocky shores, this is a great place for tide pooling. A few miles past Lip Lip, reach East Beach, a county park and launch. Few facilities are available. For the next several miles, high bluffs rise above the beach, providing solitude and empty beaches, even on the nicest summer days.

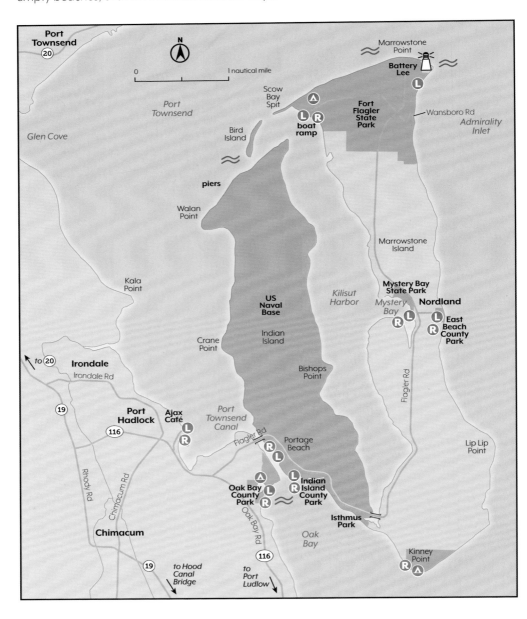

As you near the lighthouse on Marrowstone Point, a wide and sandy crescent beach indicates you have entered Fort Flagler State Park. A low sandy point juts out into Puget Sound below the bluffs, giving the lighthouse an extended view into Admiralty Inlet. Fishing and beachcombing are popular near the point. Give anglers extra space when passing by. There are no facilities aside from a restroom and picnic table. An eddy occurs on the south side of the point on flood tides, and on ebbs expect a strong pull to the point. Give the point a wide berth in heavy wind, which can produce chop near the shore. Keep your eye on passing ships, as they can produce a sizeable surf wave on the north side.

A noisy tide rip north of the point can be heard from the bluffs above. Keep your distance if you're not comfortable with rough water—but for those who are, it's a fun source of standing waves.

On the north side of Marrowstone Point where the bluff rises above the beach again, look for a concrete bunker hanging from the cliff. This is the 1903-era Battery Lee, a searchlight battery with dark tunnels that I once enjoyed while playing hooky at a music camp there in the 1970s. Above Battery Lee you can find several larger coastal defense fortifications once equipped with twelve-inch guns designed to fire a shell 15 miles into Admiralty Inlet. Dark tunnels and slit-window pill boxes make for an interesting side trip. A rough trail in the woods below Battery Lee leads up the hill. Above the bluffs, gain a commanding view of Port Townsend, Whidbey Island, and Mount Rainer far to the south.

High bluffs continue along Marrowstone Point all the way to the state park campground a few miles west. Here the flood current splits in half as it hits the shore, sending some to the east and the rest to the west. Occasional chunks of concrete can be found on the beach, remnants of the fort above. The beach is mostly gravel, with some sand and larger rocks. The state park has full facilities, including a small store.

Birders will enjoy Scow Bay Spit, which extends east into Kilisut Harbor from Fort Flagler. On a flood, shoot the current through the gap in the spit and head south toward the mostly bucolic Kilisut Harbor. From here, choose whether to turn south into Kilisut Harbor or continue west to go around Indian Island. (see Trip 40, Indian Island).

For an alternative day trip, launch from East Beach and paddle to Marrowstone Point. Or launch from Indian Island or Oak Bay on a low tide to enjoy the tide pooling at Lip Lip Point. If you like to surf, launch at Marrowstone Point and time southbound shipping traffic for surf on the east side of the point below Battery Lee. Bring a helmet if you do; the beach here is rocky.

# 42. Port Townsend to Point Wilson

Explorer Captain George Vancouver noted that the current location of Port Townsend, located on the northern tip of Quimper Peninsula, had a "fine deep harbor." Prior to Vancouver, long-time residents were primarily members of the Klallam (or S'Klallam) Tribe. They called the location Kah Tai. Like many towns in the Puget Sound area, Port Towsend (or "PT," as the locals call it) got its start in the 1850s. By the 1880s, it was the hub for commerce in the region. Prior to development, the shore was primarily below the bluff with a sandy spit wrapping around it. This area was built out to create the town and docks. In 1887, Tacoma was chosen to be the northwest link to the transcontinental line of the Union Pacific railroad. Soon commerce began to wane in PT and during the 1893 depression, the town's population plummeted from seven thousand to two thousand nearly overnight. In 1898, the US government chose PT to be part of the "Triangle of Fire," a ring of coastal defense forts aimed at keeping invading ships at bay. Fort Worden's guns aimed across the Strait of Juan de Fuca for years until they were rendered obsolete by the advancement of airplane technology. In the 1970s, PT's property values were cheap, which attracted artists of all kinds who built a strong creative community. Today Fort Worden's Centrum organization uses the former fort's grounds to bring world-class cultural events to the area, including a fiddling festival, a jazz and blues festival, and a much-renowned film festival.

**Duration:** Part day to full day.

**Rating:** *Protected*, *Moderate*, or *Exposed*. In some conditions, waters are *Protected* and in others they are slightly *Moderate*, making this a good place for new and experienced kayakers alike. The paddling is easy and scenic with few likely challenges.

**Navigation Aids:** SeaTrails WA 103; NOAA charts 18465 (1:80,000), 18471 (1:40,000); Port Townsend tide table (subtract 30 minutes).

**Planning Considerations:** Wind from the south or northwest can affect this route. Ship wakes may break on the shore inside Point Wilson.

## GETTING THERE AND LAUNCHING

**Port Townsend Boat Haven:** Entering Port Townsend on State Route 20 (Sims Way), drive to the bottom of the big hill toward downtown. At the bottom, take a right onto Haines Place. Follow this through the shipyard to the water. You'll see a small shorefront parking strip with beach access. Parking is day-use only. Watch for bicycles on the trail along the waterfront. At low tides, the carry to the beach can be about 100 yards. Visit https://portofpt.com/boat-haven-marina for additional information.

**Point Hudson Marina Launch:** Located on the southeast corner of downtown by a full-service marina improved in 2023, this is a great launch for paddling near the city center. You can also use it to access destinations such as Fort Flagler or Point Wilson. The launch has plenty of parking, restrooms, laundry, showers, and camping. Restaurants and other services are a short walk from the marina. Watch for breaking waves on the point where the launch beach rounds the corner east toward the waterfront. Visit https://portofpt.com/point-hudson-marina-rv-park for additional information.

**Fort Worden State Park:** From downtown Port Townsend, take Water Street through the city center. Just before Point Hudson Marina, take a left on Monroe Street. Follow Monroe north and bear right onto Jackson Street. Jackson goes up the hill and curves left into Q Street. Take a right on Walnut Street and follow it as it curves left into W Street. Look for signs to enter Fort Worden State Park. Once in the park, follow signs to the beach. As you go down the hill to the

*1898-era gun battery at Fort Worden with views of Port Townsend in the distance*

beach, park by the wharf and small boat marina. A boat ramp leads to the water in a very protected launch; the wharf protects it on three sides. Three Cascadia Marine Trail sites are in the main camping area below the bluff south of the dock. Fireplaces are available; toilets and water are opposite the pier; and showers are in the campground. A seasonal food concession stand is by the Marine Science Center.

### ROUTE

If launching from Port Townsend Boat Haven, be cautious of the ferry terminal. Give ferries a wide berth and never cross in front of a moving boat.

Enjoy views of downtown historic Port Townsend and its grand Victorian architecture. A town with deep roots in boatbuilding, you may see various types of wooden boats moored or sailing nearby. On a sunny day, look for the Cascades to the east and the steep sandstone bluffs of Marrowstone Island and Fort Flagler to the south.

As you paddle west past Point Hudson, the bluffs begin to rise majestically above Admiralty Inlet. Madrona trees stretch out over the embankment with a few homes above. About a mile from downtown, the bluffs lower to the border of Fort Worden State Park. From the water, you can see the old fort's officer's quarters above you. The beach below is sandy and crescent shaped. A sandy beach on the south side of the quartermaster's wharf makes a good rest stop. You can find a restroom across the street and in summer a small café offers basic snacks. Beyond the wharf, the sandy beach curves toward Point Wilson and its historic lighthouse, built in 1915. Prominently placed on the tip of the point, the lighthouse can be seen for miles even without its blinking light. On busy summer days, anglers can be seen lined up around the point—give them plenty of room. Ship wakes wrap around the point and into the bay providing surfable waves. Land

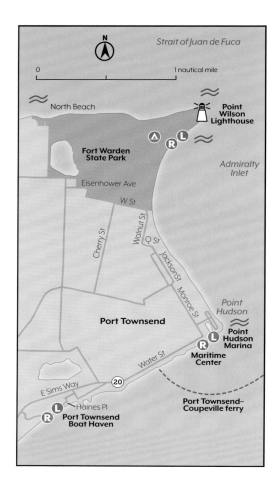

N

Strait of Juan de Fuca

0          1 nautical mile

North Beach

Point Wilson Lighthouse

Fort Warden State Park

Admiralty Inlet

Eisenhower Ave

W St

Walnut St

Cherry St

Q St

Jackson St

Monroe St

Port Townsend

Point Hudson

Point Hudson Marina

Maritime Center

Water St

E Sims Way

20

Haines Pl

Port Townsend Boat Haven

Port Townsend–Coupeville ferry

anywhere along here to take a stroll to the lighthouse or to explore the pre–World War I gun emplacements on the point. On the forested bluff above the beach, several rows of concrete gun emplacements provide a commanding view of the Strait of Juan de Fuca and Admiralty Inlet. Check the Jefferson County Historical Society's website for more information: jchsmuseum.org.

Point Wilson was known by the Chimacum as Kam-kam-ho and the S'Klallam called it Kam-Kam. The waters off Point Wilson can get very rough from wind and ocean swell. Don't venture around the point unless you have strong experience in tidal currents, rough water, and surf. A noticeable tide rip occurs northwest of the point—fun surfable standing waves for some, a hazard to others. Several kayakers have needed to be rescued off the point in recent years. Currents can pull unsuspecting paddlers into the frigid, fast-moving waters of Admiralty Inlet. Experienced paddlers might want to venture around the point toward North Beach on the western border of the park. The beach in between is composed of gravel and boulders. Watch for breaking waves at North Beach. Current can run a few knots along this stretch. Plan your trip with the current to avoid a long slog back to your launch.

# 43. Sequim Bay, Protection Island, and Diamond Point Loop

Three-quarters of the seabirds in Puget Sound nest on Protection Island, including about seventeen thousand pairs of rhinoceros auklets, glaucous-winged gulls, pelagic cormorants, tufted puffins, pigeon guillemots, double-crested cormorants, and black oystercatchers. The island is also a pupping and hauling area for about six hundred harbor seals. The word "Sequim" comes from Sxckiyan, the name of the S'Klallam village once situated at the entrance to the bay. Some translate this as "quiet waters," but the actual meaning is "place for going to shoot," a reference to the rich local hunting areas. The village reportedly dated back six hundred years but in 1875 had just ten lodges and forty residents, far fewer than in previous times due to epidemics brought over by early European explorers. Explorer George Vancouver named Protection Island, noting how it protected the entry to Discovery Bay. With a colorful history, the government owned and sold Protection Island in the 1860s. It was a farm for a while, and then in the 1940s an out-of-control beach fire burned the entire island. The island almost became a 1100-unit housing development in 1968, until environmentalists stopped construction. In 1988, the island became a National Wildlife Refuge partially managed by the US Fish and Wildlife Service and the Washington State Department of Fish and Wildlife. To protect wildlife, there is no public access on the island, and paddlers must stay 200 yards offshore. The last time I was there, I could hear the island birds a mile away at Diamond Point, and I saw a whale breaching in the distance. Read more about Sequim Bay history online at giventoglide.com/-sequim-bay.html.

**Duration:** Part day to full day.

**Rating:** *Protected*, *Moderate*, or *Exposed*. Confined waters and alongshore routes make this a good place for new kayakers. The paddling is easy and scenic with few likely challenges.

**Navigation Aids:** SeaTrails WA 103; NOAA charts 18465 (1:80,000), 18471 (1:40,000); Port Townsend tide table (subtract 30 minutes).

**Planning Considerations:** A rising tide is best for exploring the lagoon behind Gibson Spit in Sequim Bay. The crossing to Protection Island can involve current, strong wind, and chop. Stay 200 yards offshore from Protection Island; landing is not permitted.

## GETTING THERE AND LAUNCHING

**John Wayne Marina:** The launch, on land that was donated to the county by John Wayne, is off US Highway 101 about 2 miles east of Sequim. Turn right (if going west) on White Feather Way and follow signs about half a mile to the marina. Use the ramp on the west side for launching. The full-service marina has a café, and there is a $15 launch fee payable at a pay machine by the ramp.

**Sequim Bay State Park:** The park lies on both sides of US 101 about 4.75 miles southeast of Sequim. Turn east off the highway, toward the water, and follow the road downhill through the campground to the boat launch. There is parking, a boat ramp, and stairs leading to the beach. A Discover Pass is required to park.

**Marlyn Nelson County Park/Port Williams:** The park is reached by turning north from US 101 onto Brown Road about a half mile west of Sequim. Drive 1 mile to Port Williams Road, turn right, and go about 2.5 miles to the park. Launch from the gravel beach or boat ramp. Parking, restrooms, and picnic tables are available.

**Diamond Point Launch:** From US 101 near Gardiner, turn north onto Diamond Point Road. Follow the road all the way to the public access beach launch, located between two houses.

*Sequim Bay and palisade posts in beach from the Sxckiyan S'Klallam village once located there. (On Battelle private property.)*

Unload your gear and then park along the west side of the road across from the estuary. No facilities available.

## ROUTES

**Sequim Bay:** *Protected.* Beginning at either Sequim Bay State Park or John Wayne Marina, paddle north along the beach. Shores between these points and the bay's entrance are wooded, with occasional homes above the gravel beaches. About 1 mile north of the marina, pass Battelle Institute's laboratories, located just inside the dredged entrance that skirts Kiapot Point at the end of Travis Spit. The spit is a long sand-and-gravel obstruction that extends from the east shore nearly to the bay's western side. Just north is a smaller one, Gibson Spit, running perpendicular to Travis Spit and further constricting the entrance. At the laboratories, you can either cut across to explore the north side of Travis Spit or continue along the shore to the lagoon and Gibson Spit. This is a narrow, dredged channel, so stay close to shore to ensure larger boats have the room they need.

If a strong flood tide is running, you may see current flowing past John Wayne Marina. From the marina, use the shore north of John Wayne Marina to find eddies to paddle toward the spits.

Use the same tactic to return to the marina if the ebb current is swift. The two spits have public tidelands: on the north side of Travis Spit and the east side of Gibson Spit. The areas above the mean high-tide line on both spits are the property of Battelle Institute. Their scientists do research here from time to time and they ask that you not trespass.

The lagoon is a fine place to ride in on a rising tide starting at about midtide. The bird-viewing is good and has a pastoral backdrop of farmlands. At high tide, you should be able to follow the tidal channels for a mile or so. The tidelands in the lagoon are also research areas, as is the drying shoal called "Middle Ground" south of Travis Spit. Stay in your boat except on the public tidelands. Though shellfish are plentiful in Sequim Bay, they cannot be harvested because of contamination.

The route from Gibson Spit to Marlyn Nelson Park follows the gravel beach north. Bluffs begin at the foot of the spit less than 1 mile south of the park. The park's present site was once Port Williams, where steamers called with freight and passenger service for the community of Sequim.

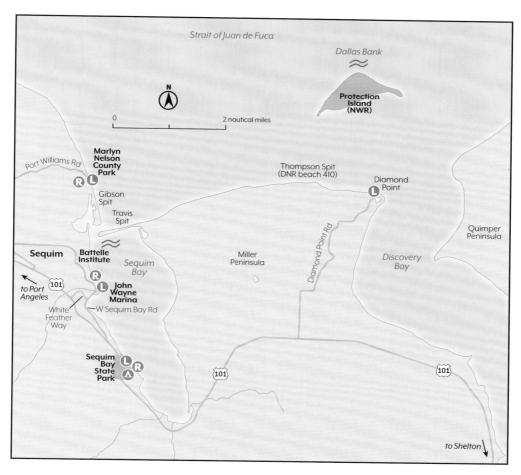

To access Protection Island from here, paddle alongside the undeveloped shore of Miller Peninsula, and if winds are low, begin your crossing to the island. As you get closer, you'll hear more and more bird sounds.

**From Diamond Point:** *Protected* or *Moderate*. Launch on the public put-in between houses. Head west along the shore past the houses. Note: The beach access road seen after launching is a private road locked by the local community. Following the shore, you'll soon reach DNR beach 410, also called Thompson Spit. This 2710-foot-long public beach makes a great rest stop. Explore an abandoned building alongside driftwood and the tidal estuary behind the beach. From here, either continue past the spit to explore the empty, untouched beaches of Miller Peninsula, possibly entering Sequim Bay, or if the conditions are right, start your crossing to Protection Island.

**Circumnavigation of Protection Island:** *Moderate* or *Exposed*. The crossing is exposed to swell and wind, which can make this paddle difficult for those not familiar with rough-water paddling. Staying 200 yards off the shore of the island, start by going around the spit that points southwest. You may see seals ducking below the water off the spit and a few brave ones following your progress. The island immediately rises to a sheer cliff facing north. The cliffs stay high until the far northeastern shore of the island. Watch for tide rips and surf caused by wind or ship wakes along the western edge, also called Dallas Bank. It's very shallow here and for some distance offshore. The east end has a long spit with an artificial harbor that opens on the southeast side.

**Alternative Route:** *Moderate* or *Exposed*. Start from Sequim Bay, paddle through Travis and Gibson Spits to halfway down Miller Peninsula. Cross to Protection Island and paddle from west to east on its northern side, then cross over to Thompson Spit on Miller Peninsula. Work your way back along the peninsula's beaches to Sequim Bay.

# 44. **Dungeness Spit**

This 5-mile-long spit is a National Wildlife Refuge set aside for waterfowl and shorebirds. As many as ten thousand birds winter in the refuge, particularly the black brant. Sandpipers and other shorebirds scour its beaches for food. Shallow Dungeness Bay, south of the spit, harbors clams and oysters, as well as the crab that takes its name. Captain George Vancouver visited here in 1792. It was once called Shipwreck Spit for the many shipwrecks that have occurred along its length. The Dungeness Lighthouse, built in 1857, was the first light station in the inland waters of the region. Originally a hundred feet tall, it was later shortened due to structural issues. The S'Klallam people lived along the Dungeness River for thousands of years. In 1872, they were forced by European American homesteaders to live for one difficult year on the spit; they were later forced to live on a reservation elsewhere. In 1868, the Tsimshian people were camping on the spit after coming back from harvesting hops in the Puyallup Valley. The S'Klallam people attacked them, killing everyone except one woman who took refuge in the lighthouse. The lighthouse is now managed by the New Dungeness Light Station Association, which rents out the building to volunteer lightkeepers.

**Duration:** Part day to full day. No camping is allowed along these shorelines. Landing is only permitted at the lighthouse and you must have a reservation.

**Rating:** *Protected* or *Moderate*, depending on route. The *Moderate* route may involve exposure to rough seas, beach surf, and tide rips.

**Navigation Aids:** SeaTrails WA 103, 301; NOAA chart 18471 (1:40,000); Port Townsend tide table (subtract about 45 minutes).

**Planning Considerations:** Best on higher tides. Tide flats south of the spit and in the lagoon are extensive at low tide. A loop around the spit is not possible due to restrictions on crossing the spit. The only landing permitted is at the lighthouse and it requires a (free) reservation. Call 360-457-8451 to reserve. Winds can be strong on the spit due to lack of cover. Prevailing winds in summer are from the northwest and in winter from the south to southeast. Fog is common in August and September. Keep a distance from harbor seals hauled out on shore.

## GETTING THERE AND LAUNCHING

**Cline Spit County Park:** From US Highway 101 in Sequim, turn north on Sequim Avenue and drive 6 miles. This becomes Sequim–Dungeness Way and later Marine Drive. After 6 miles, the spit comes into view on the right. Turn down a side road that drops sharply over the bluff to Cline Spit County Park. Launch from the gravel beach north of the parking area. The ramp has restrooms, garbage cans, and plenty of parking. For additional information, call Clallam County Parks at 360-417-2291.

**Dungeness Boat Launch on Oyster House Road:** This boat ramp is located a half mile east of Cline Spit (see above) off Marine Drive. It has extensive parking, full restrooms, garbage cans, and a covered bird-viewing platform.

An alternative route is to take Kitchen–Dick Road off US 101, west of Sequim. After 3.6 miles, take a right on Lotzgesell Road. After a winding 2.4 miles, take a left on Clark Road and follow it to Marine Drive. Take a right on Marine Drive and go 0.6 mile to the Oyster House Road access; you will see a sign leading to the boat ramp on your left.

No camping is allowed on the spit. The closest camping is at the Dungeness Recreation Area, a Clallam County park not far away. To get there, continue driving west on Marine Drive beyond the turnoff to Cline Spit County Park. Marine Drive turns left and becomes Cays Road. Turn right on Lotzgesell Road and follow it to the park entrance.

You can only land on the spit at the Dungeness Lighthouse—and only between the yellow poles on the southeast side. The end of the spit is off-limits, but it is ok to land on a section of the western beach of the spit. Landing requires a free reservation; call 360-457-8451. There is a $100 fine for landing elsewhere on the spit. Learn more online at newdungenesslighthouse.com/boating-to-the-lighthouse.

**3 Crabs Road:** It is not recommended to launch from 3 Crabs Road, as it is a sensitive recovery area and an extensive mudflat at low tides. The 3 Crabs Restaurant was demolished in 2014.

## ROUTES

**Cline Spit to Dungeness Lighthouse:** *Protected.* A loop trip is not possible since portaging across the spit at the lagoon is not allowed. Always keep outside the "Area Closed" signs. In windy weather, you may prefer to stick to the lagoon north and east of Cline Spit, which affords sheltered paddling and easy viewing of the shoreline south of the spit. The south side of the spit is usually calm except in southerly winds. The waters on either side of Graveyard Spit are closed from October 1 to May 14; call ahead to confirm these dates.

The manned lighthouse at the end of the spit is open to the public for daily tours. The climb up the tower's spiral staircase is worthwhile in its own right; the view along the spit is even better.

**Outer Spit:** *Moderate.* In calm weather, consider paddling around the end of the spit into the Strait of Juan de Fuca proper. The feasibility of this depends on the sea conditions. If the waves are too big, retreat to the south side of the spit. Currents passing over the bar at the end of the spit and interacting with the eddies behind it can produce tide rips on both the flood and ebb. You may be able to avoid them by cutting across close to shore unless seas are rough. Ebb

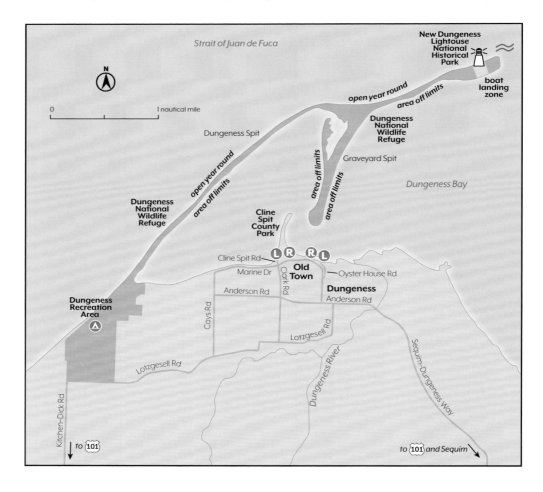

*Dungeness Spit's barren shoreline*

current and Dungeness River flow can pull you into the strait—pay attention to your position and avoid paddling here if you're unfamiliar with paddling in current.

Paddling the northern side of Dungeness Spit gives you a close-up look at this wild, driftwood-strewn beach. Stay as close in as the surf or, where enforced, a 100-yard buffer allows. Keep an eye offshore for wakes from the constant stream of ships passing in and out of the Strait of Juan de Fuca, as these will break farther out. Give beached harbor seals a wide berth in accordance with the Marine Mammal Protection Act.

# 45. Lake Crescent

Carved by glaciers during the last ice age, the 624-feet-deep and 7-mile-long Lake Crescent is the second deepest lake in Washington. The lake was separated from nearby Lake Sutherland by a huge landslide seven thousand years ago. A Klallam Tribe legend supports the theory, stating that Mount Storm King was angered by warring tribes and threw a large boulder, separating the two lakes. Located in Olympic National Park, the lake's clear turquoise waters are the result of a lack of nitrogen, which prevents the growth of algae. The landslide caused two anadromous fish populations to become landlocked, eventually evolving into the blue-colored Beardslee trout (a relative of the rainbow trout) and the Crescenti cutthroat trout. The lake has plenty of options for paddlers of all skill levels, including downwinding in winter for experienced paddlers.

**Duration:** Half day to overnight.

**Rating:** *Protected* to *Moderate*.

**Navigation:** Sea Trails 301; NOAA charts 18465 (1:80,000), 18480 (1:176,253).

**Planning Considerations:** The lake can be glassy and calm, or the westerly or easterly winds can whip up large wind waves. Make sure to check wind apps to plan for a forecast that works for your skills or interest. You have a choice of three boat ramps: at the Log Cabin Resort, at Storm King Ranger Station near the Lake Crescent Lodge, and at Fairholme. Put-ins include the above ramps plus Lake Crescent Lodge, Bovee's Meadow behind the lodge, East Beach, and numerous pullouts along the highway. Lake Crescent Lodge and Log Cabin Resort have paddle craft rentals. Read the National Park Service brochure online at nps.gov/olym/planyourvisit/lake-crescent-area-brochure.htm for more information. Camping is available at Fairholme and Log Cabin Resort.

*Paddlers on Lake Crescent*

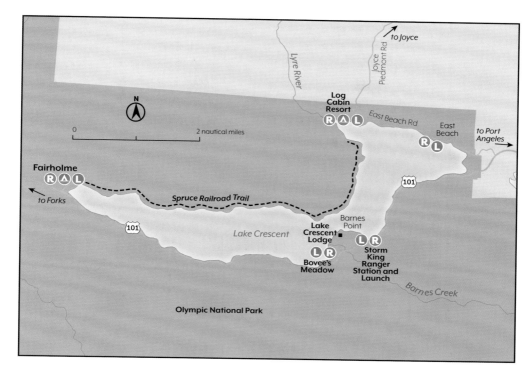

## GETTING THERE AND LAUNCHING

**Bovee's Meadow and Storm King Ranger Station:** The most direct route from Port Angeles is to take US Highway 101 west of town. Reach the lake in 16 miles and in 21 miles reach Lake Crescent Lodge; take a right off the highway here. Then take a left and follow signs to the beach access at Bovee's Meadow or turn right to the boat ramp at the Storm King Ranger Station. From Forks, follow US 101 toward Port Angeles to the lake.

Both launches have restrooms and easy access to Lake Crescent Lodge. While it is possible to launch from the busy parking lot at the lodge, it's usually full in summer and the only restrooms are inside the lodge. Note: Lake Crescent Lodge closes for a period in winter.

**Fairholme Campground:** Fairholme is on the very west end of the lake along Highway 101. From Lake Crescent Lodge, continue west on US 101. From Forks, you'll spot Fairholme as you near the lake. There are restrooms, a dock, boat ramp, camping, and a store in summer.

**Log Cabin Resort:** For a more scenic route—or if coming from Port Angeles, Neah Bay, or Salt Creek Recreation Area—take State Route 112, which follows the Strait of Juan de Fuca to Joyce. Visit the historic Joyce General Store for supplies and the largest candy collection in the state. At the Crescent School, turn onto Joyce Access Road/Joyce Piedmont Road. The road becomes narrow East Beach Road. The Log Cabin Resort, operated by Olympic National Park, is on the right as you reach the lake. The resort has camping, cabins, a store, and a boat ramp.

**East Beach:** Access East Beach Road from either US 101 or from Joyce. The park has a beach, picnic tables, and restrooms.

**ROUTE**

Choose your own route. My favorite is launching from Bovee's Meadow and paddling past the Barnes Creek mouth, then moving along the shore past Lake Crescent Lodge and Barnes Point, and finally crossing over to the north side to follow the scenic, tree-lined shoreline along Spruce Railroad Trail to Devil's Punchbowl. The Punchbowl is a popular swimming spot in summer.

Bovee's Meadow is a nice, protected bay in most wind conditions and gets quite warm in summer. The forested beach is a quiet spot. East Beach provides access from the east side of the lake, away from the busy Lake Crescent Lodge.

Make sure to enjoy the old-growth forest adjacent to Bovee's Meadow and Marymere Falls by the Storm King Ranger Station.

If the wind is blowing, you can usually find a wind-protected section to paddle on since the lake has plenty of contours. During westerly winds, launch at the Storm King boat ramp; Barnes Point will protect this area from winds. Launch in Bovee's Meadow on easterly winds to enjoy a calm bay west of Lake Crescent Lodge. The multiple launch spots make a downwinding shuttle easy.

# 46. Freshwater Bay to Salt Creek Recreation Area

At Freshwater Bay, you can get a taste of Washington's outer coast just a few miles west of Port Angeles. Swells penetrating the Strait of Juan de Fuca are still large enough here to create challenging surf on the beaches. A double sea arch bored by the waves is a testament to the power of the water along this route. Depending on the swell size, landings are possible on many tiny gravel beaches that are inaccessible from the cliffs above. The preservation of the uplands as the Department of Natural Resources's Striped Peak Area makes this one of the wildest stretches along the Strait of Juan de Fuca coast close to Port Angeles. Possible routes include short day trips, a full day trip, or even an overnight.

**Duration:** Part day to overnight. (Add time for a car shuttle or double the route distance for a paddled return.)

**Rating:** *Protected*, *Moderate*, or *Exposed*. Surf and strong currents are likely. Surf may prevent landings along the route and require you to paddle while possibly exposed to the effects of wind and opposing current for the full distance between Crescent and Freshwater Bays.

**Navigation Aids:** SeaTrails WA 301; NOAA chart 18465 (1:80,000); Race Rocks current table (adjusted for Angeles Point) or the Canadian *Current Atlas*.

**Planning Considerations:** Travel with the current direction or at times of little current as forecasted in the current tables or the *Current Atlas*. Alongshore currents can exceed 2 knots. Breaking swells may prevent using inshore eddies to work upstream. A large swell may produce large surf at Crescent Bay and may also prevent landings along the way. Avoid paddling when weather conditions include strong east or west winds for the Strait of Juan de Fuca. If paddling to Crescent Beach, learn surf etiquette to prevent collisions with other surfers. Consider taking a local sea-kayak tour from Adventures Through Kayaking to familiarize yourself with the area prior to paddling on your own.

## GETTING THERE AND LAUNCHING

This route can be accessed from either Freshwater Bay to the east or Salt Creek Recreation Area to the west. Camping is available at Salt Creek Recreation Area and Crescent Beach and RV Park. An easy 9-mile vehicle shuttle can be made between the two parks.

**Freshwater Bay:** Drive on State Route 112 west from its junction with US Highway 101 just a few miles west of Port Angeles. After 5 miles, turn right on Freshwater Bay Road and follow it 3 miles to Freshwater Bay County Park. Launch on a gravel beach to the left of the launching ramp. Yield to anglers launching boats—this launch can be very busy in summer. This day-use park has a vault toilet and picnic tables but no other services. Freshwater Bay is very protected and is a great place to go when other areas are too rough. No parking permits needed.

**Salt Creek Recreation Area:** Continue another 3 miles beyond the turnoff to Freshwater Bay on SR 112 to Camp Hayden Road. Turn right and go 3 miles to Salt Creek Recreation Area. Continue straight into the park for camping, or curve left downhill to the day-use launch. The launch has a restroom and a small parking lot that can fill up on sunny weekends. During low tides, the carry to the beach can be 300 yards. During medium to high tides, you can paddle or take the current of Salt Creek to the beach. The west (left) side of the creek is strictly enforced private property.

Salt Creek Campground provides several campsites, many of which are sited spectacularly at the edge of sea cliffs with panoramic views of the strait, and it offers access to extensive tide pools at Tongue Point. This area has unique coast defense artillery installations that are well worth a visit. Unlike others farther inland, these were built during World War II rather than prior to World War I. You can see Crescent Beach and the sea stack from the viewpoint, which you can reach via the road running through the large gun emplacement. Take the first left in the park to access this route. For additional information, call 360-928-3441 or visit wa-clallamcounty. civicplus.com/Facilities/Facility/Details/Salt-Creek-Recreation-Area-26.

**Crescent Beach and RV Park:** Use the same directions above to access Salt Creek Recreation Area. As you reach the day-use launch, continue driving down the road paralleling the beach. In about one-eighth of a mile, turn left into Crescent Beach and RV Park. You must register to enter the park. Pay a modest fee to use the beach and the facility's showers, restroom, parking, and laundry room. For camping fees and more information, call 1-866-690-3344 or visit crescentbeachrv.com. The RV Park owns all the beach west of Salt Creek adjacent to the recreation area and extending to the other side of the bay, Agate Point, and beyond.

## ROUTES

**Freshwater Bay:** *Protected* or *Moderate*. Freshwater Bay by the boat ramp is very protected, making it great for paddlers of all skill levels. The beach is mostly sandy and surrounded by rocky tide pools on its west (left) side. Even at high tide, the water here is quite shallow 100 yards or so offshore. Give boaters the right-of-way on the boat ramp and below, where they have to use a paddle in the shallow water to get to shore. Paddle near the shore, exploring the rocks and thick-forested tree line above. Northeast winds can affect the bay. This route is popular with local sea kayaking tour companies. Beginner paddlers should not go beyond Observatory Point on the northwest corner of the bay.

Paddle east in Freshwater Bay, exploring the bay's thick kelp beds and empty, rugged beaches below tall, wooded bluffs. East of the boat ramp, find an erratic boulder left by an ice-age glacier. While it can be calm, the bay can also have large waves generated from wind and swell. Strong flood currents and wind can create a bay-wide gyro or eddy that can confuse paddlers unaware of the situation. In this case, a straight line isn't the most efficient way to your destination. Use shore currents and wind to paddle back to the boat ramp.

**Paddling West to Salt Creek Recreation Area:** *Exposed*. The *Exposed* rating is merited by the swells, wind, and current, which can make landings along this 4-mile route difficult. Conditions may require you to paddle from one end to the other without stopping.

Planning with the current is more important here than along other routes where it is possible to use eddies to travel against contrary flows. Unless the swells are very small, surge and shore break prevent using the eddies inside the kelp; this can force you to travel along the outside of the beds, where the current is strong.

Round Observatory Point with care. A large rock pillar called Bachelor Rock is connected to the point at lower tides. Surf and wind waves can break on the rock. Only go between if you know you can make it. The inside section just below the point has a lower depression, allowing for a crossing if you don't mind an occasional scrape or two on your hull. West of the point, a pocket beach with vertical walls reaching up nearly fifty feet appears, giving you a taste of the terrain for the next 3.5 miles. Do not go ashore on this first beach, as it is private property. West of here, the shore is private property, but beaches are accessible. Halfway to Salt Creek, it becomes DNR beach 419, which is public access.

Magnificent sheer rock cliffs topped with cedar, fir, and madronas tower above the many pocket beaches in this section. The rocks extending from Freshwater Bay to Tongue Point are part of the Crescent terrane and are tertiary volcanic and sedimentary rocks that are roughly 52.9 million years old. A local geologist friend described these as *tholeiitic basaltic* and *tuffaceous* rocks.

Swell and wind waves pound the shoreline and fill the surge channels, creating challenging paddling conditions. Paddlers who enjoy "rock gardening" come here to play in the surge as it draws in and out of rock slots, sea caves, and rocks just under the waterline. Local sea-kayak guides keep their inexperienced paddlers far on the outside of the action to safely view from a distance. Extensive kelp beds border this entire coastline.

Look for abundant sea life ranging from birds, harbor seals, and the occasional orca to huge schools of smelt threading through the undersea forests of kelp. Starfish, anemones, and, in summer, jellyfish can be spotted in the waters below you. In calm conditions and at lower

*Kayakers exploring Bachelor Rock off Observatory Point*

tides, take a rest stop or lunch break in one of the many pocket beaches. One of the most interesting landing spots is at the midpoint of the route, near a double arch best reached from a beach just to the east. Near the end of this stretch, a rocky point jutting out to the northwest hides a protected beach called Hidden Cove (also known as Secret Beach), accessed via a trail from Salt Creek Recreation Area. Look for a waterfall in the trees above the beach near the trail. West of here, the shoreline cliffs drop in elevation and their features flatten as you near Tongue Point.

If the conditions are flat and the tide is high, you can paddle over Tongue Point below the cliff. If the tide is low, go around the point, watching for incoming waves. Sometimes on an incoming tide, a scissor wave (two waves colliding from two directions) rips down from the point to the cliff and can throw a kayak in the air a few feet, possibly capsizing it. A few of my friends enjoy this feature and go there specifically for the effect. Less experienced paddlers should go around the point. If surf and breakers off the point are large, go wide around it or even determine if you need to turn around. Several rocks sit just below the waterline on both sides of the point—navigate carefully. Paddlers with rudders or skegs should watch for the thick kelp beds on the west side of the point.

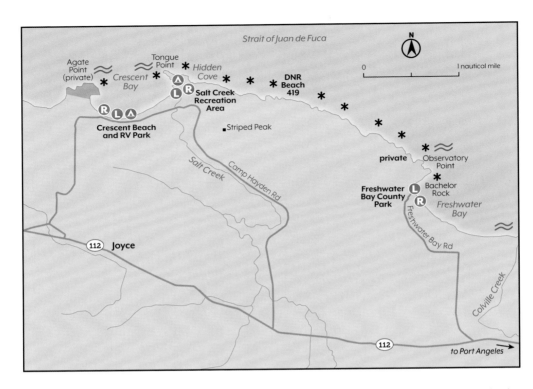

Tongue Point is a marine sanctuary and is also one of the best tide-pooling spots in the state. Do not take any sea life from this area. Two stairways lead to the beach east of the point. If the wave action is light, you can use these to end your trip or take a break.

On the west side of Tongue Point begins Crescent Beach. The park's iconic sea stack lies below the cliffs just inside the point. Another stairway leads down from the park onto this side of the point; this access is too steep and narrow for hauling out gear. The western edge of the bay was a thriving logging town in the late nineteenth century with several hundred residents, a modern motel, a saloon, a store, and a long wharf where Mosquito Fleet ferries landed. Remnants of the wharf can be seen at low tides.

To enter Crescent Beach if there's no wave action, paddle to shore on either side of the sea stack, depending on tide level, and land on the east (left if you're facing the beach) side of the creek. If the tide is low, paddle around the west (right) side of the island to land, as shallow reefs lie between it and the cliff. Make sure you don't land on the west (right) side of the creek. This is strictly enforced private property. The landowners regularly patrol the beach and will threaten criminal trespassing if you land here. The private property includes the beach below the low-tide line, which is uncommon for this region.

If surfers are in the water, give them a lot of space when going through to land. And if the waves are too big for your skill level, determine if landing here is the right choice. In the past decade, the popularity of this beach for surfing has increased considerably and unskilled kayakers have gained a reputation for creating a stir. A seventeen-foot sea kayak barreling out of control on a wave toward unsuspecting surfers is a frightening experience. Learn about surfing etiquette (see Resources) prior to paddling in any popular surfing area.

If the surf is up and you can find a spot far from others, this is a great beach to practice your wave-riding skills. The beach is sandy, and the waves are generally well-formed. Wave size varies widely, from flat calm days to winter surf to fifteen-foot closeouts. Surf on the strait is inconsistent compared to the open ocean beaches, so good planning is required to get waves. If you're going there to surf, look for a medium tide from four to six feet, a west or northwest swell under twelve seconds, and little wind. At less than a four-foot tide level, closeout waves will form. Onshore wind (wind going toward shore) creates closeout conditions or "mushy" waves—fine for kayakers but less preferred by board surfers. Watch for the rip on the west or outside edge of the sea stack on an ebb, especially after a big rain—a few unlucky boaters have been sucked out into the strait here.

# 47. Pillar Point and Pysht River

Pillar Point is a marine headland with two prominent "pillars," tall rock formations from the Miocene Epoch consisting of sedimentary rocks of the Clallam Formation. The USGS predicts the two pillars will be sea stacks in the future. Pillar Point borders the west side of the Pysht River mouth and estuary. Located 52 miles west of Port Angeles, the day-use park is operated by Clallam County. Enjoy views of 740-foot Pillar Point and Vancouver Island across the Strait of Juan de Fuca.

*Pillar Point rock formation is likely a future sea stack.*

Pillar Point once harbored a Klallam village. Pysht means "fish" in Chinook jargon or "against the wind and current" in Coast Salish. In Klallam, Pysht means "where the wind is blowing in all directions," and it was listed on British Admiralty charts in the mid-1800s as "Ketsoth Village." In 1886, a logging company acquired Pysht to mill spruce and it later became busy producing airplanes for World War I. The Klallam village was demolished in the 1920s to build a lumber mill; in the process, the river was channelized in places. In 2009, the North Olympic Land Trust, the Makah and Klallam Tribes, and others began working to restore the lower 10 miles of the river. Today, the Pysht River supports nine species of freshwater fish and five species of salmon.

**Duration:** Half to full day.

**Rating:** *Protected*, *Moderate*, or *Exposed*.

**Navigation Aids:** SeaTrails WA 103, 101; NOAA chart 18460 (1:00,000); Race Rocks current table (adjusted for Angeles Point) or the Canadian *Current Atlas*.

**Planning Considerations:** Pillar Point Park is day-use only and closes at dusk. A small boat ramp, vault restrooms, picnic tables, and parking are available. No permits required. Time your trip for higher tides, as the entire bay below the parking lot and the lower Pysht River can dry, leaving an extensive mudflat. A specific river channel is deep all the time; following it will mostly keep you out of the shallow mudflats (see the Route description below for more details). Wind can increase suddenly on the strait west of Pillar Point.

### GETTING THERE AND LAUNCHING

From Port Angeles, follow US Highway 101 and then State Route 112 west past Joyce for about 37 miles to the park. The Joyce General Store is the last gas and services until Clallam Bay. The road is very rough past Twin and Deep Creek and often washes out in winter. Launch from the beach or boat ramp. You can also reach the park from the west. From Clallam Bay on SR 112, turn left onto SR 112. From US 101 east of Forks, take a left on SR 113 and then a right on SR 112. Pillar Point Recreation Area is about 13 miles east.

### ROUTE

Pillar Point is a unique trip with coastal paddling, a protected river estuary, and the slow-winding Pysht River to explore. Aim for higher tides or a flood tide to avoid getting stuck in the mudflat that extends across to Pillar Point. At lower tides, the river channel may be deep enough if you are rudderless or have your skeg up. Paddle across the bay to Pillar Point and marvel at the huge rock pillars rising around you. One rock pillar can be seen from Pillar Point Park, which faces east and another is around the point facing west. Waves may break on the west side of the river channel on medium tides if a west swell is running. Continue west along the shoreline, exploring pocket beaches and thick forest above while keeping an eye out for seabirds and marine life. On a paddle here, I've spotted sea lions, harbor seals, otters, and several species of birds. Watch for rocks below the surface and thick kelp beds, as well as incoming swell. The point wraps around into a small bay 1.3 miles from the first pillar. A few small beaches offer places to pull out for a break. This section is as interesting as the cliff section west of Freshwater Bay (see Trip 46), but you'll see fewer paddlers.

If you want a longer trip, you can continue west toward Slip Point and Clallam Bay and return or run a shuttle. You will need to watch for shallow reef and waves around Slip Point, which is 9.8 miles from Pillar Point Recreation Area. Take out by the lighthouse or farther past the sandbar at Clallam Bay Spit Community Park, where the Clallam River meets the bay at a primitive pullout and lot about 1 mile west of Slip Point (see Trip 48, Clallam Bay Spit Community Beach County Park).

A good *Protected* route from Pillar Point Recreation Area takes you farther into the bay and up the Pysht River. If you launch from Pillar Point Recreation Area on a lower tide, you can find the river channel about 175 yards west of the park. Follow the channel deeper into the bay to connect with the main river channel, which flows out to the southwest. Make sure to follow this channel back when you return if the tide is ebbing. If you launch on a higher tide, aim southwest to find the river mouth. The lower river channel winds through an estuary littered with large, barnacled-covered maple and conifer tree stumps, some lying on sandbars. As the river curves south, old pilings from past logging operations begin to appear along the shore and in the middle of the channel. Watch for trees lying across sections of the river. The current runs 1 to 3 knots. As the river enters the forest, moss-covered cedars and firs line the shore. At about a mile, the river channel is lined with vertical pilings on both sides and a creek enters from the right. After this section, the riverbank reverts to sand and thick

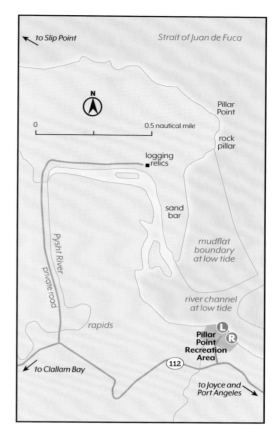

forest. During low tides, rocks create a small rapid at 1.5 miles, which can be passed or portaged. Just above, a rock shelf stretches nearly across the river, but the portage is easy on the right side. You'll paddle over the shelf at higher tides. Soon after, the Pysht Tree Farm buildings come into view. The river narrows above, with more wood across or in the channel.

# 48. Clallam Bay Spit Community Beach County Park

This thirty-three-acre park on the road to Neah Bay features a backwater river estuary, a back bay, and exposed ocean beach. The slow-moving Clallam River flows into a waterway separated from the Strait of Juan de Fuca by a mile-long sandbar; you can enjoy an easy paddle in the waterway or a spicier option just over the sandbar. It's not uncommon to hear sea lions barking in the distance on rocky Slip Point or from an offshore buoy. You may also spot an eagle or osprey. The Clallam River supports coho, chum, and winter steelhead, but the often-closed sandbar doesn't always allow them to access the strait.

**Duration:** Half day.

**Rating:** *Protected.*

**Navigation Aids:** SeaTrails WA 301; NOAA charts 18460 (1:100,000), 18480 (1:176,253).

**Planning Considerations:** Clallam River is Class 1, meaning it doesn't have rapids, and so is an option for beginners. It is best when the water level is higher fall through spring. Summer tends to be brackish. The river only occasionally breaks through the sandbar to Clallam Bay. River levels vary throughout the year. Avoid trees and branches lying across the river if you venture upstream. Watch for surf on the Clallam Bay side. Both launches are run by Clallam County.

### GETTING THERE AND LAUNCHING

To get to Clallam Bay from Port Angeles, you have the option of looping south around Lake Crescent or following a more direct route along the Strait of Juan de Fuca. To go past Lake Crescent, follow US Highway 101 west and then take a right in Sappho onto State Route 113, merge onto State Route 112, and follow it to Clallam Bay. To follow the Strait of Juan de Fuca, take US 101 west for 5 miles and then take a right on SR 112, following it to Clallam Bay. The upper part of the park, which doesn't have water access but does have restrooms, is at 16716 Frontier Street, Clallam Bay.

**Salt Air Street (Clallam Bay East):** Once in Clallam Bay, take a right on Frontier Street, a left on Fisherman Street, and another left onto Salt Air Street. The day-use-only parking is limited, and no facilities are available. Enter the river from the beach.

*Clallam Bay's East County Park sand bar with distant Slip Point Lighthouse*

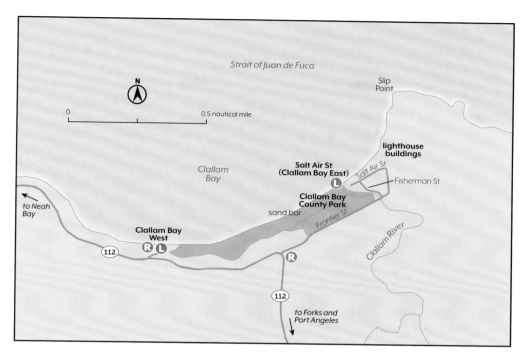

**Clallam Bay West:** This launch, which is about 0.15 mile past the community of Clallam Bay, has more parking space but no restrooms. Drive down the short, steep road to the parking lot. Access the river by walking about 100 yards past the metal telephone pole; wheels may work for kayakers. Or go over the sandbar directly to the beach.

## ROUTE

Clallam Bay County Park is a great option for beginners seeking a quiet, protected backwater or for more experienced paddlers who want to ply the open water on the Strait of Juan de Fuca, only a few steps away. Launch from either end of the Clallam River to enjoy an easygoing float with minimal (if any) current. Paddle under the walkway that used to connect the park to the sandbar. On the east end, look for the Slip Point Lighthouse buildings below towering Slip Point. The river level varies, so check it before launching. In late summer, it can run low and get a bit murky. Paddle up the river, keeping an eye out for strainers (trees) crossing over.

Those with surf and open-water experience can step over the sandbar to paddle Clallam Bay. There may be a few flat days here on calm summer days. Northwest and westerly swell or wind swell can get in here; check the surf forecast and wind apps prior to heading out. Slip Point to the east is a reef with occasional surf—only experienced paddlers should venture here. The exposed shoreline east of the point will eventually take you to Pillar Point in 8 miles (see Trip 47, Pillar Point and Pysht River).

Consult *Day Hiking: Olympic Peninsula* by Craig Romano for walking and hiking options along Clallam Bay Spit.

# 49. **Ozette Lake**

Located in Olympic National Park in the northwest corner of the state, Ozette Lake is the third-largest natural lake in the country and the largest undeveloped lake in Washington State. Known for its remoteness and quiet, Ozette Lake also harbors thirteen species of fish. The lake was called Kahouk by the Makah people, which means "large lake." There are two launches: one from Swan Bay and the other in Ozette Campground near the Ozette Loop trailhead, which leads to the coastal beaches of Cape Alava and Sand Point. Due to the lake's large size, winds can whip up large waves, and because it's over 300 feet deep, it stays cold most of the year. Camping is available in three areas, including Tivoli Island. You can also take two primitive trails from the lake to the coastal beaches.

**Duration:** Half day to overnight.

**Rating:** *Protected* to *Moderate*.

**Navigation Aids:** SeaTrails WA 103; NOAA charts 18460 (1:100,000), 18484 (1:10,000).

**Planning Considerations:** The lake is open all year and will have the most activity in summer. A wilderness permit is required for any backcountry camping in the park, which includes Ericsons Bay and Tivoli Island. Each of these has a capacity of twelve people. Visit recreation.gov/permits/4098362 for details about wilderness permits. Bear canisters are also required; for more information visit nps.gov/olym/planyourvisit/wic.htm. Fires are not allowed in backcountry sites. Camping at the Ozette Ranger Station is first come, first served. The campground has fifteen sites with restrooms and water. Check the wind forecast prior to your departure. Make sure to filter or bring your own water: the lake's water has a tan tint, which is just from leaf tannins, but it is also known to contain Giardia and Cryptosporidium.

## GETTING THERE AND LAUNCHING

To get to Ozette Lake from Port Angeles, you have the option of looping south around Lake Crescent or following a more direct route along the Strait of Juan de Fuca. To go past Lake Crescent, follow US Highway 101 west and then take a right in Sappho onto State Route 113, go left onto SR 112, and follow it to Clallam Bay/Sekiu. A few miles past Sekiu, take a left on Ozette Lake Road and follow it to Ozette Lake.

To follow the Strait of Juan de Fuca, take US 101 west for five miles out of Port Angeles and then take a right on SR 112, following it to Clallam Bay/Sekiu. A few miles past Sekiu, take a left on Ozette Lake Road and follow it to Ozette Lake.

The left turn for the Swan Bay boat ramp is 3.6 miles south of Ozette Campground. Note: These routes can be washed out in winter; make sure to check both before leaving. Get last-minute supplies at the Lost Resort on Hoko Ozette Road, open spring through fall; you can visit them online at lostresort.net.

*A perfect launch spot on Erickson's Bay with view of Tivoli Island*

**Swan Bay Boat Ramp:** This is a gravel launch in Olympic National Park. Take a left on Swan Bay Road 3.6 miles before you reach the Ozette Ranger Station and drive 0.8 mile to the ramp and restroom.

**Ozette Campground and Ranger Station:** This grassy launch is next to the campground and has limited parking. Drop your gear, check your permits for overnight stays, and park in the main hikers' lot a short distance away. Restrooms are located near the lot.

## ROUTE

Whether you are interested in a casual day trip or a longer overnight, Ozette Lake has options for everyone. Launching from the north end of the lake at the Ozette Campground and Ranger Station, you have two additional options for camping. The closest, Ericsons Bay, is 4 miles away, but it is also the most popular; it has a nice sandy beach and views of distant Tivoli Island. In the off-season, you'll have it to yourself. The site is limited to twelve people and has one pit toilet in the trees to the west. Make sure to set tents on preexisting bare ground. The primitive trail to Sand Point is 0.65 mile south of the Ericsons Bay campground, around the little forested point; look for orange signs in the trees. The 1.5-mile-long trail is not maintained by the park, so be ready to get muddy and do some bushwacking. Bring hiking boots, as the trail is rough. Old-growth trees line the heavily forested trail. The Washington Trails Association (WTA) provides online trail reports at wta.org/go-hiking/hikes/ericsons-bay.

You can find another campsite on beautiful Tivoli Island, 5.5 miles from the Ozette Ranger Station launch. It is also limited to twelve people but has no toilets. Bury waste six to eight inches deep and two hundred feet from the campsite. Consider packing out waste. Set tents only on preexisting bare ground. Practice Leave No Trace principles during your stay.

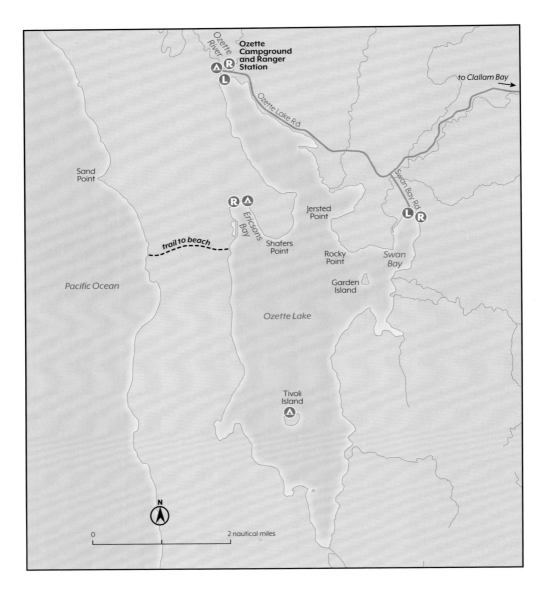

If you launch from Swan Bay, the campsite at Ericsons Bay is 3.8 miles away and the Tivoli Island campsite is 3.5 miles away. As you launch, enjoy the undeveloped, mixed-tree-lined shorelines and Garden Island. At Rocky and Jersted Points, you may spot rustic fishing cabins in the trees. The 1-mile crossing to Shafers Point can be windy on a northerly or southerly wind. Each of these points and bays offers good wind protection.

OPPOSITE **Point Doughty on the northwest tip of Orcas Island (Trip 58)**

# San Juan Islands

The San Juan archipelago, featuring 175 named islands and islets (400 total, including unnamed rocks), provides beginning paddlers with many protected bays and coves, while advanced paddlers can enjoy the open water with swift currents. It's a very dynamic place to explore. Archaeological evidence shows people arrived at the islands fourteen thousand years ago, with shell middens and house sites dating back at least nine thousand years. Anthropologists have identified these people as Northern Straits Salish, including Saanich, Samish, Songhees, and Lummi. Spanish explorers arrived in the 1790s and named many of the islands. The transition from an undeveloped landscape began in 1853 as settlers and logging operations began to appear.

# 50. **Cypress Island**

The wild ruggedness of Cypress Island, along with the chance for a hike to catch the panoramic views from Eagle Cliff, contribute to its popularity with kayakers. You can spend the night outdoors in this rough beauty at either of two seasonal, public camping areas with Cascadia Marine sites. Cypress Island has a bonus that is unique in the San Juan Islands: ferry trips are not required. The Department of Natural Resources (DNR) owns about four-fifths of the island and manages it primarily for recreation. Plan for one to two nights out to the island's two campsites or circumnavigate the entire island.

**Duration:** Full day to overnight.

**Rating:** *Moderate.*

**Navigation Aids:** SeaTrails WA 001, 005; NOAA charts 18423 SC or 18421 (both 1:80,000), 18430 (1:25,000); Rosario Strait current tables (with corrections for Bellingham Channel, Strawberry Island, Guemes Channel, or Shannon Point, depending on your location) or the Canadian *Current Atlas.*

**Planning Considerations:** The trail to Eagle Cliff is normally closed from February to July 15 because of peregrine falcon breeding activities. Strong currents can create very dangerous localized conditions off Cypress Head in Bellingham Channel; avoid big tides or aim for slack current in this area. Currents strongly affect traveling speeds on all sides of the island—use flood current for going north and ebb current for the return.

## GETTING THERE AND LAUNCHING

You have three launches to choose from in Anacortes: the ferry dock for Guemes Island, downtown Anacortes inside Cap Sante, and Washington Park.

**Anacortes Ferry Dock (to Guemes Island):** From Commercial Avenue, take a left on 6th Street, which will take you to the dock. Look for Kiwanis Waterfront Park. Unload your boat from the day-use park on the west side of the dock, which allows two-hour parking. When launching, watch for ferry and recreational boating traffic in the channel. After unloading, park on residential streets for overnight trips.

**Anacortes (Cap Sante):** Use Seafarers' Memorial Park just south of the marina. Parking here is day-use only. Check with nearby marinas for overnight parking. Call the harbor office for additional information at 360-293-0694. To get to Seafarers' Park, turn right (east) from Commercial Avenue onto 15th Street. Turn left on Q Avenue and then right on Seafarers Way along the south edge of the marina. It is an easy carry to the gravel beach. Restrooms are available.

Rotary Park has day use parking on the north end of the marina with an easy launch down a concrete ramp to the water. To get to Rotary Park, turn east from Commercial Avenue onto 4th Street, then take a right on T Avenue and follow it to the gravel lot. Restrooms are available in the marina.

*Kayaker off Cypress Head with views of distant Lummi Island*

**Cap Sante Marina:** The marina has three lots with long term parking with no fees or permits. Parking in the lot on the north end adjacent to Rotary Park is good for thirty days. The triangle-shaped gravel lot on Q Avenue and 9th Street offers ten-day parking. And the lot on 11th Street closest to the Marina Office offers seventy-two-hour parking. Restrooms are at the marina.

**Washington Park:** From Anacortes, follow signs for the San Juan Island ferry, about 4 miles west of town. From Commercial Avenue, take a left on 12th Street (State Route 20), which becomes Oakes Avenue. Enjoy views to your right of Guemes and Cypress Islands and Bellingham Channel. At the Anacortes ferry terminal, continue going straight at the Y intersection. The road becomes Sunset Avenue. Follow Sunset Avenue to Washington Park.

Overnight parking is allowed in lot "B" for up to fourteen days. To get closest to the beach, drive down to the day-use parking lot "A" to unload, then carry your boat across the lawn to the gravel beach. Move your car to the overnight "B" lot. Call the marina office at 360-661-3611 for additional information. Be cautious of the boat ramp activity on busy weekends. The park is owned by the city of Anacortes and also offers car camping.

## ROUTE

**Circumnavigation:** A complete circumnavigation of Cypress Island is approximately 15 miles. Use the Canadian *Current Atlas* to visualize and plan your trip around the currents in Bellingham and Guemes Channels and in Rosario Strait. The tidal stage affects which launch point you should use.

Camping is closed, and no facilities are available on Strawberry Island, positioned off the southwest corner of Cypress Island. Watch for recreational boating traffic when crossing Guemes Channel. Fast-moving current can send the boats closer to you than expected. Boat wakes can also get quite large when opposing strong current.

The easiest launch in Anacortes is on the west side of the Guemes Island ferry dock. Launch on slack, the end of the ebb current, or early in the flood current and cross over to Guemes Island. Follow the Guemes Island shore west, then north, and finally cross over to Cypress Island.

The launch point in downtown Anacortes is at Seafarer's Memorial Park. Time it so you get the tail end of the ebb or wait for slack in Guemes Channel and then let the flood take you north up Bellingham Channel. Round Cap Sante and cross the 0.5-mile-wide Guemes Channel, usually possible on most tide stages, and then work west along Guemes Island and up its western shore. Wait until the current slacks before crossing Bellingham Channel to Cypress Island.

The Guemes Island ferry dock and Seafarer's Park launches are safer and more amenable to a range of tide stages than the Washington Park put-in near Fidalgo Head. On flood currents, Washington Park may be an easier launch point, as you can ride the current flowing northward into Bellingham Channel. Watch for outgoing and incoming ferry traffic at the terminal just east of the park.

Currents sweep strongly around this body of land, and the crossing from here to Cypress Island is more than 2 miles. As the ebb current sets southwest, reaching Cypress Island from the Fidalgo Head/Shannon Point area on even average tides can be almost impossible. There is a good possibility of being swept out into Rosario Strait in the process. This situation would be very rough with a southerly wind.

Reach Cypress Head midway up Bellingham Channel and 4.6 miles from Washington Park. This protuberance creates back eddies, strong eddy lines, and associated rips that can be very dangerous, particularly on large ebbs. If you approach while the current is flowing, hug the shoreline. The back eddy extends 100 feet off Cypress Head and the safest route is right along the shore inside the kelp.

Cypress Head is a DNR recreation site with a Cascadia Marine Trail designation: it has five free sites, two picnic areas, a composting toilet, and fire rings. Water is not available. Campsites are in the woods on the head and at the neck connecting it to the main island—a great place to watch the action in a big ebb exchange. Hear porpoises pass and the sound of the current running on big exchanges. Enjoy views to the north of the undeveloped Cone and Sinclair Islands, with Lummi Island in the distance to the northeast. The swift currents off Cypress Head may be beneficial to those seeking to practice their skills in moving water.

Landings are at the rock-and-gravel beaches on both the north and south sides of the neck. The campsites on the west end of the neck are the most convenient to reach from the beaches, but the more distant sites in the woods offer better weather protection. Use minimum impact camping techniques.

About 2.5 miles north of Cypress Head, arrive at Pelican Beach, another DNR area designated with Cascadia Marine Trail status. This area was originally developed with help from the

Pelican Fleet: a club of people who own Pelican boats, a type of beachable cruising sailboat often found hauled up on this fine pebble beach. One of the nicest features here is Eagle Cliff, a spectacular 840-foot overlook of the entire Rosario Strait area, very popular with campers who climb up for the sunsets. The trail is a little more than 1 mile long. The climb is easy except for the last few hundred yards. The open-meadowed uplands around Eagle Cliff invite independent exploration with an alternative loop to another overlook. The trail to Eagle Cliff is closed, however, from February to mid-July because of peregrine falcon nesting. Other walks accessible from the campground include trails to Duck Lake or Eagle Harbor.

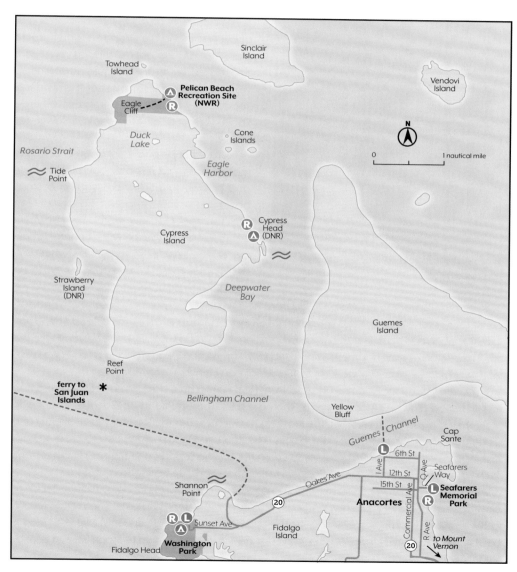

*Kayak on the tombolo connecting Cypress Head to the island*

At the beach there are five to ten camping spaces. Though more can be accommodated, the narrow beach strip quickly becomes very crowded on sunny weekends, typically with kayakers. Behind is a covered picnic shelter and vault toilets, but water is not available. Camping is not allowed on the beach beyond the campsite limits, and fires must be built only in the firepits.

The currents along the Rosario Strait side of Cypress Island are strong enough to merit planning around them, though there are enough eddies in this irregular shoreline to work against them for most of the distance. Topography is at its most impressive here—Eagle Cliff and other precipices tower far above.

Strawberry Island is yet another DNR recreation area, but it is only open for day use and has no facilities. Access it via a small beach at the south end that is gravel at high tide but rocky at low water. As elsewhere along Rosario Strait, be wary of huge breaking wakes from passing tankers when you beach your boat. A trail continues north up the island to an overlook.

If you plan to paddle to Fidalgo Head from Reef Point at Cypress Island's southern end, formulate tactics for crossing. Keep the powerful offshore currents in mind. On a flood tide, crossing to the Washington Park area can be exhausting, even impossible. Ebbs, however, make this easy, barring any strong southerly winds and with some course correction to counteract westerly drift. Watch for boating and ferry traffic, which can be heavy on weekends.

If you are bound for Guemes Channel from Reef Point, use a slack or early flood current to cross to Yellow Bluff on Guemes Island. Then get a lift from the flood up Guemes Channel to the ferry landing. In calm weather, the crossing to Guemes Channel can be made directly and quickly from Reef Point with the right timing. You can use the last of the ebb to cross toward Washington Park and position yourself to catch the southerly portion of the new flood current, which will sweep you into Guemes Channel rather than north up Bellingham Channel.

**Alternative route:** For a shorter trip, you can paddle to Cypress Head or Pelican Beach to enjoy idyllic camping or just a day among the craggy, madrona-lined cliffs. Then return following the same route, making any necessary adjustments for current or wind. Cypress Head is about 4.5 miles one-way from Washington Park. Add another 2.5 miles to reach Pelican Beach.

# 51. **James Island Park**

Rugged James Island State Park has plenty of trails and enough secluded coves to keep you busy for more than an overnight stay. Camping includes a Cascadia Marine Trail site along with public camping facilities. For variety, you have two options for travel routes from Lopez Island—and if you feel up to it, you can also make the exposed Rosario Strait crossing from Fidalgo Head to James Island, avoiding any San Juan Island ferry hassles. This trip can be combined with Obstruction Pass and Doe Bay (see Trip 52, Obstruction Pass) or perhaps with a circumnavigation of Blakely Island.

**Duration:** Overnight.

**Rating:** *Moderate* or *Exposed*. The *Moderate* route involves some currents and possible tide rips. The *Exposed* route requires a 3-mile, open-water crossing with currents, tide rips, and shipping traffic.

**Navigation Aids:** SeaTrails WA 001, 002; NOAA charts 18423 SC or 18421 (both 1:80,000), 18430 (1:25,000); Rosario Strait current tables with corrections for Thatcher Pass.

**Planning Considerations:** Currents affect ease of travel and safety on both routes. Raccoons are a problem on the island; make sure you secure your gear and food.

## GETTING THERE AND LAUNCHING

Two approaches begin from Lopez Island, while a third originates from Washington Park on Fidalgo Head in Anacortes.

**Spencer Spit State Park (Lopez Island):** Starting from Lopez Island requires driving a car aboard the ferry, as there is no public access to the beach at the Lopez Island ferry terminal for foot passengers with kayaks. Drive south from the ferry landing on Ferry Road a little more than 1 mile to Port Stanley Road, which is across the highway from Odlin County Park (which has a Cascadia Marine Trail site). Turn left and follow this road for approximately 3 miles as it winds past Shoal and Swifts Bays. Turn left onto Baker View Road and follow it another mile to the state park entrance.

Within Spencer Spit State Park, pass the registration booth and follow the main road to a gated gravel road. Follow this narrow road as it drops steeply down to a small lot just south of the lagoon. There is a 50-yard carry to the beach. After unloading boats and gear, move cars back up to the parking lot. A Discover Pass is required. No garbage or recycling receptacles are available at this park—you must pack out what you pack in. The main park is not open in the winter, but you can still access the Cascadia Marine Trail site from the water. Outdoor Adventure Center operates kayaking tours from the spit in the summer. You can visit their website at outdooradventurecenter.com/kayaking/lopez-island-sea-kayak-tour.

*James Island from Thatcher Pass*

**Hunter Bay Boat Ramp (Lopez Island):** From the ferry, take Ferry Road south to Center Road. Follow it to the south side of the island and take a left on Mud Bay Road. In about a mile, take another left on Islandale Road. Drive for a curvy 1.5 miles through a thickly forested residential area to the boat ramp. Parking and a pit toilet are available. The ramp may be busy with boaters in fishing season.

**Washington Park (Fidalgo Island):** From Anacortes, follow signs for the San Juan Island ferry, about 4 miles west of town. From Commercial Avenue, take a left on 12th Street (State Route 20), which becomes Oakes Avenue. Enjoy views to your right of Guemes and Cypress Islands and Bellingham Channel. At the Anacortes ferry terminal, continue going straight at the Y intersection. The road becomes Sunset Avenue, and you soon enter the park. Park in the "A" lot to carry your boat across the lawn to the gravel beach. Then move your car to the "B" lot to park. There is a daily parking fee.

### ROUTES

**Spencer Spit to James Island:** *Moderate*. The one-way paddling distance via Thatcher Pass is 4 miles. If you travel via Lopez Pass around the south end of Decatur Island, the one-way distance is 7 miles.

Currents west of Blakely Island are weak and the waterway there is fairly well protected from wind-driven seas. However, East Sound, to the north and almost bisecting Orcas Island, can develop very strong, intensified northerly winds that may extend south as far as this route on warm, fair-weather afternoons. Currents in Thatcher Pass rarely exceed 1 knot and it can usually be paddled safely in any stage of the tide. However, currents are strong enough to warrant coordinating with the flow direction. The flood current flows west through Thatcher Pass.

For a longer route, loop south around Decatur Island, threading through narrow inter-island passageways and enjoying views of this quiet, pastoral island. As with Blakely Island to the north, there is no public ferry service to Decatur Island. Places to go ashore here include a small, undeveloped island state park just north of the spit east of Lopez Pass and extensive, publicly owned tidelands bounded above by private property. These tidelands include the shores of Center Island, which has some gravel pocket beaches. Another public tideland covers over 2 miles of sand-and-gravel beach, with one intermediate strip of private tideland, on the east side of Decatur Island between Lopez Pass and Decatur Head. The shore break here can be quite large when a southerly wind is blowing.

James Island has three camping areas with multiple sites at each, including one with Cascadia Marine Trail status. A network of trails roams over the island's steep, rocky hills and a secluded beach sits on the south shore. The island's drawback is the rapacious raccoon population that lurks in wait for all visitors. Campsites are accessible from either the eastern or western coves. Water is available on the island in the main campground. The central area between the coves is the most popular with boaters, and it has a small picnic shelter. However, wind can

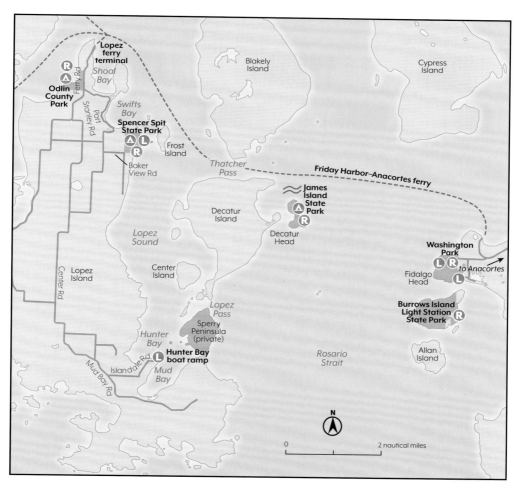

howl across this isthmus from either direction. At the eastern campsites, the southern side of the cove offers more protection.

The secluded Cascadia Marine Trail site between the main west beach and east beach is the most popular with paddlers. The trees that surround the site also make it the best protected in bad weather. Beyond the outhouse, a trail leads across the island to the eastern cove. The island is known for "commando" raccoons, who will do anything to get into your food and gear. Kayak guides have resorted to tying zippers together and wrapping gear in two tarps bound by rope.

**Fidalgo Head to James Island:** *Exposed*. The one-way distance is 3.5 miles, 3 miles of which are open Rosario Strait waters. Currents in this area of the strait can exceed 2.5 knots and are usually strongest on the southern flowing ebb. Hence, southerly winds can make this an extremely dangerous body of water on a falling tide, and tanker and tug-and-barge traffic add to the hazard. Crossings should be made only in auspicious conditions; otherwise use the ferry. Be especially careful in the area north of James Island, where dangerous rips can form when the westward-flowing ebb from Thatcher Pass and the southward current in the strait meet an opposing wind. One kayak fatality here was apparently due to this situation. NOAA chart 18423 SC provides the following warning for Rosario Strait, presumably applying to Thatcher, Lopez, Peavine, and Obstruction Passes: "On the ebb tide, southerly winds cause dangerous tide rips off the entrance to the passes."

If conditions and your skills are appropriate for the Rosario Strait crossing, time your start relative to the currents. Since your drift from the current will be considerable in all but very small tides, start the crossing about thirty minutes before slack so that the currents will be minimal and will cancel each other out before and after the slack. Currents are particularly swift off Fidalgo Head.

# 52. **Obstruction Pass**

Convoluted shores, steep hillsides of madrona, and rocky meadows make Obstruction Pass prime San Juan Islands paddling country. Currents in its passageways are strong enough for some exciting rides and require a measure of caution. Alternative launch points around this area make a variety of trips possible, from short local paddles to one-night or longer adventures. A Cascadia Marine Trail (CMT) site is within the state park. By adding another day to the itinerary, you can combine it with the Cypress Island route to the east (see Trip 50) or the James Island route to the south (see Trip 51).

**Duration:** Part day to overnight.
**Rating:** *Moderate*. The area has currents with associated tide rips and eddy lines, though the areas of swiftest flow can be avoided.

**Navigation Aids:** SeaTrails WA 001, 002, 004; NOAA charts 18423 SC or 18421 (both 1:80,000), 18430 (1:25,000); Rosario Strait current tables with corrections for Obstruction Pass.

**Planning Considerations:** See the Fidalgo Head to James Island route in Trip 51, James Island, for safety considerations in the passes leading to Rosario Strait and including Obstruction Pass. Obstruction Pass State Park has no launching access.

## GETTING THERE AND LAUNCHING

Launch from Spencer Spit State Park on Lopez Island or from two alternative launches on Orcas Island.

**Spencer Spit State Park (Lopez Island):** Starting from Lopez Island requires driving a car aboard the ferry, as there is no public access to the beach at the Lopez Island ferry terminal for foot passengers. Drive south from the ferry landing on Ferry Road a little more than 1 mile to Port Stanley Road, which is across the highway from Odlin County Park (which has a CMT site). Turn left and follow this road for approximately 3 miles as it winds past Shoal and Swifts Bays. Turn left onto Baker View Road and follow it another mile to the state park entrance.

Within Spencer Spit State Park, pass the registration booth and follow the main road to a gated gravel road. Follow this narrow road as it drops steeply down to a small lot just south of the lagoon. There is a 50-yard carry to the beach. After unloading boats and gear, move cars back up to the parking lot. A Discover Pass is required. No garbage or recycling receptacles are available at this park—you must pack out what you pack in. The main park is not open in the winter, but you can still access the CMT site from the water.

*Early morning mist in Obstruction Pass with Mount Baker in the distance*

**Obstruction Pass (Orcas Island):** The closest launch site is the Obstruction Pass boat ramp. This site is approximately 20 miles from the Orcas Island ferry dock by road. After leaving the ferry, follow the road to Eastsound and then toward Olga. Approximately a quarter mile before Olga, turn left onto Point Lawrence Road where signs point to Obstruction Pass and Doe Bay. After another quarter mile, reach a fork in the road; go right for Obstruction Pass. (Left leads to Doe Bay.) Use this ramp for day-trip paddling only, as no overnight parking for the general public is allowed here. There are additional limited parking spots, both day use and seventy-two hour, but this is a very busy place. Next to the boat ramp is the Lieber Haven Resort

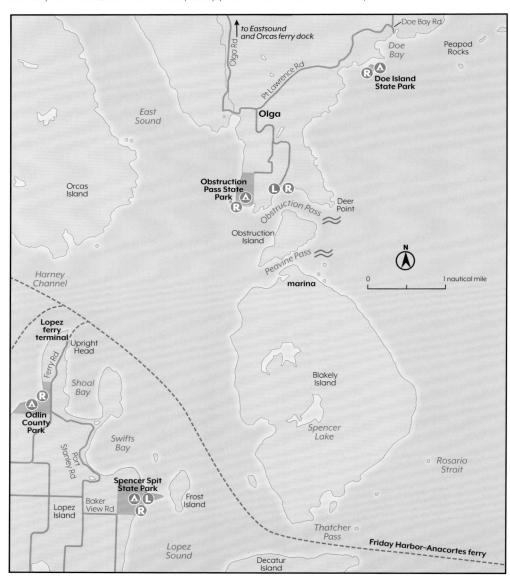

with a marina that offers kayak and other boat rentals and has most of the amenities you might need. Visit their website at lieberhavenresort.com.

**Doe Bay Village Resort (Orcas Island):** This launch is for guests only. Follow the directions above for Obstruction Pass, except this time keep left at the fork on Point Lawrence Road and follow it to Doe Bay Road. Turn right into Doe Bay Resort. A popular retreat for people with an inclination toward natural living, Doe Bay's cabins, saunas, and hot tubs are busy year-round.

## ROUTES

**Spencer Spit to Obstruction Pass:** *Moderate.* The one-way distance is 4.5 miles. Cross from Spencer Spit and Frost Island and follow the rocky shores of Blakely Island. The uplands of this large island are privately owned, but most of its tidelands are public. To avoid conflicts with residents, do not land in the coves along the western shore or near homes elsewhere. Fine, secluded gravel beaches line its predominantly wild shores. Stay below the high-tide line.

At the west end of Peavine Pass, Blakely Island Marina offers groceries, ice cream, espresso, and beer from Memorial Day to Labor Day weekend. Showers, laundry, and restrooms are also seasonally available, but there is no overnight camping or ferry service on the island. Visit the marina website at blakelyislandgeneralstore.com. Land on the beach to the left of the fuel float. Paraclete and Island Express Charters can also deliver kayaks to the island.

Obstruction Pass State Park offers camping (including a CMT site) and an extensive trail system. Located in a cove about a half mile west of the pass, it is also accessible from the road via a 0.5-mile-long trail. Above the pebble beach, you can find nine campsites, picnic tables, fireplaces, and vault toilets (but no water).

Unless you are confident in your fast-current boat-handling skills, use Obstruction Pass instead of Peavine Pass for travel to and from Rosario Strait. Currents average about 1 knot in Obstruction Pass, and in Peavine Pass, over 2 knots on the ebb. Both flow east on the flood toward Rosario Strait. Interestingly, this is opposite from the flow in Thatcher Pass, which is westerly on the flood.

**Doe Bay to Obstruction Pass:** *Moderate.* The one-way distance is 3.8 miles. You can also combine this with the route described above for an 8-mile overnight trip. However, you will probably want to travel into the San Juans by ferry the day prior to ensure you have enough time for paddling.

Doe Island is a six-acre state park located about 1 mile south of Doe Bay. It has a float during the summer season and mixed rock-and-gravel beaches on the northwest and southeast sides. Five first-come, first-served campsites are available, each with a table, stove, and vault toilet. The best site is in a hollow on the north end of the island. No water is provided. Visit the park website at parks.wa.gov/498/Doe-Island.

The Orcas Island shoreline is private between Doe Bay and Deer Point. However, most of the tidelands are public with occasional gravel pocket beaches along the predominantly rock coast. You should be able to find beaches away from nearby homes.

**Blakely Island Circumnavigation:** *Moderate.* The distance starting from Spencer Spit is about 12 miles, 8 miles of which are from Obstruction Pass to Spencer Spit via the east side of Blakely Island. A leisurely two-night trip with a stop at James Island is an option.

The eastern leg of the circumnavigation is significantly more exposed: fewer places to go ashore, strong currents, probable tide rips, and exposure to wind waves from either north or south. Tidelands are public along the entire east shore of Blakely Island and steep, rocky slopes above limit residential use. But they also limit the number of pocket beaches you will find. Watch for shore break on these beaches; be especially mindful of breaking tanker wakes. A powerful eddy line and associated tide rips may form during strong ebb currents in Rosario Strait at the easternmost point of Blakely Island. The current here is reported to turn to the flood an hour later than at Strawberry Island to the east.

# 53. Lopez Island: Fisherman Bay

Located in Lopez Village, the island's main business center, Fisherman Bay is a protected lagoon surrounded by shops, homes, an active marina, and a few open spaces. The bay opens to San Juan Channel with marvelous views of Shaw Island to the north and San Juan Island to the west. Locals are known for the "Lopez Wave," making the island one of the most friendly in the region.

**Duration:** Part day.

**Rating:** *Protected.*

**Navigation Aids:** SeaTrails WA 002; NOAA charts 18434, 18400. Check currents for San Juan Channel.

**Planning Considerations:** Watch for fast-moving current and boat traffic at the mouth of the bay. Plan for higher tides to explore the bay's south end. If you're paddling into the bay from other islands, Lopez Village has lodging and full facilities for resupplying your trip.

## GETTING THERE AND LAUNCHING

From the ferry, take Ferry Road south for 2 miles. At the T intersection, continue to the right to Fisherman Bay Road. Follow it until you see signs for Lopez Village and take a right on Lopez Road, which takes you into town.

**Weeks Point Way Launch:** As you pass shops in Lopez Village, take a left onto Weeks Point Way. Drive for a few hundred feet past houses and take a right into the empty public access lot, which has spaces for about four cars. Used by locals as a handheld boat launch, this access brings you right to the mouth of the bay. Watch for fast current on larger tidal exchanges. Respect homeowners on both sides of the access area.

**Lopez Road Launch:** As you near the west end of town after Weeks Point Way, turn left into the parking lot by the shops just above the water. There are steps leading to the beach and a few parking spots. If Lopez Road curves up a slight hill to the right, you've gone too far.

**Lopez Islander Marina Launch:** Take Fisherman Bay Road south of Lopez Village about a quarter mile to the Lopez Islander Resort and Marina. This is a protected launch deep inside the

*Fisherman Bay's harbor entrance on a busy summer day*

bay adjacent to a full-facility marina. There is a fee to launch and park. Check with the marina office for information: call 360-468-2233 or visit their website at lopezfun.com/marina. Across the street, Lopez Island Sea Kayak offers tours, instruction, and both kayak and SUP rentals. Visit them online at lopezkayaks.com or call 360-468-2847.

## ROUTE

With its narrow and shallow opening, the bay is a known hazard to boaters. Paddlers will enjoy the thrill of riding up to 3 knots of current into or out of the bay during larger tidal exchanges. During slack or periods of less current, the channel offers idyllic views of Lopez Village, as well as beachfront residences along Weeks Point. A large sand spit on the west side of the channel protects the bay from wind and chop in San Juan Channel. Paddle inside the bay past recreational boats and the Lopez Islander Marina, choosing your own route. Toward the southwest corner of the bay, another sand spit nearly connects to the other side, providing another narrow channel to explore. At low tides, this part of the bay dries into mudflats.

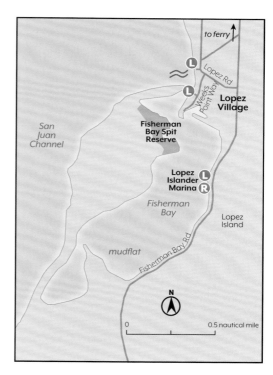

# 54. Lopez Island: Mackaye Harbor

With an annual rainfall of just twenty-two inches, Lopez Island is in the banana belt of Washington. Mackaye Harbor on the island's southwest side has an arid landscape in summer with golden meadows, warm water, and calm bays. It's an idyllic place for paddlers of all levels. Boaters mostly avoid the harbor and its bays due to shallow depths and numerous exposed and hidden rocks. Nearby Long, Charles, and Iceberg Islands are part of the San Juan Islands National Wildlife Refuge, off-limits for landing. Advanced paddlers can use the bay to enter current-laden Cattle Pass and then cross to San Juan Island, or to visit the rock garden south of Iceberg Point.

**Duration:** Part day.

**Rating:** *Protected*. An optional visit to Iceberg Point is *Moderate* to *Exposed*.

**Navigation Aids:** SeaTrails WA 002; NOAA charts 18434, 18400. Check currents for San Juan Channel.

**Planning Considerations:** Novice paddlers should stay in the inner sections of Outer Bay, Barlow Bay, and Mackaye Harbor. Stay 200 yards offshore from the San Juan Islands National Wildlife Refuge islands at the entry to both Mackaye Harbor and Outer Bay.

*Protected inner Mackaye Harbor*

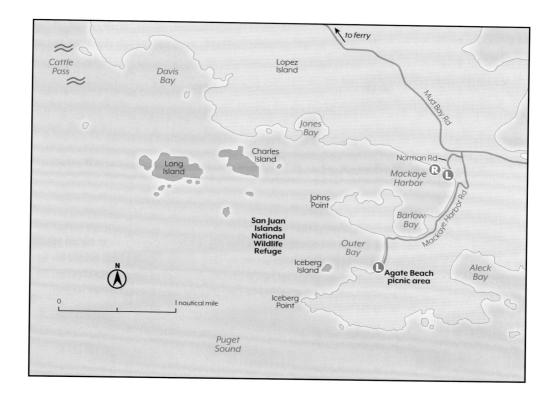

## GETTING THERE AND LAUNCHING

**Norman Road Boat Ramp:** From the Lopez ferry dock, take Ferry Road south about a mile and curve left onto Center Road. Drive for several miles and take a left on Lopez Sound Road, followed by an immediate right on Mud Bay Road. Turn right on Mackaye Harbor Road and then another quick right on Norman Road, which takes you to the boat ramp. The ramp has an outhouse but no other facilities. This is the only launch on the harbor with long-term parking.

**Agate Beach Picnic Area:** From Mackaye Harbor Road, continue south, passing a few beach homes, a B&B, and then Barlow Bay. The road eventually curves into Outer Bay. Look for Agate Beach Picnic Area on your left. There is a small day-use lot. Launch across the street below the stairs.

## ROUTES

**Mackaye Harbor:** *Protected.* Mackaye Harbor offers several options for day trips. Launching at Norman Road gives you access to wide sandy beaches to the southeast and rocky shorelines covered with sea life to the north. Johns Point on the southwest corner of the harbor has great pocket beaches. Tucked in the southeast corner of Mackaye Harbor, Barlow Bay is very protected from winds and shows evidence of a busier time, when Mackaye Harbor was home to the Lopez Island fishing fleet. The docks on the bay are privately owned.

The beach at Outer Bay is sandy and crescent shaped. Look for otters playing just off the beach. Enjoy views of the windswept, barren islands offshore, some of which are part of the wildlife refuge, including Round Rock, Secar Rock, and Hall Island.

**Iceberg Point:** *Moderate* to *Exposed*. Experienced paddlers may enjoy playing in the rocks and pocket beaches south of Outer Bay around Iceberg Point. Wind and swell from the strait can create conditions here similar to that of the outer coast.

# 55. Shaw Island: Circumnavigation

Located in the heart of the San Juan Islands, Shaw Island typically has the highest concentration of kayakers in the area during summer. Mild currents and alongshore paddling with few cross-ings make some routes here popular for less-experienced paddlers, particularly those kayak camping for the first time. Route options include an easy day, a short overnight, and a longer circumnavigation of Shaw Island with stops at neighboring parks and Cascadia Marine Trail sites. You can also easily include Jones Island as part of your route (see Trip 60, Jones Island).

**Duration:** Full day to multiple nights.

**Rating:** *Protected* or *Moderate*. A one-day protected route can be made from Odlin County Park to Indian Cove and back. The *Moderate* circumnavigation route involves currents and some open water that may become quite rough, particularly when current and wind directions oppose each other.

**Navigation Aids:** SeaTrails WA 002, 003, 004; NOAA charts 18423 SC or 18421 (both 1:80,000), 18434 (1:25,000). The San Juan Channel current table or Canadian *Current Atlas* is helpful for the circumnavigation route; Port Townsend tide tables (add about 30 minutes) are handy for Indian Cove.

**Planning Considerations:** For paddlers wheeling their watercraft aboard the ferry, convenient water access is now limited to Friday Harbor. Access at the Shaw Island ferry isn't possible, and at Orcas Island it is not always certain. Timing with the currents, a fairly complex task here made easiest by the *Current Atlas*, will greatly affect your speed and effort on the circumnavigation route. Plan for a high-tide arrival or departure at Indian Cove to avoid walking the mudflats. Campsites at Indian Cove and Jones Island are usually all spoken for on summer weekends. The Shaw General Store allows you to dock at the marina and has all the provisions you may need, including great pizza. You can visit their website at shawgeneralstore.com.

## GETTING THERE AND LAUNCHING

The route described starts from Odlin County Park on Lopez Island. From the Lopez ferry termi-nal, drive a little more than 1 mile south on Ferry Road to Odlin County Park and its easy access

*Paddle boarder off Shaw Island near Indian Cove*

to the sandy beach. The campground includes one Cascadia Marine Trail site (eight people, three tents) with overflow hiker/biker sites, as well as vault toilets and fires pits. Cars may be parked for a daily fee; pay the caretaker at the residence near the entrance.

Alternatively, the circumnavigation route can also start and end at the ferry stop in Friday Harbor or from Deer Harbor or West Sound on Orcas Island (see Trip 60, Jones Island, for a description of these launch sites).

## ROUTE

The Shaw Island circumnavigation route is approximately 14 miles, beginning at Odlin County Park and proceeding counterclockwise. Add 2 miles for a side trip to Turn Island and 3 miles for Jones Island. If you launch at Deer Harbor, add 2 miles. Five places to camp are distributed around and on Shaw Island—Odlin County Park, Blind Island, Jones Island, Turn Island, and Indian Cove—allowing you to partition the trip into two or three equal paddling days.

From Odlin County Park, paddle about 1.9 miles across Upright Channel to Indian Cove. For the most interesting route, follow the Lopez Island shore south from Odlin County Park to Flat Point, then cross the 0.25-mile-wide narrows to Canoe Island and finally Indian Cove.

A little more than 1 mile south of Odlin County Park, the day-use only Upright Channel Beach Access, managed by the Department of Natural Resources, has toilets and four picnic sites but no water. This 700-foot-long gravel beach with forested uplands sits just east of the residences near Flat Point.

Watch carefully for boat traffic before crossing from the spit at Flat Point to Canoe Island, especially the ferries going to and from Friday Harbor. Currents in Upright Channel generally are weak but may have some force here. The flood flows north. Though Canoe Island beaches are public below mean high tide, the uplands are not. The owners, who operate a youth camp specializing in French language and culture, strongly discourage visitors.

Shaw Island County Park, encompassing western Indian Cove and part of the peninsula that separates it from Reef Net Bay, offers camping, trail sites, picnicking, and more secluded stops ashore. Find the campsites along a road that starts near a low bank to the east and climbs to a bluff to the west. Steps at intervals along the beach climb to the campsites, with the most easterly ones more readily accessible from the water. Sharing a site with others is a definite possibility during peak summer weekends. Water, vault toilets, and a cooking shelter are provided, and hammocks are allowed in specific sites. The reservation system runs between March and October 15. Learn more at sanjuanco.com/523/Shaw-Island. Avoid arriving and departing near low tides, as the foreshore in Indian Cove becomes a muddy tide flat.

To make this a one-day *Protected* trip, you can return the same way you paddled or make a loop by following the Shaw Island shore north along Upright Channel. Then, opposite Odlin County Park, make the direct 1-mile crossing back to your start.

The Shaw Island shore north of Indian Cove is rocky and for the most part wild, continuing east into Harney Channel. Currents in Harney Channel are stronger than in Upright Channel but still pose few problems. The flood current here flows west.

Blind Island State Park, with a designated Cascadia Marine Trail site, is about a half mile west of the Shaw Island landing and 3.5 miles from Odlin County Park. Facilities on this three-acre island include a composting toilet, picnic tables, and fire pits but no water. Two state park sites and four Cascadia Marine Trail sites are available. Landings can be made on rocky beaches at the southwest and southeast ends of the island. The few trees on the island include cherry, apple, and filbert, left from an old homestead. Please do not disturb the resting birds. Chest-high brush shielding some of the sites is the only wind protection. Because it is small, Blind Island can feel crowded when only a few parties are camped there. The Shaw General Store is a good place to stop for pizza and restrooms. It's okay to use the store dock to visit, but this is not a launch.

For the route west from Blind Island to Neck Point, including a possible side trip to Jones Island via Yellow and the Wasp Islands, see Trip 60, Jones Island. Jones Island is 5.5 miles from Blind Island.

The small islets north and south of Neck Point are very popular with seals. It is not uncommon to see two dozen or so hauled out here. Both islets are part of the San Juan Islands National Wildlife Refuge, so do not approach closer than 200 yards.

Rounding Neck Point and heading southeast along Shaw Island's west-facing shore, the San Juan Channel current can be quite strong, especially at the points that protrude into the waterway. You can find eddy systems alongshore for much of the way, with extensive eddies in the vicinity of Parks Bay. Most of the northern portion of this shore is developed with summer residences, but there are some points of interest. At Point George, a one-thousand-plus-acre biological preserve, owned by the University of Washington (UW), extends south and west almost

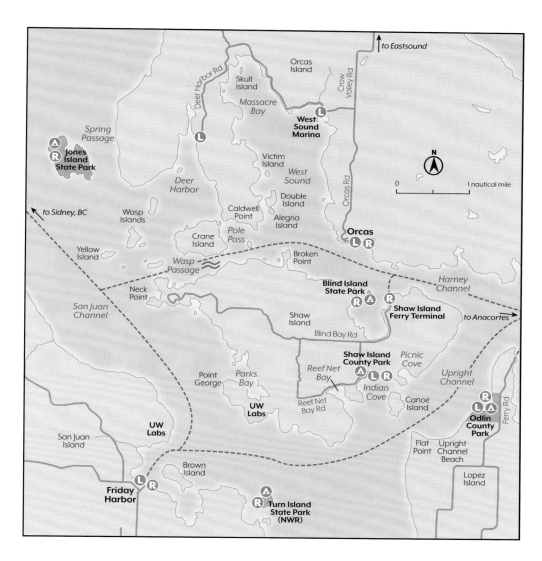

to Reef Net Bay. Managed by the UW's Friday Harbor Laboratories, this preserve is off-limits to the public in the uplands and tidelands. But as you paddle by, you can still enjoy the forests and meadows.

Turn Island State Park, located a little over 1 mile south of Shaw Island across San Juan Channel, offers an opportunity for camping or a respite along this otherwise no-access portion of the circumnavigation. Located 3.1 miles from Shaw Island County Park, this state park is a good place to spend your first night if you had an afternoon start from Friday Harbor.

Be careful crossing San Juan Channel to and from Turn Island. Currents are strong enough to require significant course adjustment to offset your drift, and steep seas can develop when the current opposes winds from either north or south. Watch for ferries and other heavy boat traffic associated with nearby Friday Harbor.

Turn Island is a unit of the San Juan Islands National Wildlife Refuge. A portion of the west end is leased to the Washington State Parks and Recreation Commission: camping is allowed only in this park area's twelve sites. No water is available, and fires are prohibited, but there are composting toilets and camp stoves are allowed. A rough trail circles the island. Keep in mind that public use of this refuge island is contingent on being compatible with wildlife. Avoid any nesting sites.

As you round the southernmost point of Shaw Island, arrive at Reef Net Bay. The tips of both points forming the bay are private land, but two pocket beaches on the west side of the bay make more-secluded landing spots. A spur road down the rocky slopes provides land access to the beaches.

From Reef Net Bay, head east to Indian Cove and then take a usually easy, protected paddle across Upright Channel back to your starting point at Odlin County Park.

# 56. **Clark Island**

Paths wind through madrona bordering this island's shore, which includes a gravel beach on one side and sand on the other, while extensive tide pools invite exploration. Because moorings here are somewhat exposed, Clark Island gets fewer overnight boaters than other state park

*Aerial view of Clark and Barnes Islands from Mount Constitution*

islands in the northern San Juans. Radically different approach routes to the island are possible. The southern route from Doe Bay on Orcas Island is shorter, though it requires a ferry ride from the mainland. Also note that the launch point at Doe Bay Resort is only available to resort guests, who get access to camping, cabins, and a soak in the resort's hot tubs. The general store is open to the public. For details, visit doebay.com. The northern route originates in the Lummi Indian Reservation between Bellingham and Ferndale. Few kayakers think to use this northeastern approach to the San Juans, but it has significant advantages.

**Duration:** Full day to overnight.

**Rating:** *Exposed*. Both routes require 1.5- to 2-mile crossings through a strong current with possible shipping traffic on the northern route. Tide rips are likely along either route.

**Navigation Aids:** SeaTrails WA 004, 005; NOAA charts 18423 SC or 18421 (both 1:80,000), 18430 (1:25,000); Rosario Strait current tables with local corrections or the Canadian *Current Atlas*.

**Planning Considerations:** For the southern route, aim for times of least current in the area between the north shore of Orcas Island and Clark Island. Pay heed to the behavior of eddies in this area and accompanying hazards. For the approach from Gooseberry Point around Lummi Island, plan for times of minimal current in Rosario Strait. Also try to avoid current flow conflicting with the likely wind direction. Currents in this area have no precise secondary reference station in the NOAA current tables; the station 1.5 miles north of Clark Island is closest. The Canadian *Current Atlas* is most useful for gauging the timing and strength of the currents on this crossing.

## GETTING THERE AND LAUNCHING

**Doe Bay Resort:** This launch is for Doe Bay Resort guests only. From the Orcas Island ferry landing, follow Orcas Road north to Eastsound. Veer right onto Main Street and drive through town. Main Street becomes Crescent Beach Drive. Take a right onto Olga Road and follow it approximately 6 miles to Olga. Take a left on Point Lawrence Road to Doe Bay Resort. A popular retreat for people with an inclination toward natural foods and living, Doe Bay's cabins, saunas, and hot tubs are busy year-round. An area for tent camping is nearby, as well as a café and a natural-foods general store. The management charges a nominal fee to camp and launch there. A soak in the hot tubs is an additional fee.

**Gooseberry Point:** From Interstate 5, take Exit 260 (Lummi Island/Slater Road) and turn west onto Slater Road. After almost 4 miles, turn left onto Haxton Way and follow it for 6.5 miles to the Lummi Island ferry landing at Gooseberry Point. For overnight parking at Gooseberry Point, the launch is north of the Lummi Island ferry and is owned by the Lummi Nation. A parking attendant is in the small building by the boat launch. Parking is a nominal fee, and the lot is monitored by a security guard. Park in the westernmost corner of the lot. Call 360-305-9703 or check lummi-island.com/ferry to confirm these details.

For Vancouver, British Columbia, and Bellingham residents, this northern approach is the most convenient way to access the northern San Juans, as well as Sucia, Matia, and Patos Islands. Seattle-area dwellers wishing to access this area will find it takes less time to drive to Gooseberry Point than to ferry to Orcas Island. During busy summer weekends, the time saved may amount to a half-day or more due to ferry traffic backups.

**Village Point:** This launch is along the road on Lummi Island, 0.6 mile north of the point off West Shore Drive. Look for two pullouts and a trail going about 50 yards to a gravel beach.

## ROUTES

**Doe Bay to Clark Island:** *Exposed.* The distance from Doe Bay to Clark Island is about 4 miles. Though the shoreline of Orcas Island north from Doe Bay makes for pretty paddling, consider a detour 0.5 mile offshore to the Peapod Rocks if weather and currents are favorable. This San Juan Islands National Wildlife Refuge unit has abundant birdlife, seals, and sometimes sea lions. Remember, no landings are permitted; keep 200 yards away from these and other refuge rocks.

Lawrence Point is Department of Natural Resources (DNR) land. You can camp here, but it's not a particularly good place for it—there are no facilities. The grassy point does make a pleasant lunch stop, though, or a place to watch the swirling currents while you wait for favorable ones. Access is via two narrow pebble beaches on the south side of the point.

The 1.5-mile crossing to Clark Island from Lawrence Point can expose you to hazards created by strong currents. Both flood and ebb tides produce large eddies around Lawrence Point, and powerful rips may occur at the boundaries with the main current streams. The Canadian *Current Atlas* gives the best picture of the complex flows in this area. Note that strong east-flowing currents move along the shore of Orcas Island on large flood exchanges in this area, the opposite of what might be expected, and they flow the same way on large ebbs too! The current can produce strong tide rips as it passes over a shoal not shown on chart 18423 SC, just east of a line between Lawrence Point and Clark Island. Time your crossing to the Lawrence Point area to arrive at slack time. Also avoid this area on ebbs if southerly winds are likely. Because there are eddies near the point, a close-in route is usually safest if you must pass by while the current is running.

**Gooseberry Point to Clark Island:** *Exposed.* The one-way paddling distance is approximately 7 miles if you go around the north end of Lummi Island. The south end makes a much longer but interesting alternative, adding about 13 miles to the trip, with a possible overnight stop at Lummi Island Natural Resources Conservation Area (see Trip 35, Lummi Island, for details).

For the northern route, begin with the 1-mile crossing of Hale Passage. Keep in mind the currents can be as strong as several knots. A flood current is advantageous for reaching the north end of the island; you can gradually work across while the moving water carries you north. The Lummi Island shore is mostly residential until you round Point Migley. Development dwindles past here, as bluffs rise along the water and conceal it from view. Strong wind opposing currents can make this section a treacherous paddle.

The 2-mile Clark Island crossing from Village Point is exposed to the Strait of Georgia to the north and Rosario Strait to the south. Swift currents with possible tide rips and busy ship-

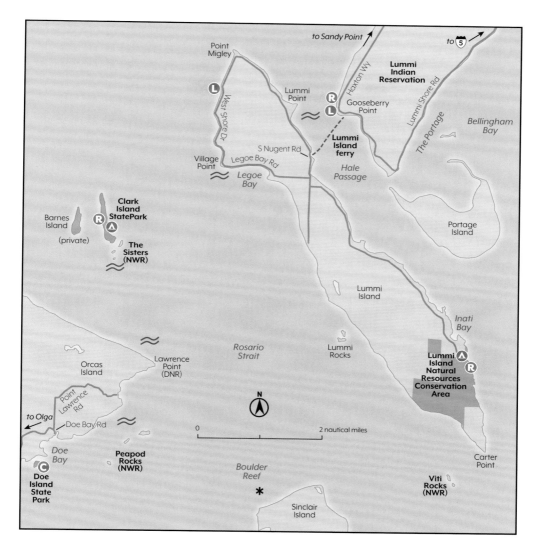

ping in Rosario Strait, particularly tankers en route to Ferndale's Cherry Point terminal, make this segment challenging. Launch north of Village Point along West Shore Drive via a public beach accessed from the road. Look for cars or a pullout along the road.

Currents move very swiftly around both ends of Clark Island and nearby privately owned Barnes Island. Watch out for tide rips. The Sisters Islands to the southeast of Clark Island are units of the San Juan Islands National Wildlife Refuge. Landings are prohibited; keep 200 yards offshore.

Paths circle the low bluffs around the southern end of Clark Island with open madrona woods onshore and extensive tide pools and flats exposed at low tide. There are no trails to the brushy north end, but rounding the cliffs and offshore rocks makes a nice paddling excursion. A sand beach sits on the island's west side and a gravel one on the east. The west beach sites are for picnicking; camping is allowed on sites most easily reached from the east.

Eight campsites are spaced out along the east beach, low enough that a loaded kayak can be dragged over the smooth gravel right into camp. No water is available on the island. The beach sites are vulnerable to bad weather; two sites in the woods at the narrowest point of the island are the best protected. Camping is first come, first served for all sites but one, which can be reserved for groups by calling Washington State Parks at 360-376-2073.

# 57. Orcas Island: Cascade and Mountain Lakes

These lakes on Orcas Island are ideal for beginners or those seeking freshwater options that are more protected than nearby saltwater trips. Enjoy warm water in summer and solitude in winter. Cascade Lake has abundant stocked rainbow trout, as well as coastal cutthroat trout, kokanee, and largemouth bass. Mountain Lake harbors eastern brook trout, kokanee, cutthroat trout, and jumbo triploid trout (stocked in the spring).

**Duration:** Half day.

**Rating:** *Protected.*

**Navigation Aids:** NOAA chart 18421 (1:80,000). For Moran State Park maps, visit parks. wa.gov/547/Moran.

**Planning Considerations:** Bring your Discover Pass. Both lakes have boat ramps and camping. Cascade Lake has paddle board and kayak rentals in summer.

## GETTING THERE AND LAUNCHING

**Cascade Lake:** From Eastsound, head east on Crescent Beach Road and take a right on Olga Road, which takes you south to Cascade Lake. The main swim beach has parking, restrooms, and (in summer) a small store. Launch to the right of the swim area on the far side of the store.

**Mountain Lake:** Near the southeast corner of Cascade Lake, take a left on Mount Constitution Road and follow it to the Mountain Lake boat ramp just past the Twin Lakes trailhead.

## ROUTES

**Cascade Lake:** Situated within Moran State Park, Cascade Lake is easily accessed from Olga Road south of Eastsound. The forest-lined lake is undeveloped and has a secluded lagoon on the west side, making it a popular swimming and paddling spot in summer. You can glide under a classic wooden footbridge stretching over the entry to the lagoon. The 3-mile Cascade Lake Loop hiking trail circles the lake. The Cascade Lake Swim Beach may be congested in sum-

*Footbridge connecting Cascade Lake to the smaller Moran Lagoon*

mer, making launching more difficult, but it's easier in the off-season. The lake has three campgrounds on the north, middle, and south sides; the boat ramp onto the lake is at Midway Campground. The northeast corner of the lake is home to Orcas Adventures, which offers kayak and paddle board rentals in summer.

**Mountain Lake:** Perched 900 feet up Mount Constitution, this lake lives up to its name. It's also the largest lake on the island. Explore forest-lined shores and the lake's three islets. The lake is colder than Cascade Lake and less crowded in summer. Motors are not allowed. Find the boat ramp by the Twin Lakes trailhead, with camping nearby. Parking is tight in summer.

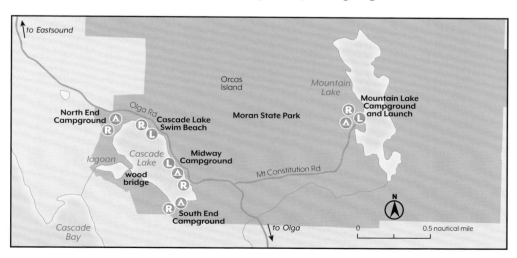

*Tide rip off Point Doughty*

# 58. **Point Doughty on Orcas Island**

Accessible only from the water, this little Department of Natural Resources (DNR) Recreation Site at Orcas Island's northwest tip has attractive madrona and fir woods, tide pools, and spectacular cliffs, complete with a small sea cave or two on the north side. The Cascadia Marine Trail's campsite has views facing south and west. Point Doughty was named for John Doughty, an officer in the 1841 Wilkes Expedition.

At the time of this writing, 1800 feet of shoreline and the former Glenwood Inn resort south of Point Doughty have been purchased by the San Juan County Conservation Land Bank in partnership with the San Juan Preservation Trust. In the future, you will be able to walk to Point Doughty from this property at low tide, and paddlers will be able to land but not camp on the property.

**Duration:** Part day to overnight.

**Rating:** *Moderate*. A north wind can create rough conditions and surf along Orcas Island's north shore. Current and tide rips are likely off the point.

**Navigation Aids:** SeaTrails WA 004; NOAA charts 18423 SC or 18421 (both 1:80,000), 18431 (1:25,000); Canadian *Current Atlas*.

**Planning Considerations:** Aim for times of least current to avoid tide rips while rounding Point Doughty. Give the point a wide berth in rough seas.

## GETTING THERE AND LAUNCHING

From the Orcas Island ferry dock, drive north to Eastsound. At Eastsound, turn north on North Beach Road and follow it to the launch (see map on page 269).

**North Beach Road End:** Launch from the gravel beach at the end of North Beach Road. Parking is free along the road but is restricted to five cars. Do not expect to find space on summer weekends, as it is an extremely popular launch. Respect the private homes on both sides. You can park in the lot for three days.

Outer Island Excursions, located just west of the North Beach launch, offers a water taxi to carry you and your boat to the islands. They also offer tours and related services. For additional information, visit outerislandx.com or call 360-376-3711.

## ROUTE

The roundtrip distance from North Beach to Point Doughty is about 4.2 miles. Follow the beach west past occasional homes and small resorts. A mile short of the point, the shore begins to rise, and sheer cliffs line the remaining distance. Rocks and shoals are extensive off Point Doughty and, together with swift currents, produce significant tide rips. A close inshore route around the point may avoid them if the seas are smooth enough to allow it. If you have rock-gardening experience, you may enjoy shooting the gap between the rocks on the point at high tides.

An unprotected moorage and largely rocky beach limit visits by other boaters, though the point is popular with scuba divers. Access is via a small beach on the south side of the point. At midtide or above, landings are on pebbles and gravel; low-tide approaches are rocky and may be hard on your boat if a southerly sea is running.

One campsite has Cascadia Marine Trail designation; the other is open to all boaters on a first-come, first-served basis. Vault toilets, picnic tables, and garbage cans are provided, but water is not available. One campsite reveals good views to the south and west, but it has poor weather protection. The other is tucked into the trees, making it a good all-weather camp, but offers no views. Trails lead east from the campsites along the south bluffs and eventually to the YMCA's Camp Orkila, 1 mile to the east, though there is no public access to the camp by land.

# 59. Patos, Sucia, and Matia Islands

This chain of state park and wildlife refuge islands is famed for its intricate geology as well as its potentially treacherous waters. Separated from other islands in the San Juan group by miles of sea and open to the expanse of the Strait of Georgia, they are relatively isolated and very beautiful.

In 2015, the first dinosaur fossil in Washington State was found on Sucia Island. The fossil was identified by Burke Museum paleontologists as a partial left femur (thigh bone) of a theropod dinosaur: a two-legged, meat-eating dinosaur similar to the Tyrannosaurus rex.

**Duration:** Overnight to multiple nights.

**Rating:** *Exposed*. Though this area is sometimes millpond-smooth, it is also well known for producing strong but erratic currents and big seas that develop from northerly winds on fair afternoons. This is no place for inexperienced paddlers!

**Navigation Aids:** SeaTrails WA 004; NOAA charts 18423 SC or 18421 (both 1:80,000), 18431 (1:25,000); Rosario Strait current tables or the Canadian *Current Atlas*.

**Planning Considerations:** All routes to these islands put paddlers at the mercy of the weather and strong currents during long crossings. Be sure to consult forecasts and be prepared to lay over on the islands during bad weather. Currents are strong throughout the area but not reliably predictable (see the discussion in the North Beach to Sucia Island route below). All campsites are marine state parks. Get information about fees at parks.wa.gov/166/Camping-fees.

## GETTING THERE AND LAUNCHING

From the Orcas Island ferry dock, drive north to Eastsound. At Eastsound, turn north on North Beach Road and follow it to the launch. There are no restrooms and limited parking. Outer Island Excursions, located just west of the North Beach launch, offers a water taxi to carry you and your boat to the islands. They also offer tours and related services. For additional information, visit outerislandx.com or call 360-376-3711.

## ROUTES

A weekend trip from North Beach to Sucia Island (about 5 miles roundtrip), with an optional excursion to Matia Island (add another 2-plus miles one way), is one of the most popular kayak outings in the San Juan Islands. Including Patos Island in the agenda adds another 5 miles or more and usually merits another overnight.

**North Beach to Sucia Island:** *Exposed*. The roundtrip distance is about 5 miles, depending on your destination on Sucia Island. The crossing from North Beach to the nearest point on Sucia Island is 2 miles. The greatest hazard en route is Parker Reef: it consists of two separate shoals located less than halfway across. The area around the reefs can develop dangerous rips in strong currents, sometimes exceeding 2 knots, which are made worse by contrary winds. A kayaking fatality has occurred here. Looks can be deceiving—the crossing may appear glassy and inviting, but it can change rapidly.

Generally, the west-flowing ebb current is the most dangerous. The Canadian *Current Atlas* shows the flood currents coming around the east and west sides of Orcas Island, meeting and weakening in this area. The timing of these currents is somewhat unreliable. There have been reports of slacks varying greatly from their predicted times and current flowing in reverse of what was predicted.

Nonetheless, this route attracts large numbers of paddlers during the summer, including novices. As the record shows, more than a few first-time kayakers have had bad experiences between Sucia and Orcas Islands, with some lucky to escape with their lives. The potential for risk remains very high and must be considered before venturing out.

Sucia Island is a cruising hub in the northern San Juan Islands for yachts and kayaks alike. You are unlikely to find solitude in the summer, but its other attractions make up for it. This island complex, in actuality at least six separate islands, can absorb a day's exploring by kayak and another day by foot along the extensive trail system. Little Sucia Island is an eagle preserve; no camping or fires are allowed. The bizarre formations of water-dissolved rock here are unsurpassed, and seals abound on and around them. Watch for rips off Johnson Point.

Kayakers visiting Sucia Island during the summer generally prefer Ewing Cove or Snoring Bay for the relative isolation from other boaters and campers that these areas afford. You can land but not camp at Ewing Cove.

Most overnight visitors to Sucia Island stay in Fossil and Echo Bays, which have extensive campsites with solar composting toilets; water is available in summer. Fossil and Echo Bays

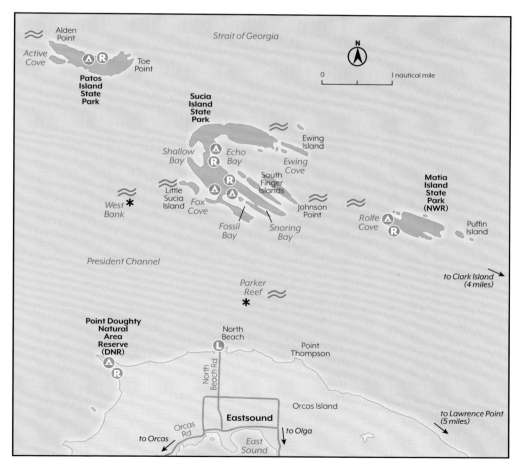

*Map is for both trips 58 and 59.*

*Rock formations along Sucia Island's south side*

also offer the best campsites for the off-season, especially since driftwood for fires piles up in Echo Bay during the winter. Low banks and mixed shell-and-gravel beaches make camping attractive for kayakers in Fossil Bay or adjoining Fox Cove. Shallow Bay, on the island's west side, also has camps, with drinking water nearby at the picnic shelters on the north side of the bay. A 125-foot portage connects Echo Bay to Shallow Bay, allowing you to visit both without having to make a long paddle around the island.

Elsewhere on the island, camp only at sites designated with a fire ring or a picnic table. Camping outside these areas is prohibited.

Campsites are often full at Sucia Island on busy summer weekends. As a San Juan Islands marine park, a special reservation service for group camping only is provided through Washington State Parks. Call 360-376-2073 well in advance to reserve. Otherwise, all camping is on a first-come, first-served basis. You can visit the park website at parks.wa.gov/594/Sucia-Island.

**North Beach or Sucia Island to Matia Island:** *Exposed.* The crossing from Orcas Island to Matia Island is slightly longer than the crossing to Sucia Island. It's about 2.5 miles one way and may involve strong currents, though the shallows at Parker Reef are easier to avoid.

A little more than 1 mile from Sucia Island, Matia Island is hard-pressed to maintain its wild quality in the face of nearby boating activity. Matia Island is owned entirely by the federal government as a national wildlife refuge for bald eagles and pelagic cormorants. Five acres at Rolfe Cove are formally leased to the Washington State Parks and Recreation Commission, which also manages the rest of the island for the US Fish and Wildlife Service.

Camping is confined to Rolfe Cove and is first come, first served. Rolfe is a very protected cove with steep walls on two sides. No open fires are allowed. Find the six well-protected sites above the gravel beach and low bluffs. A composting toilet is nearby, but no water is provided on the island (water can be found on Sucia Island from April to September). Nearby Eagle Cove is outside the state park lease area and is closed to camping. Exploring ashore should be confined to a trail loop that runs down the center of the island and returns on the south side.

The many coves around Matia Island are best visited by boat to limit the refuge's onshore disturbance. On the south side, look for the "hermit's cove," which holds remnants of a solitary island dweller's structures dating back to the 1920s. At the southeast corner, visit coves with pebble beaches. Refuge managers ask that you avoid the cove at the east end of the island facing Puffin Island because of the eagles that nest there. Keep at least 200 yards offshore of Puffin Island to avoid disturbing that refuge as well.

**North Beach or Sucia Island to Patos Island:** *Exposed.* Paddle to Patos Island from North Beach by following the Orcas Island shore west to Point Doughty, then cross a little more than 4 miles of open water. Strong currents and tide rips are possible along this route. The safer but longer alternative is to head for Sucia Island first, then cut across to Patos Island at the time of slack water. Both routes are safer and far easier on the flood current. Watch for rips in the area of West Bank marked by an extensive kelp bed.

Patos Island is one of the wildest islands in the northern chain. A small portion of the island on the west side is managed by Washington State and the remainder is managed by the Bureau of Land Management's Wenatchee office. Four acres at Alden Point include a Coast Guard light station, which was established in 1893. All recreational use is confined to the west end of the island at Active Cove, which features a 1.5-mile loop trail. Facilities include seven campsites, one picnic site, one composting toilet, and one vault toilet. No water or garbage service is provided. Campers must register at the bulletin board near the beach.

Patos Island merits a circumnavigation, taking care to avoid disturbing the eagles and other wildlife along the way. On the south shore, notice bluffs and low cliffs with interestingly eroded sandstone conglomerate rocks, characteristic of this island chain. The east end has two coves with pebble beaches and long rock reefs. At low tide, you can see them a long distance from shore, giving Toe Point its name. Pebble beaches compose most of the northern shoreline.

**Great Rectangle Route:** *Exposed.* The paddling distance is about 25 miles. Integrate the string of Patos, Sucia, and Matia Islands into a large rectangle route including Clark Island (see Trip 56), with the fourth side formed by the entire north shore of Orcas Island. Camping is available on all five islands, including Point Doughty on northwestern Orcas Island (see Trip 58). Plan on at least two or, better yet, three nights for this trip.

Getting from Matia Island to Clark Island involves a 4-mile crossing with active currents between Clark and Orcas Islands, making both crossings precarious in unfavorable conditions. (See Trip 56, Clark Island, for a description of currents between Clark and Orcas Islands.) In unsettled weather, it's safer to cut this area out of the rectangle.

The north shore of Orcas Island forms the return leg of the rectangle route. Though this 6-mile-long linear shoreline between Lawrence Point and North Beach appears unexciting on the chart, it is gratifying to follow. Few spots are available for an emergency camp, so do your best to plan for fair weather. Most of the shore is very steep with either wooded scree slopes or cliffs rising up from sea level. Occasional narrow gravel beaches crop up at the base, but rarely is there anywhere to go above.

The coast is wild—look for otters and hauled-out seals—and has a few surprise bits of history. At one point, an old limestone kiln is fitted so unobtrusively into the steep slope that most boaters probably miss it. Farther on, pass an extensive, overgrown quarry long since covered by a vigorous young fir forest. Near Moran State Park, look for a San Juan Islands rarity—a waterfall spilling into the sea at high tide. Houses finally appear during the final third of the way to North Beach.

# 60. **Jones Island**

Sandy beaches, trails meandering through madrona groves and meadows, and a resident deer herd that mingles with campers make Jones Island one of the most popular San Juan Island destinations for kayakers. Other boaters enjoy it, too, so much so that campsites are often scarce on summer weekends. You can combine this trip with a circumnavigation of Shaw Island (see Trip 55) and a paddle through the Wasp Islands. Jones Island was named by the Wilkes Expedition in 1841 in honor of Captain Jacob Jones.

**Duration:** Full day or overnight.

**Rating:** *Moderate*. The trip involves a 0.5-mile open-water crossing in currents up to 2 knots.

**Navigation Aids:** SeaTrails WA 002, 003, 004; NOAA charts 18423 SC or 18421 (both 1:80,000), 18434 (1:25,000). The San Juan Channel current table or Canadian *Current Atlas* are useful for timing the route for favorable flows.

**Planning Considerations:** Arrive early to secure a campsite on summer weekends. Coordinate with currents in Wasp Passage, Pole Pass, and, if Friday Harbor is a trip terminus, San Juan Channel. Raccoons on Jones Island can be a problem. For kayakers wheeling their watercraft aboard the ferry, convenient water access is now limited to Friday Harbor. Launching near the ferry dock at Shaw Island is no longer possible, and at Orcas Island questionable. However, three routes are still described below using these launches as starting points, in the hopes that they or nearby alternatives will become available through the efforts of organizations such as the Washington Water Trails Association. Including these routes also allows you to integrate them into a Shaw Island circumnavigation or other trips of your own design. In summer, watch for heavy boat traffic.

## GETTING THERE AND LAUNCHING

Take the San Juan Islands ferry to either Orcas Island or San Juan Island, depending on where you want to start.

**West Sound (Orcas Island):** From the ferry, take Orcas Road north. Take a left on Deer Harbor Road and follow it for about a mile to West Sound. After the marina, but just before the

*Paddlers threading through the Wasp Islands*

T intersection at Crow Valley Road, find a pullout on the north side of the road where kayakers park. Launch on the beach below the metal stairway that is adjacent to the marina dock. There are no facilities, but a restaurant is nearby.

**Deer Harbor (Orcas Island):** Continue past West Sound on Deer Harbor Road a few more miles to Deer Harbor. Just before Deer Harbor, the Deer Harbor Preserve is a great day-use spot but allows no camping. Note the lot fills on summer days as overflow marina parking. At low tides, there's a mudflat to launch from. A bit farther down the road, the Deer Harbor launch site provides the closest access to Jones Island. Driving to Deer Harbor to launch reduces the one-way paddling distance to Jones Island to about 2 miles. Water access is at Deer Harbor Marina, which charges a fee to launch and to park; pay at the store. All the basic amenities are here, including restrooms with showers, water, a boat-cleaning hose, a small store, a public telephone, and sea kayak rentals. Call the marina for additional information at 360-376-3037. Cayou Quay Marina offers overnight parking, but it must be preapproved by the marina office several days prior. Learn more online at cayouquay.com.

**Orcas Island Ferry Landing:** Access the water from the west side of the ferry dock at the county launch. If you're exiting the ferry, find it to the immediate left on the ramp before Orcas Road. Water access is off a high dock. Park far above in pay parking.

**Friday Harbor (San Juan Island):** The launch is the dinghy dock at the public wharf north of the ferry landing. Pay a launch fee at the marina, which has two kayak launch slots, public restrooms, and coin-operated showers. In the summer, parking in Friday Harbor is extremely scarce and boating traffic can be very busy. Keep clear of ferry traffic.

**Shaw Island:** No launching is allowed at the ferry terminal. The closest access point is at Shaw Island County Park on the south side of the island, 2 miles from the ferry. Plan on driving if you use this option; it is too far to wheel a kayak unless you are extremely determined. From the ferry, take Blind Bay Road south. Take a left on Reef Net Bay Road and look for signs for Shaw Island County Park, which offers camping.

## ROUTES

**Deer Harbor to Jones Island:** *Moderate.* The paddling distance is about 2 miles one way. Follow the western shore of Deer Harbor toward Steep Point, passing rocky shores covered with madronas, cliffs, and occasional homes. All the shoreline along this route is private, so plan to stay in your boat until you reach Jones Island. This route would qualify for a *Protected* rating if not for the Spring Passage crossing. Here currents can reach almost 2 knots. You may need to ferry upstream at a large angle to hold your position during the crossing. Seas in the passage can get quite rough when the wind opposes the current. Tide rips are also possible. To be safest, time this crossing for when currents are flowing in the same direction as the wind.

Jones Island State Park is a very popular destination for kayakers and other boaters. Approach from the south and take out in the cove for a short walk to the Cascadia Marine Trail campsite, which has two sites (up to eight people each), a picnic table, a composting toilet, and a fire pit. Water is only available in summer. The park has other primitive campsites scattered around the island, connected by 2 miles of island trails. Reservations can be made for groups only by calling Washington State Parks at 360-902-8844. Other campsites are first come, first served and difficult to find on summer weekends.

Most powerboaters prefer the more protected northern cove where there is a dock. Protect your gear and food from the island's posse of commando raccoons, which will do anything to gain access to your food.

**Friday Harbor to Jones Island:** *Moderate.* The paddling distance is 6.2 miles one way. This route is often used by kayakers riding the ferries as foot passengers. Aside from Yellow Island, no public shorelines exist along the route, but with favorable current and wind, this trip should take less than two hours. Currents in this part of San Juan Channel can attain about 1 knot; planning to use them is worthwhile. Watch for ferry and recreational boating traffic when crossing to Jones Island.

The shoreline of Shaw Island is the more interesting side to follow (see Trip 55, Shaw Island: Circumnavigation, for more details) and under the appropriate conditions, you can return by crossing to the San Juan Island side at Point George. Point George and Parks Bay behind it are part of a University of Washington biological preserve; landings are not allowed.

**West Sound on Orcas Island to Jones Island via Pole Pass:** *Moderate.* The paddling distance is 5.5 miles one way from the public launch west of the West Sound Marina. Take a short side trip north to Massacre Bay to view Skull Island and the migratory waterfowl that fill the bay. Then head south to paddle along the inside of Victim Island, Double Island, and Alegria Island, enjoying views of 1500-foot-high Turtleback Mountain to the north. Victim and Skull Islands were named after the bloody Indian war of 1858, when the Haidas from British Columbia ventured south to catch slaves. One hundred local Lummi people were killed. Human remains from this period were found at Haida Point in 1900.

Round Caldwell Point and enter Pole Pass on the inside of Crane Island. Pole Pass is a little tide race that can run at more than 2 knots for a short distance. It is rarely dangerous, but boat wakes in the riffles on the downstream side can make it quite rough. You can go through against the current because it is quite weak in the approaches. Use eddies on the Orcas Island side; a hard push is required for the short distance in the narrows against the flow. Be especially

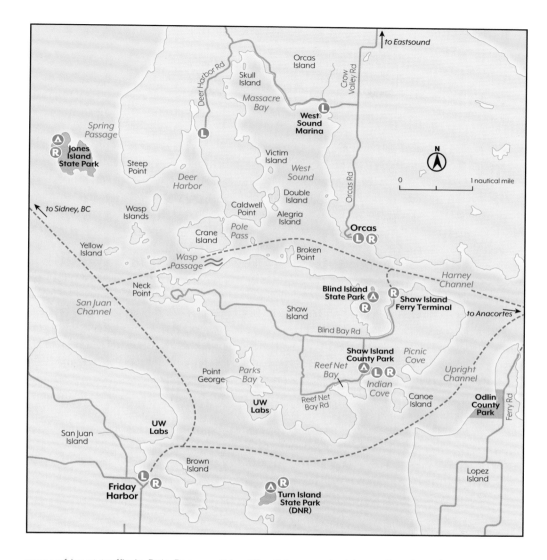

wary of boat traffic in Pole Pass, as it is difficult to see what is coming the other way as you approach. Currents in the passages between Shaw and Orcas Islands generally flow westward during the flood tide and eastward during the ebb.

Currents in this area are rarely fast enough to be hazardous but can substantially affect paddling effort. Except for Blind Island State Park (see Trip 55, Shaw Island: Circumnavigation, for details) and the public tidelands at Broken Point, there is no public access ashore along this route. However, it can be covered in less than two hours with favorable currents.

**Orcas, Shaw, and San Juan Islands to Jones Island via the Wasp Islands:** *Moderate.* Use NOAA chart 18434. When paddling to Jones Island, take a side trip to the Wasp Islands, a series of rocky islets with a colorful history and great wildlife viewing. Located north of Wasp Passage on the west side of Crane Island, the name Wasp came from a warship in the War of 1812. Wasp Passage is known as the "rockpile" by locals.

Scattered with rocks and islets, the Wasp Islands make for interesting and scenic paddling. Most of the Wasp Islands are privately owned and a few smaller ones are part of the San Juan National Wildlife Refuge, in which landings are prohibited. Coon Island's pocket beaches and 2000 feet of the southern portion of McDonnell Island are public tidelands. The public areas are only below the mean high-water level.

Currents in this area are moderate. Wasp Passage runs swiftly enough to produce rips in the area of Crane Island. The major hazard here is the ferry that takes this route between Friday Harbor and Orcas Island. It can come around the corner quite suddenly from either direction. Do not dawdle in midchannel at Wasp Passage, and keep your group tightly together for all channel crossings. Also watch out for ferry wakes colliding with an opposing current (when the ferry is traveling against the current), as these can become steep and nasty breakers. The wake will smooth out after entering eddies along the sides of the passage.

The Shaw Island shore of Wasp Passage is a fine place to practice using shore eddies to travel against the current. Note that the currents in this area run counter to what might be expected; they flow west into San Juan Channel on the flood tide. Boat wakes may increase the size of the tide rips. Expect heavy recreational boat traffic in summer. In 1946, Lew and Tib Dodd purchased Yellow Island and built a cabin out of driftwood. A guest house and sauna on the west shore are now gone. In 1960, Lew died on the island and his ashes were buried on his favorite spot on Hummingbird Hill. Tib lived on the island for six months out of the year until 1978. The Nature Conservancy now owns Yellow Island and works to protect the island's wildflowers. Flowers begin to bloom in late March and are at their best from mid-April through early summer. Resident caretakers live in the cabin on the southwest shore.

Yellow Island has limited access and no camping, restrooms, or other facilities are available. Collecting plants or intertidal life, smoking, pets, picnicking, and fires are prohibited. The island is open from 10 AM to 4 PM year-round. Only land on the southeast beach below the Dodd cabin. The east spit is open to landings only in the spring and fall. Do not beach watercraft on the west spit. For more information, call The Nature Conservancy in Seattle at 206-343-4344.

# 61. **South and West San Juan Island**

Paddlers come here for two distinct reasons. The first is whales: Haro Strait is the best place to see orcas in the summer, and Lime Kiln Point State Park was developed primarily for public observation of the whales that pass offshore regularly. The second reason paddlers visit is the barren beauty: the largely treeless southwestern coast of San Juan Island is unique in the Northwest. The exposure to southerly and westerly winds and big seas along its beaches make it all the wilder. To the north, western San Juan Island has a gentler face with inter-island channels and the accessible historical attractions of English Camp. Around 1990, an ancient Lummi winter village site was excavated on Garrison Bay at the site of English Camp. The Coast Salish name for this area is Pe'pi'ow'elh. It's estimated that dwellings shaped by piled shells existed here as early as AD 100. By AD 1500, two plank-style longhouses were built, approximately thirty feet wide and forty-five feet long. Large shell middens lie under the Parade Ground of the English Camp site. Cattle Point on the south side of the island has evidence of discarded shells dating as far back as five thousand years.

**Duration:** Part day to multiple nights.

**Rating:** *Moderate* or *Exposed. Exposed* routes involve strong currents with probable tide rips, characteristically strong winds with fully developed seas, and resulting surf on the beaches. See the description of wind patterns under the South Beach to Griffin Bay via Cattle Point route below.

**Navigation Aids:** SeaTrails WA 002, 003; NOAA charts 18423 SC or 18421 (both 1:80,000), 18433 or 18434 (both 1:25,000); San Juan Channel current table.

**Planning Considerations:** Avoid mid- to late afternoons for paddling west of Cattle Point when westerlies from the Strait of Juan de Fuca are strongest. Plan your trips according to the currents, which can be strong in certain areas on the island. Heavy fog in August can make visibility difficult along the west and south sides of the island.

## GETTING THERE AND LAUNCHING

You have several options for launching on the island whether you're doing a day trip, shuttle, overnight, or 30-mile circumnavigation.

**Friday Harbor:** The launch is the dinghy dock at the public wharf north of the ferry landing. Pay a launch fee at the marina, which has two kayak launch slots, public restrooms, and coin-operated showers. In summer, parking in Friday Harbor is extremely scarce and boating traffic can be very busy. Keep clear of ferry traffic. Call the marina office for additional information at 360-378-2688.

**Roche Harbor:** From the Friday Harbor ferry landing, drive about 10 miles to Roche Harbor. Take Spring Street two blocks through town to 2nd Street and turn right. After three blocks, 2nd Street bears left, becoming Guard Street. After one block, turn right onto Tucker Avenue. At the fork, bear left onto Roche Harbor Road and follow it to Roche Harbor.

You can launch on the south side of the main dock by the parking lot. San Juan Outfitters offers kayak and SUP rentals in front of the resort mid-May through September. Reservations are required; call 800-450-6858 or 360-378-1323. To contact the Roche Harbor Resort Marina, call 800-586-3590.

**English Camp:** Drive about 8.2 miles from Friday Harbor to English Camp. From the ferry landing, follow Spring Street to 2nd Street and turn right. Follow this street, bearing left where it becomes Guard Street. This eventually becomes Beaverton Valley Road and then West Valley Road. Turn off to the left for the entrance to English Camp and go down the hill to the lot.

*English Camp blockhouse and gardens on Garrison Bay*

Boats will have to be carried several hundred yards along a gravel walkway and lawn, smooth enough for carts, to the dinghy dock on the bay's north side. Restrooms and interpretive facilities are open in summer.

**San Juan County Park:** Follow the directions above for English Camp to West Valley Road, but this time turn left onto Mitchell Bay Road about 9.3 miles from Friday Harbor. Then turn left on Westside Road and follow it to the park at Smallpox Bay. A small parking lot gives easy access to the gravel beach where you can drop your gear. Above, overnight parking is available for boaters and paddlers of smaller watercraft; check with the park office for the best place to park. Campsites, restrooms, and water are available, including a Cascadia Marine Trail site and raccoon-proof food storage. Kayak racks are behind the restrooms. For more details, visit the San Juan County Parks website at sanjuanco.com/430/Parks-Recreation-Fair. Heavy paddling traffic in recent years has put public water access on the west side of the island in jeopardy. Call the San Juan County Park's line for additional information at 360-378-8420.

**Eagle Cove:** This launch point is just north of the American Camp portion of San Juan Island National Historical Park. From the Friday Harbor ferry landing, follow Spring Street three blocks to a Y intersection and go left on Argyle Avenue. This becomes Cattle Point Road and reaches the park after about 5 miles. Just before the park entrance, turn right onto Eagle Cove Road and go a half mile to the parking lot. Boats must be carried 100 yards downhill on a some-times-slippery path to the gravel beach. This launch point has more protection from surf than the beaches at Salmon Banks Lane farther south.

**Fourth of July Beach:** Traveling south in American Camp, the next launch spot is Fourth of July Beach. It provides access to the southeast shore of the island in Griffin Bay. Turn left off Cattle Point Road 1 mile south of the park entrance and drive to the small picnic area lot with a restroom. The beach is about 100 yards beyond the lot on a gravel path and is busy on warm weekends. Tidal currents can be swift off the beach.

**South Beach:** A huge parking area gives easy access to continuous gravel beaches facing southwest. Reach this launch by turning right off Cattle Point Road onto Pickett's Lane a short distance south of the Fourth of July Beach intersection. Launches can be rough here in even a moderate wind.

**Cattle Point Picnic Area:** This day-use launch gives access to the southern tip of the island and the tidal rapids at Shark Reef. Continue 0.75 mile past the eastern edge of American Camp to the small lot on the right. Boats must be carried 50 yards down a steep embankment to a sandy beach. Cattle Point offers some protection against surf at the west end of the beach.

## ROUTES

**South Beach to Griffin Bay via Cattle Point:** *Exposed*. The paddling distance is 5 miles one way. Logistically, this is the easiest route, as the 1.5-mile walk between the launch and take-out points eliminates the need for a car shuttle. You can take a lunch stop at the picnic area by Cattle Point, which early Lummi people called Tl'i'kweneng. Plan for plenty of time in Griffin Bay to explore its three lagoons. To read wildlife-viewing guidelines for San Juan National Historic Park, visit nps.gov/sajh/index.htm.

The *Exposed* rating is based on both currents and wind. Currents at San Juan Channel's south entrance can reach 5 knots, when heavy tide rips are likely, especially around Goose Island and Deadman Island on the Lopez Island side. Staying close inshore on the San Juan Island side may prove best. The current usually flows east off Cattle Point because a large eddy forms there during the ebb cycle. This, combined with the typical fair-weather wind pattern, suggests paddling from west to east. A flood current is most favorable.

The Haro Strait side of southern San Juan Island is exposed to bad-weather winds from the south and is a very windy area even in fair weather. When high pressure builds, strong offshore winds inflowing from the Strait of Juan de Fuca often produce westerlies of up to 25 knots in the afternoon. They are strongest from about 2:00 PM to 6:00 PM. A little farther north in the strait, they become southwesterlies. At the north end of San Juan Island, the effects of the strait are diminished where northwesterlies blow. Pacific swells can penetrate through the Strait of Juan de Fuca and, amplified by local wind, develop considerable surf on southwestern San Juan Island beaches, such as South Beach. Locals have been known to find good surfing here.

If wind makes travel west around Cattle Point imprudent, consider beginning at Cattle Point Picnic Area, which cuts the paddling distance to 3 miles. With three high-tide lagoons and a maze of old roads meandering through the woods above and between them, there is plenty to explore in Griffin Bay. If the currents are close to slack, you can add 2 miles to the route by paddling across the channel narrows to Lopez Island. Here you can visit the undeveloped Shark Reef Sanctuary just south of Kings Point. If you enjoy playing in tidal rapids, visit Shark Reef on a strong tide exchange.

**Smallpox Bay (San Juan County Park) to Lime Kiln Point:** *Exposed*. The roundtrip paddling distance is 4 miles, often in fast-moving current with a few tide rips. This route can be paddled one way with a 3-mile car shuttle to Deadman Bay just south of Lime Kiln Point State Park. Please respect private property above the beach. To go ashore at the park, continue around the point and land on the north end of the beach at Deadman Bay. Deadman is part of the San Juan Preservation Trust. Shores along the way to Lime Kiln Point are consistently rocky, with residences here and there. In a bight just north of the point, the old lime kilns are easily identified by the white piles of material on the hillside.

This is the best coastline for whales. The population of orcas called the Southern Residents are listed as endangered by the Endangered Species Act. These whales frequent Puget Sound and the San Juan Islands in the summer and fall. They include at least three separate extended orca families: the J, K, and L pods. Strict paddling and boating regulations have been imposed to protect the whales. A voluntary motorboat exclusion zone stretches from Mitchell Bay to the north end of Eagle Point. This requires motorboats to stay a quarter of a mile offshore in most areas and a half mile offshore by Lime Kiln Point. Read about the Kayak Education and Leadership Program (KELP) before entering these waters. For additional information, visit bewhalewise.org. Do not paddle within 200 yards of the whales and never position yourself in their path of travel or behind them. You should also paddle at minimum speed within 400 yards of the animals.

Facilities and interpretive displays at Lime Kiln Point State Park are geared toward whale watching. On a busy summer day, hundreds of people may line the viewing areas in the park. Whale-watching boats and kayaking tours ply the waters offshore. Minke and pilot whales, Dall's and harbor porpoises, and even the occasional gray whale are sighted here, along with daily sightings of the orca pods.

**Roche Harbor to English Camp via Mosquito Pass:** *Moderate*. The roundtrip paddling distance is 5 miles. If you take a 4-mile car shuttle, the one-way paddling distance is 2.5 miles. This entire route is very well protected from winds, making it an excellent paddle in most weather conditions. However, currents in Mosquito Pass can be strong and erratic: there are no predictions for them in the current guides. Inexperienced paddlers should stay close to the eastern side of the channel near Mosquito Pass. This is probably the easiest route for going through against the current. South of the pass, turn left to enter even more protected waters in Garrison Bay. Land on the dinghy dock on the north side of the beach. A visitor center is in the white barracks building just inshore from the blockhouse. Restrooms are nearby in the parking lot above.

**Great San Juan Island Tour:** *Exposed*. A circumnavigation of the island is about 30 miles. Shorter partial circuits include Cattle Point to Roche Harbor (17 miles) and Smallpox Bay to Friday Harbor (20 miles). Campsites around San Juan Island are sparse and irregularly spaced, with a 14-mile gap at the southwest portion. Choices include campsites at Turn Island State Park southeast of Friday Harbor (see Trip 55, Shaw Island: Circumnavigation, for details), as well as three Cascadia Marine Trail sites—Griffin Bay Recreation Site, San Juan County Park at Smallpox

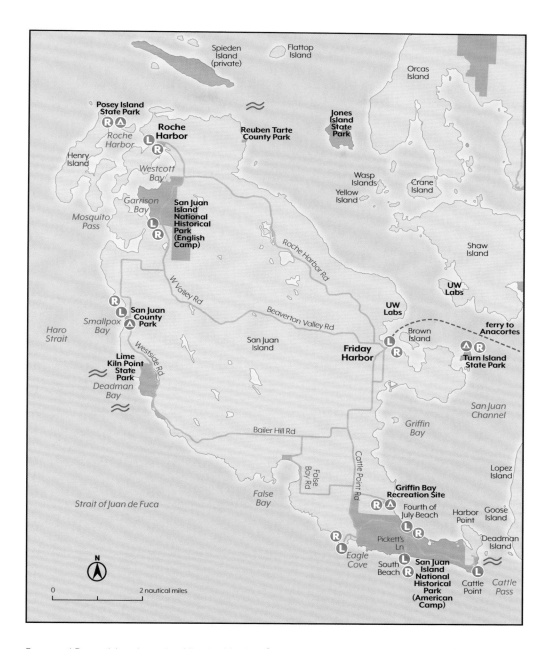

Bay, and Posey Island north of Roche Harbor (see Trip 62, Stuart Island, for details). There is no paddling launch at Snug Harbor on the northwest side of the island.

The Griffin Bay campsite, a Cascadia Marine Trail site, is just south of Low Point in a meadow area directly inshore from Halftide Rocks. Vault toilets, picnic tables, and four campsites sit 400 yards inland at the trees. There is no water. The grassy path is smooth enough for boat carts if you feel the need to keep your boat nearby. There is no formal access to this recreation site from the road, and private property borders it.

The site on Posey Island is a mile northwest of Roche Harbor Resort and can be very busy in summer. It has two sites (with a maximum of sixteen people), picnic tables, a fire ring, a vault toilet, and no water. Reservations are recommended if you want a campsite. Reserve your spot online at washington.goingtocamp.com.

San Juan County Park in Smallpox Bay is a very popular campground with eighteen common sites and one Cascadia Marine Trail site, often full during the summer months. Fortunately, they have a reservation system and a group area for those who arrive on human-powered craft. Look for the kayak rack behind the restrooms. For additional information, call 360-378-8420 or visit sanjuanco.com/Parks/sanjuan.aspx.

# 62. **Stuart Island**

Paddling to Stuart Island is among the "wildest" of the San Juan Island trips for two reasons: this destination is in a rarely experienced natural state, and the tidal forces are some of the strongest in the region. This is no place for novices. You are likely to encounter some excitement just paddling to and from Stuart Island, and its shorelines, two park areas, and Cascadia Marine Trail tent sites are sure to make the visit a pleasure.

**Duration:** Overnight or longer; two nights recommended.

**Rating:** *Protected* or *Exposed*. Strong currents and tide rips are likely throughout this area.

**Navigation Aids:** SeaTrails WA 003; NOAA charts 18423 SC or 18421 (both 1:80,000), 18432 (1:25,000); San Juan Channel current tables with corrections for Limestone Point, Admiralty Inlet current tables with corrections for Turn Point, or the Canadian *Current Atlas*.

**Planning Considerations:** Currents in this area are very strong, and powerful tide rips form in all weather conditions. Coordinating travel with currents is essential for both efficiency and safety, particularly when there are larger-than-average tides.

## GETTING THERE AND LAUNCHING

Launch from San Juan Island at either Roche Harbor or Friday Harbor.

**Roche Harbor:** From the Friday Harbor ferry landing, drive about 10 miles north to Roche Harbor. Take Spring Street two blocks through town to 2nd Street and turn right. After three blocks, 2nd Street bears left, becoming Guard Street. After one block, turn right onto Tucker Avenue. At the fork, bear left onto Roche Harbor Road and follow it to Roche Harbor.

Launching at the Roche Harbor Resort is allowed from the boat ramp at the far end of the parking area west of the main resort facilities. Restrooms, a shower, water, and provisions are

*Spieden Island and distant Stuart Island from Jones Island*

available. San Juan Outfitters rents kayaks and SUPs at the resort; you can call them at 866-810-1483. Contact Roche Harbor Resort for additional information by calling 800-451-8910.

**Reuben Tarte County Park:** Located on the northeast corner of the island, this launch provides easy northside access to paddle past Spieden Island to Stuart Island. There's one restroom and a gear drop-off area by the beach. Park above by the street. From Friday Harbor, head northwest on 2nd Street North. Turn right on Tucker Avenue and then right on Rouleau Road. Take a right on Limestone Point Road, followed by another right on San Juan Drive. Finally, turn left onto Reuben Tarte Road.

**Friday Harbor:** Use the public dinghy dock north of the ferry landing. Pay a fee at the marina office; you can contact them at 360-378-2688. Overnight parking is very limited and almost unobtainable in Friday Harbor during the summer. An alternative launch point is Deer Harbor on Orcas Island (see Trip 60, Jones Island, for details).

## ROUTES

**Roche Harbor to Stuart Island:** *Exposed.* The roundtrip paddling distance is 10 miles. This is the shortest, least hazardous, and most popular approach to Stuart Island. Add 10 miles to the roundtrip distance if launching from Friday Harbor.

Paddling between San Juan Island and Stuart Island probably requires more careful timing with the currents than anywhere else in the San Juan Islands. Though the crossings are generally

1 mile or less, the strong currents that run through these channels and the associated tide rips earn this trip its *Exposed* rating. However, since tidal cycles are predictable, careful planning and timing can make this a safer trip than *Exposed* trips with longer crossings and associated bad-weather exposure.

The primary hazards occur in Spieden Channel. At the eastern end of the channel, between Green Point on Spieden Island and Limestone Point on San Juan Island, runs some of the fastest water in the San Juan Islands; it can be over 5 knots on the year's biggest tides. Most significant are two powerful and extensive tide rips that form off both points on both the flood and ebb sets of the tide. The rip off Limestone Point forms 100 yards or more offshore, but the Green Point rip extends quite close to Spieden Island's shoreline. Less severe rips form at the western end of the channel in the vicinity of Danger Shoal, Center Reef, and Sentinel Island.

The channels north of Spieden Island on either side of the Cactus Islands also run very swiftly, though you will find no local reference stations for them in the current tables. Currents here and in the northern San Juan Channel are somewhat fickle, particularly after the tide changes and patterns of flow around each side of San Juan Island are not yet established. One kayaker bound for Jones Island from Flattop Island reported being carried to Spieden Island on the flood current when it should have been flowing in the opposite direction.

Since the total distance from San Juan Island to Stuart Island is too far to paddle in a single slack current period, give the most low-current priority to Spieden Channel. Then you may round Spieden Island in whichever direction is the most convenient, keeping in mind the possible rips close to Green Point. Do not land on Spieden Island, as it's private property. In 1970, the Jonas Brothers, taxidermists from Seattle, purchased the island and renamed it "Safari Island." They imported exotic animals, such as sika deer, Spanish goats, Corsican mouflon, and Indian blackbuck and spent their free time driving around sipping martinis while hunting them. Environmentalists forced them to shut down operations, and the island was sold to another private landowner. Many of the imported species still roam the island.

Currents in Spieden Channel are slower between Davison Head and Sentinel Island than farther to the east. A good time to start is at the tail end of a flood tide, next riding the ebb current west along Spieden Island, and finally taking advantage of that same ebb current to reach Reid Harbor by compensating to the northeast against its flow.

Most of the small islands and rocks north of Spieden Island are within the San Juan Islands National Wildlife Refuge; do not approach them. If you have a late start from Roche Harbor or run late on the return, you can stay overnight at the Cascadia Marine Trail group site on tiny Posey Island State Park outside the harbor's two approaches. A composting vault toilet and a couple of picnic tables are provided; water is not available. The tent sites are located on the south, east, and west sides, with the trees and brush at the center providing some wind protection. The maximum number of campers allowed at one time is sixteen, and it is strictly enforced on this fragile island. Since Posey Island is close to Roche Harbor's many summer homes, you can expect company in the summer from young partyers who like to bring their music with them.

For camping on Stuart Island, both Reid and Prevost Harbors are suitable for paddlers. Both are within Stuart Island State Park, one of the few marine parks in the San Juan Islands where

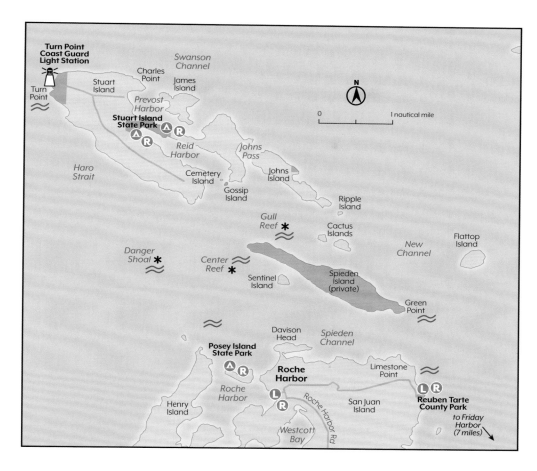

you can count on finding fresh water; the well rarely runs dry, yet park managers only provide assurances in the summer boating season. The landing beach here dries for a fair distance—great for clam diggers, but not so good for gear-laden kayakers on minus tides.

Three Cascadia Marine Trail tent sites at Reid Harbor can hold up to eight people each. Find them on the right (north) side of the marsh at the head of the bay. The rest of the sites are located on Prevost Harbor or on the ridge that separates Prevost and Reid Harbors. Composting toilets are near the docks at both Reid and Prevost Harbors. Pit toilets are available at the head of Reid Harbor. For camping details, visit wwta.org/sites/stuart-island-sp and be sure to read the comments.

Allowing a day's layover at Stuart Island for some exploration by foot or boat is strongly recommended. Hiking the island's ample trails and little-used, unpaved country roads is a pleasure. There are also fine opportunities for daylong paddling loops, skirting the island from one harbor to the other via Johns Pass to the east or Turn Point to the west.

If you circumnavigate Stuart Island, note that currents flow around both ends of the island on their way to or from the Strait of Georgia. With the right timing, both of the following trips can be made with favorable currents for almost the entire distance. Consult the Canadian *Current Atlas* for specifics.

**Reid Harbor to Prevost Harbor via Johns Pass One-Day Loop:** *Protected*. The total paddling distance is 4.5 miles. The Johns Pass loop is easier and shorter than the Turn Point loop (see below). Most of this shoreline is residential. Except for Johns Pass, currents along the shore are usually benign, hence the *Protected* rating. Tiny, state-owned Gossip and Cemetery Islands at Reid Harbor's entrance are the only opportunities for shore exploration along this route.

**Prevost Harbor to Reid Habor via Turn Point One-Day Loop:** *Exposed*. The total paddling distance is 7 miles. The western circuit around Turn Point is exceptionally appealing for its wild, rugged shores and boisterous Haro Strait waters. But remember, the steep shores with few safe landings, the strong currents racing around the point, and the open north and south fetches with potential for rough seas require good skills and experience.

As you paddle out from Prevost Harbor, the pastoral civility of Stuart Island is left behind at Charles Point. From here to Turn Point, you will encounter a progression of rocky kelp beds, sea crags, and overhanging vegetation. Extensive eddies occupy most of these beds all the way to the point and progress is fairly easy, even against the current. These waters are prime fishing grounds for both bottom fish and salmon.

Turn Point is a ten-acre Coast Guard light station surrounded by a fifty-three-acre park managed by the Bureau of Land Management (BLM). The light facility is now automated and diverse tenants, such as Stuart Island teachers and whale researchers, occasionally occupy the former residences. The parkland is undeveloped with no recreational facilities. Camping is not allowed, but it does provide excellent day hiking. A popular 5-mile roundtrip hike runs between here and Reid and Prevost Harbors via an unpaved road.

Turn Point offers few easy landing sites for visiting the light station. Though the rocks have eroded into flat shelves, you need to be adept at landing on rocks in the waves that are usually present. Also beware of the powerful wakes of ships that pass quite close offshore.

Find a much more practical landing, with a rough trail access to the point, at a small gravel beach about a quarter mile to the south, just beyond some spectacular sea cliffs and still within the park. Secure your boat well above the drift logs and passing freighters' wakes. Plan to be gone for at least one hour if you intend to visit the point.

The rough, little-used trail switchbacks steeply up from the beach. Follow the gully above the beach uphill for about 100 yards to a well-defined trail that climbs across the hillside to the left through open fir and madrona woods. Climb upward for another 300 yards, passing open, grassy meadows above and below, a perfect spot for secluded sunbathing. Reach a high, bald hilltop with sweeping views over Haro Strait, Boundary Pass, and the Canadian Gulf Islands beyond. Walk down to the cliff edge to see Turn Point Light Station below. Look a few yards behind this bald hilltop to find the unpaved road linking the light station to Reid and Prevost Harbors. Follow it to the left and downhill to the point.

OPPOSITE  *Taking a break at Chivers Point on Wallace Island (Trip 71)*

# Victoria and The Gulf Islands

Victoria and the Gulf Islands offer paddlers a wide range of trips from quiet, protected bays to fast-moving currents and island camping. Victoria trips allow for great city views and easy escapes along the Strait of Juan de Fuca or northward toward the Saanich Peninsula. The Gulf Islands make you feel much farther away with quiet bays, many islands to explore, and quaint small villages.

# 63. **Victoria Harbor**

Captain James Cook is the first European known to have visited what is now Victoria. It wasn't until 1843, when the Hudson Bay Company began to operate out of the harbor, that Victoria began to grow as a town. Today, Victoria is a bustling city surrounded by water. Known for its British-like charm, the city's tourism industry keeps the downtown corridor buzzing. Victoria's paddling opportunities are equally exciting, with a variety of water bodies in or within a short distance of town.

**Duration:** Part day to full day.

**Rating:** *Protected.*

**Navigation Aids:** NOAA chart 18400 (1:200,000); Canadian Hydrographic Service charts 3412 Victoria Harbor (1:5,000), 3440 (1:40,000), 3424 (1:10,000); Victoria Harbor tide table.

**Planning Considerations:** Stay clear of the considerable boating and seaplane traffic in Victoria Harbor, especially in summer. Bring along a Public Port of Victoria Traffic Scheme map when paddling here, and make sure to paddle along the shore for the entire trip. Plan around the tides when paddling in the lower reaches of the Gorge Waterway. Currents creating a tidal rapid up to 11 knots can rip under the Tillicum Bridge.

## GETTING THERE AND LAUNCHING

To get to Victoria from the United States, you have a few options. The *Victoria Clipper*, a hydrofoil, runs daily from Seattle (visit its website at clippervacations.com/ferry). The *Clipper* doesn't accept kayaks or SUPs, but Ocean River Sports in Victoria has kayak and SUP rentals, as well as paddling tours. Kenmore Air, a seaplane service, offers daily flights from several Northwest towns to Victoria (visit kenmoreair.com for details). Another option is to take the Tsawwassen ferry near Vancouver to Schwartz Bay on the Saanich Peninsula, north of Victoria. Or take the ferry from Anacortes through the San Juan Islands to Sidney, British Columbia, also north of Victoria. For both, you can find more information at bcferries.com. If you're coming from the Olympic Peninsula, a good option is to take the Black Ball Ferry (cohoferry.com/main) from Port Angeles to Victoria. Canadian Customs is north of the Empress Hotel on the waterfront below Wharf Street.

**Victoria–James Bay Angler's Association:** From the downtown waterfront area, take Belleville Street west two blocks and turn left onto Oswego Street in front of the Black Ball Ferry terminal. Go eight blocks to the water. Turn right on Dallas Road and drive about five blocks. On your left, look for the James Bay Angler's Association boat ramp. To use the ramp, you must pay a modest daily (or yearly) fee. The parking lot is small, and there are no facilities. The ramp puts you just inside the Ogden Point breakwater. A seaplane airport is next to the ramp—be cautious

*Paddlers enjoy inner Victoria Harbor.*

of seaplane activity as you launch. This launch grants access to Inner Harbor paddling and is also good for going outside the breakwater.

**Victoria–Ocean River Sports:** A few blocks north of downtown Victoria at 400 Swift Street, this paddling shop has a public launch on the Gorge Waterway. From the waterfront in Victoria, take Wharf Street north to Store Street. Ocean River Sports is three more blocks on your left. You can rent canoes, kayaks, and SUPs here. For additional information, call 800-909-4233 or visit oceanriver.com.

**Fisherman's Wharf Park:** Located near the ferry along the David Foster walking path (12 Erie Street), this day-use park has restrooms and street parking with a two-hour limit. Very busy in summer, this is a launch site for the Victoria Waterways Loop trail. You can rent a kayak from Kelp Reef Kayaking; visit kelpreef.com for details.

**Songhees Point:** Located in west Victoria at 50 Songhees Road, this gravel launch is near a popular day-use walking path. Limited street parking.

**Victoria–Gorge Waterway Park:** To access the upper Gorge Waterway, this long strip park has several options for launching. From downtown Victoria, take Government Street north. Veer left on Gorge Road East, which becomes Gorge Road West. At 1.9 miles, you'll see the park on your left extending several blocks. Take a peek at the current flowing under the Tillicum Bridge just south of the Victoria Canoe and Kayak Club.

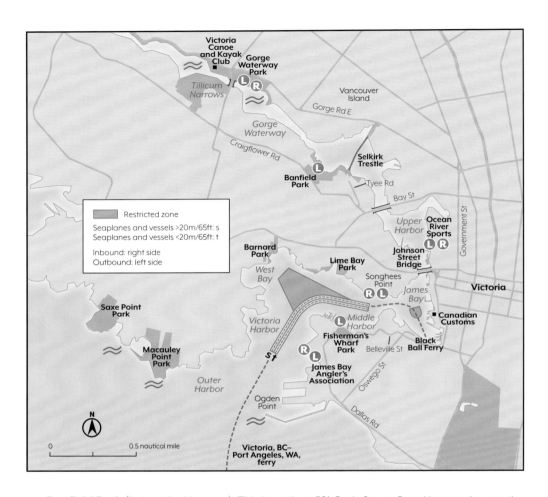

**Banfield Park** (below the Narrows): This launch at 521 Craigflower Road is very close to the Gorge but has a steep stairway down to a small dock, with a lower dock for easier in and out. No restrooms and only about five parking spots are available. From Victoria, take Trans-Canada Highway 1 north and take a left on Bay Street. Turn right on Tyee Road, which becomes Skinner Street, and follow it to the park.

## ROUTES

Look at the Public Port of Victoria Traffic Scheme map before paddling here. The harbor is busy with boating traffic from ferries, mini tourist boats, seaplanes, shipping traffic, and other small craft like yours. Paddle close to the shore while in the harbor and never assume you have the right-of-way over boats and seaplanes. Also check the Victoria tide tables if you decide to paddle up the Gorge Waterway or near the mouth of Victoria Harbor—current can affect progress in these places. Inside the main harbor, the water is generally calm and protected. A good place for paddlers of all skill levels, the harbor presents you with views of the Empress Hotel, the Royal BC Museum, and the dome of the capitol building. North of the Empress Hotel are several marinas and waterfront restaurants. As you paddle away from downtown, the harbor narrows and then opens again as you float past colorful houseboats. Small islands in the harbor's northern reaches by Lime Bay Park and Barnard Park beg to be explored.

As you reach the harbor entry to the Strait of Juan de Fuca, the shore becomes rocky and less developed on the north side at Macaulay Point Park and north to Saxe Point Park. Pay attention to the current here. Refracted waves can bounce off the exterior of the Ogden Point breakwater in windy conditions or from boating traffic in a phenomenon called clapotis. These conditions can be tough going if you're unfamiliar with rough-water paddling. For experienced paddlers, this can be a fun place to play.

**Victoria Waterways Loop:** If you're looking for a full tour of the harbor and Gorge Waterway and a bit of a challenge, try this 22-kilometer water trail. The circular route includes a 1 km portage across Portage Park in View Royal and the Old Island Highway. For details, visit oceanriver.com/victoria-waterways-loop.

# 64. **The Gorge Waterway**

Located in the heart of Victoria, the Gorge Waterway is a 6-mile-long natural saltwater canal that winds and bends through residential neighborhoods and empties into Victoria Harbor. The gorge was used for thousands of years by the Songhees First Nation people as a source to catch coho salmon and herring. A 4100-year-old midden of shells, charcoal, and scorched rock sits under the south end of the Tillicum Bridge. The Canal of Camosack, as it was known in the 1800s, is now called Tillicum Narrows. Here the shore narrows to a 45-foot-wide bottleneck, forcing the tidal current to flush through at higher speeds. Current has been reported ripping through here at 11 knots—enough to create a wild whitewater rapid below the bridge. The rest of the Gorge is wider and very calm, ideal for novice paddlers or those seeking a casual, easy paddle.

**Duration:** Part day.

**Rating:** *Protected* or *Moderate*.

**Navigation Aids:** NOAA chart 18400 (1:200,000); Canadian Hydrographic Service chart 3412 Victoria Harbor (1:5,000); Public Port of Victoria Traffic Scheme map; Victoria Harbor tide table.

**Planning Considerations:** Read the Victoria tide table for this trip. If you're paddling through Tillicum Narrows and are uncomfortable with fast-moving currents, go at slack. The ebb current here is the strongest and can create turbulent whitewater during large tidal exchanges.

## GETTING THERE AND LAUNCHING

**Victoria–Ocean River Sports:** A few blocks north of downtown Victoria at 400 Swift Street, this paddling shop has a public launch on the Gorge Waterway. From the waterfront in Victoria, take Wharf Street north to Store Street. Ocean River Sports is three more blocks on your left. You can rent canoes, kayaks, and SUPs here. For additional information, call 800-909-4233 or visit oceanriver.com.

**Victoria–Gorge Waterway Park:** To access the upper Gorge Waterway, this long strip park has several options for launching. From downtown Victoria, take Government Street north. Veer left on Gorge Road East, which becomes Gorge Road West. At 1.9 miles, you'll see the park on your left extending several blocks. Take a look at the current flowing under the Tillicum Bridge just south of the Victoria Canoe and Kayak Club.

**Banfield Park (below the Narrows):** This launch at 521 Craigflower Road is very close to the Gorge but has a steep stairway down to a small dock, with a lowered dock for easier in and out. No restrooms and only about five parking spots are available. From Victoria, take Trans-

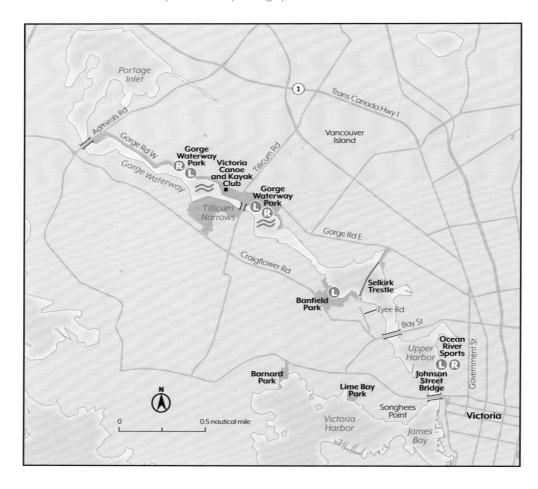

Canada Highway 1 north and take a left on Bay Street. Turn right on Tyee Road, which becomes Skinner Street, and follow it to the park.

**ROUTE**

Check your tide table before launching. A flood may add a push up the gorge; an ebb will help take you back to the harbor. Paddling against a strong tidal exchange could be a lot of work.

From Victoria Harbor, the paddle begins north of the stout-looking Johnson Street Bridge. Explore the area's industrial scenery, then pass under the bridge for the Galloping Goose Trail, a walking and biking trail. The gorge opens here, with an interesting inlet on the right and a nice, wooded park on the left. The gorge narrows again as you pass waterfront homes and their docks. About 1.3 miles from the start, the Tillicum Road bridge comes into view. The narrow gap here speeds up the current. On lighter tidal flows, the ride under the bridge can be a fun

*Kayakers play in the tidal rapids at Tillicum Narrows on the Gorge Waterway*

free ride; in heavier flows, dangerous rapids can occur here. Make sure you time your paddle so you either pass through at slack or at a level that is appropriate for your skill level. Local kayakers with whitewater skills love to play in the rapids on the ebb. As the ebb gets low, the rapids get too rough for even experienced paddlers. Check with Lee at Best Coast Outfitters for more details about this feature; find contact information at bestcoastoutfitters.com.

As you pass upriver through the Tillicum Narrows, the Victoria Canoe and Kayak Club appears on your right. Also on your right is the Gorge Waterway Park, a long walkway with several possible launches. The rest of the route is residential, moving through bucolic, lake-like sections—some narrow, some wider. Five miles from your launch, the gorge opens into Portage Inlet, a large lake-like body of water surrounded by homes. Portage Inlet is an important bird area known for its shallow water and low salinity. Its extensive eelgrass beds and mudflats provide rich foraging grounds for shorebirds. Canada geese breed here; also look for double-crested cormorants, which feed on spawning herring.

# 65. **Outer Harbor to Cadboro Bay and Trial, Oak Bay, and Discovery Islands**

A short drive or paddle from downtown Victoria to Outer Harbor opens the door to a variety of trips with spectacular scenery for paddlers of all skill levels. The Outer Harbor has several convenient put-ins, a curvy shoreline, and protected bays with sandy beaches. The islands offshore are ideal if you're an experienced paddler seeking a long day trip or challenging conditions with turbulent water. For an overnight adventure, paddle through swift currents to Discovery Island.

**Duration:** Part day, full day, or overnight.

**Rating:** *Protected*, *Moderate*, or *Exposed*.

**Navigation Aids:** NOAA chart 18400 (1:200,000); Canadian Hydrographic Service charts 3412 Victoria Harbor (1:5,000), 3440 (1:40,000), 3424 (1:10,000), 7130 Oak Bay Station; Victoria Harbor tide tables (add 22 minutes for Plumper Passage).

**Planning Considerations:** Check tide and current tables, as well as wind and ocean swell forecasts, prior to launching. Exposure to the Strait of Juan de Fuca can bring unexpected weather.

### GETTING THERE AND LAUNCHING

**Victoria (Inner Harbor)–James Bay Angler's Association:** From the downtown waterfront area, take Belleville Street west two blocks and turn left onto Oswego Street in front of the Black Ball Ferry terminal. Go eight blocks to the water. Turn right on Dallas Road and drive about five blocks. On your left, look for the James Bay Angler's Association boat ramp. To use the ramp, you must pay a modest daily (or yearly) fee. The parking lot is small and there are no facilities. The ramp puts you just inside the Ogden Point breakwater. A seaplane airport is next to the ramp—be cautious of seaplane activity as you launch. This launch grants access to Inner Harbor paddling and is also good for going outside the breakwater. When leaving the harbor for the Strait of Juan de Fuca, watch for rips and rough water from the strait side of Ogden Point. Current leaving the harbor can collide with wind and boat wakes, creating turbulent conditions.

**Clover Point Park:** From the waterfront in Victoria, go east on Fairfield Road, then take a right on Cook Street and drive to the water. At Dallas Road, turn left and follow the road to Clover Point Park. Clover Point extends into the strait and is easy to find. Drive to the point and park. There is a steep, paved boat ramp at the end. Watch for wind at this launch.

**McNeill Bay Launches:** Take a winding, 3.8-mile drive through Victoria to McNeill Bay. From the downtown waterfront, drive east on Fairfield Road, which later becomes Beach Drive. As the water comes into view, Beach Drive veers left along the waterfront at McNeill Bay. Look for the

*Rugged, picturesque beaches await paddlers on Discovery Island.*

cobble beach. You can also access McNeill Bay from the west via Dallas Road. (Note: There are several roadside launches east of here, including Gonzales Bay.)

**Oak Bay Launches:** From the waterfront in downtown Victoria, take Pandora Avenue east. Pandora Avenue soon becomes Oak Bay Avenue. At 2.7 miles, veer left onto Prospect Place, which will curve right, become San Carlos Avenue, and then connect with Beach Drive. Take a left at Beach Drive and drive for 0.3 mile to Willows Park on the right. To access the launch, go down the steps to get below the seawall. Or you can drive another 0.6 mile beyond Willows Park to Uplands Park, which has two concrete boat ramps. Other launches from Oak Bay include Oak Bay Marina (on the south side of the bay) and the Esplanade (halfway between Uplands and Willow Parks). There is limited street parking along Beach Drive. Ocean River Sports has a "kayak shack" rental location at 1327 Beach Drive, which is open May to October; you can call them at 250-381-4233 ext 2. Find additional launches on Oak Bay at bcmarinetrails.org.

**Cadboro Bay Road:** From the University of Victoria, take Sinclair Road south. Take a left on Cadboro Bay Road and enter Cadboro-Gyro Park. There are restrooms and a parking lot.

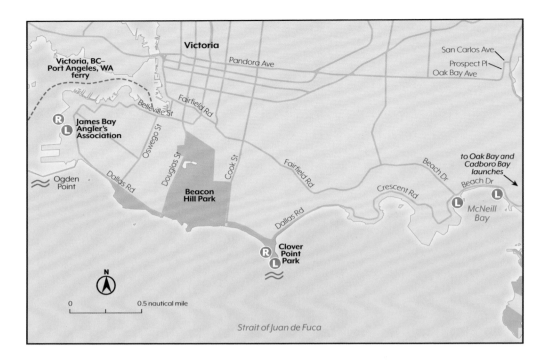

## ROUTES

**Victoria Harbor to Cadboro Bay:** *Protected*, *Moderate*, or *Exposed*. Choose your route and launch. This is a beautiful, winding area to paddle with easy access, urban views, undeveloped offshore islands, and picturesque, white-sand bays. On a hot summer day, the lovely, crescent-shaped, sandy coves are reminiscent of Southern California. Enjoy views of the snow-capped Olympic Mountains in Washington State to the south across the Strait of Juan de Fuca. Novice paddlers can enjoy turquoise-colored protected bays, while advanced paddlers seeking an adrenaline rush can surf large winter wind waves or play in the tidal rapids off Trial and Chatham Islands. You can paddle a short distance or go all the way to Cadboro Bay from Odgen Point, about 10.6 miles. Three ecological reserves are along this route: Ten Mile Point, Oak Bay Islands, and Trial Islands. Landing is prohibited at all three reserves.

**The Trial Islands Ecological Reserve:** *Exposed*. Enterprise Channel, which separates the Trial Islands Ecological Reserve from shore, is only a 0.2-mile crossing but has currents ranging between 3 and 6 knots. The islands are known for their rare plant life; species growing here are more common in southern Oregon or California. Look for Hooker's onion, shooting star, death camas, blue-eyed Mary, chocolate lily, and sea blush. Also keep an eye out for wildlife, including harbor seals, cormorants, eagles, hawks, and herons. Staines Point, on the major Trial Island's southern tip, boasts a historic lighthouse built in 1906, still in use today. Swift tidal rapids occur off the point and can be quite rough, particularly on the flood tide. Do not land.

**Oak Bay Islands Ecological Reserve:** *Moderate* or *Exposed*. The Oak Bay Islands Ecological Reserve includes the Chain Islets, Great Chain Island, Alpha Island, Jemmy Jones Island, and an offshore section of Ten Mile Point to the east. The Chain Islets and Great Chain Island have British Columbia's largest breeding population of glaucous-winged gulls and the third-largest colony of double-crested cormorants. The cormorants are on the BC Ministry of Sustainable Resource Management's (MSRM) "Red" list, meaning they're endangered or threatened in British Columbia. Watch for other birdlife, too, including pigeon guillemots, black oystercatchers, and pelagic cormorants. Great Chain Island is a little more than a mile off Oak Bay Marina. On the west

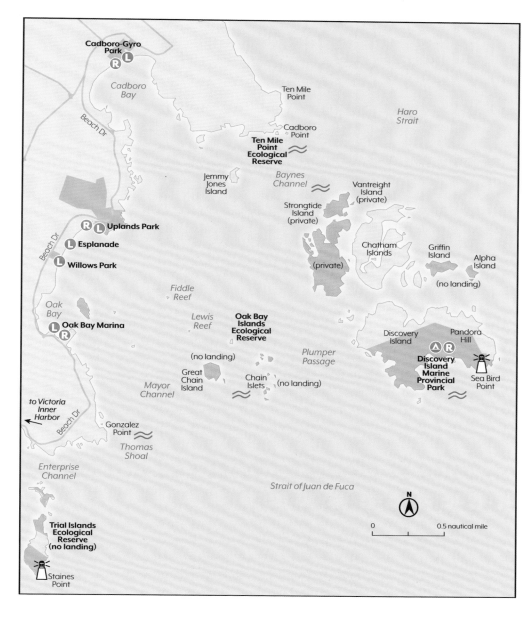

side of the island, Mayor Channel can run up to 3 knots, with the flood running north and the ebb running south. If you come from the north, watch for the "Goal Posts": two reefs, Lewis and Fiddle, both marked by buoys. If coming from the south, keep an eye out for Thomas Shoal southeast of Gonzales Point. Do not land on the islands.

**Discovery Island Marine Provincial Park and Chatham Islands:** *Exposed.* Located 2.6 miles from Oak Bay Marina, Discovery and Chatham Islands offer a nice day trip or overnight paddling option for experienced paddlers. Explore over shallow reefs, through narrow passageways, by rocky shores, and around small islets. Garry oak and arbutus trees line the shores of the Chatham Islands, which are thankfully undeveloped. Stronger current can work its way through the various islets and passageways, making for a fun paddle for those skilled in moving water. The islands also mark where Haro Strait and the Strait of Juan de Fuca connect. The northern part of Discovery Island and all the Chatham Islands are a First Nations reserve. Griffin and Alpha Islands, both ecological reserves, are tucked between the eastern sides of Discovery and Chatham Islands; landing is prohibited. Strongtide and Vantreight Islands, on the north side of the Chatham Islands, are private.

Camping is only allowed on the south side of Discovery Island—in Rudlin Bay or in a large field southwest of Pandora Hill. Boaters generally avoid Rudlin Bay due to several shallow reefs offshore. Facilities include a pit toilet, picnic tables, and information kiosk. No campfires are allowed, and a small fee applies per person. Hiking trails lead from the 1885-era lighthouse on Sea Bird Point to the western shore of the park going up to Pandora Hill. Enjoy sweeping views of the Olympic Mountains and surrounding areas from the top of Pandora Hill.

Traveling to the islands requires knowledge of open-water crossings, sometimes in fast-moving current. Plumper Passage separates Great Chain Island from Discovery Island. Here the slack tide can be short, and the flood can run for three hours and forty-five minutes, leaving about seven hours before slack begins again. Rips and rough water are common.

Baynes Channel separates the Chatham Islands from Cadboro Point by 0.8 mile, which can be a rough ride especially during large tidal exchanges. Current can run from 4 to 6 knots by Strongtide Island, where rips are common, and up to 2 to 3 knots on the southern section of the channel. The flood currents flow northeast, while the ebb currents flow southwest. Reefs are numerous off Cadboro Point and may create surface disturbances with stronger tides and wind.

# 66. **Albert Head to Witty's Lagoon and Sitting Lady Falls**

A hidden gem along the Strait of Juan de Fuca, begin this trip from a sandy beach on Albert Head Lagoon. Then round a rocky headland topped with coastal defense batteries from World War II, wind through a group of interesting islets, venture into the rich tidal estuary and birding destination of Witty's Lagoon and continue onward to a beautiful waterfall.

**Duration:** Half day to full day.

**Rating:** *Protected* or *Moderate*.

**Navigation Aids:** Canadian Hydrographic Service charts 3410 (1:20,000), 3411 (1:12,000), 3440 (1:40,000); NOAA chart 18400 (1:200,000); Victoria and Esquimalt tide tables; Race Passage current tables.

**Planning Considerations:** High tides are required to enter Witty's Lagoon. Watch for wind from the west and south. Wind-opposing current can make rounding Albert Head a rough ride, especially in opposing tide.

## GETTING THERE AND LAUNCHING

**Albert Head Lagoon Park:** From Victoria, take Trans-Canada Highway 1 north and take Exit 10 toward View Royal/Colwood. Merge onto Burnside Road West and continue onto Island Highway/Old Island Highway South, which becomes Sooke Road. Turn left on Metchosin Road and eventually left again onto Farhill Road, which becomes Park Drive. Turn right on Delgada Road and follow it to the park, which has about five parking spots but no facilities.

   **Taylor Beach:** Follow the directions above to Metchosin Road and then continue straight onto William Head Road. Take a left on Taylor Road and follow it to the beach. There are a few parking spots but no facilities.

## ROUTES

**Albert Head Lagoon Park:** *Protected* to *Moderate.* This wildlife refuge managed by the Capitol Regional District is known for migrating waterfowl, such as mute swans, herons, and turkey vul-

*Sitting Lady Falls inside Witty's Lagoon*

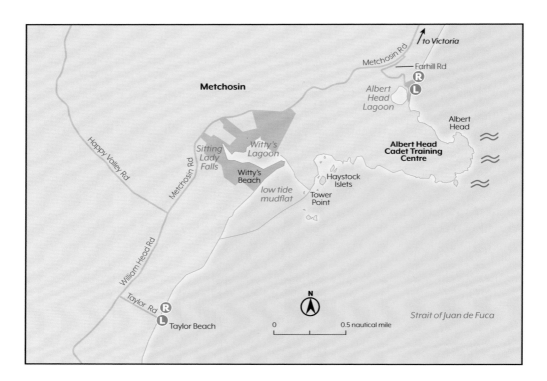

tures. Two streams feed the lagoon from the surrounding watershed, which is lined with Garry oak, fir trees, and salal. Launch from the beach head toward Albert Head. Explore small pocket beaches and islets along the rocky shoreline below steep Albert Head, also a prime area for viewing marine wildlife. Above is Albert Head Cadet Training Centre, a military base used in World War II as a coastal defense fort with three MK10 9.2-inch counter-bombardment cannons, since removed. On the west side of Albert Head, paddle out to several small rock islands, called the Haystock Islets, plus two more sandy pocket beaches popular with locals. Since the rocks look like haystacks, a typo may have been made at some point. Tower Point separates the rocky shoreline of Albert Head from the sandy salt marsh of Witty's Lagoon.

Tower Point is composed of pillow lava, a reminder of the geological history of this area. Enter Witty's Lagoon just around the west side of Tower Point. Time your entry into the lagoon for high tides and slack, keeping in mind the bay is slow to fill during flood tides. If you miss the tide, the beach below the lagoon can dry out for about 200 yards. Explore the inner shorelines of the lagoon, known to be a birder's paradise; over 160 species have been documented here. Bring your binoculars to view at a safe distance. Search for belted kingfishers, orange-crowned warblers, and dark-eyed juncos. Toward the back end of the lagoon, Sitting Lady Falls flows over lava rock. The waterfall is a trickle in summer but flows fully the rest of the year. Farther west of the lagoon is a clothing-optional beach marked by an overhanging tree.

**Taylor Beach:** *Moderate*. You can access Witty's Lagoon quicker by launching from Taylor Beach, making it a good option if you want a shorter trip or wish to avoid rounding Albert Head.

Accessing the lagoon sooner is desirable because the water empties on the ebb. Watch for breakers from wind or westerly swell when launching.

Witty's Beach is not a good launch, as it takes a long walk and a steep, three-level metal stairway to access the beach.

# 67. **Beecher Bay (aka Belcher Bay)**

This protected bay near Sooke offers a picturesque, tucked-away paddle. Visit erratic boulders and pocket beaches in madrona- and conifer-lined back bays. Explore rocky islets lining the bay's eastern shore and Fraser and Village Islands near the opening of the bay.

The bay's original inhabitants were the Sc'ianew (Beecher Bay) First Nation. The name Sc'ianew is pronounced "CHEA-nuh" and translates to "the place of big fish." At one point the band had four different dialects. The Sc'ianew operate Cheanuh Marina, along with the adjoining Spirit Bay development, and share their land with the public.

Experienced paddlers can access the bay from Whiffin Spit and East Sooke Park to the west (see Trip 68, Sooke Harbor) or Taylor Beach to the east (see Trip 66, Albert Head to Witty's Lagoon and Sitting Lady Falls). Note maps and charts may list the bay as Beecher, Belcher, or Becher.

*Beecher Marina and bay views*

**Duration:** Part day to full day.

**Rating:** *Protected*, *Moderate*, or *Exposed*.

**Navigation Aids:** Canadian Hydrographic Service charts 3410 (1:20,000), 3411 (1:12,000), 3440 (1:40,000); NOAA chart 18400 (1:200,000).

**Planning Considerations:** Beginners should avoid the outer bay during southerly and westerly winds and large westerly swell. Be careful paddling around the log rafts on the inner corners of the bay. Avoid paddling to offshore Race Rocks unless you're an expert paddler.

## GETTING THERE AND LAUNCHING

**Cheanuh Marina:** Drive about 20 miles west from Victoria to Cheanuh Marina. From downtown, take Trans-Canada Highway 1 north and take Exit 10 toward View Royal/Colwood. Merge onto Burnside Road West and continue onto Island Highway/Old Island Highway South, which becomes Sooke Road. Turn left on Metchosin Road and then right on Happy Valley Road. Take a left onto Rocky Point Road and continue onto East Sooke Road. Finally, turn left onto Spirit Bay Road, followed by another quick left on Marina Drive. Park in the gravel lot across from the marina, which has basic supplies, water, a hose, and restrooms. Pay a launch fee in the marina office and enter the water from the boat ramp.

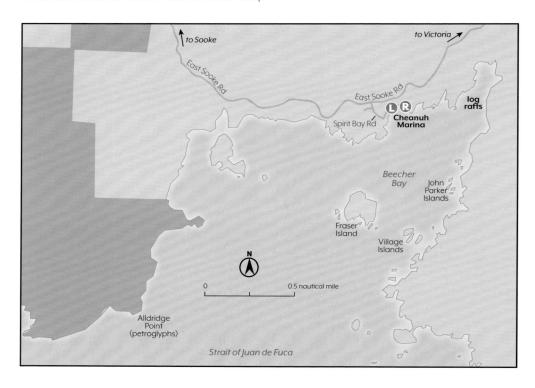

## ROUTE

The total paddling distance for a trip around Beecher Bay is about 3.3 miles. Launch from Cheanuh Marina and explore the bay's rocky shore with its mini coves and pocket beaches. Follow the shore to the east (left) as you venture farther into the bay, enjoying the sea and bird life. Be sure to give log rafts a wide berth. A few homes look down on the bay, some with docks. Look for a boat above in the trees that is also a small cottage. Paddle to the very back of the bay to view a huge erratic boulder tucked into a protected pocket beach. Continue to follow the bay's east shore to small islets and a rugged shoreline leading to the John Parker Islands, Village Islands, and Fraser Island. Stay north of Fraser and Village Islands to avoid possible ocean swell and wind waves from the Strait of Juan de Fuca. The Alldridge Point petroglyphs on the bay's southwest corner should only be accessed by expert paddlers with experience in rough water, current, and waves. When you're ready, circle back around to Cheanuh Marina, watching for incoming boat traffic. Behind the marina, find a hose by the restrooms to clean your gear.

# 68. Sooke Harbor

Eighteen miles west of Victoria is a very protected body of water called Sooke Basin. Sooke was named for the first inhabitants of the area, the T'Sou-ke people (locals pronounce the name as "Sook"). The inside of the harbor is calm and lined with beach homes and docks. The exterior of the basin, which parallels the Strait of Juan de Fuca, has a different personality: rugged shores pounded by the wind and ocean swell, both common on the strait. The town of Sooke is the main center for supplies, and numerous B&Bs can be found along its shores. The bay is protected by a narrow, sandy stretch of beach called Whiffin Spit, popular with locals for an afternoon walk. East Sooke Regional Park sits on the outside of the harbor. The park is an advanced coastal paddler's paradise with pocket beaches, caves, fast current, and a sense of wildness within a short drive of the city.

**Duration:** Part day to overnight.

**Rating:** *Protected* or *Exposed*.

**Navigation Aids:** Canadian Hydrographic Service charts 3410 (1:20,000), 3411 (1:12,000), 3440 (1:40,000); NOAA chart 18400 (1:200,000).

**Planning Considerations:** Sooke is great for novice paddlers or those seeking calm waters. Note that Sooke Basin is the inner part, and Sooke Harbor is by the town of Sooke. Watch for boaters in summer. East Sooke requires experience with outer coastal paddling and currents.

## GETTING THERE AND LAUNCHING

From Victoria, take British Columbia Highway 14 west to Sooke, approximately 18 miles. Driving can be slow going in the first half until you begin to shed the city behind you.

*East Sooke Regional Park on a windy summer day*

**Whiffin Spit Launch/Quimper Park:** Take BC 14 west to the town of Sooke and shortly after, take a left on Whiffin Spit Road. Follow the road through a residential area for about a mile into Quimper Park, just past the Sooke Harbor House. The paved, day-use parking lot is tight on sunny days, but there is additional street parking available. Launch on either side of the sandy spit over small rocks and driftwood. Most of the beach below the walking area is sandy. Whiffin Spit is on the south side of Sooke Harbor. Watch for strong currents east of the spit. For more details about Whiffin Spit, visit bcmarinetrails.org/map_site/11277.

**Sooke Public Boat Ramp:** Located in the business district at 6933 West Coast Road, this launch is close to services and has parking and a boat ramp. Fee required. For details, visit sooke.ca/our-community/boatlaunch.

**Coopers Cove:** Find this launch inside the bay on Sooke Road. It offers a public boat ramp and an easy launch, but the gravel beach floods at high water. For more launch information, visit bcmarinetrails.org/map_site/11278. Nearby Rush Adventures offers kayak and paddle board rentals; you can learn more about them online at rush-adventures.com.

**Anderson Cove:** This launch by East Sooke Regional Park is in a very picturesque section of the bay, but it dries at a minus-four tide. To reach it, take BC 14 to Gillespie Road. Keep following Gillespie Road south and then turn right on East Sooke Road.

## ROUTES

**Sooke Basin:** *Protected.* Explore the curvy and jagged shoreline of the south and east sides of the basin. A few small coves like Anderson Cove and Roche Cove offer a closer look and a wind break. A little tidal current may give you a slight push into Roche Cove. Investigate the mini-islands and Capsize Rock at low tides. Coopers Cove is a very protected launch, making it a great place for beginners or those seeking an idyllic, wind-free paddle. As you paddle west

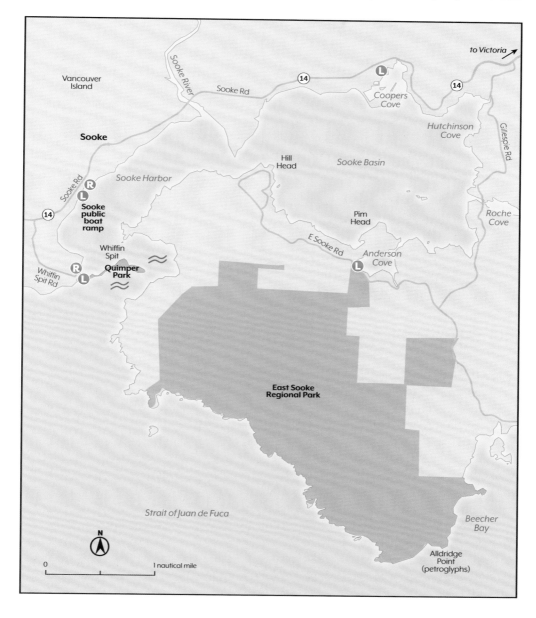

toward the harbor, look for a point sticking out into the basin, nearly splitting the two bodies of water in half. This is the beginning of Sooke Harbor. Behind the point is Sooke River, a melancholy Class I (no rapids) river. Paddle up the river on a flood tide to enjoy the river's slow current and winding curves. Take the ebb down the river for a free ride back to the harbor. On the other side of the river, beach homes and docks line the shoreline.

**Sooke Harbor:** *Protected.* In the town of Sooke, you'll pass a marina and a few homes with docks. Look for Whiffin Spit to the south, extending from the west shore nearly across the harbor entry to the east. The spit is popular with afternoon walkers, bicyclists, and paddlers seeking a rest stop. The Strait of Juan de Fuca is beyond the spit. Paddle around the outside of Whiffin Spit, enjoying views of the Olympic Mountains in Washington State, and follow the shoreline west along the strait. Currents can run up to 4 knots in the opening. Keep an eye out for entering ocean swell. If the wind and ocean swell are active, stay in the harbor unless you have outer-coast paddling skills. Much like anywhere along this stretch, the waters can be glassy calm or have full-on storm conditions. In 1790, the Spanish explorer Manual Quimper spotted a few tall poles along the beach here, used by the T'sou-ke First Nations people for suspending nets to catch birds. In the same year, a village was reported north of the spit.

**East Sooke Regional Park:** *Exposed.* East Sooke Regional Park, which begins on the eastern entry to the harbor, resembles the wild coastline from the west side of Vancouver Island. The rocky, windswept wilderness offers pocket beaches, caves, petroglyphs, sheltered coves, and solitude only a short distance from the urban center of Victoria. When the current and wind are strong or ocean swell is penetrating the shore, only advanced paddlers should venture here. Check current tables, weather, and swell forecasts (and buoys) before heading out. At Alldridge Point, a petroglyph of a fish dating back 200 to 3000 years is etched on a flat rock above the shoreline. The elements are gradually eroding the image.

# 69. **Brentwood Bay to Tod Inlet**

Close to both Victoria and Sidney, this trip starts in the busy Marina at Brentwood Bay and ends in a quiet, protected, tree-lined inlet. While it's a popular boating destination in summer, find yourself in solitude in the off season. The area surrounding Gowlland Tod Provincial Park resembles a remote coastal inlet. You can also explore tiny Butchart Cove, bordering the famous Butchart Gardens and Daphne Islet.

Tod Inlet's storied history includes two W̱SÁNEĆ (Saanich) First Nation village sites dating back 1500 years. Up to twelve shell middens line the shores of Gowlland Tod Provincial Park. First Nations people called the area SṈIDȻEȽ (pronounced "sneed-kwith"), which translates to "place of the blue grouse," symbolizing its plentiful resources.

In 1904, Robert Pim Butchart opened the Portland Cement Company in Tod Inlet, employing Canadian Chinese, Sikh, European, and First Nation workers in a series of lime quarries and kilns. After the company closed in 1921, Butchart opened his gardens, employing Canadian Chinese workers. Today, boaters visit the inlet to view the frequent fireworks displays put on by Butchart Gardens.

*Looking into protected Tod Inlet*

**Duration:** Half day to full day.

**Rating:** *Protected.*

**Navigation Aids:** Canadian Hydrographic Service chart 3441 (1:40,000).

**Planning Considerations:** This is a one-way trip to Tod Inlet, which has picnic tables and pit toilets. Keep an eye out for boats in summer.

## GETTING THERE AND LAUNCHING

**"The Beach" at Verdier Park** (Brentwood Bay, BC): From Victoria, take Burnside Road East north, which becomes Interurban Road. Turn left onto BC Highway 17A/West Saanich Road and follow it north for about 6 miles to a roundabout. At the roundabout, take the third exit onto Verdier Avenue and follow it to its end. "The Beach" park is on your left and has limited parking, restrooms, a lawn area, and easy beach access down a concrete ramp.

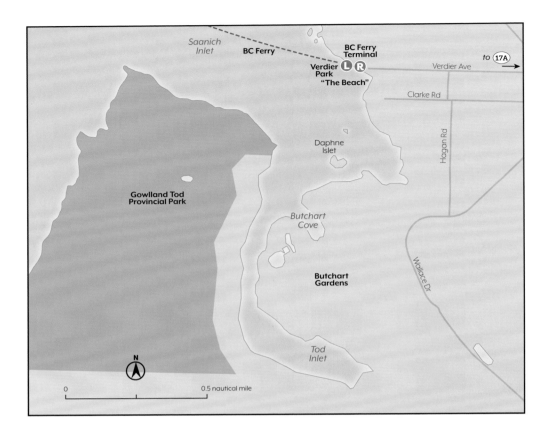

**ROUTE**

Make a quick escape to a quiet back bay within beautiful Gowlland Tod Provincial Park. This is a great paddle for beginners and those seeking a waterway protected from most winds. Conveniently located between Sidney and Victoria, the 1.8-mile paddle from Brentwood Bay to Tod Inlet starts in the busy marina. The noise soon drops away as you paddle along tree-lined shorelines in Butchart Cove, past Butchart Gardens, and on to Gowlland Tod Provincial Park. End your trip in secluded Tod Inlet. Look for culturally modified trees along the shoreline.

# 70. **Portland Island**

Originally a First Nations camp, Hawaiian immigrants called "Kanakas" settled the island in the mid-1800s. In 1958, Princess Margaret received the island as a gift when she visited the province. She returned it to British Columbia as a provincial park in 1967. Now a national park reserve, it's known for its sandy beaches, little coves, hiking trails through thick forests, orchards, and easy access to the Saanich Peninsula. At low tides, you can observe the excellent intertidal life along the northwest shore of the island below Kanaka Bluff.

**Duration:** Full day to overnight.

**Rating:** *Moderate.* Currents can be strong enough to produce tide rips and rough seas when opposing wind. Boat and ferry traffic is heavy.

**Navigation Aids:** Canadian Hydrographic Service cruising atlas 3313 (charts in spiral-bound format) or 3441 (both 1:40,000); H&R Nautical Ventures Small-Craft Nautical Maps: Sooke to Victoria and the Gulf Islands (strip charts mostly 1:40,000); CHS current tables (Volume 5) for Race Passage with corrections for Swanson Channel; Canadian *Current Atlas.*

**Planning Considerations:** Now included in the Gulf Islands National Park Reserve and the BC Marine Trail system, the island receives heavy use at its three designated fee-based camping areas. Arrive early to secure your site on summer weekends. Travel with current flow; the flood moves north and the ebb south. The fee for wheeling a kayak onto the BC Ferries varies, so check rates on the routes you plan to use. Make sure to arrive early and line up your boat on the side with the motorcycles; you'll be directed onto the car deck.

## GETTING THERE AND LAUNCHING

The launch site at Sidney is adjacent to the Washington State Ferries terminal (to and from Anacortes), and the launch at Swartz Bay is by the BC Ferries terminals. Follow signs to the appropriate one.

**Sidney–Tulista Park:** Use the beach just south of the launch ramp for the Washington State Ferries terminal. When you exit the ferry, take a left on Ocean Avenue, then another immediate left on 5th Street. Look for park signs. The busy boat ramp requires fees. A gravel beach is at

*Paddle boarders exploring the shore of Portland Island*

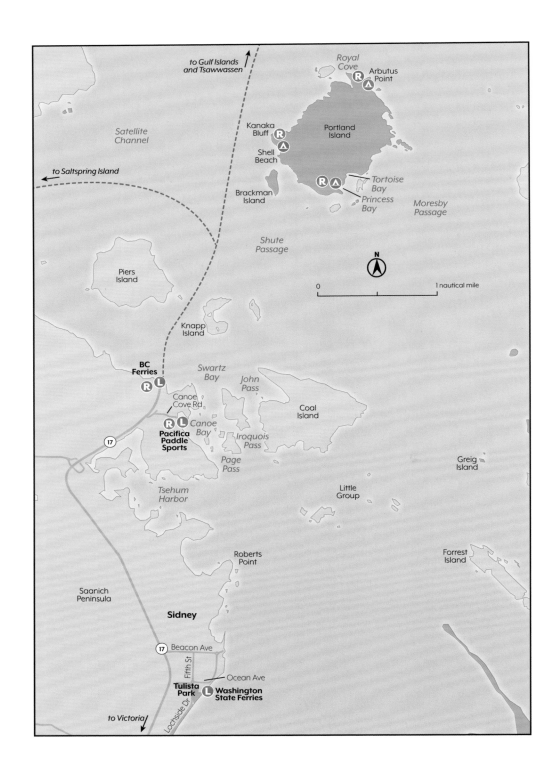

to Gulf Islands
and Tsawwassen

*Royal Cove*

Arbutus
Point

*Satellite
Channel*

Kanaka
Bluff

*Portland
Island*

Shell
Beach

to Saltspring Island

Brackman
Island

*Tortoise
Bay*

*Princess
Bay*

*Moresby
Passage*

*Shute
Passage*

N

*Piers
Island*

0                    1 nautical mile

Knapp
Island

**BC
Ferries**

*Swartz
Bay*

*John
Pass*

Canoe
Cove Rd

*Coal
Island*

*Canoe
Bay*

**Pacifica
Paddle
Sports**

*Iroquois
Pass*

17

*Page
Pass*

*Greig
Island*

*Tsehum
Harbor*

Little
Group

Roberts
Point

*Forrest
Island*

Saanich
Peninsula

**Sidney**

17   Beacon Ave

Fifth St

Ocean Ave

**Tulista
Park**   **Washington
State Ferries**

to Victoria

Lochside Dr

the north end of the park, and toilets and a picnic shelter are available. Parking can hold three vehicles for up to twenty-four hours. More long-stay pay parking can be found at the corner of Bevan Avenue and 2nd Street.

**Swartz Bay:** Use the Swartz Bay public wharf to launch. The wharf is just east of the BC Ferries terminal. If you've come in from Tsawwassen, go south on BC 17 and take the first exit off the highway, then turn back onto BC 17 heading north. Take the Dolphin Road exit and follow the ferry-terminal fence to Barnacle Road. You'll soon see the wharf with its limited parking. If you've wheeled your kayak off the ferry, walk it directly to the wharf and launch on the gravel beach nearby. When launching here, watch for ferry traffic and never cross the path of an incoming ferry.

**Pacifica Paddle Sports:** Find this launch near the Swartz Bay ferry at the end of Canoe Cove Road. At the end of E Dock, Pacifica Paddle Sports offers kayak, SUP, and canoe rentals and tours. You can launch your own craft for a small fee. Ask for a parking pass. For more details, visit pacificapaddle.com/swartz-bay.

### ROUTE

The one-way distance from Swartz Bay to Portland Island is 2 miles; it's 4 miles from Tulista Park in Sidney. If you start in Sidney, you can sightsee through John, Iroquois, or Page Passes, where sumptuous homes and moored yachts line the shores. No matter where you start, you should go east of Knapp Island to avoid the busy ferry lanes on the west. Currents in Shute Passage flood northwest at up to 1.5 knots, and on the ebb, they move in the opposite direction at the same speed. This requires a substantial ferry-angle course adjustment to control the amount you are set by it. The Canadian *Current Atlas* is very helpful for timing with this current.

Portland Island has several First Nations shell middens along its beaches. Do not disturb the middens. Enjoy the extensive trail system; it can take up to three hours to cross the island. The island has campsites at Arbutus Point, Princess Bay, and Shell Beach. Shell Beach is on the south side, protected by Brackman Island. Arbutus Point has tent pads in the forest on the north side of the island. Princess Bay has no views and requires hauling gear up the stairs that originate at the dinghy dock. Camping is in an old, grassy orchard. Facilities include pit toilets and picnic tables but no water. Unless a fire ban is in effect, you can build campfires in designated rings, but it's best to rely on your cookstove on this wildfire-prone island.

# 71. Salt Spring Island to Wallace Island

Off the northeast corner of Salt Spring Island, Wallace Island Marine Provincial Park sits 1.6 miles across Houston Passage. This easy paddle is great for all skill levels. The narrow island has several protected coves, an easy portage over the middle, and hiking trails through thick forest. The coves are popular with boaters, so expect a crowd on a sunny weekend. But as a paddler, you can easily find enough privacy in the island's numerous pocket beaches and rocky alcoves, feeling much farther away than you are.

*Perfect landing spot in Conover Cove*

**Duration:** Part day to overnight.

**Rating:** *Protected* or *Moderate*.

**Navigation Aids:** Canadian Hydrographic Service chart 3442 (1:40,000); CHS current table for Active Pass.

**Planning Considerations:** Summer weekends can be crowded on the island. Although current is light in Houston Passage, wind opposing current may create rough conditions.

## GETTING THERE AND LAUNCHING

**Fernwood Launches:** From Ganges, take the curvy Robinson Road northeast out of town. Robinson Road becomes Walkers Hook Road and follows the shoreline along Trincomali Channel. In 3.4 miles, arrive in Fernwood, a tiny community with a store and a café. On your right is a government dock. There are two launches in Fernwood. Drive past the dock and on your right look for a small pullout alongside the road. A shaky wooden stairway leads to the gravel-and-sand beach. Or about a quarter of a mile farther north, find a boat ramp with limited parking. The beach gets muddy at low tides. The south end of Wallace Island is directly across from Fernwood.

You can also easily access Wallace Island from Galiano and Thetis Islands, each with short crossings.

**Arbutus Road:** 225 Arbutus Road. Find this road-end launch at the very northern point of Salt Spring Island. From Ganges, drive north on Lower Ganges Road, which becomes North End Road. Turn right on Southey Point Road and then left on Arbutus Road, following it to the end. No facilities are available and street parking is limited. Launch over sandstone into a mini cove.

## ROUTE

If you launch from Fernwood, paddle 1 mile across Houston Passage to the south end of Wallace Island at Panther Point. Light current runs through with little effect on paddling. Rocks above and just below the waterline at Panther Point sunk the coal ship Panther in 1847. The protected cove inside the point empties out in low tides but makes a beautiful rest stop, with easy walking access to Conover Cove. Paddle around the east side of the island, passing several small off-shore rocks, some covered in harbor seals, starfish, and anemones. You'll soon come to a little cove with a small gravel landing area. A campsite is above the beach in a grassy area. You can also portage from here over to Conover Cove. The picnic shelter above the cove is covered in driftwood art, well worth a peek. Restrooms are on the hill above. Conover Cove has tents sites for eight-plus people, a picnic table and shelter, pit and vault toilets, and a food cache. No water is available, and fires are prohibited. Camping fees apply year-round.

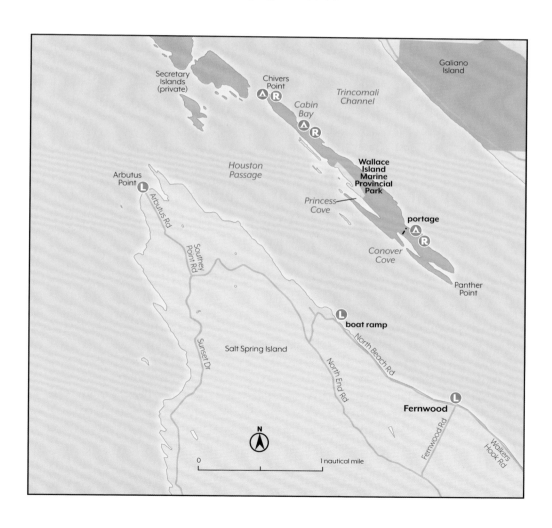

Continuing down the east side of the island, the rocky shore becomes a wall with twisting madrona trees perched on the edge. Near the northeast end, reach Cabin Bay, with two campsites tucked into a sheltered rocky cove. The campsites are on the flat area and fit two or three tents. There is no water, but a pit toilet at Chivers Point is a ten-minute walk away. Chivers Point, at the north end of the island, is surrounded by long, rocky reefs. A path leads up to nine wooden camping pads, a vault toilet, a picnic table for each pad, and a food cache. No fires permitted or water available. For all Wallace Island campsites, you can pre-pay for a camping permit, but specific campsites are not reservable. For fees and more information, visit bcparks.ca/wallace-island-marine-park.

When you're ready, round Chivers Point and head south down Houston Passage. The Secretary Islands to the north are private; landing is prohibited. Pass several slender rock shelves—one parallels the island for some distance. At higher tides, paddle through the slot, staying close to shore to enjoy the sea life and geology. Enter Princess Cove, a popular gunkhole for boaters that extends nearly 1800 feet. Walk the gravel passageway connecting to Conover Cove to the south. Two offshore reefs offer a chance for more exploration, especially at low tides when more sea life will be visible.

# 72. **Salt Spring Island to Prevost Island**

Named for Captain James Charles Prevost, the captain of the HMS *Satellite* 1857–1860, this island tucked between Pender and Salt Spring has all the benefits of all the Gulf Islands wrapped into one location. From shaped sandstone to remote-feeling pocket beaches, a historic lighthouse to madrone-lined shores to endless deep inlets to explore. There is only one campsite in protected James Bay. Feral goats are commonly seen on the island's steep shores.

**Duration:** Half-day to overnight

**Rating:** *Protected* to *Moderate*.

**Navigational Aids:** Canadian Hydrographic Service Chart 3442 (1:40,000). Fulford Harbor or Ganges Harbor tide tables. Currents: Race Passage. Secondary: Trincomali Channel.

**Planning Considerations:** Southerly winds could be of concern. In summer BC Ferries run frequently along Swanson Channel and from Salt Spring's Long Harbor. Use marine traffic apps and ferry schedules to track. During high tides, James Bay (Gulf Islands National Park Preserve) is the most easily accessed beach. Pull your paddle craft high on the beaches to avoid passing ferry wakes.

*Portlock Point Lighthouse on Prevost Island*

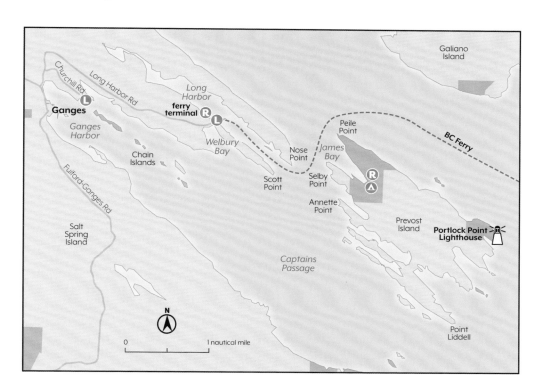

**GETTING THERE AND LAUNCHING**

With no ferries to the island, access is only by paddle craft or boat. The safest crossing is from Ganges Harbor or Long Harbor on Salt Spring Island.

**ROUTE**

**James Bay Campsite.** Launching from Churchill Road (See Trip 73, Salt Spring Island–Chain Islands), paddle along the Chain Islands veering east at Scott Point. Watching for sea planes in Ganges Harbor and ferry traffic to and from Long Harbor, cross to Nose Point then two-thirds of a mile to Selby Point on Prevost Island. Paddle the remaining half mile to the James Bay campsite on the right side of the bay. The site has a sandy beach at high water, mud and eel grass at low tides, and is a long carry in. Camping is on grass in an old orchard with three picnic tables, a food cache, composting table, and no fires.

The circumnavigation of the island is 8 miles. Take your time to explore the island's rugged arbutus and Garry Oak–lined shores and protected inlets. The many deep bays provide protection from the wind and peacefulness. Visit the 1896 era Portlock Point Lighthouse on the island's southeast shore. Land at Richardson Bay to access the lighthouse hiking trail. The landing is on a steep, sandy, and gravel beach at the end of a long, protected cove with a few rocks.

If launching from Pender Island (See Trip 74, Pender, Saturna, and Mayne Islands), note that ferry traffic is heavier in this area.

# 73. Salt Spring Island to Chain Islands

Like a string of pearls, the Chain Islands in protected Ganges Harbor allow you to easily explore and sample a variety of island habitats. From Gulf Island sandstone to colorful arbutus trees hanging over the shore, natural beauty is everywhere, and the abundant waterfowl and marine life make the islands a joy to visit. The launches are easily accessed from Ganges and because it's a short paddle into the islands, this is a great trip for beginners.

In Ganges Harbor on July 4, 1860, a canoe of Bella Bella First Nations people invited by fifty Cowichans attacked and killed several settlers, taking a few as slaves. The US-Canadian boundary nearby was determined in 1872.

**Duration:** Half day.

**Rating:** *Protected* to *Moderate*.

**Navigation Aids:** Canadian Hydrographic Service chart 3442 (1:40,000); Fulford Harbor or Ganges Harbor tide tables.

**Planning Considerations:** Southerly and northeasterly winds are the only concerns. Watch out for seaplanes launching from Ganges Harbor and boating traffic in summer.

## GETTING THERE AND LAUNCHING

**Churchill Road:** From Ganges, take Lower Ganges Road north and turn right on Upper Ganges Road. Turn right on Churchill Road and follow it to the end. Launch on Ganges Harbor; the launch may be flooded on high tides. Roadside day parking is available for about twenty vehicles. No overnight parking permitted.

**Welbury Bay Park:** From Ganges, take Lower Ganges Road north and turn right on Upper Ganges Road. Turn right on Long Harbor Road. The launch is just before the turn to Scott Point Drive. Forty-eight-hour parking is nearby on Long Harbor Road. Restrooms and picnic tables are nearby. Water is at the ferry terminal. The ramp to the water has a guardrail but is not cart friendly.

## ROUTE

If you launch from Churchill Road, you can avoid much of the busy boating traffic and paddle directly to Powder Islet, the first of the chain. The second islet, Goat Island, is private but has a picturesque shoreline with sandstone formations, tiny coves and pocket beaches, and madrona trees above. Continue to Deadman Islands, also private; look for a house on the north

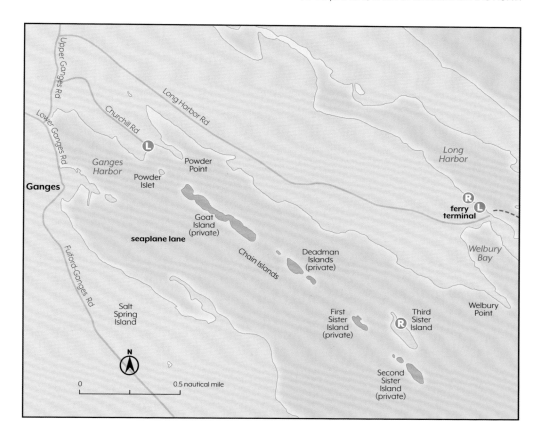

*Creative outhouse on Third Sister Island, Chain Islands*

end of the main island. In the nineteenth century, the Deadman Islands were used as a First Nations burial area. Have fun exploring the surrounding smaller islets and watching for bird life.

Next up are First and Second Sister Islands, which are private but with interesting shores. Also called Castle Island, a wealthy Scot built a small castle-like house on First Sister Island years ago but left it to ruin. The "castle" remains can be seen from the water. Third Sister Island is public; you can spot it from a distance by the white sand-and-shell beach on its north end. This is Chocolate Beach, named for chocolate lilies. After you land, pass the metal "No Fires" sign and walk up the trail to the funky outhouse on the island's east side. The trail continues up the island's spine with channel views through twisty madrona trees.

# 74. **Pender, Saturna, and Mayne Islands**

This part of the southern Gulf Islands offers the most opportunities for small-channel paddling. Swift currents in some passages make them inappropriate for the inexperienced. Many route variations are possible, especially if you carry kayaks aboard the BC Ferries. You have many different island stops to choose from for beginning and ending your paddling trip.

In 1794, Captain George Vancouver and his crew camped at Georgina Point on Mayne Island and left behind a coin and a knife, found one hundred years later. Active Pass was named for the USS *Active*, the first steam vessel to go through the pass.

**Duration:** Part day to overnight.

**Rating:** *Moderate* or *Moderate +*. Currents in parts of this area are strong, with at least two local tide races. The most challenging one is avoidable.

**Navigation Aids:** Canadian Hydrographic Service cruising atlas 3313 (charts in spiral-bound format) or 3442 (both 1:40,000), 3477 (1:15,000); H&R Nautical Ventures Small-Craft Nautical Maps: Sooke to Victoria and the Gulf Islands (strip charts mostly 1:40,000); CHS current tables (Volume 5) for Active Pass with corrections for Georgeson and Boat Passages; current tables for Race Passage with corrections for Swanson Channel; Canadian *Current Atlas*.

**Planning Considerations:** Travel with current flows as much as possible. The flood goes northward in Pender Canal and northwest in Plumper Sound. These have no current predictions but can be estimated from those in Swanson Channel. BC ferries have limited daily service to Mayne and Saturna Islands. There is no public kayak camping on Mayne Island.

## GETTING THERE AND LAUNCHING

Unless you integrate this trip with the Portland Island route to the west (see Trip 70, Portland Island), you will have to take the BC Ferries to either Pender, Mayne, or Saturna Islands. If you are coming from the mainland at Tsawwassen, you will have to transfer ferries at Mayne Island or Swartz Bay to reach Saturna Island.

### Pender Island

**Otter Bay Launch:** From the ferry terminal, the closest launch is 0.3 mile away at the Otter Bay Marina. Drive to the top of the hill above the terminal and take a right on MacKinnon Road. Immediately look for the small, poorly placed sign for Otter Bay Marina on your right. The road drops sharply down a hill to the full-service marina. The launch is a sandy beach at high tides or rock at low tides; there is also a boat ramp. There is no fee to launch or park. Contact the marina office by calling 250-629-3579 or visit otterbay-marina.ca.

**Port Browning Launch:** From the ferry landing, drive to the top of the hill above the terminal, turn right on MacKinnon Road, another right on Otter Bay Road, and then a third right on Bedwell Harbor Road. Follow the road for about 2 miles. Bedwell Harbor Road soon passes the town center, a good place to get groceries, coffee, and other supplies. Take a left on Hamilton Road. Follow the road into Port Browning, on your left at the bottom of the hill. Facilities include a marina, library, kayak shop, pub, and café. Camping in the large field is available by checking in with the marina office. Launch from the beach below the field and café. To learn more, visit portbrowning.ca.

**Mortimer Spit Launch:** After the town of Port Browning, take Canal Road south. Follow Canal Road for several miles and eventually cross Pender Canal Bridge (one lane). Continue left beyond the bridge to Mortimer Spit Road, which comes up very quickly on your left. This day-use site has a restroom near the road. Launch from any side of the spit, watching for boat traffic entering Pender Canal. Nearby is Xelisen, an Aboriginal site bisected by the construction of the canal.

**Medicine Beach Launch:** From Port Browning, take Canal Road south. Before the bridge, take a right on Wallace Road. Take a left on Schooner Way and follow it to the beach. Find six parking spots and a beach launch near the end of Schooner Way. A small grocery store is one block north.

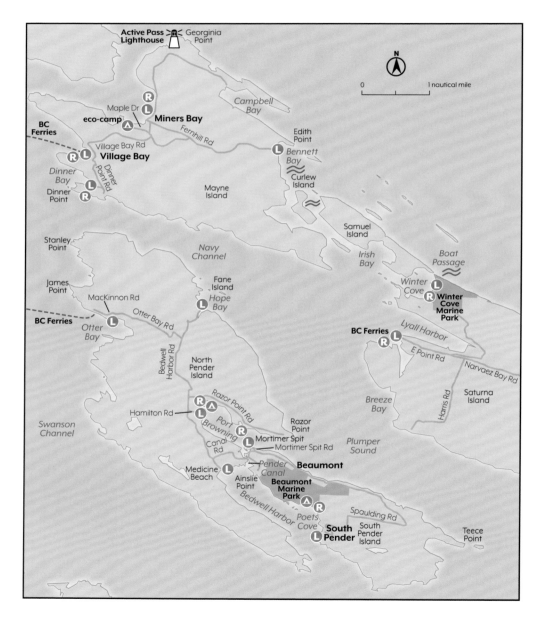

*Tidal stream between Curlew and Samuel Islands*

**Poets Cove Launch:** Continue south past Mortimer Spit on Canal Road. In a few scenic miles, take a right on Spalding Road and follow it to Poets Cove Resort and Spa. Park anywhere and launch at the beaches below the resort. If you want to park overnight, check with the resort office. There's a kayak rental on the right below the steep cliffs. A full-service marina and resort, Poets Cove has lodging, restaurants, and an outdoor pool to relax in. Beaumont Marine Park is a short paddle to the north of the resort. Poets Cove also has a Canadian Customs office. For additional information, visit poetscove.com.

**Hope Bay Launch:** From Pender town center, take Bedwell Harbor Road north a few miles to Hope Bay. Or from the ferry, go up the hill and take a right on MacKinnon Road and then another right on Otter Bay Road. In about a mile, take a left on Bedwell Harbor Road and follow it to Hope Bay. Park along the road and launch 50 yards west of the café along the gravel-stone beach. Check with the café for overnight parking.

### Mayne Island

**Village Bay Launch:** Foot passengers can wheel their boats on and off at Village Bay on Mayne Island. After leaving the ferry by foot, immediately turn left through a gate leading to a path to the beach. If driving from the ferry terminal, take a right on Dalton Drive. Turn right on Mariners Way and then turn right again on Callaghan Crescent. Below is a boat ramp on the south side of Village Bay. Vault toilet and picnic tables are available.

**Dinner Bay Launch:** From the BC Ferries terminal in Village Bay, take a right on Dalton Drive, followed by a left on Merryman, and then a right back onto Dalton Drive. Turn right on Mariners Way and then left on Dinner Bay Road. Follow this road 0.3 mile to Dinner Bay Park. The launch is from a sandy beach below the park, providing easy access to either Navy Channel or a protected bay for beginners to enjoy. Restrooms available.

**Miners Bay Launch:** From the BC Ferries terminal in Village Bay, take a left onto Village Bay Road and follow this winding route for 1.4 miles to Miners Bay. Take a left on Fernhill Road and a right on Georgina Point Road, which leads you into the main commercial district for Mayne Island.

Miners Bay has the only water-accessed, nonmotorized public watercraft camping on the island. Picnic tables, gazebo, and flush toilets are at the library building. The beach floods at high tide. Beware of strong currents outside of the bay.

**Mayne Island Camping:** This twenty-two-acre private resort offers camping and one cottage for rent. They have fifteen walk-in campsites and 1800 feet of shoreline, plus a tree shower. Only open during summer. To learn more, visit mayneislandcamping.com.

**Bennett Bay Launch:** From the ferry, take Village Bay Road to Fernhill Road. Turn right and follow Fernhill Road east for several miles. Fernhill Road becomes Bennett Bay Road, which will take you to the beach. Bennett Bay is an easy launch from a flat, rock-shelf beach. Look for old-growth fir and garry oak as well as a meadow nearby.

### Saturna Island

**Ferry Terminal Launch:** From the ferry terminal on Lyall Harbor, turn left to the public wharf. This is the easiest launch on the island. Inquire locally about overnight parking options. A store is located just above the ferry dock at Saturna.

**Winter Cove Launch:** A public day-use area with a boat ramp and gravel beach provides access for the northeast side of Saturna Island. Follow E. Point Road from the ferry terminal to Winter Cove Road and turn right. Boat Passage is just beyond the launch. Picnic tables and pit toilets are available.

## ROUTES

You have three route options: paddle locally in Port Browning and Bedwell Harbor, use a full day to explore between Saturna and Mayne Islands, or take an extended overnight route that includes both of the above. Enjoy idyllic, protected coves, play in tidal rapids like Boat Passage, or run the speedy current of Pender Canal.

**Port Browning and Bedwell Harbor:** *Moderate*. The roundtrip distance is 4 to 6 miles. You can make this a day trip or an overnight, with camping at Beaumont Marine Park or Port Browning. Launch from Port Browning.

This trip would fall within the *Protected* rating were it not for the current in Pender Canal, which can run up to 4 knots for a short distance under the bridge. There are no predictions about the current's schedule other than it flows north on the flood. This passage requires some care, but it should be no problem for paddlers with average boat-handling skills. Whether you go through with or against the current, look carefully for powerboats coming through the cut; they must maintain speed to have maneuverability in the current and have limited deep water in which to avoid you. Bigger boats going through against the current make large, breaking wakes on the beaches. You should be able to find eddies in both the north and south approaches to the canal. Avoid paddling through the narrow slots between bridge supports unless you have strong skills with fast-moving currents.

The canal area, which was a portage until it was dredged at the turn of the century, was a long-used Salish townsite. An archaeological team dug here for several years in the 1970s. The bridge was built in 1955. Enjoy examples of modern architecture well blended with the natural surroundings as you paddle south of the canal into Bedwell Harbor.

Beaumont Marine Park is also a Gulf Islands National Park Reserve. The park begins on the northern shore of Bedwell Harbor at Ainslie Point. Find several nice beaches for a break ashore, with an extensive trail system that leads toward 800-foot Mount Norman. From there, you can enjoy panoramic views of the nearby Gulf Islands. The park's shoreline is composed of little pocket beaches and craggy, steep shores with madrona trees overhanging the water.

The Coast Salish have a rich history on the island dating back five thousand years. Shell middens and burial sites can be seen within the park, sometimes under picnic areas. In 2011, a burial site was robbed at the park. Make sure not to disturb the middens. Pit toilets and tables are the extent of the facilities. One mile south of the park, Poets Cove Resort has a full-service marina and resort facilities. You can launch and park there overnight for no charge. Check in with the office to let them know you're using the lot. There is also a Canadian Customs office should you want to paddle in from the United States. Pender Island Kayak Adventures offers kayak and SUP rentals at Poets Cove and Port Browning. To learn more, visit kayakpenderisland.com.

Alternative launches for this trip include Medicine Beach on the northwest end of Bedwell Harbor and Mortimer Spit on South Pender, just east of the bridge. Both are day-use only.

**Explore Between Mayne and Saturna Islands:** *Moderate.* The distance from the Saturna ferry landing to Winter Cove can be as little as 3 miles roundtrip, or you can lengthen it to about 7 miles with a circumnavigation of Samuel Island. A trip to Winter Cove avoids significant currents but allows a close-up look at fast water in little Boat Passage, which can sometimes reach up to 8 knots. If you enjoy playing in tidal rapids, you can have a lot of fun in the passage. Give the right-of-way to boaters, who have to maintain a constant speed through the passage to negotiate the current.

The east side of Winter Cove is a day-use-only marine park. Find a gravel beach just east of Boat Passage for access to trails to a view of the passage and the Strait of Georgia beyond.

Only attempt a circumnavigation of Samuel Island if you are comfortable with strong currents and sharp eddy lines, or if you plan to traverse its tide races at slack, especially Boat Passage. If your skills are up to it, you can run Boat Passage in midstream with few problems. Going through against the flow is difficult without portaging, as there are no eddies. Currents at the western end of Samuel Island are slower but still provide challenging eddies and possible tide rips between Samuel and Curlew Islands. Currents can flow up to several knots between Curlew and Samuel Islands.

**Village Bay, Winter Cove, and Bedwell Harbor Triangle Loop:** *Moderate.* This loop trip involves about 20 miles of paddling. Travel in the Pender Islands and between Mayne and Saturna Islands as described above. Use Swanson Channel predictions for Plumper Sound and Navy Channel, but note that Navy Channel floods east at a maximum of 3 knots from Swanson

Channel, meeting the west-flowing flood current from Plumper Sound off Hope Bay. Current speeds in Plumper Sound between Saturna and South Pender Islands can reach 3 knots.

Consider alternative launches to avoid weather issues or for a preferable current flow. For example, Hope Bay on northeast Pender provides a shorter crossing to Mayne Island.

# 75. **Galiano Island and Montague Harbor**

Titled the "Gem of the Gulf Islands," Galiano Island is renowned for its sunsets. Sixteen miles long and two miles wide, the island is also known for its many curvy-shaped, Tafoni sandstone shorelines and bluffs. Tafoni is a Corsican term meaning "little holes." A major boating destination in summer, Montague Harbor can get busy, but it is easy to escape and find your own place along its long shores, especially in the off-season. Looking for a bite? Take the Hummingbird Bus with "Tommy Transit" to the Hummingbird Pub. Long before Spanish explorer Dionisio Alcalá Galiano arrived on the island's shores in 1792, the Penelakut Island Hul'qumi'num First Nations lived in this area. Their territory stretched from Galiano Island to Tent Island, and shell middens surrounding Montague Bay date back three thousand years.

**Duration:** Half day to overnight.

**Rating:** *Protected* to *Moderate*. The *Moderate* is for winds that may develop north of Montague Harbor.

**Navigation Aids:** Canadian Hydrographic Service chart 3442; NOAA charts 18421 (1:80,000), 18400 (1:200,000); Fulford Harbor or Montague Harbor tide tables; Race Passage or Trincomali Channel current tables.

**Planning Considerations:** Montague Harbor is protected but very busy in summer with boaters. Watch for winds and clapotis (reverb) along the rocky shores north of Montague. Stay clear of Active and Portier Passes unless skilled with strong tidal currents. Camping is available in Montague Harbor Marine Provincial Park all year but is only reservable from May 13 to September 23. Water is available from March 15 to October 31. There is a boat ramp on the north side of the park.

## GETTING THERE AND LAUNCHING

To get to the Sturdies Bay ferry terminal on Galiano Island, you can take BC Ferries from Tsawwassen near Vancouver or Swartz Bay on Vancouver Island. See Trips 58, 59, or 60 for paddling in from other islands.

**Montague Harbor Marine Provincial Park Launch:** From the Sturdies Bay ferry terminal on Galiano Island, take Sturdies Bay Road to Georgeson Bay Road. Turn right on Montague Road and follow it to Montague Harbor Marine Park. Find the boat ramp on the north side

*Galiano Island sandstone*

and a dock and beach access on the south side. Both have parking, with restrooms and water nearby. The marina has a store and other services. Check the park website for parking and launch fees at bcparks.ca/montague-harbour-marine-park.

**Retreat Cove Launch:** From the Sturdies Bay ferry terminal, take Sturdies Bay Road to Georgeson Bay Road. Turn right on Montague Road and then later take another right onto Clanton Road. Veer left onto Porlier Pass Road. Finally, take a left on Retreat Cove Road and follow it to its end, where you'll find a high dock on small cove. No facilities available.

**Hummingbird Bus:** "You have to take the bus!" From mid-June to mid-September, Tommy Transit runs an old red bus from Montague Harbor to the Hummingbird Pub every hour from 5 PM to 11 PM. He's known for his colorful personality, singing, and providing entertainment along the way. Learn more by visiting hummingbirdpub.com/home/pub-bus.

If you're without a kayak or want a local's perspective on exploring the island, Gulf Island Kayaking offers tours of Montague Harbor and the sandstone shores to the north. You can call them at 250-539-2442 or visit their website at seakayak.ca.

## ROUTE

Choose your route. If you launch from Montague Harbor Marine Park, first explore protected Montague Bay, which is nearly a mile long. The south side has a few houses with docks. Montague Harbor Marina sits on the east side and Montague Harbor Marine Provincial Park on the north side. Notice the park's interesting shorelines; its two white-shell beaches are actually ancient shell middens from the Penelakut Island Hul'qumi'num First Nations people. A salt lagoon splits the park in half, with a view looking north up the island. Ignoring the powerlines above, enjoy exploring the rocky western shores of the park. A shell-covered pocket beach on Gray Peninsula faces Parker Island, which is mostly developed. Keep an eye out for a popular sandstone formation, Mushroom Rock.

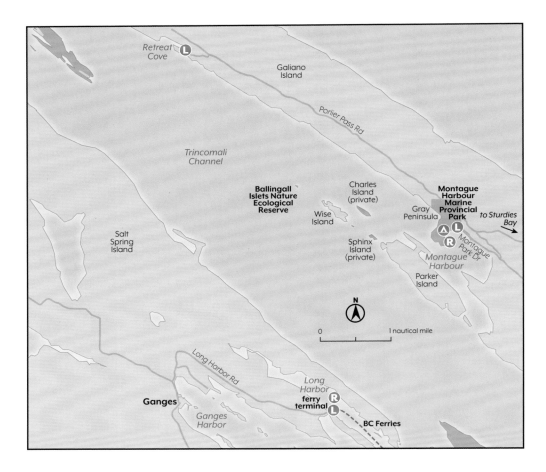

Cross to Parker Island to investigate its shores and protected pocket beaches. As you paddle north of Parker Island, encounter a series of small islands: Julia, Sphinx, and Charles Islands (which are all private) and Wise Island (which is developed). Beyond is the Ballingall Islets Nature Ecological Reserve, opened in 1963 to protect colonies of nesting glaucous-winged gulls, pigeon guillemots, and pelagic cormorants. Unfortunately, nests haven't been spotted here since 1987, but the reserve stands in hopes the birds reestablish themselves. No access is allowed. Cross east to the Galiano Island shore or return to Montague Harbor.

In Retreat Cove, 4.5 miles north of Montague Harbor, inspect the sandstone caves by the dock across from Retreat Island. Soon after Retreat Island, large sandstone cliffs rise above the water, invoking awe and showcasing the island's geology at Bodega Ridge Provincial Park. A varied sandstone shoreline continues to the north end of the island, where you'll find Porlier Pass and campsites around Dionisio Point—both only ideal for paddlers experienced with strong tidal current. Tidal current can increase closer toward Dionisio Point.

OPPOSITE *Exploring the quiet back channels of Widgeon Creek (Trip 80)*

# Vancouver, British Columbia

With majestic fjords north of the city and the mighty Fraser River to the south, paddlers will find endless opportunities around Vancouver, British Columbia. Explore the slow-moving waterway of Widgeon Creek with towering mountains rising above. Or venture into Indian Arm's fjord with its waterfalls and tree-topped islets. Paddle through the heart of urban Vancouver on False Creek and English Bay. Or enjoy a drift on the lower Fraser River past fishing boats and houseboats while also keeping an eye open for waterfowl and harbor seals.

*Swans along the South Arm Marshes, in Ladner, British Columbia*

# 76. Fraser River, Ladner Marsh, and Deas Island

The longest river in British Columbia, Fraser River runs for 851 miles and ends at the Strait of Georgia in southwest Vancouver. Ladner Marsh and Deas Island and slough provide close-up views into the lower Fraser River. Houseboats, marinas, and commercial fishing boats line the shore around Ladner. Offshore, four islands split the Fraser River channel, sending the main channel above and another channel below. Glacier and alluvial deposits 100 meters below sea level arrived more than ten thousand years ago, establishing what is now the Fraser River Lowland. Following an ice age, additional alluvial deposits brought the land to its current level. The original inhabitants of this area were the Stó:lō people, also sometimes translated as Staulo. The latter name was adopted by the Halkomelem-speaking peoples of the lower mainland, whose former dialect was Dakelh. The river's name in the Dakelh language is Lhtakoh. The first non-Native people to arrive here were Spanish explorers in 1792, and Simon Fraser mapped the entire watershed in 1808.

**Duration:** Half day to full day.

**Rating:** *Protected* to *Moderate*. The *Moderate* rating is for needing to know tides and paddling in river and tidal current.

**Navigation Aids:** NOAA chart 18400 (1:200,000); Canadian Hydrographic Service charts 3492 (1:80,000), 3490 (1:20,000).

**Planning Considerations:** Higher tides (13 feet) are preferred in order to view all channels and make it less likely to get stuck in the mud. Aim for an incoming tide. Watch for wind against tidal current and power boats in warmer months, which can throw up large waves. For Deas Park, look up the Deas Slough Recreational Use Schedules for updated info on whether paddlers or water skiers can use the waterway. Check the BC Marine Trail site for duck and goose hunting seasons here, which can be a hazard to paddlers.

## GETTING THERE AND LAUNCHING

**Captain's Cove Marina:** From BC Highway 99 south, exit to River Road. Turn right on Admiral Boulevard and then left on Admiral Way. Finally, turn right onto Launch Way.

From BC 99 north, exit west on BC Highway 17A. Turn right on Ladner Trunk Road and then right on Elliott Street. Take a right on River Road and then a left on Ferry Road, following it to the boat ramp.

**Deas Island Regional Park** (6090 Deas Island Rd.): From BC 99, exit to BC 17A north and continue on 62B Street. Turn left on Deas Island Road. Find the park, dock, and launch soon after on your left. Parking and restrooms available. In lower tides, this launch may be muddy.

**Ladner's Wharf:** From BC 99, exit on BC 17A and then turn right on Ladner Trunk Road. Take a right on Elliott Street and follow it to its end, where you'll find a few parking spots and a lower dock for launching.

**Wellington Point Boat Ramp** (3653 River Rd. W.): From BC 17A, take Ladner Trunk Road, which becomes 47A Avenue and then River Road West, to the launch. Amenities include restrooms, picnic tables, and parking.

## ROUTES

**Deas Island Peninsula and Slough:** *Protected.* Follow this route up the Deas Slough of the Fraser River adjacent to Deas Island. The slough is a dead-end arm of Fraser River that starts at Captain's Cove Marina. Due to the large number of both water-skiers and paddlers here, the park issues a Deas Slough Recreational Use Schedule, which provides schedules for each activity. Make sure to check it prior to launching. The peninsula was named for Jonathan Sullivan Deas, a tinsmith who ran a cannery on the Fraser River until 1878.

Launching from Captain's Cove Marina, paddle to the right past the marina, watching for boat traffic. Continue up the slough under the BC 99 bridge, observing beaches and ample birdlife. You can also launch from Deas Island Regional Park, which provides a similar but more protected experience with less initial boat traffic. Deas Island offers many walking and bicycling trails, and its shores are good for observing wildlife.

**Ladner Marsh:** *Protected* to *Moderate.* The *Moderate* rating is for river and tidal current and possible boat wakes and wind. Launch from Ladner's Wharf and choose your own route. Explore the dead-end channel around the launch, passing a few marinas. Aim for higher tides

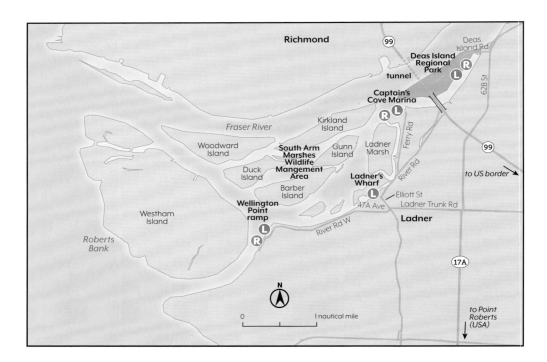

on the flood for exploring the narrow channels of Barber, Kirkland, and Gunn Islands. Only experienced paddlers should venture around Westham Island.

If you're feeling adventurous and have experience in current, paddle southwest along the Ladner shoreline past houseboats and commercial fishing boats. Directly across from Ladner, two small islands are worth investigating if you're not interested in a longer paddle. The Wellington Point boat launch is to the southwest, just before the channel takes a left along Westham Island and offers an option for running a shuttle to or from Ladner's Wharf. Before arriving at the Wellington launch, cross over to Barber Island, taking the first or second channel between Barber and Duck Islands north back toward Ladner. Enjoy this quiet, backwater channel with rich marine and birdlife. Then take the river current down from the east side of the islands and back to Ladner's Wharf or Wellington Point boat ramp.

The Ladner's Wharf round-trip around the islands is 5 miles and takes about two to three hours, depending on your pace. Note that tidal current can reverse outgoing river current on strong floods and king tides. Swans are frequently seen along these routes—they tend to be more aggressive in spring.

# 77. **English Bay**

From English Bay, you can relish panoramic skyline views of downtown Vancouver, Stanley Park, and the majestic North Shore Mountains, as well as distant western views of the Gulf Islands.

Experienced paddlers can round Point Grey below the University of British Columbia for a more coastal feel. If you're a beginner, or just want an inner-city paddling experience, you can enter False Creek to the southeast (see Trip 78, False Creek).

**Duration:** Half day.

**Rating:** *Protected*, *Moderate*, or *Exposed*. The *Exposed* rating is for wind in the bay and around Point Grey, plus ship and boat traffic.

**Navigation Aids:** Canadian Hydrographic Service charts 3311 Sunshine Coast–Vancouver Harbor to Desolation Sound (1:40.000), 3493 Vancouver Harbor, Western Portion (1:10:000), 3481 Approaches to Vancouver Harbor (1:25,000); CHS tide tables (Volume 5).

**Planning Considerations:** The main concerns are wind and boat or ship traffic. For a quieter experience in summer, launch on a Sunday morning. Rent kayaks or surf skis from the Jericho Beach Kayak Center. For details, visit jerichobeachkayak.com. Jericho Beach Kayak also hosts a webcam; if you want a sneak peak of current conditions, visit jerichobeachkayak.com/about-us/webcam.

## GETTING THERE AND LAUNCHING

**Jericho Beach:** Located west of Jericho Sailing Center, this sandy beach launch has flush toilets, parking, a concrete ramp, paddle craft rentals, and a swimming beach. This is mile 0 at the start of the BC Marine Trail. From BC Highway 99, take West 4th Avenue and look for signs for Jericho Beach. Jericho Beach Kayak Center is a bit farther away. To reach it, continue on West 4th Avenue, taking a right on Northwest Marine Drive and then a right on Discovery Street. Launching from Jericho Beach allows you to explore west or east toward downtown Vancouver.

   **Vanier Park Launch:** This is a good launch for entering False Creek if English Bay is too windy. It's also a short trip to explore the eastern shore of English Bay below skyscrapers and

*Vancouver skyline from Spanish Banks on English Bay*

upward to Stanley Park. Note that paddle craft are not allowed under the Lions Gate Bridge due to fast tidal current. From Burrard Street, exit onto Cornwall Avenue. Then turn north (right) on Chestnut Street. A final right turn on Whyte Avenue takes you to the boat ramp and parking.

## ROUTES

**Jericho Beach to False Creek:** This urban paddle goes toward the city, following a rocky and gravel beach below homes until you reach sandy Kitsilano Beach and Vanier Park. Enjoy epic views of the Vancouver skyline, distant Stanley Park, and Cypress and Grouse Mountains to the north. Large ships dominate the bay while waiting to unload. Head up the east shore to English Bay Beach, a sandy landing option for a rest directly below skyscrapers. The shores of Stanley Park vary from rocky to sandy. Do not enter under Lions Gate Bridge—it's off-limits to paddlers.

**Jericho Beach to Point Grey:** This route is for experienced paddlers. Venture west from Jericho Beach, paddling out of the bay and toward Point Grey through more exposed waters. Enjoy this quick escape from the city with medium-high, tree-lined bluffs. Immediately west of Jericho Beach, look for sandy Locarno and Spanish Banks Beaches. Watch for wind and boat wakes on Spanish Banks Beach due to the extensive low-tide sandy shelf that can reach out. Beyond Spanish Banks, the route opens to the Strait of Georgia. Paddle past Acadia Beach and Foreshore Park as it wraps around Point Grey. The beach here is a sampling of the next few miles: tall,

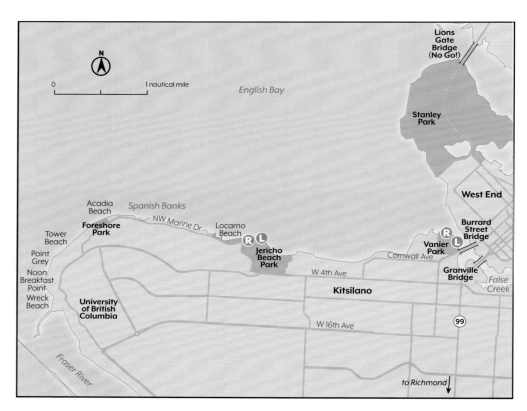

tree-lined bluffs with a mix of sandy and rocky beaches piled with driftwood. The Foreshore Trail, a beach hiking trail, begins near here. Continue south toward Point Grey to spot the World War II searchlight structure at Tower Beach and another a bit farther south. Both beaches may receive wind and boat waves due to offshore sandbars and shallow areas. The next beach, at Noon Breakfast Point, sits below a tall, sandy bluff. Just around the point is clothing-optional Wreck Beach, which at low tides extends out far with a sandy beach. End your route here, as the Fraser River mouth is at the end of the jetty and extensive log rafts may be stored behind.

# 78. **False Creek**

Savor spectacular inner-city views of Vancouver as you paddle under three bridges and float past the glass dome of Science World, BC Place stadium, Rogers Arena, colorful houseboats, and much more. The waterway is busy with water taxis, members of various paddling and rowing clubs, and other paddlers. Protected by most winds, this is a great spot for paddlers of all skill levels. False Creek was named by George Henry Richards during his hydrographic survey from 1856 to 1863. While conducting his research, he initially thought he was going along a creek but later found out it was just an inlet, hence its name. The waterway once extended to Clark Drive but was filled in over time by development. The Vancouver area was originally inhabited by the Downriver Halkomelem-speaking people—the Tsleil-Waututh. After European contact, there were only forty-one left due to epidemics. Soon after, a group of Tsleil-Waututh lived in False Creek. Over the next one hundred years, the waterway become a hub for industry.

**Duration:** Half day.

**Rating:** *Protected.*

**Navigation Aids:** Canadian Hydrographic Service chart 3493 (1:10,000).

**Planning Considerations:** Watch for boats and racing paddling craft from local clubs. False Creek is about 1.69 miles long.

### GETTING THERE AND LAUNCHING

**Vanier Boat Launch** (1000 Chestnut St.): This is the easiest launch, with a protected sandy beach and concrete boat ramps. Pay to park. Amenities include toilets and picnic tables. From Burrard Street, exit onto Cornwall Avenue. Then turn north (right) on Chestnut Street. A final right turn on Whyte Avenue takes you to the boat ramp and parking.

### ROUTE

Launch from Vanier Boat Launch, watching for boating traffic as you head southeast into False Creek. At about 0.33 mile, pass under the Burrard Street Bridge to Granville Island, a busy marketplace full of energy on busy weekends. Water taxis and boats are moored here and may be

*Canadian pride and waterfront homes along False Creek in Vancouver*

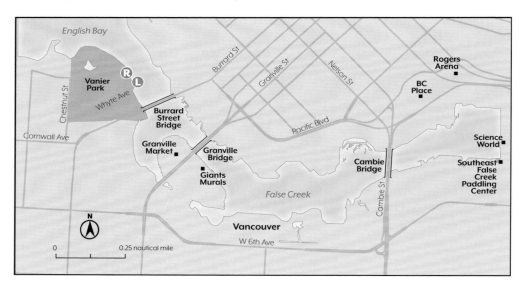

cruising around the island. As you pass under the Granville Bridge, the "Giants Murals" appear, painted on the silos of a concrete factory. Duck into the mini bays on both sides of the island (not really an island) to view quieter parts of the bay away from boating traffic. At 1.2 miles, paddle under the Cambie Bridge opening toward the end of the waterway. Look for the spectacular glass geo-dome of Science World and the impressive Southeast False Creek Paddling Centre docks. Across the inlet, BC Place stadium and Rogers Arena dominate the shoreline, along with rows of skyscrapers and apartment buildings. Watch for mini ferries that run across the waterway.

# 79. Deep Cove and Indian Arm

Thirty minutes east of Vancouver, Indian Arm (or in Halkomelem, səl̓ilw̓ət) is a 12-mile-long glacier fjord carved by the last ice age. Known for its beauty and waterfalls, enjoy this waterway's varied paddling options, from short day trips to multiday overnights. The Say Nuth Khaw Yum Provincial Park (also known as Indian Arm Provincial Park) was created in 1995 as part of the Government of British Columbia's Lower Mainland Nature Legacy Program. The park is located on the east shores of Indian Arm within Tsleil-Waututh Nation traditional territory. The northwestern corner borders Mount Seymour Provincial Park. The book *The Starship and the Canoe* by Kenneth Brower tells of baidarka kayak builder George Dyson's early days living in Belcarra, in a treehouse ninety-eight-feet high constructed from materials he salvaged from the beach. This is where he built the forty-eight-foot long baidarka known as *Mount Fairweather*.

**Duration:** Half day to overnight.

**Rating:** *Protected* to *Moderate*.

**Navigation Aids:** Canadian Hydrographic Service chart 3495 (1:80,000); tide tables for Deep Cove and Buntzen Lake; CHS current tables (Volume 5).

**Planning Considerations:** Check tides and wind forecasts. Indian Arm can be calm or windy; the conditions determine the required skill level. You'll have the most views traveling the fjord on the west or east sides. There are both day trip and overnight options, but the only overnight parking is on the street. Bring fresh water and watch for heavy boating traffic. Deep Cove Kayak offers paddle craft rentals and kayak tours. For details, visit their website at deepcovekayak.com. Deep Cove Kayak also hosts a webcam; if you want a sneak peak of current conditions visit deepcovekayak.com/webcams. On the webcam feed, Jug Island is on the right and Raccoon Island in the middle.

## GETTING THERE AND LAUNCHING

**Deep Cove Park:** Most paddlers launch from Deep Cove. From North Vancouver, take Dollarton Highway east. At Mount Seymour Parkway, Dollarton Highway becomes Deep Cove Road. Turn right on Naughton Avenue, which becomes Rockcliff Road. Launch from the park on the right side of Deep Cove Kayak.

**Panorama Park** (2200 Panorama Dr.): From North Vancouver, take Dollarton Highway east. At Mount Seymour Parkway, Dollarton Highway becomes Deep Cove Road. Turn right on Naughton Avenue and then left on Panorama Drive. Amenities include parking, restrooms, and picnic tables.

**Belcarra Picnic Area (təmtəmíxʷtən)** (4500 Tum Tumay Whueton Dr.): Originally the largest of Tsleil-Waututh 's ancestral villages, this launch is operated by Metro Vancouver Parks and has restrooms, picnic tables, changing rooms, showers, and overnight street parking. From downtown Vancouver, take BC Highway 7A (or from the east, BC 7 until it becomes BC 7A). Take

*Threading between Twin Islands and the mainland on Indian Arm*

loco Road north and turn right on 1st Avenue. Stay left at the fork to go onto Bedwell Bay Road and then veer left on Tum Tumay Whueton Drive, following it to the Belcarra Picnic Area.

## ROUTES

Choose your route: a short day trip, a longer day trip, or an overnight at one of the two campsites north of Deep Cove. There are several options.

## DAY TRIPS

**Jug Island:** Paddle 1.2 miles across Indian Arm toward Cosy Cove, Jug Island Beach, and Jug Island. Sandy Jug Island Beach and tree-topped Jug Island are great quick escapes. There is a toilet above the beach and a hiking trail into Belcarra Regional Park. You'll find seastars on the shores along Cosy Cove. Explore the point east of Jug Island and into Bedwell Bay. Belcarra Park extends down the west side and homes line the east side. Vancouver Water Ski Club has a dock midway down Belcarra Park, promising busy boat traffic in warmer months. Watch for boats and northerly winds.

    **Raccoon Island:** Rest up and enjoy the views on this tiny island 1.8 miles from Deep Cove. It offers primitive camping but also makes a fun day trip. From here, you can also continue to Twin Islands or beyond.

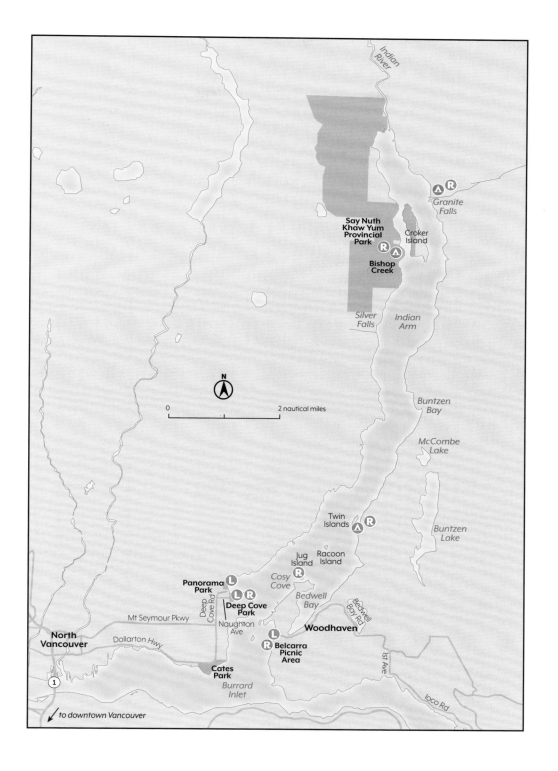

Indian River

Granite Falls

Say Nuth Khaw Yum Provincial Park

Croker Island

Bishop Creek

Silver Falls

Indian Arm

Buntzen Bay

McCombe Lake

N

0        2 nautical miles

Buntzen Lake

Twin Islands

Racoon Island

Jug Island

Cosy Cove

Bedwell Bay

Bedwell Bay Rd

Panorama Park

Deep Cove Park

Deep Cove Rd

Mt Seymour Pkwy

Naughton Ave

Woodhaven

North Vancouver

Dollarton Hwy

Belcarra Picnic Area

1st Ave

Cates Park

Burrard Inlet

Ioco Rd

1

to downtown Vancouver

**LONGER DAY TRIPS AND OVERNIGHT OPTIONS**

**Twin Islands Campsite:** This is the first camping option, located northeast of Deep Cove, and it tends to be busy in summer with boats and paddlers. From Deep Cove and Jug Island, the distance is 2.5 miles. At lower tides, you will have difficulty landing against its rocky shores. There is a small dock on the main island's east side. Amenities include camping (no fees), a composting toilet, a dock, and seventeen wooden tent pads. No fires are allowed. Soon after Twin Islands sits the Buntzen Powerhouse, which can create strong currents at its base due to the flow of McCombe and Buntzen Lakes above.

**Silver Falls:** Paddle 6 miles north of Deep Cove to view beautiful Silver Falls off Elsay Creek. Tucked into a cove, it is not easily seen from the water, and a narrow channel and steep rocky shoreline make landing difficult.

**Bishop Creek Campground:** Paddle 8.6 miles from Deep Cove to reach this campsite by Croker Island. Bishop Creek Campground is grassy and has twenty campsites, two pit toilets, and a metal food cache near the northside toilet. No camping fees. No fires are allowed, but water is available seasonally.

**Indian River:** On the north end of Indian Arm, Indian River is a six-hour (11.1-mile) trip from Deep Cove. Bald eagles are common in the fall when chum salmon are running. Also look for harbor seals, birds, and other marine life. Explore the estuary and river at high tides to avoid getting stuck in the mudflats. Vancouver Yacht Club's Wigwam Inn is an interesting sight in an otherwise seemingly untouched wilderness.

**Granite Falls Campsite:** On the northeast corner of Indian Arm, Granite Falls is 10.5 miles from Deep Cove. Gain epic views next to a spectacular, 165-foot waterfall tumbling down the mountain. The popular, grassy campsite has an easy sand-and-gravel landing, a dock, a small float, two composting toilets, two pit toilets, and is exposed to southerlies. Water is available in the creek; no fires or camping fees.

# 80. **Pitt River to Widgeon Creek and Falls**

This delightful trip east of Vancouver is a popular summer paddling destination. Enjoy a slow, meandering creek paddle as you soak in epic mountain views. Widgeon Creek flows into the beginning of the Pitt River, and just above is Pitt Lake, the second-longest lake in the region and the largest tidal lake in North America. Look for mink, river otters, and abundant birdlife. You can also hike above Widgeon Creek Campground to tumbling Widgeon Falls, either as a day trip or as part of an overnight adventure.

**Duration:** Half day to overnight.

**Rating:** *Protected* to *Moderate*. The *Moderate* rating is for the river mouth at the launch, which can be rough with wind opposing tides.

**Navigation Aids:** Canadian Hydrographic Service chart 3062 (1:25,000); NOAA chart 1807 (1:1,200,000). Tides are difficult to predict; per *BC Marine Trails*: "Some estimate 4 to 6 hours later than Point Atkinson or 2.5 to 4.5 hours later than New Westminster depending on flow in Fraser."

**Planning Considerations:** Widgeon Creek is tidal. To explore the estuary and upper river without getting stuck in mud, aim for higher tides and paddling in on a flood. Tides are difficult to predict for this area, so plan to arrive early. The area can be busy in summer. You may see clams along the shores, but note they've tested positive for coliform in the past. Pitt Lake 4 Canoe Rental rents kayaks and canoes at the launch. For details, visit them online at pitt-lake-canoe-rental.business.site.

## GETTING THERE AND LAUNCHING

**Grant Narrows Park at Pitt-Addington:** Take BC Highway 7A east of Vancouver and turn left on Old Dewdney Trunk Road. Then take a left on Harris Road, a right on McNeil Road, and a left on Rannie Road. Follow Rannie Road to Grant Narrows Park at Pitt-Addington, which has two concrete boat ramps, a float, mud beaches, a picnic shelter, and tables. No camping is available. Day-use, non-trailer parking is free, with overflow parking along the road. Pay a fee for overnight parking; the gate closes at dusk.

*Exploring Widgeon Creek*

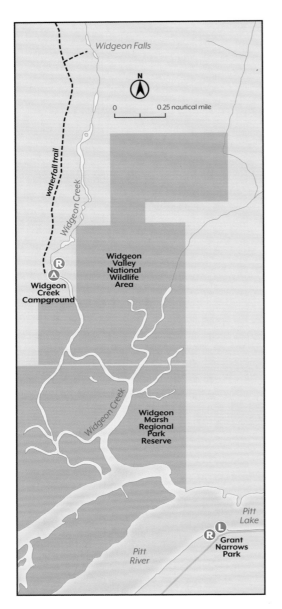

## ROUTE

Launch from Grant Narrows Park for the 0.3-mile crossing to Widgeon Creek. Since this is where Pitt Lake becomes Pitt River, there may be some bumps if the wind is opposing tidal currents. Aim upstream or use a ferry angle if the current is running south. Once across, enter the creek mouth and enjoy the slow pace of the marsh while spotting birds and marine life as you navigate upstream. The creek current is light. At the fork about one mile upstream, head left to reach Widgeon Creek Campground. The campsite, about 2 miles upstream from the creek mouth, has six gravel tent pads, picnic tables, two pit toilets, three steel bear-proof food-cache lockers, and mesh-cage lockers. No fees required and no fires allowed. Make sure to camp in the designated camping areas. Some paddlers who chose to camp on the creek banks here have been awakened by rising tides. Bring bug spray in summer.

**Hiking to Widgeon Falls:** This cascading waterfall is worth the 6-mile roundtrip hike. Widgeon Falls adds to the magnificent variety of sights in this area. With a gentle upward grade, most complete the roundtrip hike in two to three hours. To get there, take the trail to Widgeon Falls from the campground. At 1.6 miles, reach a trail junction. Stay left, following signs to the falls.

*Paddle boarder on Freshwater Bay, Strait of Juan de Fuca, near Port Angeles*

# Acknowledgments

I would like to dedicate this edition to my mentor Jim Ramey, who was a big influence on both my life and my business, with his decades of outdoor industry experience and his passion for water sports.

Many thanks to my partner, Christy Cox, for your assistance and for being so patient and supportive of accomplishing this revision in such a short time frame, as well as for being my shore support while I was on-water researching trips. Also, thanks to my parents for their support during this project. My sincere thanks to David Parks, USGS geologist and wetland scientist; Lee Richardson of Best Coast Outfitters in Victoria, BC; Paul Grey of BC Marine Trails; BC SUP coach Norm Hann for trip-idea help; Andrée Hurley of the Washington Water Trails Association; kayak coach Robert Nissenbaum for his assistance with rewriting the Tides and Currents section; David Burch of Starpath Publications; Randel Washburne; John Kuntz of the Olympic Outdoor Center; Matt Dawson of Urban Surf; Mike Darbyshire of Deep Cove Kayak; EJ Lange of Jericho Beach Kayak; Victor Okunev of SUP Touring NW; Rod Sternagel, South Puget Sound rower; and Karl Kruger of Kruger Expeditions. Lastly, my editors at Mountaineers Books, Lori Hobkirk and Kate Rogers, for keeping this book moving forward.

# Resources

## Sample Planning Checklist

### SEVERAL MONTHS TO A YEAR BEFORE:

- Once you decide to get into paddling, find a course or program from a reputable certified paddling school or coach. Learn and practice basic paddling, including self- and group-rescue skills, as well as tides, currents, and marine weather forecasting.
- After taking one or a few paddling classes, look into purchasing a boat or board for your trips. You'll be able to make a smarter purchase after you have some experience on water or with guidance from an instructor.

### A MONTH PLUS BEFORE:

- Determine what type of trip you want to take within your skill level.
- Check each piece of your paddling and camping gear to make sure it's current.
- Work with a paddling school or your trip partners to refresh your stroke and self- and group-rescue skills.
- If the trip length is a longer distance than what you're used to, start training by paddling longer distances than usual. Gradually build up your stamina for the trip distance or longer.
- Pay attention to your hydration and nutrition needs, adjusting as needed.
- Create a checklist of all your gear and food. Share it with your paddle partners.

### THREE WEEKS BEFORE:

- For the length and duration of your trip, determine your nutrition and hydration needs.
- Continue to check your gear and food list. Make a list of gear needed for a day trip or multiple nights.
- Do a shakedown trip prior to your departure with your paddling partners. This means taking a day trip or overnight to test your load and make sure your craft is ready for a trip. Is the load balanced properly in your boat or board? Does your gear fit? Too much gear? Are you going to get along with your paddling partners? Practice rescues with your group using your loaded boats or boards.
- Keep up your paddle stamina training to get comfortable with your trip distance or longer.
- Choose a route within your and your group's skill level. Group skill level and stamina determine trip distance and whether to take a Protected, Moderate, or Exposed route. Risk management comes into play here: the group should determine a route that everyone has the skills to safely complete. Choose an easier route if a group member doesn't have the right skills.
- Choose a backup route in case the main route won't work due to weather or if a group member needs to drop out.
- Determine if your launch location requires a parking permit or any fees for overnight parking.
- Research your campsites for overnight trips. Does your campsite require any fees and reservations? Does it have water and other particulars?
- Research your ferry route. Does the ferry require reservations or have any requirements for hand-loading gear?
- If tides and currents will affect your trip, start checking tides and current tables for the dates and times you're interested in. Tide levels will help determine whether you'll have enough water to land in certain locations or if you can avoid a long carry. Timing currents will make or break your trip in regard to route planning.
- Think about how you're going to carry your gear to shore from your boat or board. Day packs, duffels, or mesh paddler's bags can help bring gear in.

### ONE WEEK BEFORE:

- Start monitoring marine weather forecasts. Most forecasts are not accurate more than three days out, but a long-distance forecast can give you a ballpark idea of what may happen.
- Check ferry schedules and connections.
- Do another shakedown trip to refine your gear load and group skills and build stamina.
- Continue to examine and get gear and food for your checklist. Who's carrying the tent? Water? Start packing your food and gear.

### DAY OR NIGHT BEFORE:

- Check the forecast. Does it look good? Questionable? Do you need to reschedule?
- Make final preparations off your checklist.
- Check in with your paddling partners. Is everyone ready to go?

**LAUNCH DAY:**

- Make a final decision about whether your trip is a go by observing marine weather forecasts from home. If it's a go, recheck the actual conditions at the launch location in person.
- Leave a float plan with a friend prior to launching. This means leaving your name, boat or board description, and trip plans, including launch location, route, and planned return time and location. List how you can be reached on-water. After your trip, confirm your return with your friend.
- Make sure everyone in your group has reliable and working on-water communication options, such as mobile phones in waterproof cases and/or VHF radios. Do a radio check at the beach or parking lot. Does your group know their hand signals?
- Check all your group's gear to confirm that hatch covers are secured, leashes are attached, PFDs are properly adjusted, water and fuel is packed, and wetsuits and dry suits are zipped up. Are the steaks packed?

---

**IMPORTANT:**

If a member of your group is not comfortable with the conditions, or forgot their life jacket or tent, don't launch.

If you drove a considerable distance and took three ferries to the launch location, but the conditions aren't suitable for the group, it's okay to cancel or reschedule the trip. Remember: going anyway could end in disaster.

---

**AFTER THE TRIP:**

- Cancel your float plan, letting your land friend know you've made it back safely.
- Review your trip with your partners. How was the journey? Any lessons learned? What could be done better next time?

# Gear Recommendations

- **Paddling Clothing.** Kokatat, NRS, and Level Six dry suits are commonly seen on the Salish Sea. I use a RipCurl Dawn Patrol 4/3mm seam-sealed full surfing wet suit for fall and winter. O'Neill also makes great seam-sealed wet suits. NRS, Vaikobi, and Giant Fish make toasty wet suit tops and bottoms. I use NRS booties, hoods, and gloves.

- **PFDs.** The Mustang Khimera is a PFD with both $CO_2$ and passive foam floatation. Add a hydration bladder to the rear of your PFD, such as a Kokatat product, which has attach-on clips that fit on most PFDs. Some products such as Vaikobi or Mocke have built-in rear sleeves for hydration bladders and hi-vis colors.
- **Kayak Sails.** Advanced Elements and WindPaddle make sails that attach to the forward deck and can fold down.
- **Sea Kayak.** There are many great plastic and composite kayaks for touring. NC Kayaks, Nigel Foster Kayaks, Eddyline Kayaks, and Sterling Kayaks are all made in the Pacific Northwest. Other popular brands include Dagger Stratos, P&H, Delta, Nigel Dennis, and Stellar.
- **Sit-On-Top Kayak or Pedal Kayak.** Swell Watercraft's Scupper sit-on-top kayaks are fourteen feet or longer for speed, have ample storage, and use a floor scupper to suck water out of the foot area while underway. Hobie boats have hatches and efficient pedal drives.
- **Stand Up Paddle Board (SUP).** SplinterSUP in Port Townsend, Washington, makes a sixteen-foot touring board with internal storage that is quite speedy. Buy a 9-inch Super Flex rubber fin from Surfco for paddling through kelp beds and lake milfoil.
- **Touring Surf Ski.** Stellar, Epic, and Carbonology make stable touring surf skis with storage hatches. Don Kiesling in Hood River, Oregon, makes a rubberized surf ski rudder for rough water, rocky and reef environments. Find Don at surfski@gmail.com.

# Online Resources

Below is a list of links to help you plan your next trip. It includes aerial maps of the region, a site that teaches you how to paddle around whales, and ferry schedules for Washington State.

## BRITISH COLUMBIA

Below is a list of a variety of online links to assist with travel, weather, and finding the appropriate charts.

- BC Ferries, www.bcferries.com, 888-223-3779
- BC Land Trust Directory, https://ltabc.ca/land-trusts/directory
- BC Ministry of Sustainable Resource Management (MSRM), www2.gov.bc.ca/gov/content/environment/plants-animals-ecosystems
- BC Parks, www.env.gov.bc.ca/bcparks/
- British Columbia Tourism, www.hellobc.com

- British Columbia Webcams by Big Wave Dave. The webcams include the Strait of Georgia. www.bigwavedave.ca/webcams.php
- Canada Border Services Agency (CBSA), www.cbsa-asfc.gc.ca/menu-eng.html; CBSA Reporting Centre phone number is 888-226-7277
- Environment Canada: BC Weather, https://weather.gc.ca/forecast/canada/index_e.html?id=BC
- Fisheries & Oceans Canada: Nautical Charts, www.charts.gc.ca/index-eng.html
- Gulf Islands National Park, www.gulfislandsnationalpark.com
- Gulf Islands National Park Reserve, http://pc.gc.ca/en/pn-np/bc/gulf
- Islands Trust Conservancy, https://islandstrust.bc.ca/conservancy

## GEOGRAPHY AND MAPS

- Aerial Shoreline Photos of Washington State, https://apps.ecology.wa.gov/shorephotoviewer/Map/ShorelinePhotoViewer
- Google Maps. Map and satellite with easy tools for measuring distance, www.google.com/maps
- onX Hunt. Use this app for determining property ownership and your location, www.onxmaps.com

## MARINE WEATHER

- Cliff Mass Weather Blog, www.cliffmass.blogspot.com
- Marine Weather Apps. Use your phone to access these marine weather apps for detailed hourly and almost-weekly forecasts, along with other data on tides, surf forecasts, and more; WindAlert can access regional NOAA buoy data.
- NOAA Marine Forecast for Puget Sound, Strait of Juan de Fuca, and Outer Coast, www.weather.gov/sew
- NOAA National Weather Service, Seattle, www.weather.gov
- PredictWind, www.predictwind.com
- SailFlow, www.sailflow.com
- Surf Forecast, www.surf-forecast.com
- Surfline, www.surfline.com
- Washington State Webcams. Download the WSDOT app or visit the WSDOT website, www.wsdot.com/traffic/Cameras/default.aspx
- WindAlert, www.windalert.com
- Windy, www.windy.com

## PADDLING WITH WHALES— REGULATIONS AND ETIQUETTE

- Be Whale Wise, www.bewhalewise.org
- KELP (Kayak Education and Leadership Program), https://whalemuseum.org/products/kelp
- Orca Network, www.orcanetwork.org
- The Whale Museum in Friday Harbor, www.whalemuseum.org

## PARKS, LAND TRUSTS, AND STATE OR GOVERNMENT AGENCIES

- Capitol Land Trust in the South Sound, https://capitollandtrust.org
- Department of Natural Resources (DNR). Many shoreline areas in the state are managed by DNR. This website will help you map them; navigate to Recreation. www.dnr.wa.gov
- Discover Pass. This pass is required for cars in state parks, public access areas, wildlife areas, and boat launches. www.discoverpass.wa.gov
- Hiram M. Chittenden Locks, www.nws.usace.army.mil/Missions/Civil-Works/Locks-and-Dams/Chittenden-Locks. Find information specific to paddlers by clicking on Boater Information > Non-motorized Vessels.
- North Olympic Land Trust for the Olympic Peninsula, https://northolympiclandtrust.org
- San Juan County Parks, www.sanjuanco.com/430/Parks-Recreation-Fair
- San Juan Preservation Trust, https://sjpt.org
- US Customs and Border Protection. Visit this website for a list of offices in northwest waters, www.cbp.gov/contact/ports/wa, or call 800-562-5943.
- Washington States Parks camping fees, parks.wa.gov/166/camping-fees
- Whidbey Camano Land Trust, www.wclt.org/protected-properties

## SHIP TRACKING APPS

- Marine Traffic App. This one is my favorite ship tracking app. www.marinetraffic.com
- Ship Finder App, https://shipfinder.co
- Vessel Finder App, www.vesselfinder.com

## SURF AND WAVE FORECASTS

If you're planning on surfing or paddling the Strait of Juan de Fuca, it's important to know what the ocean swell is doing. The following sites can help you determine the swell size, direction, period, wind speed and direction, and other important information. West and northwest swells create the most waves along the south shore of the Strait of Juan de Fuca. Southwest swells and no wind often leave the Washington side quite calm. There are several other sites out there—find what works best for you.

- NOAA Angeles Point Buoy Data, www.ndbc.noaa. gov/station_page.php?station=46267
- NOAA National Data Buoy Center, www.ndbc. noaa.gov/data/Forecasts/FZUS56.KSEW.html
- NOAA Neah Bay Buoy Data, www.ndbc.noaa.gov/ station_page.php?station=46087
- Surf Forecast, www.surf-forecast.com
- Surfline, www.surfline.com

## SURFING ETIQUETTE

All paddlers traveling in a surf zone should know how to surf and practice surf etiquette. The below resources will introduce you to the basics of being a safer surfer.

- Almond, Elliot. *Surfing: Mastering Waves from Basic to Intermediate* (Seattle: Mountaineers Books, 2009), www.mountaineers.org/books/books/surfing-mastering-waves-from-basic-to-intermediate.
- Learn to Surf Lesson 12: Surfing Etiquette (Video), www.youtube.com/watch?v=SXhGp07uAMs
- Surfing Handbook, www.surfinghandbook.com/ knowledge/surfing-etiquette

## TIDES AND CURRENTS

Below are online resources to help you find the tide levels and current directions for both British Columbia and Washington State. Try out a few to see what works best for you and your region or destination.

- Aye Tides App, www.hahnsoftware.com
- British Columbia Tides and Currents, www.tides. gc.ca/en/tides-currents-and-water-levels
- Current Atlas for Puget Sound. This website shows current directions in graphic form. www.deepzoom.com
- Dairiki Tides App, www.dairiki.org/tides
- Navionics Boating App. Use this app for determining current, tides, and wind. www.navionics.com/ usa/apps/navionics-boating
- NOAA Tidal Current Tables, www.tidesandcurrents. noaa.gov/tide_predictions.shtml
- Ports and Passes. Visit this website to learn about and buy the book. https://portsandpasses.com
- Saltwater Tides, https://www.saltwatertides.com/ dynamic.dir/washingtonsites.html
- Tides Near Me App, https://apps.apple.com/us/ app/tides-near-me/id585223877

## TRANSPORTATION

- Washington State Ferries. Download the WSDOT app, which also has Hood Canal Bridge closure alerts, or visit the website, www.wsdot.wa.gov/ ferries. Statewide information, 888-808-7977.

## WATER TRAILS & MARINE CAMPSITES

Water trails allow camping and public launching access for nonmotorized watercraft in regions where public access is diminishing rapidly.

- BC Marine Trails, www.bcmarinetrails.org
- Kitsap Peninsula National Water Trail, https://kitsappeninsulawatertrails.com/maps
- Washington Water Trails Association. At the time of writing, WWTA is researching extending the trail west of Port Angeles to Neah Bay, www.wwta.org

# Useful Publications

Below is a list of excellent how-to books, manuals, guidebooks, and references available for improving your paddling skills and for travel in Pacific Northwest waters.

## GENERAL PADDLING

Alderson, Doug. *Sea Kayaker's Savvy Paddler: More than 500 Tips for Better Kayaking*. Camden, ME: Ragged Mountain Press, 2001.

Broze, Matt, and George Gronseth. *Sea Kayaker's Deep Trouble: True Stories and Their Lessons from* Sea Kayaker *Magazine*. New York: McGraw-Hill, 1997.

Burch, David. *Fundamentals of Kayak Navigation*. 4th ed. Boston: Globe Pequot Press, 2008.

Casey, Rob. *Stand Up Paddling: Flat Water to Rivers and Surf*. Seattle: Mountaineers Books, 2011.

Dowd, John. *Sea Kayaking: A Manual for Long Distance Touring*. 5th ed. Seattle: Greystone Books, 2004 (revised).

Henderson, Dan. *Sea Kayaking: Basic Skills to Advanced Paddling Techniques*. Seattle: Mountaineers Books, 2012.

Lull, John. *Sea Kayaking Safety and Rescue*. Berkeley, CA: Wilderness Press, 2001.

Mattos, Bill. *Kayak Surfing*. Guilford, CT: Falcon, 2009.

Washburne, Randel. *The Coastal Kayaker's Manual: A Complete Guide to Skills, Gear, and Sea Sense*. 3rd ed. Old Saybrook, CT: Globe Pequot Press, 1998.

## MAPS

- Maptech Nautical Charts. These are "flip-fold" waterproof navigational charts small enough to carry on a kayak, canoe, or SUP. www.maptech.com

- SeaTrails Maps. Waterproof maps designed for paddlers and other small boaters, these blend the features of nautical charts and topographic maps with updated information about parks and other attractions ashore. Available for Washington waters in regional sets or individual sheets. www.nwoc.com/shop/item.asp?itemid=367
- The Green-Duwamish River Map. Duwamish River Community Coalition, 2010. https://www.drcc.org

## MARINE WEATHER

Burch, David. *Modern Marine Weather*. Seattle: Starpath School of Navigation, 2008.

Lilly, Kenneth E., Jr. *Marine Weather of Western Washington*. Seattle: Starpath School of Navigation, 1983. www.starpath.com.

Mass, Cliff. *The Weather of the Pacific Northwest*. 2nd ed. Seattle: University of Washington Press, 2021.

Renner, Jeff. *Northwest Marine Weather: From the Columbia River to Cape Scott*. Seattle: Mountaineers Books, 1994.

## PADDLING IN BRITISH COLUMBIA

Chettleburgh, Peter. *An Explorer's Guide: Marine Parks of British Columbia*. Vancouver, BC: Special Interest Publications, 1985.

Cummings, Al, and Jo Bailey-Cummings. *Gunkholing in the Gulf Islands*. Edmonds, WA: Nor'westing, 1989.

Grey, Paul, and Gary Backlund. *Easykayaker: A Guide to Laid-Back Vancouver Island Paddling*. Pender Harbour, BC: Harbour Publishing, 2002.

Ince, John, and Hedi Kottner. *Sea Kayaking Canada's West Coast*. Seattle: Mountaineers Books, 1992 (revised).

Kimantas, John. *The Wild Coast 3, A Kayaking Hiking and Recreation Guide for BC's South Coast and East Vancouver Island*, vol. 3. North Vancouver, BC: Whitecap Books, 2010.

McGee, Peter, ed. *Kayak Routes of the Pacific Northwest Coast*. Vancouver, BC: Greystone Books, 2004.

Mueller, Marge, and Ted Mueller. *British Columbia's Gulf Islands: Afoot and Afloat*. Seattle: Mountaineers Books, 2000.

Obee, Bruce. *The Gulf Islands Explorer*. North Vancouver, BC: Whitecap Books, 1997 (revised).

Snowden, Mary A. *Sea Kayak the Gulf Islands*. 3rd ed. Surrey, BC: Rocky Mountains Books, 2010.

Vassilopoulos, Peter. *The Gulf Islands Cruising Guide*. Nanaimo, BC: Pacific Marine Publishing, 2006.

## PADDLING IN WASHINGTON STATE

Cummings, Al, and Jo Bailey-Cummings. *Gunkholing in the San Juans*. Edmonds, WA: Nor'westing, 1989.

Hahn, Jennifer. *Pacific Feast: A Cook's Guide to West Coast Foraging and Cuisine*. Seattle: Mountaineers Books, 2010.

Korb, Gary. *A Paddler's Guide to the Olympic Peninsula*. Self-published, 1997.

McGee, Peter, ed. *Kayak Routes of the Pacific Northwest Coast*. Vancouver, BC: Greystone Books, 2004.

Mueller, Marge, and Ted Mueller. *Middle Puget Sound and Hood Canal: Afoot and Afloat*. 2nd ed. Seattle: Mountaineers Books, 2006.

——. *North Puget Sound: Afoot and Afloat*. 3rd ed. Seattle: Mountaineers Books, 1995.

——. *The San Juan Islands: Afoot and Afloat*. 4th ed. Seattle: Mountaineers Books, 2003.

——. *Seattle's Lakes, Bays & Waterways: Including the Eastside*. Seattle: Mountaineers Books, 1999.

——. *South Puget Sound: Afoot and Afloat*. 4th ed. Seattle: Mountaineers Books, 1996.

Nyberg, Carl, and Jo Bailey. *Gunkholing in South Puget Sound: A Comprehensive Cruising Guide from Kingston/Edmonds South to Olympia*. Seattle: San Juan Enterprises Inc, 1997.

Rogers, Joel. *Watertrail: The Hidden Path through Puget Sound*. Seattle: Sasquatch Books, 1998.

Sept, J. Duane. *The Beachcomber's Guide to Seashore Life in the Pacific Northwest*. Madeira Park, BC: Harbour Publishing, 2009.

Thrush, Cole. *Native Seattle: Histories from the Crossing-Over Place*. Seattle: University of Washington Press, 2017.

Washington Water Trails Association. *Washington Water Marine Trail Guidebook*. 2007.

Yates, Steve. *Marine Wildlife: From Puget Sound through the Inside Passage*. Seattle: Sasquatch Books, 1998.

## SALISH SEA AND PUGET SOUND HISTORY

Blumenthal, Richard W. *Maritime Place Names: Inland Washington Waters*. Seattle: Inland Waters Publishing, 2012.

Brower, Kenneth. *The Starship and the Canoe*. Seattle: Mountaineers Books, 2020.

Cummings, B. J. *The River That Made Seattle*. Seattle: University of Washington Press, 2022.

Hansen, David M. *Battle Ready: The National Coast Defense System and the Fortification of Puget Sound, 1894–1925*. Pullman: Washington State University Press, 2014.

Thrush, Coll. *Native Seattle: Histories from the Crossing-Over Place*. Seattle: University of Washington Press, 2017.

Waterman, T. T. *Puget Sound Geography*. Independently published, 2001.

Williams, David. *Homewaters: A Human and Natural History of Puget Sound*. Seattle: University of Washington Press, 2022.

Williams, David, and Jennifer Ott. *Waterway: The Story of Seattle's Locks and Ship Canal*. Seattle: History Link, 2017.

Wray, Jacilee, ed. *Native Peoples of the Olympic Peninsula*. Norman: University of Oklahoma Press, 2015.

## TIDES AND CURRENTS

Burch, David. *Tidal Currents of Puget Sound, Graphic Current Charts and Flow Patterns*. Seattle: Starpath Publication, 2009.

Canadian Hydrographic Service. *Current Atlas: Juan de Fuca Strait to Strait of Georgia*. Ottawa: Canadian Hydrographic Service Department of Fisheries and Oceans, 1983. This atlas provides the most accurate and detailed information on tidal currents in this complex region. For a given hour and tidal range, the user is directed to a chart showing the currents. The calculations required to arrive at the correct chart make this resource a bit difficult to use. (See *Waggoner Tables* for a simplified method of finding the proper current chart.) www.charts.gc.ca/index-eng.html

Current Atlas Tables from Emanuel Borsboom's Personal Web. www.epiphyte.ca/proj/currents

Department of Natural Resources, State of Washington. Public tideland. https://www.dnr.wa.gov

*Tidelog*, Puget Sound Edition. Tiburon, CA: Pacific Publishers, published annually. http://tidelog.com. This is a useful combination of tide and current information for the year. It provides daily tidal curves showing slacks and associated current strengths, plus lunar and solar phases as they affect tides. It also includes current charts for Puget Sound and current schedules for Deception Pass and the Tacoma Narrows.

*Waggoner Tables*. Anacortes, WA: Weatherly Press, published annually. www.waggonerguide.com. Use these tables in conjunction with the helpful Canadian Hydrographic Service's *Current Atlas: Juan de Fuca Strait to Strait of Georgia*. These tables provide direct access to the proper current chart at any hour of any day without need for calculations or adjustment for daylight saving time. www.waggonerguidebooks.com/store/p400/CurrentAtlasTables.html

*Blood star at low tide on Tongue Point, Salt Creek Recreation Area*

# Index

# About the Author

**Rob Casey** has honed his kayaking, surf ski, and stand up paddling knowledge with more than two decades of year-round experience in all water conditions—from flatwater to rivers to surf. Rob is the founder and former director of the Professional Stand Up Paddle Association (PSUPA), and owner of Salmon Bay Paddle in Seattle, which offers personalized small-group sea kayaking, surf ski, and SUP instruction.

Rob is the author of the first book on stand up paddle instruction, *Stand Up Paddling: Flatwater to Surf and Rivers*. A photographer for many years, Rob has been a regular contributor to several paddling and other outdoor publications. He lives in Seattle's Ballard neighborhood and Port Angeles, Washington. You can visit his website at www.salmonbaypaddle.com or www.robcasey.net. Follow Rob on Instagram: @salmonbaypaddle and @robcaseyphoto. Join his "Paddling the Salish Sea" Facebook group at www.facebook.com/groups/1322209787977756.

**MOUNTAINEERS BOOKS,** including its two imprints, Skipstone and Braided River, is a leading publisher of quality outdoor recreation, sustainability, and conservation titles. As a 501(c)(3) nonprofit, we are committed to supporting the environmental and educational goals of our organization by providing expert information on human-powered adventure, sustainable practices at home and on the trail, and preservation of wilderness.

Our publications are made possible through the generosity of donors, and through sales of 700 titles on outdoor recreation, sustainable lifestyle, and conservation. To donate, purchase books, or learn more, visit us online:

### MOUNTAINEERS BOOKS

1001 SW Klickitat Way, Suite 201 • Seattle, WA 98134

800-553-4453 • mbooks@mountaineersbooks.org • www.mountaineersbooks.org

*An independent nonprofit publisher since 1960*

Mountaineers Books is proud to support the Leave No Trace Center for Outdoor Ethics, whose mission is to promote and inspire responsible outdoor recreation through education, research, and partnerships. The Leave No Trace program is focused specifically on human-powered (nonmotorized) recreation. For more information, visit www.lnt.org.

### YOU MAY ALSO LIKE: